THE COLORBLIND SCREEN

The Colorblind Screen

Television in Post-Racial America

Edited by Sarah Nilsen and Sarah E. Turner

NEW YORK UNIVERSITY PRESS

New York and London

NEW YORK UNIVERSITY PRESS
New York and London
www.nyupress.org

References to Internet websites (URLs) were accurate at the time of writing.
Neither the author nor New York University Press is responsible for URLs that
may have expired or changed since the manuscript was prepared.

Library of Congress Cataloging-in-Publication Data

The colorblind screen : television in post-racial America / edited by Sarah Nilsen and Sarah
E. Turner.
pages cm
Includes bibliographical references and index.
ISBN 978-1-4798-0976-9 (cloth : alk. paper) — ISBN 978-1-4798-9153-5 (pbk.   )
1. Minorities on television. 2. Race relations on television. 3. Racism on television.
4. Television broadcasting—Social aspects—United States. I. Nilsen, Sarah, editor of
compilation. II. Turner, Sarah E., editor of compilation.
PN1992.8.M54C86 2014
791.45'6552--dc23

2013043414

New York University Press books

Manufactured in the United States of America

10 9 8 7 6 5 4 3 2 1

Also available as an ebook

CONTENTS

Introduction

SARAH NILSEN AND SARAH E. TURNER

During his keynote address to the 2004 Democratic National Convention, then senator Barack Obama made the claim that "there is not a liberal America and a conservative America. There is the United States of America. There is not a Black America and a White America and Latino America and Asian America: There's the United States of America." These often-cited lines encapsulate the hope of a politician and a people who aspired to move the country past the color line to a time of unity through diversity. Obama himself acknowledges in the opening moments of his speech that his "presence on this stage is pretty unlikely." And yet, America and the world grasped that moment and that image, carrying them to election night in 2008 and again in 2012. Ironically, however, in the country's determination to both hold on to and project the image of a colorblind America, the reality of the country's racialized differences and inequities was overlooked.

Obama's comment invites multiple interpretations. Is he a post-racial president, neither black nor white? Liberals see the speech as a symbol of progress, signifying that America really has escaped its racist past, while cultural theorists might read it as evidence of the problematic allegiance to the ideals of colorblindness. For example, cultural critic and philosopher Cornel West claims that "by necessity, Obama has had to downplay his blackness to appease the white moderates and independents and speak to their anxieties" (33). The interpretive moment marked by this speech highlights the complex cultural moment of twenty-first-century America. Despite, or perhaps indirectly as a result of, the election of a biracial president, race still plays a dominant role in this culture, and, as legal scholar Kimberlé Crenshaw reminds us, "racism is a central ideological underpinning of American society" (1336).

A steady flow of academic studies continues to document the significant racial gaps in equity that permeate the core domains of social life and concrete social behaviors in America, such as housing and segregation, the labor market, close interpersonal relationships, politics, incarceration, and education (see Bobo and Charles). Much of this research has entered into the public discourse through mainstream media. As a survey of recent *New York Times* headlines reveals,[1] even with the recent election of Barack Obama to a historic second term, race relations in this country are far from reconciled. The social contradictions manifested in the celebration of the reelection of the nation's first biracial president and the persistent disregard for the socioeconomic inequities experienced by blacks and Hispanics illustrate the tensions that define what many refer to as post-racial America.

Racial attitudes in the United States have shifted significantly during the past four decades. In twenty-first-century America, the overt racism of the Jim Crow period has been replaced by significant social changes in public attitudes towards race. And yet racism persists amid deep divisions over appropriate social policy responses to racial inequality. Colorblind ideology must be understood as the outcome of a rhetorical strategy deployed in the wake of the modern civil rights movement in the early 1960s. In 1968, then presidential candidate Richard Nixon "pioneered the use of race as a primary weapon of conservative electoral politics [by] relying on carefully selected symbols, rhetorical pronouncements, and 'code words' that appealed to white voters nervous about racial change without alienating moderates who had opposed Jim Crow segregation and discrimination" (Horton 192). Neoconservative politicians insisted that the passage of the Civil Rights Act of 1964 and the Voting Rights Act of 1965 had successfully eradicated any remaining structural barriers to the advancement of the African American community. Therefore, any remaining racial inequalities were the product of individual choice rather than social policy; subsequently, concerted efforts to eradicate these inequalities were seen as antithetical to the equal protection clause of the Fourteenth Amendment. Nathan Glazer, in his influential and foundational neoconservative book on racial issues *Affirmative Discrimination: Ethnic Inequality and Public Policy* (1975), laid the groundwork for this new conservative position on race that would persist to this day. He argued that the Civil Rights Act of 1964 "could only be read as instituting into law Judge Harlan's famous dissent in *Plessy v. Ferguson*: 'Our Constitution is color-blind'" (221). He concluded that "it is now our task to work with the intellectual, judicial, and political institutions of the country to reestablish the simple and clear understanding that rights attach to the individual, not the group, and that public policy must be exercised without distinction of race, color, or national origin" (221).

In the 1980s, under the administration of President Ronald Reagan, the neoconservative revisionist appropriation of the concept of color-blindness would "blossom into a new and heavily promoted conservative discourse that combined an attack on race-conscious policies such as affirmative action with an implicitly racialized attack on social welfare programs for the poor" (Horton 204). Colorblind ideology thus needs to be understood as an ideological rhetorical stance that serves to distort the goals of the civil rights movement by claiming that the movement's objective was the eradication of racial considerations while also reassuring the dominant white culture that colorblindness represents a position of tolerance and acceptance for the equal treatment of all individuals regardless of the color of their skin. As Horton explains:

> Culturally, conservative political ideas have become overwhelmingly dominant. Even the history of the Civil Rights movement has been largely rewritten to support the conservative crusade for color-blindness and against affirmative action. Even more problematically, any memory that the movement was in fact dedicated to building an interracial coalition committed to the joint pursuit of racial and class equity seems to have been completely erased from public consciousness. (228)

The impact of the neoconservative appropriation of colorblind discourse on American society has been richly documented by sociologists who argue that the paradoxical and complex state of racial ideology today can be understood within a colorblind racial framework: a contemporary set of beliefs that posit that racism is a thing of the past and that race and racism do not play an important role in current social and economic realities. Sociologists have identified the central beliefs of colorblind racism this way:

(1) most people do not even notice race anymore; (2) racial parity has for the most part been achieved; (3) any persistent patterns of racial inequality are the result of individual and/or group-level shortcomings rather than structural ones; (4) most people do not care about racial differences; and (5) therefore, there is no need for institutional remedies (such as affirmative action) to redress persistent racialized outcomes. (Forman and Lewis)

Even though studies by the American Psychological Association (APA) have concluded that "research conducted for more than two decades strongly supports the view that we cannot be, nor should we be, colorblind," a majority of white Americans espouse a colorblind racial worldview and endorse (at least publicly) the broad goals of integration, equality and equal treatment without regard to race (3).

Colorblindness is a political tool, serving to reify and legitimize racism and protect certain racial privileges by denying and minimizing the effects of systematic and institutionalized racism on racial and ethnic minorities. Television, as the primary discursive medium today, plays a central role in the articulation, construction, and contestation of racialized identities in the United States. Even with the continuing fragmentation of the media landscape, watching TV remains the number one leisure activity that occupies the most time in the lives of Americans. While negative racial stereotypes do continue to circulate within the media, the dominant mode of televisual racialization has shifted to a colorblind ideology that foregrounds racial differences in order to celebrate multicultural assimilation while simultaneously denying the significant social, economic, and political realities and inequalities that continue to define race relations today. This colorblind mode of racial representation on television is not new and can be traced to *The Cosby Show* (1984–92). Sut Jhally's oft-cited 1992 study of the show, *Enlightened Racism,* revealed that the majority of white audiences that viewed the show believed that African Americans had the same socioeconomic opportunities as whites and that racial inequities were a product of individual failure rather than systemic racism.

The overtly negative racial stereotyping of early television programming has been replaced with what Kweisi Mifume, the then president of the National Association for the Advancement of Colored People (NAACP), described in July 1999 as a "virtual whiteout." The television networks' announcements that year of a fall lineup with no people of color in prominent roles led to calls for widespread changes within the industry. And yet the most recent update, in 2008, of the NAACP's reports on the broadcast television industry showed only "incremental progress for African Americans and Hispanics in the industry, little to no progress for Asian Americans and Native Americans, and persistent gross underrepresentation of minorities across the spectrum. . . . Although progress cannot be denied, the entertainment industry continues to be a reminder of America's segregated past" (*Out of Focus* 4). Over the past few decades, television producers have employed a variety of colorblind strategies in order to counter charges of racism and racial insensitivity. One of the most dominant and persistent trends is diversity casting, which showcases a multicultural cast without acknowledging or addressing cultural and social differences. These rainbow casts typically remain supporting players for the overwhelmingly white leads who continue to dominate television programming. The 2012 casting of Kerry Washington in the ABC series *Scandal* was the first time in almost forty years that a network drama contained an African American female lead. Her casting immediately prompted much debate about whether her character represents a new era of "postracial television, in which cast members are ethnically diverse but are not defined by their race or ethnicity" (Vega). Another colorblind trend in television is the casting of actors who are marked as racially ambiguous and therefore removed from any identifiable cultural identity. As Ron Berger, the chief executive of a major trend research company, explained, "Today what's ethnically neutral, diverse or ambiguous has tremendous appeal. Both in the mainstream and at the high end of the marketplace, what is perceived as good, desirable, successful is often a face whose heritage is hard to pin down" (qtd. in La Ferla).

As this collection documents, the dominance of colorblindness in television has been crucial in sustaining and supporting contemporary racial structures by making the reality of "substantial and widening racial economic inequalities, high levels of racial residential segregation, and persistent discrimination experienced across class lines in the Black community" invisible (Bobo, Kluegel, and Smith 40). The successful dissemination by neoconservatives of a colorblind ideology in

American culture has resulted in a majority of young whites becoming more and more comfortable with racial and ethnic inequality. In their research, sociologists Forman and Lewis have documented a disturbing reality that they label as racial apathy: "White people today often know little about the realities of life for many minorities, and what they do know is full of inaccurate information and mistaken assumptions. This not knowing is not, however, innocent" (180).

More than thirty-five years ago, the miniseries *Roots* premiered on ABC. The series won nine Emmy Awards, a Golden Globe, and a Peabody Award and received an unprecedented Nielsen rating for its finale, holding the record to this day as the third-highest-rated U.S. television program ever. The moment of shared national awareness that greeted the broadcast of *Roots* stands in stark contrast to a more recent television show that attempted to document the structural impact of racism on American society, HBO's *The Wire* (2002–8). Though widely hailed by critics and academics as outstanding, the series never earned an Emmy Award, and it garnered such poor Nielsen ratings by its final season that it barely registered on the ratings scale. As Robert Bianco argued in *USA Today*, "From start to finish, *The Wire* has been one of the best series ever produced for American television, one in which the commitment to honesty and authenticity has never wavered. Despite that quality, its subject matter—nothing less than the failure of the world's most powerful nation to solve the fundamental problems of its urban centers—was never likely to pull in a mass, casual audience." David Simon, the creator of *The Wire*, attributed the low viewership of the series to its predominantly black cast of characters. In a farewell letter to his HBO audience, Simon asked, "Why, if there is any truth to anything presented in *The Wire*, . . . does that truth go unaddressed by our political culture, by most of our mass media, and by our society in general?" Simon explains in his affirmation that "[we] are a culture without the will to seriously examine our own problems. . . . As a culture, we seek simple solutions." The following chapters, then, explore the ways in which the colorblind screen has served to present to viewers an image of the world that secures and encourages rather than challenges that racial apathy and those simple solutions. Central to all the chapters in the collection is the concern with manifestations of colorblindness in media: what each of the authors sees as the role and complicity of the media in perpetuating a comforting, if problematic, sense of sameness while at the same time enabling the continuation of racial apathy. Moreover, many of the chapters see as central to the idea and ideals of a colorblind, post-racial America the election of Barack Obama.

In the opening chapter, Doane argues the case for a more nuanced view of colorblind racial ideology, one that moves beyond a focus on the denial of racism and instead recognizes the ability to hold simultaneous—and contradictory—positions: for example, that racial inequality and white privilege persist, but that racism is not widespread. This allows for such conflicting phenomena as colorblind diversity, white victimization, the condemnation of racists, and reverse exceptionalism, all buttressed by an overarching belief that American society is fundamentally meritocratic. Throughout this analysis, he draws upon examples from recent media portrayals to illustrate the complexity of racial ideology in the contemporary United States. Mukherjee's chapter follows Doane's and focuses specifically on the evolution of the term "post-racial" and traces the discursive and rhetorical career of the term "colorblindness" to demonstrate how an appropriation of the ideology of colorblindness by the Right led to an embrace of a post-racial ideology. Embracing this post-racial ideology in turn has enabled a nationwide racial apathy and led to problematic policies and politicized rhetoric. Bonilla-Silva and Ashe's chapter examines the discursive strategies utilized by both the media and popular culture in their commentaries on the Obama moment, strategies Bonilla-Silva refers to as a "racial grammar" that serves as a formidable political tool for the maintenance of racial order. Through a close examination of housing policies, he demonstrates the subtle institutionalized impact of colorblind policies and what he calls "post-racial nonsense."

Both Peck and Leonard and Hazelwood give close readings of iconic figures in American popular culture to highlight the ways in which race is read and utilized by audiences, fans, and television programming. Peck examines Oprah Winfrey's thirteen-episode series "Racism in 1992" through an analysis of Oprah's discursive claim that she "transcends race." Peck's chapter highlights the interconnection between the rise over the last quarter century of the neoliberal political-economic project and the emergence of a post–civil rights racial ideology of colorblindness that is part of the fundamental reformulation of thinking about the problem of race in American society. By examining the rhetorical strategies of professional sports commentators and writers responding to the NBA lockout and LeBron James's decision to leave the Cleveland Cavaliers, Leonard and Hazelwood explore the role and production of race, specifically black male bodies, in professional sports television programming, as well as in the imagination of the largely white viewing audience. Alsultany and Ibrahim consider the representational strategies post-9/11 television uses to depict Arabs and Muslims. Alsultany's chapter focuses on television dramas that utilize the War on Terror as their central theme. By mapping a list of representational strategies she argues have become standard since 9/11, she examines the means by which writers and producers of TV dramas both represent Arabs/Muslims as terrorists and also seek not to reproduce the stereotype of Arabs/Muslims as terrorists. Ibrahim utilizes qualitative audience studies to analyze the ways in which Arab and Muslim and non-Arab and non-Muslim audiences read and react to contemporary depictions of Arab and Muslim characters on a variety of cable television comedies. In her chapter, Ibrahim argues that the portrayal and subsequent audience readings of Arabs and Muslims on television are never neutral but instead are "always-already" predetermined by both American politics and network bias, and her analysis of the discussion demonstrates how visual and verbal frames are used to determine these "always-already" readings.

The third part of the book considers specific shows and their widespread popularity while problematizing that popularity and the implicit reliance upon colorblind ideology utilized by the writers and producers of these shows in order to inscribe whiteness. Nilsen questions the acclaim *Mad Men* has received for its "supposed" historical authenticity and political correctness. She analyzes the racial discourse employed by the show's creators that creates a narratization of racism in America as constitutive of a distinctive historical moment, the early 1960s, and yet denies the actual social and political significance of the civil rights movement at the time. King's chapter continues the work of the collection—to problematize the role of colorblindness—albeit through a unique lens: he offers a close reading of a series of blogs and discussion posts found on the original and most influential white supremacist site stormfront.org in order to posit the ways in which colorblindness, as a hegemonic formation, nurtures the articulation of latent and emergent political and racialized ideologies that allow white supremacists to proselytize through the medium of television. Turner's chapter analyzes the "new buddy movement" that pairs black female characters in supporting roles with white female leads in two Disney Channel shows, demonstrating that Disney presents diversity in such a way as to reify the position and privilege of white culture and the white cast members. Drawing on recent Pew Center reports that document income inequities along lines of race, her argument suggests that viewers read these shows through a colorblind lens and see diversity without seeing (or understanding) difference.

The final part of the book examines the manner in which interracial relationships are rendered in the media during a period defined by post-racial identity formations. Davé offers a close reading of episodes from television shows that feature Indian weddings such as *The Simpsons* (1989–), *The Office* (2005–13), and *Miss Match* (2003–4) to argue that the twenty-first-century television portrayal of arranged marriages provides a narrative that dissolves rather than emphasizes the foreign nature of the arrangement process in American culture and instead shows a compatibility between American and Indian ideas of matchmaking. Kretsedemas utilizes audience studies and focus groups to examine viewers' ability and willingness to decode racial subtexts in *Ugly Betty*. His findings suggest that while audiences do react positively to the Latina/o main characters, they were unable or resistant to recognize disparities between lighter- and darker-skinned Latina/o characters. Finally, Huh's chapter examines the "supposedly" colorblind and gender-neutral casting of the Sci-Fi Channel's *Battlestar Galactica* series in order to articulate what she refers to as twenty-first-century racial anxiety: racial passing. Drawing on nineteenth-century detective fiction as well as twentieth-century passing narratives, Huh argues that the racial diversity and multiethnic characters of the show both critique and maintain cultural fears of miscegenation and racial erasure in post-racial America. We hope that this collection will contribute to the discourses and discussions around colorblind racism within the field of media studies.

Notes

1. "Hollywood's Whiteout," *New York Times,* 11 Feb. 2011; "Dr. King Weeps from His Grave," *New York Times,* 25 Aug. 2011; "No Smooth Ride on TV Networks' Road to Diversity," *New York Times,* 18 Mar. 2009; AP Poll: Majority Harbors

Prejudice against Blacks—AP, 27 Oct. 2012; "Worsening Wealth Inequality by Race," *CNNMoney,* 21 June 2012; "The Too Black, Too White Presidency," *New York Times,* 2 Sept. 2011; "Fear of a Black President," *Atlantic,* Sept. 2009; "Oscar Voters Overwhelmingly White, Male," *LA Times,* 19 Feb. 2012; "Segregation Prominent in Schools, Study Finds," *New York Times,* 19 Sept. 2012; "Wealth Gaps Rise to Record Highs between Whites, Blacks and Hispanics," *Pew Research Center Publications,* 26 July 2011; "5 Old-Timey Prejudices That Still Show Up in Every Movie," *Cracked.com,* 15 Nov. 2011; "Obama Elected President as Racial Barrier Falls," *New York Times,* 4 Nov. 2008; "Is Obama's America Reflected on U.S. TV? Don't Even Go There," *Globe and Mail,* 12 Nov. 2012; "Study Finds Record Number of Gay Characters on U.S. Television," *Globe and Mail,* 5 Oct. 2012; Motoko Rich, "Segregation Prominent in Schools, Study Finds," *New York Times,* 19 Sept. 2012.

WORKS CITED

American Psychological Association. *Can—or Should—America Be Color-Blind? Psychological Research Reveals Fallacies in a Color-Blind Response to Racism* [Pamphlet]. Washington, DC: American Psychological Association, 1997.

Bianco, Robert. "Too Few Were Plugged In, but HBO's 'The Wire' Was Electric." *USA Today* (March 5, 2008) <http://usatoday30.usatoday.com/life/television/news/2008-03-05-the-wire_N.htm> January 17, 2013.

Bobo, Lawrence, and Camille Charles. "Race in the American Mind: From the Moynihan Report to the Obama Candidacy." *Annals of the American Academy of Political and Social Science* 621.1 (2009): 243–59.

Bobo, Lawrence, James Kluegel, and Ryan Smith. "Laissez-Faire Racism: The Crystallization of a Kinder, Gentler, Antiblack Ideology." Ed. Stephen Tuch and Jack Martin. *Racial Attitudes in the 1990s: Continuity and Change.* Westport, CT: Praeger, 1997. 15–44.

Crenshaw, Kimberlé Williams. "Race, Reform, and Retrenchment: Transformation and Legitimation in Antidiscrimination Law." *Harvard Law Review* 101 (1988): 1331–1387.

Forman, Tyrone A., and Amanda E. Lewis. "Racial Apathy and Hurricane Katrina: The Social Anatomy of Prejudice in the Post–Civil Rights Era." *DuBois Review* 3:1 (2006): 175–202.

Glazer, Nathan. *Affirmative Discrimination: Ethnic Inequality and Public Policy.* New York: Basic Books, 1975.

Horton, Carol. *Race and the Making of American Liberalism.* New York: Oxford University Press, 2005.

Jhally, Sut. *Enlightened Racism: The Cosby Show, Audiences, and the Myth of the American Dream.* Boulder, CO: Westview Press, 1992.

La Ferla, Ruth. "Generation E.A.: Ethnically Ambiguous." *New York Times* (December 28, 2003) <http://www.nytimes.com/2003/12/28/style/generation-ea-ethnicallyambiguous.html?pagewanted=all&src=pm> January 15, 2013.

Obama, Barack. "2004 Democratic National Convention Keynote Address." Delivered 27 July, Fleet Center, Boston. *Americanrhetoric.com.* 2008.

Out of Focus—Out of Sync Take 4: A Report on the Television Industry. Baltimore: National Association for the Advancement of Colored People, 2008.

Simon, David. "A Final Thank You to the *Wire* Fans." <http://www.hbo.com/the-wire/index.html#/the-wire/inside/interviews/article/finale-letter-from-david-simon.html/> January 17, 2013.

Vega, Tanzina. "A Show Makes Friends and History." *New York Times* (January 16, 2013) <http://www.nytimes.com/2013/01/17/arts/television/scandal-on-abc-is-breaking-barriers.html?ref=tanzinavega&_r=0> January 17, 2013.

West, Cornel. "Interview with Cornel West." *Playboy* 8 (2010): 33–36, 106, 108.

PART I

Theories of Colorblindness

1

Shades of Colorblindness

Rethinking Racial Ideology in the United States

ASHLEY ("WOODY") DOANE

Colorblindness—the claim that race no longer "matters" in American society—serves as the dominant framework for making claims about the role of race in the United States. For many analysts (Carr; Bonilla-Silva *White Supremacy, Racism without Racists;* Brown et al.; Doane "Rethinking Whiteness Studies"; Gallagher "Color-Blind Privilege"), it has become *the* primary framework for understanding race in the twenty-first century. At the core of colorblindness is the belief that because the civil rights movement was nearly a half century ago and white attitudes have demonstrably changed, racism is no longer embedded in the U.S. social structure and no longer serves as an obstacle to success. If racial inequality persists, then it is due to actions (or inactions) on the part of minority group members.

It is also important to recognize that—as Michael Omi and Howard Winant have argued in their seminal book *Racial Formation in the United States* (1986)—racial ideologies are constantly being rearticulated in response to political and social challenges. And as Eduardo Bonilla-Silva observes, the "loose character" of the elements of colorblind racial ideology "allows for accommodation of contradictions, exceptions, and new information" (*Racism without Racists* 10). This means that colorblindness is not static—that it can adapt to new situations. Moreover, while colorblindness can be described as a dominant or hegemonic ideology in the United States in 2012, it is certainly not monolithic. I would suggest that it is opposed (at a minimum) by a perspective that claims that racism *is* embedded in the social and political institutions of the United States (a perspective that—following Feagin—we might refer to as "systemic racism") and a perspective that articulates an overt form of white supremacy or white nationalism. In short, colorblind racial ideology is continually evolving or changing in response to both changing social and political circumstances and counterclaims made by proponents of opposing ideologies.

As I have noted elsewhere (Doane "What Is Racism?," "The Changing Politics," "New Song"), this political struggle occurs via racial discourse—the collective text and talk of society in terms of issues of race. Public and private discourse serves as the link between macro-level racial ideologies and the micro-level understandings of groups and individuals—it is how our ideas about race both spread and evolve. Contemporary racial ideologies are communicated and contested through various media both print and electronic. In the twenty-first century, the ubiquity of the screen (television and computer) and the speed (and accessibility) of the Internet both mean that racial discourse occurs at an increasingly rapid pace. If we think of racial discourse as a political arena, one in which ideologies are rearticulated as actors respond to both the challenges of racial events and the arguments of their ideological opponents, then we need to acknowledge that it is undergoing constant evolution.

For the purposes of this book, it is also useful to consider the relationship between the media and colorblind racial ideology. In general, the media can be viewed as an institution, a set of social arrangements whose main role or function is to transmit information among and between social groups. Yet institutions reflect the divisions of wealth and power and the dominant ideologies of the larger society (Herman and Chomsky). Because the contemporary media exists in an increasingly globalized, postindustrial capitalist society, media outlets are increasingly consolidated under the control of a few large corporate actors (McChesney). This also means that media is a *product* and that decisions regarding programming and news coverage are driven, or at least shaped, by profit considerations (ratings, circulation, advertising, competition). Stories are followed not only for their newsworthiness but also for their presumed marketability. Individual actors—writers, directors, producers, editors, and reporters—find that their roles (and their career prospects) take place within this context.

What does this mean for colorblind racial ideology? As the dominant explanation for the role of race in the United States, colorblindness shapes the lens through which the media presents racial issues to the larger society. To the extent that colorblindness downplays systemic racism and claims that racism is an individual issue, the media will then reflect this perspective. In particular, this would mean that news coverage would focus more upon individual acts of racism (e.g., hate crimes or racially insensitive language) than subtle systemic issues (e.g., the disproportionate impact of mortgage lending on blacks and Latinos).[1]

My goal in this chapter is not to attempt a reanalysis of the nature of colorblind racial ideology—although we do need to recognize that frames and storylines are constantly evolving. While Bonilla-Silva (*Racism without Racists*) has called attention to the fluid nature of colorblind racial ideology, I believe there is a general tendency among analysts to focus upon the structure of colorblindness rather than the ways in which it adapts and changes.[2] I argue the case for a more nuanced view of colorblind racial ideology, one that moves beyond a simple focus on the denial of racism and instead emphasizes the ability to hold simultaneous—and contradictory—positions—for example, that racial inequality and white privilege persist, but that racism is not widespread. This allows for such conflicting phenomena as colorblind diversity, the condemnation of racists, minority racism/white victimization, racial awareness in a "colorblind" society, and reverse exceptionalism, all supported by an overarching belief that American society is fundamentally meritocratic. I conclude with the assertion that colorblind racial ideology is best understood as a fluid set of claims about the nature of race in the United States.

Seeing Color in a Colorblind World: Colorblind Diversity

Contrary to its name, colorblind racial ideology is *not* about the inability to see color or the lack of awareness of race. Even the often-used line "I don't care if they are black, white, purple, or green" demonstrates both an awareness of color/race and a centering of the black-white binary.[3] The point of colorblindness is how we see color/race: in a "colorblind" world, race is most often (but not always) defined as a characteristic of *individuals* in a world where racism is no longer a major factor and race plays no meaningful role in the distribution of resources. In essence, race is reduced—in theory but not in practice—to another descriptor along the lines of "tall" or "left-handed." To paraphrase Bonilla-Silva (*Racism without Racists*), what is left is "race without races."

Interestingly, the view of race as an individual characteristic opens the door for colorblindness to embrace racial diversity. Over the past few decades, the idea of "diversity" has taken on iconic status in American society (Doane "The Changing Politics"; Bell and Hartmann; Sherwood). Communities, corporations, educational institutions, the military, and others have embraced the virtues of diversity and inclusion. Perhaps nowhere is this more evident than in the media, as the "colorblind screen" (the title of this volume) displays diversity everywhere. Contemporary viewers see images of diversity (often carefully chosen) on news staffs, in advertisements, sports coverage, entertainment, and popular shows (crime, "reality" television), and even through the self-presentation of colleges and universities (on ads during football games and on university websites). This is not to imply that representation of peoples of color in the media is even remotely approaching parity, but that given the often hypervisibility of peoples of color to whites, the impact of diversity is likely to be exaggerated.

What makes diversity work from a colorblind standpoint is that it ostensibly supports its main ideological linchpin—the claim that race no longer matters. If we see that peoples of color are visible participants in most spheres of life—and the "colorblind" eye has a tendency to exaggerate diversity—then have we not made great strides toward racial equality? If we turn on the television and see multimillionaire minority athletes and entertainers, then is racism truly a barrier? And if we see minority justices, high-ranking government officials, and, since 2008, a black president, have we not truly realized Martin Luther King Jr.'s dream of living in a land where people are judged not by the color of their skin but by the content of their character? It is through this logic that diversity and colorblindness are intertwined.

For individuals, diversity is generally very compatible with a colorblind worldview. As Joyce Bell and Douglas Hartmann found, many people saw diversity as making life "more interesting" or "more exciting" (899). It then becomes possible to "consume" diversity through a kind of cultural tourism—going out for "ethnic" food, attending a multicultural festival—which in turn further solidifies the feeling of living in a post-racial society. For example, as Jason Rodriquez demonstrated, colorblind ideology enabled white youths to engage with and even appropriate hip-hop. Eduardo Bonilla-Silva (*Racism without Racists*) discovered that white respondents often emphasized the nature of diversity in their lives—having friends of color, living in a diverse neighborhood—even if the degree of diversity or friendship was greatly exaggerated. In the decades since the civil rights movement, it is increasingly socially desirable for individuals to embrace diversity to substantiate their nonracist or post-racial standpoint. Beyond the psychological benefits of feeling virtuous (most of us want to live in a society where race does not matter), "doing" diversity also provides individuals with a credential to use in racially challenging situations.

Diversity, however, has its limits. What is often implicit (or explicit) is the assumption that diversity involves a degree of assimilation to white middle-class/upper-middle-class norms (Bell and Hartmann). It is as if colorblindness has finally expanded the "melting pot" beyond its Eurocentric focus (Zangwill) to include blacks, Latinos, and Asians. To the extent that diversity rests upon assimilation, it is truly symbolic. There are also quantitative limits: token or symbolic inclusion is one thing, but the white majority has shown itself to become increasingly uncomfortable with being in the numerical minority in social settings, schools, neighborhoods, and the United States as a whole (Gallagher "White Racial Formation," "Miscounting Race"; Farley and Frey; Alba, Rumbaut, and Marotz). Diversity is fine in a colorblind world, as long as things do not become too diverse.

What is most important about "colorblind diversity"—beyond the way in which it reinforces the claim that we have moved beyond race—is the absence of any meaningful challenge to the racial status quo. Diverse casts and commercials, successful athletes and entertainers can all coexist along with racial disparities in income, wealth, poverty, education, and incarceration. The inclusion and upward mobility of "diverse" individuals do not necessarily challenge the logic and the structure of an unequal racial order. Even the election of Barack Obama to the presidency—often cast as the symbolic pinnacle of American society—does not change the larger picture (Bonilla-Silva "The 2008 Elections"). As Gary Younge observed when discussing the brief elevation of African American Herman Cain to "frontrunner" status in the 2011–12 Republican primary campaign, "So long as the system remains intact, the identity of those administering it holds only symbolic relevance" (10).

Racism in a Colorblind World

Given that one of the cornerstones of colorblind ideology is the rejection of race as a meaningful force in society, it would be reasonable to conclude that racism would be on the periphery of the colorblind landscape—something to be downplayed or denied. In the post–civil rights era, ideologies of racial superiority and overt displays of racism are generally universally condemned. Indeed, charges of racism and the label of "racist" carry a social stigma that is so extreme that individuals will go to great lengths to avoid them. Speakers use rhetorical shields (e.g., I am not a racist, but . . .), code words, and other tactics (including embracing diversity) in an attempt to inoculate themselves against possible accusations of racism (Bonilla-Silva *Racism without Racists;* Bonilla-Silva and Forman). When claims of racism are made, a strong defensive reaction is evoked, and the focus of discussion shifts from the issue at hand to the charge itself (Doane "Contested Terrain," "What Is Racism?"). What follows is a series of claims and counterclaims, where persons leveling accusations of racism can be problematized as engaging in "name-calling," being "oversensitive," or "playing the race card" (Essed; Doane "Contested Terrain").

Nevertheless, colorblindness and claims of racism can coexist quite comfortably. In the colorblind world, racism is defined not as a group-based system of oppression that is embedded in social institutions but instead as *individual* prejudice or discrimination. This individualization of racism means that it is generally viewed as the isolated acts of "ignorant" individuals or extremist "hate groups" on the fringes of society. Even seemingly institutional acts—for example, racial profiling by police—can be reduced to the actions of racist individuals. The near-universal condemnation of these actions can then be taken as evidence of the fact that the United States has truly moved beyond race. If action is needed, it is more education to address racial "ignorance."

So what happens when a potential case of racism emerges? In the "colorblind" society, this involves *individual* actions—most often racially charged or insensitive statements. Here, a few high-profile national cases can prove instructive:

- In November 2006, actor and comedian Michael Richards, best known for his role as Cosmo Kramer in the popular television sitcom *Seinfeld,* responded to hecklers during his stand-up routine in a Hollywood comedy club with a series of racial epithets and a reference to lynching before walking off the stage. As video recordings of the incident spread across the country, Richards responded with apologies on the *Late Show with David Letterman,* on civil rights leader Rev. Jesse Jackson's radio show, and in a telephone call to activist Rev. Al Sharpton (Farhi; CBS News "Jesse Jackson"; CNN "Sharpton"). Richards explained the tirade as the result of flying into a "rage" and asserted that he was "not a racist" (MSNBC); however, he subsequently announced his retirement from comedy and has generally remained out of the public eye.
- In early April 2007, radio personality Don Imus sparked a firestorm after making racially derogatory remarks about players from the NCAA tournament runner-up Rutgers University women's basketball team. After a week of debate, which included an apology by Imus and calls for his firing by Rev. Jackson and Rev. Sharpton, CBS first suspended Imus for two weeks and then fired him (CBS News "CBS Fires Don Imus"). After a period off the air, Imus eventually returned to radio later that year with another network and has continued broadcasting up to the present.
- In January 2008, Golf Channel anchor Kelly Tilghman commented that young golfers who wanted to challenge star golfer Tiger Woods for supremacy in the world of golf should "lynch him in a back alley." As word of the comment spread and a national discussion began, Tilghman's situation was helped by a statement from Woods that "there was no ill-intent in her comments" (Golf). Despite calls for her firing, including from Rev. Sharpton, the Golf Channel responded by suspending Tilghman for two weeks and stating that there was "no place on our network for offensive language like this" (Golf). Tilghman continues to work as an anchor and commentator on the Golf Channel.

Each of these cases serves as a "racial morality play" in three acts: a cycle of transgression, "trial," and either exoneration or atonement/ punishment. In the contemporary United States, racial transgressions may be public words and acts, or less visible writings that are unearthed at a later date (sometimes by political opponents). The "trial" is public and takes place in newspapers, on television, talk radio, and websites (including YouTube), and in the blogosphere. Outcomes are determined by a range of factors (this is an issue worthy of separate investigation), including the power of advocates, responses of the parties involved, economic interests, and media coverage. This cycle of crime and punishment, especially when it involves public figures, is also attractive to a media that is concerned with audience attention. A resolution is reached, and the media's (and society's) gaze turns elsewhere, much in the same manner that other news stories lose their currency after a brief period of interest.

With respect to colorblind racial ideology, what is significant is that whatever the outcome of the racial morality play, the institutions involved (e.g., CBS, the Golf Channel) and, by extension, the larger community have reaffirmed their commitment to "tolerance" and "diversity"—to being "nonracist." Following the classical sociologist Émile Durkheim, it is a transgression that ultimately strengthens the social order. What is overlooked is that *none of this remotely addresses larger issues of structural racism and racial inequality.* Any mention of such issues is consigned to the periphery of public discourse amid the overarching focus on the charge of racism. And in the end, the dominant claim that society is colorblind emerges all the stronger because society has "dealt" with racism.

This process also takes place on smaller stages—the regional, local, and even institutional levels.[4] One such event occurred in my local media. Following a lengthy federal investigation, four East Haven, Connecticut, police officers were charged with a range of crimes involving the long-term abuse of power (harassment of motorists, false arrests, illegal searches, and intimidation) toward the city's Latino community (Altimari, Buffa, and Owens). At the conclusion of a media interview, the city's mayor responded to a question about what he was going to do for the Latino community by saying, "I might have tacos when I go home" (Hernandez and Charlton). Not surprisingly, this remark produced a barrage of criticism from community activists, the governor (who called the mayor's comments "repugnant"), and the largest statewide newspaper, the *Hartford Courant,* which ran a lead editorial titled "The Mayor Is an Idiot" (Muñoz; "The Mayor Is an Idiot"). The mayor apologized, and defenders cited his dedication to the community, but calls for his resignation continued, including a protest that involved delivering hundreds of tacos to the mayor's office (Muñoz, Hernandez, and Colli). Whether or not the mayor will ride out the storm (another outcome of the morality play) remains to be determined.[5] What did happen, however, is that the larger issues of police abuse and systemic racism were deflected; for example, a comment by the president of the local NAACP that "the issue of racism is embedded in the community. It's pervasive" (Muñoz) was buried in the inside pages of the newspaper and not addressed in the larger debate. Once again, the story of the individual "racist" was much more compelling to the media and its audience than the broader sociological issues.

There is another dimension to this process through which the "colorblind society" cleanses itself of racism. Because societal racism is viewed as a thing of the past, and because racism is defined as a deed (prejudice and/or discrimination) committed by a dwindling number of isolated individuals, it then "logically" follows that *anyone*—white, black, Latino, Asian, or Native American—can be racist (Doane "What Is Racism?"). In other words, black racism, white racism, and Latino and other racisms are all on a par with each other in an analytical framework that is torn from history and separated from social institutions. This idea is so embedded in American society that to suggest—as a university professor did when proposing a course titled "White Racism"—that the only relevant form of racism in the United States is white racism is to invite an avalanche of criticism (Doane "What Is Racism?"). The idea of "minority racism" has become a basic tenet of colorblind racial ideology, which in turn means that people of color can also be subjected to the "racial morality play."

Once again, a few recent examples of so-called minority racism help illustrate this point:

- During the 2008 presidential campaign, racism became an issue when the media—led by ABC News—began airing video recordings and citing quotations from sermons given by then-candidate Barack Obama's pastor—the Reverend Jeremiah Wright—over a twenty-year period. In segments shown on television, Wright was harshly critical of racism in American society, with such statements as "The government gives them the drugs, builds bigger prisons, passes a three-strike law and then wants us to sing 'God Bless America.' No, no, no, God damn America, that's in the Bible for killing innocent people. God damn America for treating our citizens as less than human. God damn America for as long as she acts like she is God and she is supreme" (Ross and El-Buri). While Obama immediately sought to distance himself from Rev. Wright's comments, the media debate that followed—including charges of racism against Wright (Limbaugh; Sowell)—threatened to derail his candidacy. In response, Obama delivered a speech on race on March 18, 2008, that was generally very well received and eventually quieted the controversy. Interestingly, in the course of the speech, Obama talked about (and essentially equated) both black anger and white resentment. He spoke of how for black Americans "the memories of humiliation and doubt and fear have not gone away, nor has the anger and bitterness of those years." After acknowledging the reality of this anger, Obama then immediately observed that "a similar anger exists within segments of the white community. Most working- and middle-class white Americans don't feel that they have been particularly privileged by their race" ("Obama's Speech on Race"). Without this device—what might be regarded as a concession to colorblind ideology— it is less likely that Obama's speech would have been so successful in ending the controversy. Later that spring, after a second controversy involving Rev. Wright and another issue involving a guest speaker, the Obamas resigned from the church and ended any affiliation with Wright (Raum).

- In the spring of 2009, President Obama nominated federal appeals court judge Sonia Sotomayor to fill a vacancy on the U.S. Supreme Court. Following her nomination, media attention focused upon a 2001 speech in which she said, "I would hope that a wise Latina woman with the richness of her experiences would more often than not reach a better conclusion than a white male who hasn't lived that life" (Savage). Opponents of the nomination criticized Sotomayor, claiming that the implication that Latinas could make better decisions proved that Sotomayor was a racist (Ellerson). The issue did come up during Sotomayor's confirmation hearings during the summer, but she deflected criticism by stating, "I want to state up front, unequivocally and without doubt: I do not believe that any ethnic, racial or gender group has an advantage in sound judging" (CNN "High Marks for Sotomayor"). Justice Sotomayor was eventually confirmed by the Senate.

- In the summer of 2010, a racially based controversy emerged when videos surfaced (posted by a conservative activist) that showed a U.S. Department of Agriculture official, Shirley Sherrod, giving a speech to a NAACP audience discussing how she withheld assistance from a white farmer the first time that one came to her for help (Fox News). In the wake of widespread criticism, the Department of Agriculture soon announced that Sherrod had resigned her position. Shortly thereafter, it was found that the clip had been taken out of context and that Sherrod was actually telling a story about how the request had evoked conflicting feelings within her (her father had been murdered by unidentified whites), but that she eventually helped the couple save their farm (Stolberg, Dewan, and Stelter). The story immediately shifted from one of racism to one of change, and embarrassed administration officials offered Sherrod an apology and a new job (which she declined).

As before, the racial morality plays ground to their various outcomes, and society's attention eventually turned elsewhere. And, as before, the colorblind society buttressed its nonracist credentials by calling to account individuals who were perceived as racist. But by putting "racists of color" on trial, colorblind America has demonstrated that racism is a ubiquitous phenomenon. And if anyone can be racist, then there is no reason to consider issues of systemic racism. Once again, the final outcome of these public discussions of racism was to affirm the hegemonic status of colorblindness.

The Contradictions of Colorblindness: From Colorblind to Black and White

Both colorblind racial ideology and the United States as a "colorblind society" are rife with contradictions. One of the purposes of ideologies is to manage contradictions, most notably conflicts between ideological claims and gaps between ideological claims and material conditions. Throughout the history of the United States, racial ideologies have worked to explain the contradictions between slavery, segregation, conquest, and exclusion and the ideals of democracy. In the twenty-first century, the role of colorblindness is to manage the contradictions between the realities of race and the ideal of a post-racial society. As I have outlined earlier, colorblind ideology has proved itself more than capable of coexisting with both "diversity" and "racism."

I think there is a tendency among social theorists and social scientists to expect too much ideological and behavioral consistency from human beings. Nowhere is this more true than with respect to race. Perhaps the ideal metaphor for our view of race in the United States is the scene in the movie *The Wizard of Oz* when Dorothy opens the door after her house has landed in Oz and the movie (initially set in Kansas) changes from black and white to color. The difference is that in the "colorblind" United States, we continually shift back and forth from colorblindness to seeing color. And, like Dorothy, we continually struggle to balance our understandings nurtured in colorblind Kansas with the challenges of life in Oz, where colors are powerfully visible.

As the idea of colorblind racial ideology has emerged as a core concept for analyzing race in the contemporary United States, those of us who study the issue tend to cast matters into a dichotomy between classical/old racism with overtly racist ideologies and new racism/colorblindness as a more subtle form of racism. I am not convinced that matters are this clear. While all evidence indicates that there has been a steep decline in those who advocate ideas of biological superiority and inferiority, the ongoing influence of racial stereotypes and "cultural racism" (claims of group-based pathologies in family, work, and educational values) suggests that we should be careful in pushing too far with claims of colorblindness. Eduardo Bonilla-Silva, who includes "cultural racism" as one of the key frames in his analysis of colorblind racial ideology, also notes the tendency of respondents to use it in a "crude" or overt manner (*Racism without Racists* 39–41).[6] When we make broad claims about group cultural deficiencies, has our worldview really changed that much? We may deny the existence of systemic racism, but we are clearly saying that race still "matters."

I would like to put forward the idea that for many individuals, it is possible to move back and forth between colorblindness and more traditional forms of racism. As some researchers have observed (Myers; Picca and Feagin), overt racism is common in private or "backstage" settings. What has changed is that the overwhelming majority of people have—despite complaints about "political correctness"—learned to be more guarded in expressing thoughts or ideas that are more openly racist. And if they are called to account, there are an array of strategies that can be used, including explanations ("I was tired" or "I wasn't thinking"), apologies (and stressing one's nonracist credentials), and a range of rhetorical devices (see Bonilla-Silva's *Racism without Racists* 53–72 on "how to talk nasty about minorities without sounding racist").

Race awareness also comes to the fore in choices that people make. As Michael Emerson, George Yancey, and Karen Chai found, the presence of blacks in a neighborhood matters—and it matters more for families with children. And once a neighborhood becomes 15 percent black, whites are very unlikely to move in. Similarly, Heather Beth Johnson and Thomas Shapiro found that "race is on the minds of white Americans, and they are thinking about it when it comes to neighborhood and school choice" (186). Images of "good neighborhoods" and "good schools" are racially bounded. Multiple other studies support this point. I contend that these decisions are reached in a framework that is *not* colorblind—even if they are masked in code words.

And, in an area often overlooked by colorblind theorists, race awareness occurs at the level of the subconscious. The media plays a key role in the creation and reproduction of racial stereotypes. Television news transmits images that highlight the perceived relationship between race and crime (Bjornstrom et al.). Drama shows reproduce racial stereotypes using nonverbal cues (Weisbuch, Pauker, and Ambady). Sportscasts reinforce the connection between race and ability (Buffington and Fraley). And research shows that job applicants with white-sounding names are 50 percent more likely to be called for interviews than applicants with African American–sounding names (Bertrand and Mullainathan). In short, even when the screen is black-and-white—when we are not focusing on race—the reception is in color.

Inequality and Colorblindness: The Ultimate Contradiction

Without a doubt, the cornerstone of colorblind racial ideology is its attempt to address the persistence of racial inequality in the United States in the twenty-first century. If race no longer matters in American society, then why—nearly fifty years after the main accomplishments of the civil rights movement—are there such stark differences in terms of income, wealth, poverty, and education? This is the ultimate contradiction, the ultimate hurdle. Any other issue is secondary. Unless colorblind racial ideology can provide a reasonable answer to this question, it fails.

Given the centrality of this issue—indeed, the claim that racism no longer matters in explaining racial inequality is often presented as one of the defining features of colorblind racial ideology—it is surprising that colorblind theorists have not devoted more analytical attention to how racial inequality is explained in contemporary American society. Bonilla-Silva has—quite correctly, in my view—emphasized "cultural racism" and "naturalization" (the claim that racial inequality is due to a combination of market forces and the aggregate choices of individuals—which "happen" to produce unequal outcomes) as two dominant frames that are used to explain racial inequality (*Racism without Racists* 2).[7] While both frames are evident in current discourse, I think there is a deeper problem. Because the cultural racism frame relies on more overt statements of racial difference, it becomes more difficult to sustain in a colorblind context. To make broad public statements about the deficient values of racial groups is to risk condemnation for being "racist." Similarly, the claim of "naturalization" is difficult to sustain because it is statistically impossible for existing racial disparities to be due to chance. It might be possible, given the general atmosphere of colorblind racial ideology, that many Americans are as unaware of the scope of racial inequality as they are of the demographic composition of the United States (I know that my students are regularly surprised by the extent of racial gaps in income, wealth, poverty, and education). Mainstream media coverage of racial inequality is generally limited to a brief mention of disparities in income, poverty, and unemployment when data are released by government agencies—and where race is generally not the focus of the article. Some antiracist organizations present studies of racial inequality; however, their work is usually buried amid more "interesting" news.[8] Nevertheless, ignorance and/or denial of racial inequality does not make a sustainable explanation.

Available research on social explanations for racial inequality shows a pattern that is notable for its inconsistency. Matthew Hunt, using General Social Survey data, traced beliefs about black/white inequality over nearly three decades.[9] Among his interesting findings was that respondents used a variety of conflicting explanations, with relatively equal percentages selecting person-centered (ability and/or motivation), structural (lack of educational opportunities and/or discrimination), and mixed (both person-centered and structural) modes of explanation. Similarly, Paul Croll (see also Hartmann, Gerteis, and Croll) found that most American Mosaic Project survey respondents used *both* structural and individual explanations to understand black disadvantages and white advantages.[10] And Heather Beth Johnson, in a qualitative study of race, wealth, and inequality, found that white respondents *simultaneously* employed structural (inherited wealth) and individual (hard work) explanations for their success.

Interestingly, all three researchers found similar mixed and contradictory patterns among respondents of color in explanations for racial inequality, although there are differences from whites in the greater use of structural as opposed to individual explanations. This is compatible with other work that finds blacks influenced by colorblindness but less so than whites, with Asian Americans and Latinos in the middle (Bonilla-Silva *Racism without Racists*; O'Brien). I contend that this illustrates the strength of the two dominant ideologies for explaining inequality in American society: colorblindness and meritocracy. I also suspect that for respondents of color, some belief in the openness of the system is necessary to retain hope for oneself and one's children. Students of color in my race classes often write in essays that there may be barriers that they will have to face, but they can be surmounted—a perspective that combines optimism and realism.

Another issue in understanding explanations of racial inequality is the defensive aspect of colorblindness. If "anyone" can be racist, then it is possible for whites, particularly during times of economic stress or when privileges are challenged, to respond in a reactive manner and claim that "they [people of color] are the racist ones" (Bonilla-Silva *Racism without Racists* 62–66). Over the past few years, claims of "minority racism"—such as those mentioned in this chapter—received considerable attention in the conservative media. Likewise, politicians inveighing against "illegal" immigrant workers, food stamps, and "sharia law" all contribute to a picture of (white) America under attack. With often exaggerated views of the scope of affirmative action, it is easy to claim that "reverse discrimination"—viewed as a violation of the norms of equality in a post-racial society—is a pervasive problem. Not surprisingly, recent studies (Norton and Sommers; Jones et al.; Blake) show that white Americans are increasingly likely to see racism against whites as a more significant social problem than racism against minorities. These studies found that a plurality of whites support the view that when it comes to racism, whites are the new victims. This is the "white resentment" that Barack Obama felt compelled to address in his 2008 speech on race ("Obama's Speech on Race"). In this context, it is certainly possible to imagine an increase in overt racial mobilization among whites in the future.

This matrix of contradictory perspectives on racial inequality presents complications for colorblind racial ideology. Indeed, to continue with the screen metaphors, explanations for racial inequality are reminiscent (for those of us of a certain age) of the early color television sets that required viewers to adjust "hue" and "tint" and still be left with a distorted image. It is more difficult to sustain the claim that race does not matter in explaining racial inequality when a significant number of Americans use—at least in part—*structural* explanations for racial inequality. While "cultural racism" and "naturalization" will continue to be used, buttressed by a seemingly global belief in meritocracy, colorblind racial ideology will need to continue to evolve if it is to maintain its hegemonic status.[11]

I think that one possible outcome will be linked to ongoing changes in the racial and ethnic demography of the United States—and the prediction that by 2050 the United States will be a "majority minority" society (Passel and Cohn). Some theorists (Bonilla-Silva "From Bi-racial"; Yancey) have predicted the eventual restructuring of racial boundaries and the U.S. racial order. In his "Latin-Americanization" thesis, Bonilla-Silva ("From Bi-racial") predicts that race in the United States will become fluid—along the lines of Latin American and Caribbean societies—which, ironically, will make racial inequality and colorblindness more difficult to challenge. Along with this restructuring of boundaries, I think it likely that social status will increasingly be determined by a socially defined combination of race and class. "Colorblind diversity" as described earlier makes it possible for whites to consider "successful" blacks and Latinos as part of the social mainstream. From the *Cosby Show* to sports to the White House, more whites are willing to accept people of color as family members, neighbors, classmates, coworkers, and even leaders—especially if they "assimilate" to white middle-class/upper-class society. Where class comes in is that while white-dominated society will increasingly be willing to accept upper-class and middle-class blacks and Latinos, it will exclude those who are poor or who live in hypersegregated and/or low-income neighborhoods.

This outcome may be described as "reverse exceptionalism." In the past, when being black carried a heavy social stigma, a successful black was viewed as "exceptional," as a "credit to his race" (which was otherwise degraded). If my prediction comes to pass, the new racial order will find blacks and Latinos increasingly accepted as a group, but those on the economic margins will be viewed as a "discredit" to their race (which is otherwise viewed positively). So instead of the "not all blacks are lazy but most are" that Bonilla-Silva describes, the discourse will shift to "many/most blacks and Latinos are hardworking, but some are really lazy" (*Racism without Racists* 48) This nuanced use of race and class would enable the use of individualistic explanations (family values, work ethic) instead of cultural racism to explain the status of lower-class blacks and Latinos without fear of being called racist (after all, the speaker has just claimed that most minorities are hardworking). In the past, the question was often "If Italians and Jews and Japanese can be successful, why can't blacks?" In the future, the question may well be "If Oprah can create an economic empire and Obama can become president, why can't other blacks and Latinos succeed?" This singling out of a small segment of minority communities is, in my opinion, well under way, particularly in areas such as poverty, welfare, and crime (Quadagno; Alexander). To the extent that "reverse exceptionalism" becomes embedded in colorblind racial ideology, racial inequality will become even more difficult to challenge.

Conclusion

What are the implications of the preceding for the "colorblind screen" and for colorblindness in general? In this chapter, I have presented a view of colorblindness that is complex—to the extent that it is appropriate to speak of "shades of colorblindness." I have argued that colorblind racial ideology is constantly being rearticulated in response to political challenges and changing social contexts. And I have attempted to demonstrate how colorblindness is fluid enough to incorporate both "diversity" and "racism." Finally, I have explored the hole in the center of colorblindness: the contradictions that lie underneath its central task, that of explaining (or explaining away) the persistence of racial inequality in the United States. I believe it is essential that those seeking to understand and critique colorblindness emphasize its complexity and fluidity as well as its structure. Our analyses must be as adaptable as the ideologies that we seek to explain.[12]

What is the road ahead for those who seek to contest the hegemony of colorblindness? It is important to continue—as this book does—to illustrate the reach of colorblindness into virtually every aspect of popular discourse and to provide a critical assessment of its claims. The work of scholars (e.g., Montagu) played an important role in undermining the intellectual credibility of classical racism. And the media, while it does not create change, can play an important role in the spread of new ideas and demands for change—as we saw during the "Arab Spring" uprisings of 2011. Yet institutions change slowly and only in response to changes in the larger society. Despite the contributions of academics and the media, it eventually took the work of social movements (e.g., the civil rights movement) to change the U.S. racial order. If change comes to the colorblind screen, it will emerge only when social movements challenging racial injustice become too powerful to ignore.

Notes

1. While the mainstream media has become increasingly controlled by large corporations, the expansion of the Internet has allowed space for voices that challenge the hegemony of colorblind racial ideology. For an example of a site that provides a critical perspective on colorblindness, see www.racismreview.com. For an analysis of the use of the Internet by white supremacists, see Daniels. The sides may be unequal, but ideological competition still takes place.

2. In many ways the study of society embodies a tension between the study of *social structure* (the organization of society at any one point in time) and the study of *social change*. Given the complexity of change, the eye of the analyst is often more readily drawn to understanding society at a particular moment.

3. Entering the *exact* phrase "I don't care if they are black, white, purple or green" into Google's advanced search produced 2,000 results. Entering the *exact* phrase "I don't care what color they are" produced 246,000 results. The point is that phrases such as these are widely used in an attempt to demonstrate the speaker's indifference to race.

4. When I asked students in my race and ethnic relations class what happened when there was a racial incident in their town or high school, the overwhelming response was that "we would have an assembly." Such events provide a forum for expressions of hurt and outrage. The assembled group then reaffirms its commitment to "tolerance," and the community moves to place the episode in the past.

5. For additional information on this episode, see www.courant.com/maturo.

6. "Cultural racism" differs from classical racism in that social and economic differences are *not* attributed to biological or genetic causes but are instead viewed as grounded in deficient group values or culture. Blame is placed on a poor work ethic, single-parent families, and a lack of commitment to education, and it is claimed that these "dysfunctional" values are then passed from one generation to the next. The problem with this is that it involves stereotyping all members of a racial group (with perhaps a few exceptions) as sharing the same negative values.

7. At the core of "naturalization" is the view that racial disparities are not due to racism or race-conscious choices but instead reflect individual preferences and

social or market forces that have "nothing to do with race." For example, as I found in a study of a school desegregation debate (Doane "Contested Terrain"), concentrations of whites in certain neighborhoods and schools were claimed to be the simple result of housing choices made by individual families. And as Bonilla-Silva (*Racism without Racists*) points out, speakers may combine naturalization with other types of explanations such as "cultural racism" in a discussion of racial issues.

8. For example, the organization United for a Fair Economy released a report of racial inequality in the United States, "State of the Dream 2012" (Sullivan et al.), on Martin Luther King Day. It was only briefly mentioned in the national media.

9. The General Social Survey (GSS) is a series of national surveys that have been conducted by the National Opinion Research Center at the University of Chicago since 1972 to track how the opinions of Americans have changed over the past four decades. It is one of the most widely used sources of survey data by social scientists. For more information, see www.gss.norc.org.

10. The American Mosaic Project was a multiyear, multimethod study of issues of diversity in the United States. Conducted by researchers at the University of Minnesota, survey results in the study came from a nationally representative sample contacted by telephone (random-digit dialing). For further details, see Edgell, Gerteis, and Hartmann.

11. I believe that meritocracy—the claim that success reflects ability and effort (but not inherited advantages)—plays an important (and understudied) role in colorblind racial ideology. While the claim of meritocracy has been used to defend class-based inequality in the United States for more than a century (and has become embedded in American culture), it has received much less attention from those studying racial ideologies. For the most part, this reflects the history of racial domination, where claims of racial superiority and inferiority were long used to justify racial differences. As Johnson has emphasized, meritocracy is important to colorblindness as the flip side of cultural racism. If we turn our attention from the disadvantages of minorities to the advantages of whites, then the first explanation that surfaces from meritocracy is the role of "hard work." In many ways, this is the hidden component of colorblindness. If so, then any meaningful challenge to colorblindness will have to contest the hegemony of meritocracy. The current challenge to the claim that meritocracy is a defining feature of American society has been mounted by the Occupy Wall Street Movement with its assertion of the fundamental unfairness of an economic system that is run for the benefit of the 1 percent of wealthiest Americans. This claim, if it gains traction in the media and in popular culture, creates new possibilities for countering colorblind ideology.

12. My point is that while theorists such as Omi and Winant and Bonilla-Silva have mentioned the fluid nature of racial ideologies, the tendency in practice is to apply existing frameworks—such as Bonilla-Silva's masterful analysis of colorblindness—rather than look for changing patterns.

WORKS CITED

Alba, Richard, Ruben G. Rumbaut, and Karen Marotz. "A Distorted Nation: Perceptions of Racial/Ethnic Group Sizes and Attitudes towards Immigrants and Other Minorities." *Social Forces* 84.2 (2005): 901–19. Print.

Alexander, Michelle. *The New Jim Crow: Mass Incarceration in the Age of Colorblindness.* New York: New Press, 2010. Print.

Altimari, Dave, Denise Buffa, and David Owens. "Cops Called Racial Bullies." *Hartford Courant* 25 Jan. 2012: A1, A6–A7. Print.

Bell, Joyce M., and Douglas Hartmann. "Diversity in Everyday Discourse: The Cultural Ambiguities and Consequences of 'Happy Talk.'" *American Sociological Review* 72.6 (2007): 895–914. Print.

Bertrand, Marianne, and Sendhil Mullainathan. "Are Emily and Greg More Employable Than Lakisha and Jamal? A Field Experiment on Labor Market Discrimination." *American Economic Review* 94.4 (2004): 991–1013. Print.

Bjornstrom, Eileen E. S., Robert L. Kaufman, Ruth D. Peterson, and Michael D. Slater. "Race and Ethnic Representations of Lawbreakers and Victims in Crime News: A National Study of Television Coverage." *Social Problems* 57.2 (2010): 269–93. Print.

Blake, John. "Are Whites Racially Oppressed?" *CNN.com.* 4 Mar. 2011. Web. 28 Jan. 2012. <http://www.cnn.com/2010/US/12/21/white.persecution/index.html>.

Bonilla-Silva, Eduardo. "From Bi-racial to Tri-racial: Towards a New System of Racial Stratification in the USA." *Ethnic and Racial Studies* 27.6 (2004): 931–50. Print.

———. *Racism without Racists: Color-Blind Racism and the Persistence of Racial Inequality in the United States.* 3rd ed. Lanham, MD: Rowman and Littlefield, 2010. Print.

———. "The 2008 Elections and the Future of Anti-racism in 21st Century Amerika or How We Got Drunk with Obama's Hope Liquor and Failed to See Reality." *Humanity and Society* 34.3 (2010): 222–32. Print.

———. *White Supremacy and Racism in the Post–Civil Rights Era.* Boulder, CO: Lynne Rienner, 2001. Print.

Bonilla-Silva, Eduardo, and Tyrone Forman. "'I'm Not a Racist but . . .' Mapping White College Students' Racial Ideology in the U.S.A. *Discourse and Society* 11.1 (2000): 53–85. Print.

Brown, Michael K., et al. *Whitewashing Race: The Myth of a Colorblind Society.* Berkeley: University of California Press, 2003. Print.

Buffington, Daniel, and Todd Fraley. "Racetalk and Sport: The Color Consciousness of Contemporary Discourse on Basketball." *Sociological Inquiry* 81.3 (2011): 333–52. Print.

Carr, Leslie G. *"Color-Blind" Racism.* Thousand Oaks, CA: Sage, 1997. Print.

CBS News. "CBS Fires Don Imus over Racial Slur." *CBSnews.com.* 12 Apr. 2007. Web. 22 Jan. 2012. < http://www.cbsnews.com/stories/2007/04/12/national/main2675273. shtml>.

———. "Jesse Jackson Talks to Michael Richards." *CBSnews.com.* 25 Nov. 2006. Web. 22 Jan. 2012. <http://www.cbsnews.com/stories/2006/11/25/entertainment/ main2208718.shtml?source=RSSattr=U.S._2208718>.

CNN. "High Marks for Sotomayor after Tough Questioning." *CNN.com.* 14 July 2009. Web. 24 Jan. 2012. < http://articles.cnn.com/2009-07-14/politics/sotomayor.hearing_1_soto-mayor-hearings-wise-latina-woman-hispanic-supreme-court?_s=PM:POLITICS>.

———. "Sharpton: Comedian's Apology Not Enough." *CNN.com.* 22 Nov. 2006. Web. 22 Jan. 2012. < http://articles.cnn.com/2006-11-22/entertainment/sharpton.richard_1_sharpton-apology-hecklers?_s=PM:SHOWBIZ>.

Croll, Paul. "Making Sense of Whiteness: From Invisibility to Colorblindness." Paper presented at the annual meeting of the American Sociological Association, Las Vegas, Nevada, Aug. 2011.

Daniels, Jessie. *Cyber Racism: White Supremacy Online and the New Attack on Civil Rights.* Lanham, MD: Rowman and Littlefield, 2009. Print.

Doane, Ashley W. "The Changing Politics of Color-Blind Racism." *Research in Race and Ethnic Relations* 14 (2007): 181–97. Print.

———. "Contested Terrain: Negotiating Racial Understandings in Public Discourse." *Humanity and Society* 20.4 (1996): 32–51. Print.

———. "New Song, Same Old Tune: Racial Discourse in the Aftermath of Hurricane Katrina." *Through the Eye of Katrina: Social Justice in the United States.* Ed. Kristin Swan and Richelle Bates. Durham, NC: Carolina Academic Press, 2010. 107–28. Print.

———. "Rethinking Whiteness Studies." *White Out: The Continuing Significance of Racism.* Ed. Ashley W. Doane and Eduardo Bonilla-Silva. New York: Routledge, 2003. 3–18. Print.

———. "What Is Racism? Racial Discourse and Racial Politics." *Critical Sociology* 32.2–3 (2006): 255–74. Print.

Durkheim, Émile. *The Rules of Sociological Method.* 8th ed. Trans. Sarah Solovay and John Mueller. Ed. George Catlin. New York: Free Press, 1933. Print.

Edgell, Penny, Joseph Gerteis and Douglas Hartmann. "Atheists as 'Other': Moral Boundaries and Cultural Membership in American Society." *American Sociological Review* 71.2 (2006): 211–34. Print.

Ellerson, Lindsey. "Gingrich Calls Sotomayor "Racist." *ABCnews.com.* 29 May 2009. Web. 24 Jan. 2012. < http://abcnews.go.com/blogs/politics/2009/05/gingrich-calls/>.

Emerson, Michael O., George Yancey, and Karen J. Chai. "Does Race Matter in Residential Segregation? Exploring the Preferences of White Americans." *American Sociological Review* 66.6 (2001): 922–35. Print.

Essed, Philomena. *Understanding Everyday Racism.* Newbury Park, CA: Sage, 1991. Print.

Farhi, Paul. "Seinfeld Comic Richards Apologizes for Racial Rant." *Washingtonpost.com.* 21 Nov. 2006. Web. 22 Jan. 2012. <http://www.washingtonpost.com/wp-dyn/content/article/2006/11/21/AR2006112100242.html>.

Farley, Reynolds, and William H. Frey. "Changes in the Segregation of Whites from Blacks during the 1980s: Small Steps toward a More Integrated Society." *American Sociological Review* 59.1 (1994): 23–45. Print.

Feagin, Joe R. *Systemic Racism: A Theory of Oppression.* New York: Routledge, 2006. Print.

Fox News. "Video Shows USDA Official Saying She Didn't Give 'Full
    Force' of Help to White Farmer." *Foxnews.com.* 20 July 2010. Web.
    24 Jan. 2012. <http://www.foxnews.com/politics/2010/07/19/
    clip-shows-usda-official-admitting-withheld-help-white-farmer/>.
Gallagher, Charles A. "Color-Blind Privilege: The Social and Political Functions of
    Erasing the Color Line in Post Race America." *Race, Gender and Class* 10.4 (2003):
    22–37. Print.
———. "Miscounting Race: Explaining Whites' Misperceptions of Racial Group Size."
    Sociological Perspectives 46.3 (2003): 381–96. Print.
———. "White Racial Formation: Into the Twenty-First Century." *Critical White Stud-
    ies.* Ed. Richard Delgado and Jean Stefancic. Philadelphia: Temple University Press,
    1997. 6–11. Print.
Golf. "Golf Channel Anchor Kelly Tilghman Suspended for
    'Lynch' Remark about Tiger Woods." *Golf.com.* 8 Jan. 2008.
    Web. 22 Jan. 2012. < http://www.golf.com/tour-and-news/
    golf-channel-anchor-kelly-tilghman-suspended-lynch-remark-about-tiger-woods>.
Hartmann, Douglas, Joseph Gerteis, and Paul R. Croll. "An Empirical Assessment of White-
    ness Theory: Hidden from How Many?" *Social Problems* 56.3 (2009): 402–24. Print.
Herman, Edward S., and Noam Chomsky. *Manufacturing Consent: The Political
    Economy of the Mass Media.* New York: Pantheon, 1988. Print.
Hernandez, Samaia, and John Charlton. "Mayor: 'Tacos' for Dinner." *Hartford Courant*
    25 Jan. 2012: A7. Print.
Hunt, Matthew O. "African American, Hispanic, and White Beliefs about Black/White
    Inequality, 1977–2004." *American Sociological Review* 72 (2007): 390–415. Print.
Johnson, Heather Beth. *The American Dream and the Power of Wealth.* New York:
    Routledge, 2006. Print.
Johnson, Heather Beth, and Thomas Shapiro. "Good Neighborhoods, Good Schools:
    Race and the 'Good Choices' of White Families." *White Out: The Continuing
    Significance of Racism.* Ed. Ashley W. Doane and Eduardo Bonilla-Silva. New York:
    Routledge, 2003. 173–87. Print.
Jones, Robert P., Daniel Cox, William A. Galston, and E. J. Dionne Jr. *What It Means to
    Be American: Attitudes in an Increasingly Diverse America Ten Years after 9/11.* Wash-
    ington, DC: Brookings Institute/Public Religion Research Institute, 2011. Print.
Limbaugh, Rush. "Obama's Double Life Exposed: His Rac-
    ist, Hatemonger Pastor." *Rushlimbaugh.com.* 13 Mar. 2008. Web.
    24 Jan. 2012. <http://www.rushlimbaugh.com/daily/2008/03/13/
    obama_s_double_life_exposed_his_racist_hatemonger_pastor2>.
"The Mayor Is an Idiot." *Hartford Courant* 26 Jan. 2012: A14. Print.
McChesney, Robert. *The Political Economy of Media: Enduring Issues, Enduring Dilem-
    mas.* New York: Monthly Review Press, 2008. Print.
Montagu, M. F. Ashley. *Man's Most Dangerous Myth: The Fallacy of Race.* 5th ed. New
    York: Oxford University Press, 1974. Print.

MSNBC. "Former 'Seinfeld' Star Apologizes for Yelling 'N' Word at Hecklers." *MSNBC.com.* 22 Nov. 2006. Web. 22 Jan. 2012. <http://today.msnbc.msn.com/id/15816126/ns/today-entertainment/t/richards-says-anger-not-racism-sparked-tirade/#>.

Muñoz, Hilda. "Mayor Issues 2nd Apology." *Hartford Courant* 26 Jan. 2012: A8. Print.

Muñoz, Hilda, Samaia Hernandez, and George Colli. "Group Delivers Tacos to Mayor." *Hartford Courant* 27 Jan. 2012: B1, B6. Print.

Myers, Kristen. *Racetalk: Racism Hiding in Plain Sight.* Lanham, MD: Rowman and Littlefield, 2005. Print.

Norton, Michael I., and Samuel R. Sommers. "Whites See Racism as a Zero-Sum Game That They Are Now Losing." *Perspectives on Psychological Science* 6.3 (2011): 215–18. Print.

"Obama's Speech on Race." *Nytimes.com.* 18 Mar. 2008. Web. 24 Jan. 2012. <http://www.nytimes.com/interactive/2008/03/18/us/politics/20080318_OBAMA_GRAPHIC.html>.

O'Brien, Eileen. *The Racial Middle: Latinos and Asian Americans Living beyond the Racial Divide.* New York: NYU Press, 2008. Print.

Omi, Michael, and Howard Winant. *Racial Formation in the United States.* New York: Routledge and Kegan Paul, 1986. Print.

Passel, Jeffrey S., and D'Vera Cohn. *U.S. Population Projections: 2005–2050.* Washington, DC: Pew Research Center, 2008. Available at <http://pewhispanic.org/files/reports/85.pdf >.

Picca, Leslie Houts, and Joe R. Feagin. *Two-Faced Racism: Whites in the Backstage and Frontstage.* New York: Routledge, 2007. Print.

Quadagno, Jill S. *The Color of Welfare: How Racism Undermined the War on Poverty.* New York: Oxford University Press, 1994. Print.

Raum, Tom. "Obama Resigns from Church after Pastor Controversy." *Boston.com.* 31 May 2008. Web. 27 Jan. 2012. < http://articles.boston.com/2008-06-01/news/29277981_1_barack-obama-press-club-appearance-pfleger>.

Rodriquez, Jason. "Color-Blind Ideology and the Cultural Appropriation of Hip-Hop." *Journal of Contemporary Ethnography* 35.6 (2006): 645–68. Print.

Ross, Brian, and Rehab El-Buri. "Obama's Pastor: God Damn America, U.S. to Blame for 9/11." *ABCNews.com.* 13 Mar. 2008. Web. 24 Jan. 2012. <http://abcnews.go.com/Blotter/DemocraticDebate/story?id=4443788&page=1#.TyYJsYESodQ>.

Savage, Charlie. "A Judge's View of Judging Is on the Record." *Nytimes.com.* 15 May 2009. Web. 25 Jan. 2012. < http://www.nytimes.com/2009/05/15/us/15judge.html>.

Sherwood, Jessica Holden. *Wealth, Whiteness, and the Matrix of Privilege.* Lanham, MD: Lexington, 2010. Print.

Sowell, Thomas. "Wright Bound." *Nationalreview.com.* 19 Mar. 2008. Web. 24 Jan. 2012. <http://www.nationalreview.com/articles/223964/wright-bound/thomas-sowell>.

Stolberg, Sheryl Gay, Shaila Dewan, and Brian Stelter. "With Apology, Fired Official Is Offered a New Job." *Nytimes.com.* 21 July 2010. Web. 4 Jan. 2010. <http://www.nytimes.com/2010/07/22/us/politics/22sherrod.html?pagewanted=print>.

Sullivan, Tim, Wanjiku Mwangi, Brian Miller, Dedrick Muhammad, and Colin Harris. "State of the Dream 2012: The Emerging Majority." *Faireconomy.org.* 12 Jan. 2012. Web. 13 Jan. 2012. <http://www.faireconomy.org/dream>.

Weisbuch, Max, Kristin Pauker, and Nalini Ambady. "The Subtle Transmission of Race Bias via Televised Nonverbal Behavior." *Science* 326.5960 (2009): 1711–14. Print.

Yancey, George. *Who Is White? Latinos, Asians and the New Black/Nonblack Divide.* Boulder, CO: Lynne Rienner, 2003. Print.

Younge, Gary. "What's Race Got to Do with Herman Cain?" *Nation* 26 Dec. 2011: 10.

Zangwill, Israel. *The Melting Pot.* New York: Macmillan, 1906. Print.

2

Rhyme and Reason

"Post-Race" and the Politics of Colorblind Racism

ROOPALI MUKHERJEE

History doesn't repeat itself, but it does rhyme.
—Mark Twain

Over the months leading up to and following the 2008 elections, political discourse, news coverage, and popular cultural expressions indulged
in a new refrain in American public discourse. Cohering around the
term "post-race," such talk took shape as the climax of an enduring
national saga, signaling transformative shifts in U.S. racial relations,
aspirations, and experiences. If discourses of colorblindness had set the
scene, its plotlines pitting "self-made" heroes against "state-made" villains (Lubiano 1992, 354), its mythic narratives setting in motion new
modalities of "racism without racists" (Bonilla-Silva 2010), then Barack
Obama's epochal significance took shape as the culmination of these
ideas: the farcical denouement—elaborate, extravagant, and improbable—of colorblindness as universal paean of the U.S. racial narrative.
Against staggering evidence of abiding, and indeed deepening, ethno-
racial inequalities impacting education, income and wealth, housing, health care, voting, and incarceration (Alexander 2010; Bobo and
Charles 2009; Cohen 2011; Forman and Lewis 2006; Haney Lopez 2010;
Heckman 2011; Hunt and Wilson 2009; Oliver and Shapiro 2006; Reed
and Louis Jr. 2009), the Obama moment organizes the "truth," however
improbable, of a new America in which race has become the difference
that makes no difference at all.

Discourses of colorblindness are crucial to articulations of post-
racialism. As Kimberlé Crenshaw has shown, the colorblind paradigm

is premised centrally on strategic erasures within which the "white norm" and silent operations of white privilege do not disappear but, rather, become "submerged" within racial consciousness (1995, 115). Such colorblind erasures turn on the technical fiction of "non-recognition" in which individuals are asked to not consider race even though, as Neil Gotanda reminds us, "it is impossible to not think about a subject without having at first thought about it at least a little" (2000, 36). These mutually reinforcing amalgams of wishful thinking, studied denials, scripted declarations, and tortured performances, Crenshaw suggests, gradually but unmistakably reenvisioned the domain of racism (1997, 97). Potently structured by what David Theo Goldberg theorizes as the ongoing march of the "neoliberalization of race," these formulations enable a range of new racisms, in other words, "racism without race, racism gone private, racism without the categories to name it as such" (Goldberg 2009, 23). Working powerfully to disconnect the legacies of white supremacy from enduring material inequalities, these new "born-again" racisms work toward "forgetting, getting over, moving on, . . . wiping away the very vocabulary necessary to recall and recollect, to make a case [or] a claim" (2009, 21).

Crucially, these modes of "e-racing" also make room for strategic "re-racings" (Crenshaw 1997) especially in the context of workplace tokenism, criminality, and national security. Like the relations between "old money" and "new money," those e-raced by the "crossover" logics of colorblindness are granted access to selective dividends of racial privilege even though, as Crenshaw points out, everyone still understands the "difference between the truly privileged and the newly entitled" (107). Renewing black discipline against those who remain outside, these re-racings corral "dangerous individuals" into the regimes of "enterprise culture" (Rose 1996, 57–58) demanding that they abdicate their reliance on race and racial grievance now reformulated as the "provenance of an unjust, irrational ascription and prejudice" (Singh 2004, 11). It is by the conjuring tricks of colorblindness thus that "race disappears but whiteness persists" (Roediger 2008).

The discursive career of colorblindness tracks larger formations of what Howard Winant (2002) identifies as a two-phased "racial break" within the history of racial modernity. The first phase, starting after World War II and culminating in the 1960s, initiated a shift or break in a worldwide racial system that had endured for centuries, and converged in and across a range of progressive antiracist movements—anticolonialism, antiapartheid, the worldwide rejection of fascism, and the U.S. civil rights movement. Together, these antiracist movements called white supremacy into question to an extent unparalleled in modern history; moreover, they brought an unprecedented slate of progressive antiracist demands to state and civic attention. By the 1970s, notes Winant, a second phase emerged, witnessing "adaptations" of centuries-old and deeply entrenched systems of racial injustice toward the "containment" of antiracist challenges (18). Enabling the development of a new racial politics, which while conceding to some of the demands of antiracist movements, served far more crucially to "adapt" modes of racial power and to "absorb" conceptual paradigms for racial reform. Repackaging the ideological structures of white supremacy away from earlier modes of intransigent, violent, and overt racisms, civil rights reforms were incorporated into the agenda of the political center, developing a comprehensive program of racial democracy that reinforced key dimensions of U.S. nationalist ideology (22). Thus, dividing movements, reasserting stability, and defusing political opposition, the "racial break" defined a "new racial common sense" (22), producing successively prominent versions of what Jodi Melamed terms postwar "official antiracisms" in the United States (2011). From racial liberalism (in the mid-1940s to the 1960s) to liberal multiculturalism (from the 1980s to the 1990s) to neoliberal multiculturalism (in the 2000s), Melamed reveals the decisive incorporation of these sanctioned antiracisms into postwar U.S. governmentality, with critical consequences. These incorporations limit official antiracist discourses to colorblind denials of racial privilege as well as stigma, and restrict the settlement of racial conflicts to liberal political terrain concealing the intersectional links between race and material inequality.

Largely tracking historical formations of the racial break, the colorblind paradigm shifted over the course of the twentieth century from a "progressive demand to a reactionary one" (Haney Lopez 2011, 809). Starting in the 1970s, massive transformations in the American economy spurred by global forces of deindustrialization, foreign competition, and rising unemployment consolidated in the potent and visceral politics of white backlash. The patrons of colorblindness, recruited from the ranks of besieged white masculinities, changed gradually from proponents of racial integration to political constituencies firmly committed to defending white supremacy. As progressive antiracist challenges were contained within postwar official antiracisms, paradigms of colorblindness assimilated into right-wing formations, repurposed by the 1990s to attack state programs designed to remedy racism, in particular, affirmative action and immigrant rights (Hasian and Delgado 1998; Mukherjee 2006; Roediger 1997; Skrentny 1996). Moving apace but separately from the liberal "retreat" from racial justice (Steinberg 1995), these reactionary currents emerged by the 2000s to target the state and demand the dismantling of administrative protocols of indexing, auditing, indeed even seeing, race (Flores, Moon, and Nakayama 2006; Goldberg 2002; HoSang 2010).

These reformulations of the colorblind paradigm from the 1970s to the 1990s revealed a growing political distance between unyielding right-wing fronts populated by "born-again" racists and "sympathy-fatigued" liberals solidly committed to the narrow parameters of sanctioned antiracisms. Far from coincidental, the arrival of post-race within this scene constitutes the "liberal embrace of colorblindness" (Haney Lopez 2011, 808) and, crucially, brings into relief a range of ethical and tactical deficits that colorblindness had accrued over the course of its political career. The emergence of a new cultural refrain like post-race, unfettered by regressive political baggage, as Sumi Cho (2009) suggests, produces powerfully integrative and cohering effects. Thus, the arrival of post-race marks a crucial moment in the discursive history of colorblindness. It offers us insights into not only the corroborating synergies between colorblindness and post-race, but equally, the strategic differences between these ideas. The giddy euphoria over post-race as it circulated in the Obama moment, then, takes form as an echo, a rumble, a rhyme, if you will, that steadies the racial "truth" of post-race to adapt, refine, and likewise contain the rationalities of colorblindness as the conceptual paradigm of official antiracisms. Thus, setting post-racial rhyme in step with colorblind reason, I focus here on a few selected moments within public discourse in the months surrounding Obama's 2008 victory to take account of the relations that link post-race and colorblindness. My focus remains on unpacking the crucially ameliorative, integrative, and reinforcing service of post-race, as it closes deficits within the colorblind paradigm. Reformulating the logics of colorblindness, the analysis considers how post-race adapts modes of racial power and absorbs paradigms of racial reform to the service of racial neoliberalism.

The Deficits of Colorblindness

By every account, Barack Obama's presidential campaign and his victory in the 2008 elections stand apart as a focal event of immense affective power. Obama's iconicity emerged buoyed by colorblind fantasies within which Americans no matter their racial lineage could reach the highest echelons of power and prestige, and where an individual's racial circumstance stood no chance against the moral force of an inclusive, race-transcendent America. Obama himself made stilted efforts to interrupt his allure within these narratives (Enck-Wanzer 2011), pointing out that "it implies that somehow my campaign represents an easy shortcut to racial reconciliation" (Wolffe and Briscoe 2007, 26). But, after decades of colorblind imperatives that demanded moving beyond race, the prospect of electing a black man to the presidency took shape as an "emotional epiphany" (Morris 2007). As media spectacles constructed the campaign as "trailblazing" and "historic" (Herbert 2008; Zeleny 2006), Obama himself took shape as a "metaphorical exclamation point—a visual assurance that the country can work for everyone" (Wallace-Wells 2006). As "the last of the republic's old barriers to entry came tumbling down" (Alter 2006, 28), the "orgy of interest" that "Obamamania" commanded shaped the election as "a particularly American achievement, an affirmation of American ideals and a celebration of American circumstances" (Wallace-Wells 2006, B01) that "put a period on the sorriest chapter in American history" (Morris 2007). As Faith Kinyua, a Kenyan green card holder living in Oakland observed, "Color has no meaning and Obama has proved it" (qtd. in Feldmann 2008, 25).

In the first instance, then, Obama's iconicity, his appearance as signal marker of a new post-racial America, performs crucial work to shore up the discursive logics of colorblindness. A particularly American achievement, Obama's victory offered his largely liberal supporters the self-congratulatory assurance that their faith in colorblind denials of racial privilege and stigma were key to his ascendance. Equally, Obama's victory metaphorically sealed shut key chapters of a shameful racial history, enabling the cathartic relief of distance separating the "sorry" past of rank racism from the blameless present of post-racialism. Reinforcing the centrist logics of sanctioned antiracisms, Obama's victory certifies key dimensions of U.S. nationalist ideology—meritocratic fairness, liberal racial magnanimity, the unerring promise of the American Dream, and the forward march of colorblindness as ethical telos of racial history—each an affirmation of American ideals and a celebration of American circumstances. Ultimately, Obama's 2008 victory staged visible evidence that a colorblind country can work for everyone, even, or perhaps especially, for African Americans.

Emerging in stark contrast to the reactionary racisms of the Birthers and the Tea Party movement, popular appeals to post-race circulated almost entirely in the leftist and liberal press (Roediger 2006). Journalists noted the ways that the post-racial figure of Obama signified a "gradual erosion of whiteness as the touchstone of what it means to be American," and the inexorable "dawning of an age [marking] the end of white America" (Hsu 2009, 47). Touching off a new "season of rage," manifest in a "vile and racist right-wing storm front" populated by "angry tea party folks" (Tucker 2009, 34), the lynch mob mentalities of these groups set themselves apart, recruiting anxious white males to their side. For *Essence* writer Cynthia Tucker, far from the "transforming effect of the first black president," the Obama victory spurred "an all-out assault by an unhinged fringe that simply doesn't believe a black man has the right to be president of the United States" (2009, 134).

Opposing these renewals of earlier modes of intransigent, violent, and overt racisms, post-race performed in exemplary ways to consolidate a broad swath of "reasonable" white liberals committed to the imperatives of colorblindness. As Sumi Cho explains, assaults on racialized social justice premised on the reactionary paradigms of born-again racisms that had consolidated from the 1990s through the 2000s had "entangled discourses of colorblindness with the transparent racial-subordination agendas" of the radical right (2009, 1598). As state-level ballot initiatives from California to Michigan ran their course, bludgeoning affirmative action with racist precision, the racial project of colorblindness strained credulity by claiming as its own the language and legacies of the black civil rights movement (Mukherjee 2006). The divisive bent of those campaigns associated colorblindness with politically regressive ends, "injuring the brand for moderate-to-liberal voters" (Cho 2009, 1598). A new concept like post-race could "do the ideological work of colorblindness without so much of its retro-regressive baggage" (1599). Crucially, it could reach key constituencies of moderate-to-liberal and youth voters whom the tainted brand of colorblindness had thus far failed to recruit. Thus, delivering fresh constituencies into the fold of colorblind racism, post-race takes shape as similar to and yet different from colorblindness. Its muscular tactics make room for self-congratulatory renewals of the colorblind paradigm, ousting the reactionary excesses of born-again racisms while invoking the moral superiority of liberal whiteness in adjudicating the political parameters of official antiracisms.

The Racial Gaze of Post-Racialism

The media buzz surrounding Obama turned particularly and repeatedly on studied appraisals of the candidate's blackness. Against scripted denials and long-established prescriptions of noticing but not considering race, of seeing and then sublimating racial categories, Obama's post-racial significance demanded declarative and self-conscious acts of seeing and recognizing his blackness. Indeed, the urgency of "seeing" Obama clearly was reflected in repeated plaints about the difficulties posed by an "enigmatic Obama," as op-eds, talk radio programs, and news reports alike weighed in on who the "real" Obama was (Canellos 2008; Balz 2008; Goodwin 2008).

As journalist Jeff Zeleny noted, although the candidate "strived to be defined by more than color alone," it was Obama's race "as much as anything that would make a presidential run historic" (2006, 1). Likewise, Jonathan Alter, noting "surging, tumultuous crowds, pumped-up Democrats, and ravenous, screaming political reporters" at a 2006 Obama appearance in New Hampshire, explained that "voters might be in the mood to try something historic and possibly redemptive. And a black president in a country that fought a civil war over race might even prove cathartic. . . . Whatever happens, the process feels uplifting . . . psychologically and generationally" (2006, 28). Similarly, reporter Benjamin Wallace-Wells predicted that electing Obama to the presidency would be "widely cheered" both as a sign of "the arrival of his race and [as] a . . . symbol of progress," noting that "the nation feels its racial sins more clearly [than its gendered crimes] and has a more urgent desire to get past them" (2006, B01).

In a similar vein, Obama drew a steady barrage of taunts from the Right as well as the Left about the differences between "black black" and "Obama black" (Chude-Sokei 2007; Mundy 2007). When Jesse Jackson suggested that Obama was "acting like he's white" by showing a tepid response to the racially inflammatory events of the Jena Six controversy (Mooney 2007; Muwakkil 2007), he was publicly reprimanded by his own son, Jesse Jackson Jr. in an op-ed that reasserted Obama's racial standing as a leader who was not simply "black" but also the right sort of black (Jackson 2007). From the Right, similarly, African American conservatives like Stanley Crouch urged caution against the rising "white paroxysm of self-congratulation" over the candidate, noting that "Obama's biracial heritage, and his lineage not being that descended from plantation slaves" served as evidence "of his 'not-quite-blackness.'" "If he . . . wins the White House," Crouch lamented, "he will have entered it through a 'side door'" (2006). Commentator Debra J. Dickerson observed similarly that Obama, "not descended from West African slaves brought to America," had nevertheless stepped into "the benefits of black progress without having borne any of the burden." "Never having been 'black' for a living," Dickerson continued, his "'black' but not black" biography allowed "white folks plausible deniability [for their] unwillingness to embrace blacks in public life . . . while making blacks fear that one day he'll go Tiger Woods on us and get all race transcendent" (2007).

As the nation's racial gaze narrowed precisely on Obama's blackness, these voices assessed the qualities of the candidate's particularly racial allure, noting his generational distance from earlier black politicians defined, to their tactical disadvantage, by their "pro-black bluster" against Obama's "black, but not just black" appeal (Mundy 2007, W10). Fixing the scopic drive of public assessment on the grain of Obama's racial standing, these voices constructed Obama as a candidate who "by the color of his skin" offered the promise of national deliverance, "the chance to turn the page on more than two centuries of painful racial history" (Wolffe and Briscoe 2007, 26). Returning compulsively to tonal assessments of Obama's blackness, these evaluations, unburdened by irony, steadied Obama's "racial bonafides" (Wolffe and Briscoe 2007) as markers of a new post-racial America.

Against colorblind imperatives of noticing but not considering race, of seeing and then sublimating racial categories, Obama's post-racial significance is premised on self-conscious assurances of racial recognition. Constructions of Obama's epochal importance require a vocal constituency of racial "insiders" who can vouch for his authenticity, in-group voices with sufficient credibility to give surety of his racial standing as "black" (Robinson 1994). Thus, Obama's iconicity became calculable and was privileged as post-racial precisely because of his blackness. His claim to the presidency hinged not on racial suppressions and sublimations that are key to the colorblind paradigm but instead on deliberative but selectively ahistorical "re-racings" of the candidate in full view of the public.

As the "educated fool from Harvard" (Moran 2008, 1) morphed into "the great white hope" (Greenberg 2008, B4), from "JFK in sepia" (Street 2008) to fist-bumping icon of "Black Folks 2.0" (Sklar 2008),[1] Obama moved from "not black enough" to "too black" and back again (Marable 2008; Page 2008). No doubt, specific episodes within these re-racings—the Jeremiah Wright episode, the fist-bump incident, and conspiracy theories that fixated on the candidate's "foreign" middle name and African lineage, his birth in Hawaii and years in Malaysia—integrated with relative ease into the transparently racist rhetoric of born-again racists. But, for the vast constituency that made up his liberal base, the racial gaze of these assessments was premised neither on nonrecognition nor on wiping away the terms of reference that made his race relevant.

Rather, these scripted declarations of Obama's blackness affirmatively, and indeed obsessively, required recognition of race, demarcated in precise terms as "socially relevant today because of yesterday's discrimination" (Haney Lopez 2011, 825). The euphoric liberal embrace of Obama turned precisely on his ability to perform as a credible black candidate who presented contemporary inequality as "merely a vestige of the past, an inertial legacy of an otherwise defeated history" (825). As cable news anchor Chris Matthews observed glibly: "There is no history of Jim Crow, no history of anger, no history of slavery. All the bad stuff in our history ain't there with this guy" (2007). Right-wing adherents of colorblind racisms played their part in these reconciliations, ready targets of liberal ire, confirming that in the post-racial vernacular, "racism" referred only to individual bigots who clasped in vain to older modes of intransigent, violent, and overt racisms. Distancing those in the nutty fringes from "proper" standards of liberal colorblindness, post-race recognizes, indeed, it fixates on, race as an artifact that resonates with historical significance in order to make room for self-serving liberal paroxysms over the defeat of its legacies.

In the Service of Racial Neoliberalism

Minutes after news anchors announced Obama's 2008 victory, conservative commentator Bill Bennett, appearing as a guest during CNN's election night coverage, parsed the significance of the moment, noting: "Well, I'll tell you one thing it means. . . . You don't take any excuses anymore from anybody who says, 'The deck is stacked. I can't do anything, there's so much built-in this and that" (Neiwert 2008). Within hours, news cameras showed young African Americans shouting, "No excuses!" as reporters documented spontaneous street celebrations in cities across the country, and a new video appeared on YouTube, pithily titled "Barack Obama Winz! No More Excuses 4 Black Folk" (Moore 2008).

The "no more excuses" theme gathered steam as the meme of the week, with substantiations in op-eds and news reports in the days that followed. "A President Obama," one observer remarked, "undermines their ability to blame discrimination for all the woes afflicting their community" (Feldmann 2008, 25). Others argued similarly that "the election of a black President . . . does make it harder to justify the claim that a racist country is the major obstacle to black advancement" ("Obama and Preferences" 2008, A18). Hollywood superstar Will Smith added racial weight to these sentiments, remarking: "I love that all of our excuses have been removed. There's no white man trying to keep you down, because if he were really trying to keep you down, he would have done everything he could to keep Obama down" (Curry 2009, A19).[2]

Fueling introspections about the continuing relevance of "the black American meta-narrative of heroic or noble victimization" (Early 2008, B11), commentators rushed to proclaim that "the 1960s are over—finally" (Harris and Vandehei 2008); these sentiments coalesced into a growing chorus that urged a move "away from what might be called the civil rights paradigm . . . focused almost exclusively on grievance" (Raspberry 2008). Voices from the Right chimed in, synchronizing the rhyming cadences of post-race with older colorblind appeals. "Obama's success certainly makes the case for any race-based preferential treatment a weak argument," one commentator noted, while another predicted that "affirmative action would be largely off the table with the new administration" (Billups and Sands 2008, A01).[3]

These "no longer necessary" tropes made potent synergies with finger-wagging "no more excuses" admonitions, finding singular proof in the Obama victory of "a fatal blow to the so-called 'Bradley effect,' [driving] a stake through the heart of that demon" (Billups and Sands 2008, A01). The myth of the racist white voter—a demon vanquished by Obama's election—now cleared ground for claims about key civil rights protections as unnecessary. One such set of protections introduced by Section Five of the Voting Rights Act of 1965 focuses on "conditions of preclearance," which require that states with especially notorious histories of discriminating against black voters get permission from the federal government before they modify any election procedures. The provision charges the U.S. Department of Justice with ensuring that any such modification neither "has the purpose nor will have the effect of denying or abridging the right to vote on account of race or color" (Savage 2009, US2).

In April 2009, less than three months after Obama was elected resident, the U.S. Supreme Court heard arguments in *Northwest Austin Municipal Utility District No. 1 v. Holder,* a case seeking relief from preclearance conditions. As voices in the press ruminated over "whether America needs the Voting Rights Act at all . . . now that a black man has won the presidency" (Biskupic 2009; see also Wallsten and Savage 2009), in June 2009, the Court ruled in favor of the appellant. The racial significance of Obama, the newly elected first black president, emerged front and center in their claims, asserting that preclearance provisions were unconstitutional because they imposed "disproportionate burdens" and "a badge of shame" based on an "ancient formula" and "conditions that existed thirty or more years ago that have been long since remedied" (Biskupic 2009). As Gregory Coleman, the lawyer arguing for the local utility board in Austin, Texas, asserted in his opening argument: "The America that has elected Barack Obama as its first African American president is far different than when Section Five was first enacted in 1965" (qtd. in Biskupic 2009).

Opening the door to questions about the absurdity of "black-only" organizations and black advocacy groups, these ruminations touched on larger threads about the feasibility and continuing relevance of the institutions of the black public sphere. Versions of these dilemmas had circulated earlier in a cover story for the *New York Times Magazine* in which the author Matt Bai pondered whether "with Obama in the White House, race-specific policies will be even harder to pursue, and a separate sphere of 'black politics' harder to maintain" (2008). Pointing to "chasms of experience that separate[d] one generation from the next," Bai noted that for younger generations, Obama's candidacy "signified . . . that black politics might now be disappearing into American politics in the same way that the Irish and Italian machines long ago joined the political mainstream" (36). These arguments proliferated with new force after Obama's victory, raising questions about the relevance of long-standing black advocacy groups like the NAACP, which, as one commentator put it, was "as anachronistic as colored-only water fountains and white-only bathrooms" (Barras 2009, B04). Black conservative John McWhorter asked, "Might it not be time to allow that our obsession with how unschooled and usually aging folks feel in their hearts about black people has become a fetish?" (2008), while another African American proclaimed with glee: "We couldn't wait for our forty acres and a mule, so we took fifty states and the White House" (Washington 2008, A4). As if closing the book on decades of grinding black political endeavor, these voices troubled core mythologies around which black solidarities had cohered, urging the dismantling of black public spaces that had served to shelter race talk and antiracist organizing.

Clearing ground for a new "post-rage" era of black politics, these articulations rendered racial grievance moot and reduced paradigms for black advocacy to little beyond a fetish. Probing the significance of Obama's victory as a "living rebuttal to Fanon's rage of the powerless" (Ignatius 2008, B7), progressive commentators cautioned that Obama's post-racial significance inaugurated new modalities to "domesticate, discipline, and contain the politics of radical opposition" (Adams 2008). Alerting readers to the ways that Obama's victory deepens the silence on the links between race and material inequalities (Fletcher 2008; Muwakkil 2007; Reed "Where Obamaism Seems to Be Going," "Obama No"; Roediger 2008; "Roundtable" 2008; Street 2008; Tilove 2008; Wickham 2008), these voices warned that the post-racial triumphalism of the Obama moment would settle into an "uncritical exuberance" that could not but sedate social action (Butler 2008). Reordered through the rhyming allures of post-race, the colorblind paradigm emerged reinvigorated, claiming a wide swath of adherents for whom the racial present had been rendered different in crucial ways from the past.

The broad ideological draw of post-race exhorts Americans to see race but only as a signal of its legacies having been defeated. It secures the nation's racial gaze on blackness to enable, in the main, self-congratulatory renewals of nationalist ideologies of merit, fairness, and freedom. The ideology of post-race theories discharges historical paradigms for progressive racial reform as "no longer necessary" for shoring up the anemic parameters of official antiracisms. It leaves poor people of every race to fend for themselves within the governing logics of enterprise culture. African Americans, in particular, have "no more excuses" when their material circumstances fail by the standards of the American Dream. They can neither invoke race to explain their condition nor can it cohere as their paradigm for reform. These decisive incorporations of post-race into neoliberal governmentality do not police the boundaries of black experiences and aspirations alone. They also reconfigure modes of racial power to admonish born-again racists and racial progressives alike into the proper conduct of colorblind racism.

Notes

1. The fist-bump controversy arose after Barack and Michelle Obama bumped fists with each other on a stage in St. Paul, Minnesota, on June 3, 2008, at a rally celebrating Obama's victory in the Democratic presidential primaries. Media pundits analyzed the gesture as a symbol of generational change, a harbinger of post-racial politics, and other more sinister interpretations. Particularly inflammatory was Fox News anchor E. D. Hill's provocative reference to the gesture as a "terrorist fist jab" (Stephey 2008). In contrast, African American writer Ta-Nehisi Coates was quoted in the *Washington Post* applauding Obama for introducing black colloquialisms like the "dap" to the political world, saying "Barack is like Black Folks 2.0" (Argetsinger and Roberts 2008; see also, Coates 2007). A few weeks later, the *New Yorker* added fuel to these fires with a caricature of the fist bump on its July 21, 2008, cover, featuring "Michelle as afro-sporting and rifle-toting Black Panther and Barack as Muslim jihadi in the Oval Office" (Stephey 2008). *New Yorker* editor David Remnick defended the cover, explaining that it was intended to satirize right-wing rumors about the Obamas, drawing attention to "the lies that have fed into the politics of fear" (Sklar 2008).

2. In June 2008, African American comedienne Wanda Sykes, appearing on *The Conan O'Brien Show,* received applause from a predominantly white studio audience when she joked that if Obama won, it would mean that black people

have no more excuses for their inferior status and would have to take personal responsibility for being disproportionately locked up in the nation's prisons.

3. Obama's election in 2008 coincided with the passage of yet another anti–affirmative action ballot measure, this one in Nebraska, and a narrow loss for a similar initiative in Colorado.

WORKS CITED

Adams, Jonathan. "The Dreadful Genius of the Obama Moment." *Colorlines.* N.p., November 10, 2008. Web. <http://colorlines.com/archives/2008/11/the_dreadful_genius_of_the_oba.html>.

Alexander, Michelle. *The New Jim Crow: Mass Incarceration in the Age of Colorblindness.* New York: New Press. 2010. Print.

Alter, Jonathan. "Is America Ready: Hillary's Hair and Hemline Won't Be Issues." *Newsweek,* 28. December 25, 2006. Print.

Argetsinger, Amy, and Roxanne Roberts. "The Fist Couple: Giving a Big Bump to Authenticity." *Washington Post* June 5, 2008. Web. < http://www.washingtonpost.com/wp-dyn/content/article/2008/06/04/AR2008060404521.html>.

Bai, Matt. "Post-Race: Is Obama the End of Black Politics?" *New York Times Magazine,* 34–41. August 10, 2008. Print.

Balz, Dan. "Obama's Ideology Proving Difficult to Pinpoint." *Washington Post,* A01. July 10, 2008. Print.

Barras, Jonetta Rose. "Why We Should Get Rid of the NAACP." *Washington Post,* B04. April 19, 2009. Print.

Billups, Andrea, and David R. Sands. "Obama Presidency Expected to Be Post-Racial." *Washington Times,* A01. November 9, 2008. Print.

Biskupic, Joan. "Supreme Court Considers Challenge to Voting Rights Act." *USA Today.* January 8, 2009. Web. <http://www.usatoday.com/news/washington/judicial/2009-01-08-court_N.htm>.

Bobo, Lawrence, and Camille Z. Charles. "Race in the American Mind: From the Moynihan Report to the Obama Candidacy." *Annals of the American Academy of Political and Social Science* 621.1 (2009): 243–59. Print.

Bonilla-Silva, Eduardo. *Racism without Racists: Color-Blind Racism and the Persistence of Racial Inequality in the United States.* 3rd ed. New York: Rowman and Littlefield, 2010. Print.

Butler, Judith. "Uncritical Exuberance." November 5, 2008. Web. <www.indybay.org/newsitems/2008/11/05/18549195.php>.

Canellos, Peter. "On Affirmative Action, Obama Intriguing but Vague." *Boston Globe.* April 29, 2008. Web. <http://www.boston.com/news/nation/articles/2008/04/29/on_affirmative_action_obama_intriguing_but_vague/>.

Cho, Sumi. "Post-Racialism." *Iowa Law Review* 94 (2009): 1589–1645. Print.

Chude-Sokei, Louis. "Shades of Black." *Los Angeles Times,* M6. February 18, 2007. Print.

Coates, Ta-Nehisi P. "Is Obama Black Enough?" *Time.* February 1, 2007. Web. <http://www.time.com/time/nation/article/0,8599,1584736,00.html>.

Cohen, Cathy J. "Millennials and the Myth of the Post-Racial Society: Black Youth, Intra-generational Divisions and the Continuing Racial Divide in American Politics." *Daedalus* 140.2 (2011): 197–205. Print.

Crenshaw, Kimberlé. "Race, Reform, and Retrenchment: Transformation and Legitimation in Anti-discrimination Law." In Kimberlé Crenshaw et al. eds. *Critical Race Theory: The Key Writings That Formed the Movement.* New York: New Press, 103–22. 1995. Print.

Crenshaw, Kimberlé. "Color-Blind Dreams and Racial Nightmares: Reconfiguring Racism in the Post-Civil Rights Era." In Toni Morrison and Claudia Brodsky LaCour, eds. *Birth of a Nation 'hood: Gaze, Script and Spectacle in the O. J. Simpson Trial.* New York: Pantheon, 97–168. 1997. Print.

Crouch, Stanley. "What Obama Isn't: Black Like Me on Race." *New York Daily News.* November 2, 2006. Web. <http://www.nydailynews.com/archives/opinions/2006/11/02/2006>.

Curry, George. "Beyond the Spin: Reflecting on Obama's Win." *Philadelphia Inquirer,* A19. January 22, 2009. Print.

Dickerson, Debra J. "Colorblind: Barack Obama Would Be the Great Black Hope in the Next Presidential Race—If He Were Actually Black." *Salon.com.* January 22, 2007. Web. <http://www.salon.com/news/opinion/feature/2007/01/22/obama>.

Early, Gerald L. "The End of Race as We Know It." *Chronicle of Higher Education* 55.7 (October 10, 2008): B11–B13. Print.

Enck-Wanzer, Darrel. "Barack Obama, the Tea Party, and the Threat of Race: On Racial Neoliberalism and Born Again Racism." *Communication, Culture and Critique* 4 (2011): 23–30. Print.

Feldmann, Linda. "Obama's Victory Signals New Push for Unity." *Christian Science Monitor,* 25. November 6, 2008. Print.

Fletcher, Bill, Jr. "Obama—History, Challenges and Possibilities." *Black Commentator.* November 6, 2008. Web. <www.BlackCommentator.com>.

Flores, Lisa A., Dreama G. Moon, and Thomas K. Nakayama. "Dynamic Rhetorics of Race: California's Racial Privacy Initiative and the Shifting Grounds of Racial Politics." *Communication and Critical/Cultural Studies* 3.3 (2006): 181–201. Print.

Forman, Tyrone, and Amanda Lewis. "Racial Apathy and Hurricane Katrina: The Social Anatomy of Prejudice in the Post–Civil Rights Era." *Du Bois Review* 3 (2006): 175–202. Print.

Goldberg David Theo. *The Racial State.* Malden, MA: Blackwell. 2002. Print.

———. *The Threat of Race: Reflections on Racial Neoliberalism.* Malden, MA: Wiley-Blackwell. 2009. Print

Goodwin, Michael. "Will the Real Obama Please Stand?" *New York Daily News,* 31. July 13, 2008. Print.

Gotanda, Neil. "A Critique of 'Our Constitution Is Colorblind.'" In Richard Delgado and Jean Stefancic, eds. *Critical Race Theory: The Cutting Edge.* 2nd ed. Philadelphia: Temple University Press, 35–38. 2000. Print.

Greenberg, David. "Why Obamamania? Because He Runs as the Great White Hope." *Washington Post*, B4. January 13, 2008. Print.

Haney Lopez, Ian F. "Is the 'Post' in Post-Racial the 'Blind' in Colorblind?" *Cardozo Law Review* 32.3 (2011): 807–31. Print.

———. "Post-Racial Racism: Racial Stratification and Mass Incarceration in the Age of Obama." *California Law Review* 98 (2010): 1023–73. Print.

Harris, John F., and Jim Vandehei. "The Obama Revolution." *Politico.com*. November 5, 2008. Web. <http://www.politico.com/news/stories/1108/15300.html>.

Hasian, Marouf, and Fernando Delgado. "The Trials and Tribulations of Racialized Critical Rhetorical Theory: Understanding the Rhetorical Ambiguities of Proposition 187." *Communication Theory* 8 (1998): 245–70. Print.

Heckman, James J. "The American Family in Black and White: A Post-Racial Strategy for Improving Skills to Promote Equality." *Daedalus* 140.2 (2011): 70–89. Print.

Herbert, Bob. "The Obama Phenomenon." *New York Times*, A15. January 5, 2008. Print.

HoSang, Daniel. *Racial Propositions: Ballot Initiatives and the Making of Postwar California*. Berkeley and Los Angeles: University of California Press. 2010. Print.

Hsu, Hua. "The End of White America." *Atlantic*, 46–55. January/February 2009. Print.

Hunt, Matthew O., and David C. Wilson. "Race/Ethnicity, Perceived Discrimination, and Beliefs about the Meaning of an Obama Presidency." *Du Bois Review* 6 (2009): 173–99.

Ignatius, David. "Obama the Healer." *Washington Post*, B7. December 14, 2008. Print.

Jackson, Jesse, Jr. "You're Wrong on Obama, Dad." *Chicago Sun-Times*, 28. December 3, 2007. Print.

Lubiano, Wahneema. "Black Ladies, Welfare Queens, and State Minstrels: Ideological War by Narrative Means." In Toni Morrison, ed. *Race-ing Justice, En-gendering Power: Essays on Anita Hill, Clarence Thomas, and the Construction of Social Reality*. New York: Pantheon, 323–63. 1992. Print.

Marable, Manning. "Racializing Obama." *Free Press*. April 16, 2008. Web. <http://freepress.org/columns/display/4/2008/1647>.

Matthews, Chris. *The Chris Matthews Show* (Television transcript). January 21, 2007. <http://www.thechrismatthewsshow.com/html/transcript/index.php?id=41&selected=1>.

McWhorter, John. "The End of Racism?" *Forbes*. November 5, 2008. Web. <http://www.forbes.com/2008/11/05/obama-racism-president-oped-cx_jm_1105mcwhorter_print.html>.

Melamed, Jodi. *Represent and Destroy: Rationalizing Violence in the New Racial Capitalism*. Minneapolis: University of Minnesota Press. 2011. Print.

Mooney, Alexander. "Jesse Jackson: Obama Needs to Bring More Attention to Jena 6." CNN. September 19, 2007. <http://www.cnn.com/2007/POLITICS/09/19/jackson.jena6/index.html>.

Moore, Kevin. "In Contempt (Comic Strip)." *Web Comics Nation*. 2008. Web. <http://www.webcomicsnation.com/kevinmoore/incontempt/series.php?view=single&ID=131823>.

Moran, Tom. "Tossing Out the Race Card." *Star-Ledger* (Newark), 1. January 10, 2008. Print.

Morris, Dick. "Obama's Selma Bounce." *Real Clear Politics* March 7, 2007. Web. <RealClearPolitics.com/articles/2007/03/obama_selma_bounce.html>.

Mukherjee, Roopali. *The Racial Order of Things: Cultural Imaginaries of the "Post-soul" Era.* Minneapolis: University of Minnesota Press. 2006. Print.

Mundy, Liza. "A Series of Fortunate Events." *Washington Post Magazine,* W10. August 12, 2007. Print.

Muwakkil, Salim. "The Squandering of Obama." *In These Times.* July 26, 2007. Web. <www.inthesetimes.com/article/3268/the_squandering_of_obama>.

Neiwert, David. "Bill Bennett: Obama's Win Means 'You Don't Take Excuses Anymore' from Minorities." *Crooks and Liars.* November 5, 2008. Web. <http://crooksandliars.com/david-neiwert/billbennett-obama-wins-means-no-mor>.

Northwest Austin Municipal Utility District No. 1 v. Holder. 557 U.S. 193, 129 S.Ct. 2504 (2009).

"Obama and Preferences." *Wall Street Journal,* A18. November 6, 2008. Print.

Oliver, Melvin, and Thomas Shapiro. *Black Wealth/White Wealth: A New Perspective on Racial Inequality.* New York: Routledge. 2006. Print.

Page, Clarence. "Barack Obama and His Pastor; First Not Black Enough; Now Is He Too Black?" *Cutting Edge.* March 31, 2008. Web. <http://www.thecuttingedgenews.com/index.php?article=400&pageid=&pagename=>.

Raspberry, William. "A Path beyond Grievance." *Washington Post.* November 11, 2008. Web. <http://www.washingtonpost.com/wp-dyn/content/article/2008/11/10/AR2008111001544.html>.

Reed, Adolph, Jr. "Obama No." *Progressive.* May 2008. Print.

———. "Where Obamaism Seems to Be Going." *Black Agenda Report,* July 16, 2008. Web. <www.blackagendareport.com>.

Reed, Wornie L., and Bertin M. Louis Jr. "No More Excuses: Problematic Responses to Barack Obama's Election." *Journal of African American Studies* 13 (2009): 97–109. Print.

Robinson, Amy. "It Takes One to Know One: Passing and Communities of Common Interest." *Critical Inquiry* 20 (1994): 715–36. Print.

Roediger, David R. "Race Will Survive the Obama Phenomenon." *Chronicle of Higher Education.* October 10, 2008. Web. <http://chronicle.com/article/Race-Will-Survive-the-Obama/21983>.

———. "The Retreat from Race and Class." *Monthly Review.* July–August 2006. Web. < http://monthlyreview.org/author/davidroediger>.

———. "White Workers, New Democrats, and Affirmative Action." In Wahneema Lubiano, ed. *The House That Race Built.* New York: Vintage, 48–65. 1997. Print.

Rose, Nicholas. "Governing Advanced Liberal Democracies." In Andrew Barry, Thomas Osborne, and Nicholas Rose, eds. *Foucault and Political Reason: Liberalism, Neo-liberalism and Rationalities of Government.* Chicago: University of Chicago Press, 37–64. 1996. Print.

"Roundtable: From King to Obama: Race in America." Social Science Research Council. April 4, 2008. Web. <http://www.ssrc.org/raceinamerica>.

Savage, David G. "Voting Rights Act Section That Singles Out South May Be Abolished." *Los Angeles Times.* April 30, 2009. Print.

Singh, Nikhil Pal. *Black Is a Country: Race and the Unfinished Struggle for Democracy.* Cambridge: Harvard University Press. 2004. Print.

Sklar, Rachel. "David Remnick on That *New Yorker* Cover." *Huffington Post.* July 21, 2008. Web. <http://www.huffingtonpost.com/2008/07/13/david-remnick-on-emnew-yo_n_112456.html>.

Skrentny, John D. *The Ironies of Affirmative Action: Politics, Culture, and Justice in America.* Chicago: University of Chicago Press. 1996. Print.

Steinberg, Stephen. *Turning Back: The Retreat from Racial Justice in American Thought and Policy.* Boston: Beacon. 1995. Print.

Stephey, M. J. "A Brief History of the Fist Bump." *Time.* June 5, 2008. Web. <http://www.time.com/time/nation/article/0,8599,1812102,00.html>.

Street, Paul. "Comment: Seven Reasons Not to Get Overly Excited about the Fact that Obama Is Black." Paul Street's blog for *Black Agenda Report.com.* June 11, 2008. Web. <http://links.org.au/node/464/970>.

Tilove, Jonathan. "For Scholars of Race, an Obama Dilemma." *Seattle Times.* August 13, 2008. Print.

Tucker, Cynthia. November. "Anger Management." *Essence,* 134. 2009. Print.

Wallace-Wells, Benjamin. "Is America Too Racist for Barack? Too Sexist for Hillary?" *Washington Post,* B01. November 12, 2006. Print.

Wallsten, Peter, and David G. Savage. "Voting Rights Act Opponents Point to Barack Obama's Election as Reason to Scale Back Civil Rights Laws." *Chicago Tribune,* C5. March 15, 2009. Print.

Washington, Adrienne T. "Take Time to Revel in Beyond Belief Black Tuesday." *Washington Times,* A4. November 7, 2008. Print.

Wickham, DeWayne. "New NAACP President's Biggest Challenge: Restoring Group's Relevancy." *USA Today,* 9A. May 20, 2008. Print.

Winant, Howard. "The Modern World Racial System." *Souls* 4.3 (2002): 17–30. Print.

Wolffe, Richard, and Daren Briscoe. "Across the Divide." *Newsweek,* 30. July 16, 2007. Print.

Zeleny, Jeff. "Testing the Water, Obama Tests His Own Limits." *New York Times,* 1. December 24, 2006. Print.

3

The End of Racism?

Colorblind Racism and Popular Media

EDUARDO BONILLA-SILVA AND AUSTIN ASHE

Introduction: Colorblindness in Obamerica

In the beginning, Obama created the heavens and the earth and America became a nation no longer divided by race.[1] A mythology that emerged in the post–civil rights era (from the 1970s onward) has become accepted dogma among whites with the election of Barack Obama: the idea that race is no longer a central factor determining the life chances of Americans. Journalists (Dowd 2009; Shapiro 2004), political advisers (Ifill 2009), some people of color (Reed and Louis 2009), and most whites (CBS 2009) have deemed the election of our first black president evidence that we have entered a "post-racial" era.

Despite the dominant white common sense about race becoming a secondary matter in the nation, media coverage of Obama's campaign and presidency has actually been saturated with discussions about race.[2] Nevertheless, Obama and his administration have all worked hard to maintain a colorblind (or race-blind) stand that fits perfectly the racial game of post–civil rights America. In contrast to the belief that his victory represents the "end of racism," we contend Obama's ascendancy to the presidency is part and parcel of the "New Racism." In fact, Bonilla-Silva has argued the Obama phenomenon can be explained as the culmination of forty years of racial transition from the Jim Crow era to what he calls the "New Racism" regime (2010; cf. Bobo, Kluegel, and Smith 1997; Essed 1991). This is the fundamental explanation behind the Obama "miracle" (Bonilla-Silva and Seamster 2011). Among other things, the age of Obama has ushered in (1) framing Obama's multiracial heritage as "exceptional";[3] (2) the strategic portrayal of Obama's family as "ethnic," rather than black; (3) the emphasis on the traditional character and stability of Obama's marriage and family, making them "exceptional" and thus "acceptable blacks"; (4) the careful construction of a nonthreatening, nonsexualized, black masculine identity; (5) the avoidance of any clear public connection to black leaders and the black community; (6) the careful retreat from any controversy that tastes of race;[4] and (7) the hesitant yet consistent hint by Obama and his administration that race is no longer the central reason behind blacks' role in America.

The potency of Obama's "hope liquor" (Bonilla-Silva 2010) has gotten the country drunk with delusions of racial harmony. Average Americans and social analysts alike argue that race has "declined in significance" (Wilson 1978; Sakamoto, Wu, and Tzeng 2000; Wakefield and Uggen 2004), yet whites and people of color remain separate and disturbingly unequal in all sorts of matters (Sampson and Sharkey 2008). To account for this contradiction—a post-racial nation with growing racial disparities—whites have developed a new racial repertoire of explanations. Instead of claiming people of color are biologically or naturally inferior as they did during the Jim Crow era, they explain their status nowadays as the products of aberrant behaviors (e.g., having too many babies) or lacking the proper work ethic, or due to non-racial market factors (Bobo and Charles 2009; Hunt 2007). More troublesome is that many minority elite commentators (e.g., Steele 2006; O. Patterson 2006; McWhorter 2001) and more than a few liberals such as comedian Bill Cosby (Cosby and Poussaint 2007) and actor Will Smith are also embracing these views (Smith 2008).[5]

The belief that America is a post-racial nation is based on a narrowly defined notion of racism. For most whites (most social scientists included), racism is fundamentally an ideological or attitudinal phenomenon. In contrast, radical and progressive scholars regard racism as a *structure*, that is, as a network of relations at the social, political, economic, and ideological levels that shapes the life chances of the various racial groups (Bonilla-Silva 1997). The foundation of this structure, as with all social structure, is material: that the group in the superordinate position (whites) accrues systemic advantages over nonwhites and thus develops an interest in the reproduction of their dominant status position. What people (again, most social scientists included) define as racism is conceptualized in this framework as racial ideology. Racial ideology helps explain and justify racial inequality in society as well as cement racial stratification.

From this vantage point, rather than arguing about whether race has "declined in significance" (Wilson 1978), increased, or not changed at all, the issue at hand is assessing if the racial structure in the United States has undergone a transformation. We argue that racial oppression in America is still "systemic" (Feagin 2006), thus affecting *all* people and institutions. Racism is not limited to "racist," uneducated, working-class people in the South, as was suggested by the media in the 2008 election, but is a structural problem affecting all of us (Bonilla-Silva 1997)—whites, as the superordinate group, receive material benefits and rewards,[6] and people of color, as the racially subordinated groups, experience systemic disadvantages. In contemporary America, the racial practices[7] and behaviors responsible for the reproduction of racial inequality are mostly subtle, apparently nonracial, and institutionalized. This new racial regime has been labeled by Bonilla-Silva as the "New Racism" (2001), and not surprisingly, the ideological anchor of this new regime, colorblind racism, is equally slippery and seemingly nonracial (Bonilla-Silva 2001; Bonilla-Silva and Doane 2003; see Caditz 1976 for an early work that captured this ideological transition).

Framing the current post-racial moment and the Obama phenomenon properly requires an understanding of how racism in the post–civil rights era fits the New Racism and its ideological anchor—colorblind racism. Our discussion of race and racism in Obamerica will consist of three parts. First, we describe the New Racism that emerged in the 1970s. Second, we explain the ideology of colorblind racism that co-emerged with the New Racism. Third, we illustrate how colorblind racism works in the popular media, which is the focus of this book. We conclude by making some general observations about the peculiar moment we live in, how it will shape the cultural and political terrain, and how we can fight the current illusion we are facing where nothing seems to be racial yet all is.

The New Racism: Jim Crow with a Smile

Just as Jim Crow racism served to justify racial oppression in the past, the New Racism upholds racial inequality in contemporary America. It is our contention that despite the profound changes that occurred in the 1960s, a new racial structure is operating that accounts for the persistence of racial inequality. The elements that constitute this new racial structure are (1) the increasingly *covert* nature of racial discourse and racial practices; (2) the avoidance of racial terminology and the ever-growing claim by whites that they experience "reverse racism"; (3) the elaboration of a racial agenda over political matters that eschew direct racial references; (4) the invisibility of most mechanisms that reproduce racial inequality; and, finally, (5) the rearticulation of some racial practices characteristic of the Jim Crow period of race relations.[8]

There are many examples of how the new character of racism has played out in the political, social, and economic institutions of America. To illustrate this reality, we will provide a brief discussion of how residential segregation and housing discrimination operated in the past and how it works today in New Racism fashion to maintain racial inequality. We show that there is little evidence suggesting that residential segregation and housing discrimination will end any time soon unless there are significant systemic and institutional transformations.

Welcome to the Neighborhood: Residential Segregation and Housing Discrimination

A close examination of research in the areas of housing, education, and everyday social interaction reveals startlingly little progress since the 1960s. Data from the 2010 U.S. census indicate that residential segregation has declined for the fourth straight decade (CensusScope 2011), but these segregation indices tell only part of the story about segregation (Zuberi and Bonilla-Silva 2008). The apparent decline fails to account for the way that social distance operates in so-called integrated neighborhoods (Mayorga 2012). Mayorga (2012) observes and analyzes social interaction between and within three racial and ethnic groups in an integrated neighborhood. By focusing on social relationships in an integrated neighborhood, she moves beyond traditional studies of segregation research that use segregation indices, such as the dissimilarity index.[9] By measuring social distance through neighborhood observations, in-depth interviews with residents, and a neighborhood-wide survey, Mayorga finds that racial segregation persists and that researchers must go beyond census-based analyses when studying racial segregation.

Furthermore, blacks are still more segregated than any other racial or ethnic group (Logan 2003; Zhao 2005; Zhao, Ondrich, and Yinger 2006)—segregation that they have experienced longer than any other group—and are segregated at every income level. The black poor, in particular, suffer the greatest degree of segregation, and this pattern of extreme isolation has remained the same through the last third of the previous century (Cashin 2004). The actual difference between the de jure racism of the Jim Crow era and the smiling face of segregation today is simply in how it is accomplished. In the past, the housing industry used overtly discriminatory practices such as real estate agents employing outright refusal or subterfuge to avoid renting or selling to black customers, federal government redlining policies, overtly discriminatory insurance and lending practices, and racially restrictive covenants on housing deeds in order to maintain segregated communities (Tauber and Tauber 1965; Tabb 1970; Massey and Denton 1993). In contrast, the covert behaviors of colorblind racism have replaced these practices and have maintained the same outcome: separate communities. The contemporary racial practices are subtle, indirect, and fluid and operate at the economic, political, social, and ideological levels. The current racial practices that reproduce racial inequality in contemporary America (1) are increasingly covert, (2) are embedded in normal operations of institutions, (3) avoid direct racial terminology, and (4) are invisible to most whites (Bonilla-Silva 1997).

Many studies have detailed the obstacles that minorities face from government agencies, real estate agents, moneylenders, and white residents. A study by the Federal Reserve Bank of Boston found that controlling for a number of variables, blacks on average were denied loans 60 percent more times than whites (Oliver and Shapiro 2006). In an overview of mortgage loan practices during the 1990s, Turner and Skidmore (1999) reported blacks received less information from loan officers, were quoted higher interest rates, and suffered higher loan denial rates. Much of the gain in home ownership among African Americans in the 1990s was achieved through subprime lenders who offered usurious rates, due in large part to the continued practice of redlining of black neighborhoods by mainstream lenders (Williams, Nesiba, and McConnell 2005; Cashin 2004).

Results from the Department of Housing and Urban Development's 1989 and 2000 *Housing Discrimination Study* (HDS) both found significant levels of racial discrimination. Reports based on the 1989 HDS found that blacks and Latinos were discriminated against in approximately *half* of their efforts to rent or buy housing (Turner, Struyk, and Yinger 1991). Using the 2000 audit of housing discrimination, Turner et al. (2002) report that, although there have been improvements since the 1989 audit, whites continue to be given more information about potential rentals and are shown more available housing units in both the rental and sales markets. This study also showed a significant increase in geographic steering that perpetuated segregation predominantly through real estate agent editorializing. Using the audit data from the 2000 HDS, Zhao (2005), controlling for the auditors' socioeconomic status, find that blacks are shown 30 percent fewer units than whites, while Latinos are shown 10 percent fewer units. Zhao (2005) also find that discrimination against blacks has actually increased by 12 percent since 1989 and is mostly due to white prejudice. In examining racial and ethnic discrimination among real estate brokers specifically, Zhao, Ondrich, and Yinger (2006) find that discrimination remains strong but has declined since 1989.

These housing studies have found that when compared with whites, blacks are shown fewer apartments, quoted higher rents, offered worse conditions, and steered to specific neighborhoods (Yinger 1986; Galster 1990; Turner, Struyk, and Yinger 1991; Turner et al. 2002; Zhao 2005; Zhao, Ondrich, and Yinger 2006). African Americans and Latinos are also differentially marketed risky subprime loans (Rugh and Massey 2010), explaining a major factor in why minorities suffered disproportionately from the recent housing bubble and wave of foreclosures. Even minorities with similar incomes and credit scores as white borrowers are found to still receive less favorable loans and are charged additional fees (Aleo and Svirsky 2008).

Segregation continues to be a serious consequence of contemporary racial practices. Framing housing discrimination as a part of America's racist past is misleading and serves to maintain the racial order. As rental markets increasingly move online, we must develop appropriate techniques for studying housing discrimination in cyberspace (Ahmed and Hammarstedt 2008). Recent audit studies have found that racism persists in the online housing market. Research examining the online rental market using racialized names (Bertrand and Mullainathan 2004;

Hanson and Hawley 2011) found significant levels of discrimination against African Americans. Landlords respond to e-mails from white names more formally and politely. They also respond more quickly and send longer e-mails to inquiries from white renters (Hanson, Hawley, and Taylor 2011). The wealth of evidence proving the continued significance of racism in the housing market is simply an example of one domain in which the New Racism upholds an unequal structure. Essential to the maintenance of this racial hierarchy is its ideological component, colorblind racism, which we discuss in detail in the next section.

The (White) Color of Colorblind Racism

Bonilla-Silva (2001) argues that the dominant racial views held by whites constitute an ideology rather than mere prejudice. By this we mean that this ideology should be understood within the context of how power relations between whites and nonwhites are maintained in the racial arena. Thus, because the civil rights movement forced changes in the way racial inequality is reproduced in the United States,[10] new explanations, accounts, and vocabulary emerged to justify the racial status quo.

According to Omi and Winant (1986), the first phase of the civil rights movement produced real although limited reforms (e.g., enactment of the Civil Rights Act of 1964 and the Voting Rights Act of 1965, and registration of millions of southern black voters). However, the economic status of most blacks was left unaffected by these reforms. To understand this significant ideological shift, we must also recognize that the civil rights rebellion, in conjunction with other social, economic, and demographic changes, dramatically altered the nature of the racial order. Today the maintenance of "white privilege" (McIntosh 1998) no longer depends on the subordinated incorporation of all individual members of racial minority groups in the economic, social, and political spheres. Instead, it is reproduced in a mostly institutional way.

For analytical purposes, racial ideology can be conceived as consisting of the following three elements: frames, styles, and racial stories. Systematic interview data are used in this section to illustrate how these three components function to create apparently nonracial explanations of race events. The data come from two similarly structured projects. The first is the 1997 Survey of Social Attitudes of College Students, based on a convenience sample of 627 college students (including 451 white students) surveyed at a large midwestern university (henceforth MU), a large southern university, and a medium-size West Coast university. The second data source is the 1998 Detroit Area Study (DAS), a probabilistic survey of 323 white and 67 black Detroit metropolitan area residents. In this section we use these data to briefly explain the functions of colorblind frames, styles, and stories (Bonilla-Silva 2010).

Frames are the unacknowledged, contextual standpoints that provide the intellectual and moral building blocks whites (and some blacks) use to explain racial matters. We discuss only the *abstract liberalism* frame in detail here;[11] this frame incorporates values associated with political and economic liberalism in an abstract and decontextualized manner. The framing of race-related issues through liberalism allows whites to present themselves as "reasonable" and even "moral" while opposing all practical approaches to deal with racial inequality. For instance, by using the tenets of the free market ideology in the abstract, whites can oppose affirmative action as a violation of the norm of equal opportunity. The following example illustrates how whites use this frame. Jim, a thirty-year-old computer software salesperson from a privileged background, explained his opposition to affirmative action as follows:

> I think it's unfair top to bottom on everybody and the whole process. It often, you know, discrimination itself is a bad word, right? But you discriminate every day. You wanna buy a beer at the store and there are six kinda beers you can get from *Natural Light* to *Sam Adams,* right? And you look at the price and you look at the kind of beer, and you . . . *it's a choice.* . . . And it's the same thing about getting into school or getting into some place. . . . I don't think [MU] has a lot of racism in the admissions process. . . . So why not just pick people that are going to do well at Midwestern University, pick people by their merit? I think we should stop the whole idea of choosing people based on their color.

Because Jim assumes decisions are like market choices (choosing between competing brands of beer), he embraces a laissez-faire position on racial discrimination. The problem with Jim's view is that labor market discrimination is alive and well (Holzer 2009), and most jobs are obtained through informal networks (Royster 2003). Jim's abstract position is further cushioned by his belief that although blacks "perceive or feel" like there is a lot of discrimination, he does not see much out there. Therefore, by upholding a strict laissez-faire view on hiring and at the same time ignoring the significant impact of discrimination in the labor market, Jim can safely voice his opposition to affirmative action in an apparently race-neutral way. This frame allows whites to be unconcerned about school and residential segregation, oppose almost any kind of government intervention to ameliorate the effects of past and contemporary discrimination, and even support their preferences for whites as partners and friends as a matter of choice.

The style of a racial ideology refers to its particular linguistic manners and rhetorical strategies or the tools that allow users to articulate the frames and stories of an ideology. Because overt racist talk in public venues is no longer tolerated, contemporary racial discussions must be done in code or with shields that allow individuals to express their views in a way that preserves their image of race neutrality.[12] In the following, we highlight a few of the stylistic components of colorblind racism.

"Semantic moves" or "strategically managed propositions" are phrases that are interjected in speech when an individual is about to state a position that is seemingly racist. Two classic examples of semantic moves are "I'm not prejudiced, but . . . " and "Some of my best friends are black."[13] A woman in her sixties used the former move in her explanation of why blacks are worse off than whites in the United States:

> Well, I'm gonna be, you understand, I'm not prejudice or racial or whatever. They're always given the smut jobs because they would do it. Then they stopped, they stopped doing [them]. The welfare system got to be very, very easy. And I'm not saying all, there's many, many white people on welfare that shouldn't be. But if you take the percentage in the Tri-City county area, you will find that the majority are white, but all you see is the black people on welfare. . . . And it was easier to collect welfare from the state rather than go out and get a job. Why work if the government's gonna take care of you? (57)

This is a classic example of how these moves are used. After she interjected the "I'm not prejudice or racial or whatever," this older woman proceeded to state her belief that blacks are lazy and welfare-dependent. The ideological value of the disclaimer is clear as it allowed this respondent to justify racial inequality in an overt way without opening herself to the charge of racism.

In addition to frames and styles, racial stories refer to the narratives whites use to articulate and bolster their racial accounts and work as story lines (generic stories without much personal content) and testimonies (stories that are seemingly personal). The racial stories associated with colorblind racism assist whites in making sense of their world in ways that reinforce the racial order. Racial storytelling is ideological because the stories are collectively produced and circulated, as if there is only one way of telling them. Racial stories thus are extremely powerful tools because they seem to lie in the realm of the given, in the matter-of-fact world.

Story lines are socially shared tales that are fable-like and incorporate a common scheme or wording. The dominant story lines of the post–civil rights era are "The past is the past," "I didn't own any slaves," "I did not get a job, or was not admitted to college, because of a minority," and "If Jews, Irish, and Italians made it, how come blacks have not?" Roland, an electrical engineer in his forties, used the first two story lines when expressing his extreme displeasure with the idea of reparations:

> I think they've gotten enough. I don't think we need to pay them any-thing or I think as long as they are afforded opportunities and avail themselves to the opportunities like everybody else. I, I don't know why we should give them any reparation for something that happened, you know . . . I can't, I *can't* help what happened in the 1400s, the 1500s, or the 1600s, when the blacks were brought over here and put into slavery. I mean, I had no control over that, neither did you, so I don't think we should do anything as far as reparations are concerned. (81)

Roland, like most whites,[14] assumes that discrimination means slavery and thus that it is something in America's remote past. By missing 150 years of racial history, Roland could voice his anger over the idea of reparations. The components of colorblind racism (styles, frames, and racial stories) have proved to be strategically attuned to maintain the

New Racism. In the next section, we discuss how the new racial discourse and racial practices are expressed in the media.

Media (Colorblind) Racism in Post–Civil Rights America

Since the mid-1980s, major media companies have transformed the entertainment industry by purchasing smaller firms to form larger conglomerates. These media conglomerates are increasingly global, with a handful of media giants dominating what we see, hear, and read (Crouteau and Hoynes 2001). CBS, Disney, News Corp, and Time Warner are among the largest of these media corporations (Kratz 2009), which continue to dominate the industry. The media is a necessary site for understanding racial ideologies because it plays such an important role in the production, reproduction, and transformation of ideologies.[15]

Clark (1969) argues that there are four stages of media representation for social groups: The first stage, *nonrecognition,* refers to no appearance at all, while the second, *ridicule,* indicates inclusion only in stereotypical images. The third stage, *protectors,* describes the moment that representation expands to include roles as police officers and detectives, and stage four, *respect,* refers to variation in media representation so that all sorts of characters are presented. This is a useful frame to start a conversation about media representation given that media is directly involved in the production and transformation of ideologies (Hall 1981). While it is true that the first black representations in television were solely stereotypical roles (Coleman 2000) and that now there are a variety of roles for people of color, blacks are still usually represented stereotypically (e.g., in the films *The Blind Side* [2009] and *The Help* [2011]), with the addition of the more "positive" but latently racist characters (Hughey 2009). While the media does not present one unified image of race, we argue that the predominant production is of a colorblind notion of race and racism.

In this section we provide a discussion of how colorblind racism is reflected in the media with examples from television and film. First, we will discuss how diverse casts can serve to support the dominant ideology through symbolic inclusion. Second, we will address how colorblind racism allows a space for the "ethnically ambiguous" to receive roles that were once restricted to whites.

Diverse for the Worst

Diversity has been articulated as a part of the liberal solution to racism. Racism in the media can therefore be seen as resolved with more diverse casts. The latest report by the Gay and Lesbian Alliance Against Defamation (GLAAD 2011) shows that overall ethnic diversity on prime-time broadcast scripted series has dropped. According to the Screen Actors Guild's most recent data (SAG 2008), African American actors held 13.3 percent of all film and television roles in 2008, down from 14.8 percent in 2007. Latinos were also slightly down in their proportion of roles from 2007–2008, particularly in lead roles (SAG 2008). Still, this numerical assessment of representation is inadequate considering that the roles for minorities are mostly symbolic. If racism in the media could be resolved by simply increasing the number of minority roles, then it would seem that racism in the media is gone for the most part. Instead, we argue that the media is directly involved in the production of racial ideology, specifically colorblind racism, and that diversity in this symbolic form is a part of the abstract liberal agenda.

In 2005, the *New York Times* published an article titled "'Grey's Anatomy' Goes Colorblind" (Fogel 2005), referring to the television series. The presence of black doctors, without addressing their racial realities, suggests that the series went "colorblind racist" instead. The creator, executive producer, and head writer of *Grey's Anatomy* is a black woman, Shonda Rhimes, who described the setting of the series as a "multicultural hub where social issues take a back seat to the more pressing problems of hospital life." *Grey's Anatomy,* like past shows (e.g., *The Cosby Show* [1984–92]), portrays a black fantasy of fully integrated black doctors. In 2005, only 8 percent of U.S. first-year medical students were black, despite blacks accounting for 15 percent of the population (Cannon 2010). Just as having "racial contacts" *does not* mean substantive integration, simply having a diverse cast does not adequately or accurately represent the racial reality of twentieth-century America.

Rhimes stated that she does not sit around with her friends and discuss race because "we're post–civil rights, post-feminist babies" (Fogel 2005). She also claims the show was written and developed with "blind-casting" where she did not have particular races in mind (Fogel 2005). Neglecting to recognize race as a social reality allows for these colorblind dreams to dominate in popular media. Television series like *Glee* and *The Office* provide evidence of the kind of symbolic inclusion that complicates the struggle for minority representation beyond a request for numerical representation. These so-called diverse casts serve to uphold the current racial structure by obscuring the real inequalities both on television and in real life.

The popular television series *Glee,* which has been rewarded for having a diverse cast, illustrates how "diversity" can exist with people of color being shown in narrow, restrictive roles.[16] Stereotypical images of people of color for comedic shorthand (Bogle 2001) characterize many television portrayals, even in supposedly "diverse" shows. *Glee* has been criticized for its stereotypical presentation of homosexuality, women, and minorities while patting itself on the back for being the most progressive show on television (Hartmann 2010). For instance, the role of Mercedes Jones, played by Amber Riley, presents the stereotypical portrayal of an overweight, lonely black woman with an attitude.[17]

The *abstract liberal* frame, referring to the presentation of racial issues in an abstract manner using the language of liberalism, is rewarded over realistic depiction of how race is lived in America. A comparison of the HBO series *The Wire* (Neal 2010) and *Grey's Anatomy* reveals how abstract liberalism is entrenched in American popular media. Shonda Rhimes, the creator of *Grey's Anatomy,* expressed a commitment to *blind-casting* while simultaneously stating in a liberal abstract manner that in "Shondaland" (her production company), "we're not going to have a black, drug-dealing single-mother selling crack" (Chozick 2011). On the other hand, *The Wire* included plenty of drug dealers and single mothers, worrying less about constructing a Utopian experience and instead dealing with the realities of race as it relates to education, politics, and imprisonment. Many viewers, including sociologist Elijah Anderson, were critical of *The Wire* because, as he stated in an interview done by the *Atlantic,* "what they have left out are the decent people" (Bowden 2008). Why aren't we instead criticizing shows like *Grey's Anatomy* and instead asking "Where is the racism?" *Grey's Anatomy* gets awarded NAACP image awards while *The Wire* does not. This focus on superficial racial representation instead of confronting the reality of racism reflects the strength of the "liberal" media industries in this period of New Racism and colorblindness.

The Rise of the Honorary Whites

The post–civil rights era has allowed a space for the rise of the neo-mulatto and the "ethnically ambiguous" (Beltrán and Fojas 2008) to fill some of the roles traditionally accorded to white actors. The rise of the "honorary white" fits with the new racial regime and highlights the *Latin Americanization thesis,* which suggests that the United States is moving toward a racial stratification system similar to many Latin American and Caribbean nations (Bonilla-Silva 2004). He suggests that the emerging triracial system will consist of "whites" at the top, an intermediary group of "honorary whites" in the middle, and a black collective at the bottom. The honorary white category is of particular interest in the following discussion.

Biracial actor Vin Diesel sees the popularity of ethnic ambiguity as a positive development because his multiracial appearance has allowed him to get more job offers, to have a greater variety of potential roles than actors who are easily identified as black or white. Toronto-born platinum-selling hip-hop artist Drake identifies as "mixed-race" and cites his background as one of the reasons for his success. When asked about his racial identity, Drake admitted to how his ambiguity benefits his career, stating, "I get a lot of love everywhere, for just being diverse, instead of straight out being [one thing]" (Rivas 2011). In the area of popular music, many performers, including both individuals who are "multiracial" and those who simply appear ambiguously raced, often have played up the "exotic look" of their light-skinned phenotype by bleaching their hair blond and wearing long, straight hairpieces. Marketing experts, such as Linda Well, editor in chief for *Allure,* point to a current "popular fascination with the racial hybrid" (La Ferla 2003).

The celebration of ethnically ambiguous characters is a reflection of a continued privilege for those actors/actresses who are considered capable of assimilating and appealing to whiteness (Beltrán and Fojas 2008). The apparent trend to cast South Asian woman as love interests of white men (*The Big Bang Theory, Numbers, The Rise of the Planet of the Apes, Greek, Scrubs, The Office, ER*) could be misread as a signal that interracial relationships are now viewed as acceptable and that racism is no longer relevant. However, South Asian women are most often found playing nonracialized roles. People of color are included while simultaneously being denied any substantial conversation concerning race and racism. Such shows that have a South Asian woman provide rhetorical ammunition to defend against criticisms and accusation of racism because they have a diverse cast.

Conclusion

The "post-racial" incubus that oozed out of the Jim Crow beast in the 1970s has grown into a full-blown monster. Nowadays the idea that race is no longer central to this country's institutions and discourse but is instead a vestige of the past has become the normative depiction of racial matters. And in so-called post-racial America, the monster proclaims that anyone can be "racist" as racism is no longer viewed as the prerogative of whites; thus blacks and Latinos can be labeled racist if associated with race-based organizations such as the NAACP or the League of United Latin American Citizens (LULAC) or if accused of playing the "race card."

In this chapter, however, we tried to slay the monster. We argued that racism—which we regard as a structural problem in the nation—is still central to the organizational matrix of America. As such, we interpreted the election of Barack Obama and the post-racial logic that he embodies not as symbols of racial progress but as part of the New Racism regime that emerged in the 1970s (Bonilla-Silva 2010). Hence, Obama's "race shuffle" ("Hey, I am black but I do not deal with race or racial politics!") fits perfectly with the new way of reproducing racial inequality. In fact, in many ways, the new racial order works better (in a more hegemonic manner) in blackface.

The transition from Jim Crow to the new racial order, we suggested, generated a new racial ideology: the ideology of colorblind racism. This ideology, like a Trojan horse, hides its real purpose. Despite its seemingly suave and genteel character ("I am not a racist, but . . . "), colorblind racism's job is to safeguard white supremacy. Instead of claiming that blacks and people of color are biologically inferior or that God made blacks subservient, whites today explain racial disparities as the result of people of color's cultural deficiencies (laziness, bad parenting, and lack of proper work ethic) or justify not doing anything to ameliorate racial inequality by invoking liberalism in an abstract and decontextualized manner ("I am all for equal opportunity, and that is why I am against affirmative action because it amounts to discrimination in reverse"). This ideological tool also developed a new "race-talk" that is elusive; hence, nowadays one can hide behind racial stories ("I did not own slaves") or use semantic moves to state racial views without opening oneself to the charge of racism ("I am not a racist, but why is it that so many blacks are poor or incarcerated?").

We briefly illustrated that the ideology of colorbind racism is directly connected to the production of television, film, and other forms of popular culture. The method of "colorblind" casting is rewarded as (white) roles are increasingly given to people of color—most often to those who appear racially ambiguous. Still, some of the old stereotypical images of blackness remain with characters like Mercedes (*Glee*) and Stanley (*The Office*), who remain underdeveloped racial signifiers. Meanwhile, a character like Bubbles (*The Wire*), who on the surface fits the typical role of black homelessness and drug addiction, is a fully developed character who defies stereotypes and instead forces the audience to think critically about issues of race and poverty. But we must point out that *The Wire* was not a financially successful TV show, and we have no reason to believe white viewers understood the depth of what was been attempted. Perhaps as in the case of *Chappelle's Show* (Cobb 2007) or hip-hop music (Rodriquez 2006), whites consumed this show as yet another way of appropriating the "Other." The need to move beyond symbolic inclusion reflects the necessity to further examine the cultural component of racism.

But the question remains: What is to be done? It is important to recognize the centrality of the culture in reproducing racial order while simultaneously fighting racism and discrimination in other venues. Continuing to consume passively and even with pleasure the various products of our "racist culture" (Goldberg 1993), as many of us do daily, makes our struggle against the new racial monster of America harder. These products reinforce the current racial script of America and poison our minds and souls. The more we are entertained with movies such as *Avatar* (a neocolonial film where the hero is a neo-Tarzan character), *The Blind Side* (a racist film similar to *Mississippi Burning*), and TV shows like *The Office, Glee,* and *Grey's Anatomy,* the more we accept unwillingly our own domination.

Our task, then, is to fight white supremacy in *all* its manifestations, and this includes the ideological terrain. Ideology is neither fixed nor permanent and can always be challenged; hence, we must develop *reverse discourses* (Weaver 2010) to counter the relentless colorblind nonsense that permeates our culture. And we must not get confused by symbolic inclusion of any kind. It is not enough that people of color are more likely to appear these days on TV or in movies because the issue that matters most is *how* we are represented and *what kind* of racial messages are conveyed. Similarly, it is not enough to have a black president when he only delivers on the color but not on the all-important flavor. By this standard we are a long way from equality in the cultural field as well as in society. Accordingly, we must remain committed and vigilant; we must fight racism in the streets as well as on the screens. In the words of Public Enemy, we must "Fight the power!" and we must do so by any means necessary!

Notes

1. Bonilla-Silva has labeled the United States since the election of President Barack Obama as *Obamerica* (Bonilla-Silva 2010).
2. The media in general, but the liberal outlets in particular (*New York Times* and *MSNBC*), have done a lot of reporting on racial incidents. However, the focus on the old-fashioned racial behavior of groups such as the Birther movement, the actions and statements of many Tea Party members, racially inflammatory comments by Republican operatives (*The Ed Schultz Show,* December 21, 2010), or the resurgence of Klan-like organizations misses the point. Although we should always be vigilant about these organizations and people, in post–civil rights America the *bulk* of racial behavior and practices work in a more suave and, thus, more formidable way. This is something we will highlight in this chapter and something Bonilla-Silva has been articulating for quite some time in his work.
3. We are all "multiracial" as we are all *Homo sapiens* and, as such, are thoroughly "mixed." This is what anthropologists and geneticists examining the human genome have concluded. And in the specific case of the recent American experience (last 200 years or so), we have mixed a lot across "racial lines." Some estimate that about 70 percent of "blacks" are *recently* mixed with "whites" and that a relatively large number of "whites" are mixed with blacks. The issue is not that Obama is "multiracial" or "biracial" but that in the post–civil rights era we can designate him as such.
4. See chapter 9 in Bonilla-Silva 2010.

5. Both Bill Cosby and Will Smith have been criticized for being too liberal and have been ardent supporters of Barack Obama for president. Smith stated in 2008 that Obama is only the second political figure he has ever thrown his support behind—the first being Nelson Mandela.

6. See chapter 1 in Bonilla-Silva 2001 for a more complete discussion on rethinking racism as structural matter and how all whites receive material benefits as members of the dominant racial group.

7. Bonilla-Silva (2001) has argued it is time to drop the notion of "discrimination" because it limits our understanding of racism and forces us to use the "prejudice problematic," that is, to individual-level analysis of racial matters (the racists) as well as to overt racial behavior (Klan-like actions by individuals and organizations).

8. For details, see chapter 4 in Bonilla-Silva 2001.

9. The index of dissimilarity is a measure developed by demographers to assess how even is the distribution of two groups in an area. The score of this index run from 0 to 100 and represents the percentage of a group that would have to move into the area to achieve evenness, hence, a score of 0 is interpreted as "no segregation" and a score of 100 as "total segregation."

10. See chapter 4 in Bonilla-Silva 2001.

11. The four central frames of this ideology are *abstract liberalism, cultural racism, minimization of racism,* and *naturalization of race-related matters* (Bonilla-Silva 2010).

12. Bonilla-Silva suggests that the style of colorblind racism has five components: avoidance of racist speech, semantic moves, projection, diminutives, and rhetorical incoherence. For a more detailed discussion, see Bonilla-Silva 2001.

13. Bonilla-Silva (2001) found that these two examples were two of the most common semantic moves used by white respondents.

14. For more examples, see Bonilla-Silva 2001.

15. Herman Gray argues that television "remains a decisive arena in which struggles for representation, and more significantly, struggles over the meanings of representation, continue to be waged at various levels of national politics, expressive culture, and moral authority" (xvii).

16. Winner of Outstanding Comedy Series by Gay and Lesbian Alliance Against Defamation (GLAAD) for 2010 and 2011, and Winner of Diversity Award from the Multicultural Motion Picture Association for 2009.

17. Kurt (played by Chris Colfer) represents the stereotypical depiction of a gay teenager and Brittany (played by Heather Morris) the "dumb blonde."

WORKS CITED

Ahmed, Ali M., and Mats Hammarstedt. "Discrimination in the Rental Housing Market: A Field Experiment on the Internet." *Journal of Urban Economics* 64.2 (2008): 362–72. Print.

Aleo, Michael, and Pablo Svirsky. "Foreclosure Fallout: The Banking Industry's Attack on Disparate Impact Race Discrimination Claims under the Fair Housing Act and the Equal Credit Opportunity Act." *Public Interest Law Journal* 18.1 (2008): n. pag. Print.

Beltrán, Mary, and Camilla Fojas. *Mixed Race Hollywood*. New York: NYU Press, 2008. Print.

Bertrand, Marianne, and Sendhil Mullainathan. "Are Emily and Greg More Employable Than Lakisha and Jamal? A Field Experiment on Labor Market Discrimination." *American Economic Review* 94.4 (2004): 991–1013. Print.

Bobo, L. D., and C. Z. Charles. "Race in the American Mind: From the Moynihan Report to the Obama Candidacy." *Annals of the American Academy of Political and Social Science* 621.1 (2009): 243–59. Print.

Bobo, Lawrence D., James R. Kluegel, and Ryan A. Smith. "Laissez-Faire Racism." *Racial Attitudes in the 1990s: Continuity and Change*. Ed. Steven A. Tuch and Jack K. Martin. Westport, CT: Praeger, 1997. N. pag. Print.

Bogle, Donald. *Toms, Coons, Mulattoes, Mammies, and Bucks: An Interpretive History of Blacks in American Films*. New York: Continuum International Group, 2001. Print.

Bonilla-Silva, Eduardo. "From Bi-racial to Tri-racial: Towards a New System of Racial Stratification in the USA." *Ethnic and Racial Studies* 27.6 (2004): 931–50. Print.

———. "The Invisible Weight of Whiteness: The Racial Grammar of Everyday Life in Contemporary America." *Ethnic and Racial Studies*. N.p.: n.p., 2012. Print.

———. *Racism without Racists: Color-Blind Racism and the Persistence of Racial Inequality in the United States*. 3rd ed. Lanham, MD: Rowman and Littlefield, 2010. Print.

———. "Rethinking Racism: Toward a Structural Interpretation." *American Sociological Review* 62 (1997): 465–80. Print.

———. *White Supremacy and Racism in the Post–Civil Rights Era*. Boulder, CO: Lynne Rienner, 2001. Print.

Bonilla-Silva, Eduardo, and Ashley Doane, eds. *Whiteout: The Continuing Significance of Racism and Whiteness*. New York: Routledge, 2003.

Bonilla-Silva, Eduardo, and Louise Seamster. *Rethinking Obama: Political, Power and Social Theory*. Ed. Julian Go. Bingley, UK: Emerald, 2011. Print.

Bowden, Mark. "The Angriest Man in Television." *Atlantic*. N.p. Retrieved Jan./Feb. 2008. Web.

Caditz, Judith. *White Liberals in Transition: Current Dilemmas of Ethnic Integration*. New York: Spectrum Publications, 1976. Print.

Cannon, Brevy. "Lack of Black Doctors Traced Primarily to Pre-college Factors, Study Finds." *UVA Today*. N.p. Retrieved from http://www.virginia.edu/uvatoday/newsRelease.php?id=11038, 2010. Web.

Cashin, Sheryll. *The Failures of Integration: How Race and Class are Undermining the American Dream*. New York: Public Affairs, 2004. Print.

CBS News. "Poll: Blacks See Improved Race Relations." Retrieved from http://www.cbsnews.com/8301-500160_162-4972532.html, 2010. Web.

Census Scope. http://www.censusscope.org.

Chozick, Amy. "Anatomy of a TV Hitmaker." *Wall Street Journal*. http://online.wsj. com/article/SB10001424052748703730804576315552637855980.html, 2011. Web.

Clark, Cedric C. "Television and Social Controls: Some Observations on the Portrayals of Ethnic Minorities." *Television Quarterly* 9.2 (1969): 18–32. Print.

Cloud, Cathy, and George Galster. "What Do We Know about Racial Discrimination in Mortgage Markets?" *Review of Black Political Economy* 21 (1993): 101–20. Print.

Cobb, William Jelani. *The Devil and Dave Chappelle*. New York: Thunder's Mouth Press, 2007. Print.

Coleman, R. R. Means. *African American Viewers and the Black Situation Comedy: Situating Racial Humor*. New York: Garland, 2000. Print.

Cosby, William H., and Alvin F. Poussaint. *Come on, People: On the Path from Victims to Victors*. Nashville, TN: Thomas Nelson, 2007. Print.

Crouteau, David R., and William D. Hoynes. *Media/Society: Industries, Images, and Audiences*. Thousand Oaks, CA: Pine Forge Press, 2003. Print.

Dowd, Maureen. "Dark, Dark, Dark." *New York Times*. Retrieved from http://www. nytimes.com/2009/02/22/opinion/22dowd.html, 2009. Web.

Duncan, Otis. "Patterns of Occupational Mobility among Negro Men." *Demography* 5 (1968): 11–22. Print.

Essed, Philomena. *Understanding Everyday Racism*. Newbury Park, CA: Sage, 1991. Print.

Farley, Reynolds, and Walter R. Allen. *The Color Line and the Quality of Life in America*. New York: Russell Sage Foundation, 1987. Print.

Feagin, Joe R. *Systemic Racism: A Theory of Oppression*. New York: Routledge, 2006. Print.

Fogel, Matthew. "'Grey's Anatomy' Goes Colorblind" *New York Times*. Retrieved from http://www.nytimes.com/2005/05/08/arts/television/08foge. html?pagewanted=print, 2005. Web.

Galster, George C. "Neighborhood Racial Change, Segregationist Sentiments, and Affirmative Marketing Policies." *Journal of Urban Economics* 27.3 (1990): 344–61. Print.

Gay & Lesbian Alliance Against Defamation (GLAAD). "Where Are We on TV Report: 2011–2012 Season." Retrieved from http://www.glaad.org/publications/ whereweareontv11, 2011. Web.

Goldberg, David Theo. *The Racial State*. Malden, MA: Blackwell, 1993. Print.

Hall, Stuart. "Notes on Deconstructing the Popular." *People's History and Socialist Theory*. Ed. Raphael Samuel. London: Routledge, 1981. 227–39. Print.

Hanson, Andrew, and Zackary Hawley. "Do Landlords Discriminate in the Rental Housing Market? Evidence from an Internet Field Experiment in US Cities." *Journal of Urban Economics* 70:2–3 (2011): 99–114. Print.

Hanson, Andrew, Zackary Hawley, and Aryn Taylor. "Subtle Discrimination in the Rental Housing Market: Evidence from E-Mail Correspondence." *Journal of Housing Economics* 20:4 (2011): 276–84.

Hartmann, Margaret. "Why Glee Still Needs to Work on Diversity." *Jezebel*. Retrieved from http://jezebel.com/5541897/why-glee-still-needs-to-work-on-diversity, 2010. Web.

Herring, Cedric, Verna Keith, and Hayward Derrick Horton. *Skin Deep: How Race and Complexion Matter in the "Colorblind" Era.* Chicago: University of Illinois Press, 2004. Print.

Holzer, Harry J. "The Labor Market and Young Black Men: Updating Moynihan's Perspective." *Annals of the American Academy of Political and Social Sciences* 621.1 (2009): 47–69.

Hughey, Matthew. "Cinethetic Racism: White Redemption and Black Stereotypes in 'Magical Negro' Films." *Social Problems* 56.3 (2009): 543–77. Print.

Hunt, Matthew. "African American, Hispanic, and White Beliefs about Black/White Inequality, 1977–2004." *American Sociological Review* 72.3 (2007): 390–415. Print.

Iceland, John, and Kyle Anne Nelson. 2008. "Hispanic Segregation in Metropolitan America: Exploring the Multiple Forms of Spatial Assimilation." *American Sociological Review* 73.5 (2001): 741–65. Web.

Ifill, Gwen. *The Breakthrough.* New York: Doubleday, 2009. Print.

Jackman, Mary, and Robert Jackman. "Racial Inequality in Home Ownership." *Social Forces* 58.4 (1980): 1221–54.

Kratz, Michelle. "Corporate Influence: How the Media Merger Trend Changed the Book Publishing Industry and the Distribution of Information." Master of Science in Publishing. Retrieved from http://digitalcommons.pace.edu/dyson_mspublishing/17, 2009. Web.

La Ferla, Ruth. "Generation E.A.: Ethnically Ambiguous." *New York Times.* Retrieved from http://www.nytimes.com/2003/12/28/style/generation-ea-ethnically-ambiguous. html?pagewanted=all&src=pm, 2003. Web.

Logan, John R. "Ethnic Diversity Grows, Neighborhood Integration Lags Behind." *Redefining Urban and Suburban America: Evidence from Census 2000.* Ed. Bruce Katz and Robert E. Lang. Washington, DC: Brookings Institution Press, 2003. N. pag. Print.

Massey, Douglas, and Nancy Denton. *American Apartheid: Segregation and the Making of the American Underclass.* Cambridge: Harvard University Press, 1993. Print.

Mayorga, Sarah Ann. Preserving the White Picket Fence: Interracial Conduct in an Integrated Neighborhood. Dissertation: Duke (2012). http://hdl.handle. net/10161/5553.

McIntosh, Peggy. "White Privilege: Unpacking the Invisible Knapsack." *Re-visioning Family Therapy: Race, Culture, and Gender in Clinical Practice.* Ed. Monica McGoldrick and Kenneth Hardy. New York: Guilford Press, 1998. 147–52. Print.

McWhorter, John H. "What's Holding Blacks Back?" *City Journal* (Winter 2001). Retrieved from http://www.cityjournal.org/html/11_1_whats_holding_blacks.html.

Neal, Mark Anthony. "'A Man without a Country': The Boundaries of Legibility, Social Capital, and Cosmopolitan Masculinity." *Criticism* 52.3&4 (2010): 399–411. Print.

Oliver, Melvin, and Thomas Shapiro. *Black Wealth/White Wealth.* New York: Routledge, 2006.

Omi, Michael, and Howard Winant. *Racial Formation in the United States: From the 1960s to the 1990s.* New York: Routledge, 1986. Print.

Pager, Devah, and Hana Shepherd. "The Sociology of Discrimination: Racial Discrimination in Employment, Housing, Credit, and Consumer Markets." *Annual Review of Sociology* 34.1 (2008): 181–209. Print.

Patterson, Ernest. *City Politics.* New York: Dodd, Mead, 1974.

Patterson, Orlando. "A Poverty of the Mind." *New York Times.* Retrieved from www. nytimes.com, March 2006. Web.

Reed, Wornie L., and Bertin M. Louis Jr. "No More Excuses." *Journal of African American Studies* 13.2 (2009): 97–109. Print.

Rivas, Jorge. "Jay Smooth Talks to Drake about Racial Identity." *Colorlines.* Retrieved from http://colorlines.com/archives/2011/11/jay_smooth_interviews_drake_about_his_ racial_indentity.html, November 9, 2011. Web.

Rodriquez, J. "Colorblind Ideology and the Cultural Appropriation of Hip-Hop." *Journal of Contemporary Ethnography* 35.6 (2006): 645–68. Print.

Ross, Stephen L., and Mary A. Turner. "Housing Discrimination in Metropolitan America: Explaining Changes between 1989 and 2000." *Social Problems* 52.2 (2005): 152–80. Print.

Royster, Deirdre A. *Race and the Invisible Hand: How White Networks Exclude Men from Blue-Collar Jobs.* Berkeley: University of California Press, 2003. Print.

Rugh, J. S., and D. S. Massey. "Racial Segregation and the American Foreclosure Crisis." *American Sociological Review* 75.5 (2010): 629–51. Print.

Sakamoto, Arthur, Huei-Hsia Wu, and Jessie M. Tzeng. "The Declining Significance of Race among American Men during the Latter Half of the Twentieth Century." *Demography* 37.1 (2000): 41–51. Print.

Sampson, Robert J., and Patrick Sharkey. "Neighborhood Selection and the Social Reproduction of Concentrated Racial Inequality." *Demography* 45.1 (2008): 1–29. Print.

Screen Actors Guild (SAG). "2007 & 2008 Casting Data Reports." Retrieved from http://www.sag.org/press-releases/october-23-2009/latest-casting-data-follows-historical-trends-and-continues-exclude-p, 2008. Web.

Shapiro, Thomas M. *The Hidden Cost of Being African-American.* Oxford: Oxford University Press, 2004. Print.

Smith, James P., and Finnis R. Welch. *Closing the Gap: Forty Years of Economic Progress for Blacks.* Santa Monica, CA: Rand Corporation, 1986. Print.

Smith, Robert C. *Racism in the Post-Civil Rights Era: Now You See It, Now You Don't.* New York: State University of New York Press, 1995. Print.

Smith, Will. Appearance on *The Oprah Winfrey Show.* Retrieved from www.oprah.com, 2008. Web.

Social Science Data Analysis Network (SSDAN). *CensusScope.* Retrieved from http:// www.censusscope.org/index.html. Print.

Sowell, Thomas. *Civil Rights: Rhetoric or Reality?* New York: Morrow, 1984. Print.

Steele, Shelby. *White Guilt.* New York: HarperCollins, 2006. Print

Street, Paul. *Barack Obama and the Future of American Politics.* Boulder, CO: Paradigm, 2009. Print.

Struyk, R. J., and M. A. Turner. "Exploring the Effects of Preferences on Urban Housing Markets." *Journal of Urban Economics* 19.2 (1986): 131–47. Print.

Tabb, William K. *The Political Economy of the Black Ghetto.* New York: Norton, 1970. Print.

Tauber, Karl E., and Alma E. Tauber. *Negroes in Cities.* Chicago: Aldine, 1965. Print.

Turner, Margery A., Stephen L. Ross, George Galster, and John Yinger. *Discrimination in Metropolitan Housing Markets.* Washington, DC: Urban Institute, 2002. Print.

Turner, Margery A., and Felicity Skidmore. *Mortgage Lending Discrimination: A Review of Existing Evidence.* Washington, DC: Urban Institute, 1999. Print.

Turner, Margery A., Raymond Struyk, and John Yinger. *The Housing Discrimination Study.* Washington, DC: Urban Institute, 1991. Print.

Wakefield, Sara, and Christopher Uggen. "The Declining Significance of Race in Federal Civil Rights Law: The Social Structure of Employment Discrimination Claims." *Sociological Inquiry* 74.1 (2004): 128–57. Print.

Weaver, Simon. "The 'Other' Laughs Back: Humour and Resistance in Anti-racist Comedy." *Sociology* 44.1 (2010): 31–48. Print.

Williams, Richard, Reynold Nesiba, and Eileen Diaz McConnell. "The Changing Face of Inequality in Home Mortgage Lending." *Social Problems* 52 (2005): 181–208. Print.

Wilson, William J. *The Declining Significance of Race.* Chicago: University of Chicago Press, 1978. Print.

———. *The Truly Disadvantaged.* Chicago: University of Chicago Press, 1987. Print.

Yinger, John. "Housing Discrimination and Residential Segregation as Causes of Poverty." *Understanding Poverty.* Ed. Sheldon H. Danziger and Robert H. Haveman. New York: Russell Sage, 2001. 359–91. Print.

———. "Measuring Discrimination with Fair Housing Audits: Caught in the Act." *American Economic Review* 76.5 (1986): 881–93. Print.

Zhao, Bo. "Does the Number of Houses a Broker Shows Depend on a Homeseeker's Race?" *Journal of Urban Economics* 57.1 (2005): 128–47. Print.

Zhao, Bo, Jan Ondrich, and John Yinger. "Why Do Real Estate Brokers Continue to Discriminate? Evidence from the 2000 Housing Discrimination Study." *Journal of Urban Economics* 59.3 (2006): 394–419. Print.

Zuberi, Tukufu, and Eduardo Bonilla-Silva. *White Logic, White Methods: Racism and Methodology.* Lanham, MD: Rowman and Littlefield, 2008.

PART II

Icons of Post-Racial America

4

Oprah Winfrey

Cultural Icon of Mainstream (White) America

JANICE PECK

On May 4, 1992, as the rioting that swept through South Central Los Angeles after the Rodney King trial was winding down, Oprah Winfrey took her show to LA, where she taped a session with a diverse audience discussing the verdict, the riots, the judicial system, and race relations. Aired in two installments, "The Rodney King Verdict: The Aftermath and the Anger" was intended to "confront the controversial issues" and "give people who rarely get heard a chance to speak." At one point in the sometimes heated conversation, a young white woman stated, "I don't really see color. . . . I try not to because everybody's an individual. People are so different. Some of them are terrible and then some of them are really nice, of all colors" ("Rodney King Verdict"). This remark— hailed by Winfrey and many in the audience as a move toward racial "healing" and reconciliation—is a testament to the rise and naturalization of colorblind ideology in late twentieth-century America.

Perhaps no other celebrity is more emblematic of the power of that ideology than Oprah Winfrey, who shortly after her show's 1986 national premiere confidently asserted in a *Spy* magazine profile, "I transcend race" (Zehme 32). By 1991, when she had become undisputed queen of daytime talk, *Ebony* declared that Winfrey, along with Bill Cosby and Arsenio Hall, brought "an authoritative presence and an ability to transcend race to television" ("Television"). Two decades later, worth billions and sitting atop a multimedia empire, she was credited with aiding the election of the nation's first black president—himself deemed a "post-racial" candidate who defies "racial stereotypes" and "transcends the racial divide" (e.g., Klein; Will; Schorr). Reflecting on Winfrey's decision to end her talk show in 2011 after a quarter-century run, *New York Times* media columnist David Carr wrote, "It could be argued—well, I'll just say it—without Oprah Winfrey, there would be no Barack Obama. Not because she endorsed him, but with her message of bootstrap accountability, she not only empowered black people, she empowered white people."

To understand Winfrey's metamorphosis since the 1980s, when she was casually described by *Time* magazine as "a black female of ample bulk" whose show exposed the "often bizarre nooks and crannies of human misfortune" (Zoglin), to the late 1990s, when *Time* included her on its list of the 100 most influential Americans of the twentieth century, it is necessary to place her journey in a broader historical context. In particular, Winfrey's ascent from mere TV talk show host to "cultural icon of mainstream America" (Brown 242) must be situated in relation to the neoliberal political-economic project, which got its start with Ronald Reagan, became fully bipartisan with the rightward shift of the Democratic Party and the election of Bill Clinton, and has indelibly shaped the contemporary U.S. political economy.

It is no coincidence that this political-economic sea change over the final quarter of the twentieth century witnessed a major reconfiguration of the problem of race founded on the conviction that since the 1960s civil rights movement, racism has receded and lingers mainly as isolated individual attitudes, rather than in institutionalized practices. In that reformulation, political scientist Claire Kim argues, "The American race problem no longer consists of White racism, which is steadily declining, but rather of racialism, defined as the misguided tendency of minorities (especially Blacks) to cry racism and/or emphasize their racial identity as a strategy for getting ahead" ("Managing the Racial Breach" 62). It thus followed that the source of America's "race problem" was no longer the white majority, which was being penalized for long-past transgressions, but racial minorities who clung to a "'cult of victimization'" to "leverage white guilt" (62). The ideology of "colorblindness" found a receptive political environment alongside this new definition of racism. If in the early twentieth century, the notion of colorblindness expressed desires for racial emancipation and an end to white supremacy, those aspirations were never fully actualized in law or policy (Haney Lopez). Instead, Eduardo Bonilla-Silva argues, in the wake of the civil rights movement a revised conception of colorblindness "emerged as part of the great racial transformation that occurred in the late sixties and early seventies," eventually becoming "the central racial ideology of the post–civil rights era" (42). In the process, the "overt bigotry," "strict segregation," "governmentally enforced discrimination" (Bobo and Smith 185; also Bobo and Charles), and assumptions about black intellectual inferiority that had characterized the Jim Crow era were replaced by a more subtle ideology based on "the assertion of essential sameness between racial and ethnic groups despite unequal social locations and distinctive histories" (Rodriquez 645).

From the beginning of her TV career, Winfrey has embraced this notion of essential sameness as she worked to project a racially non-threatening image. In January 1987, six months after the national premiere of *The Oprah Winfrey Show,* she received her first magazine cover story in *People Weekly.* Recounting her time at historically black Tennessee State University, Winfrey stressed her differences with classmates who were "into black power and anger." As she asserted, "Race is not an issue. It has never been an issue with me. . . . Truth is, I've never felt prevented from doing anything because I was either black or a woman" (Richman 58). In making clear that she was free of racial resentment and had not been personally harmed by racism—while distinguishing herself from black Americans who felt otherwise—Winfrey proved early on to be a model of racial reassurance for the white audience she hoped to attract. Claire Kim argues that the "black-white divide on racial matters is one of the most profound and enduring in American society." In particular, black and white Americans "differ fundamentally as to what constitutes the race problem, how severe it is, and what to do about it" ("Managing the Racial Breach" 57). Given this divide, it is not surprising that a black entertainer hoping to attract a mass audience might adopt a public persona that *Newsday* described as "a comfortable and unthreatening bridge between the white and black cultures" (Firstman 4). In this way, the queen of talk set out to forge a relationship with her predominantly white, female, middle-class followers whose legendary devotion to her would come to stand as proof that racism was being eclipsed (Mediamark; "Oprah.com").

The ability to evoke a "para-social relationship" and its "intimacy at a distance" (Horton and Wohl) with a majority white audience reflects Winfrey's skill at simultaneously embracing her black heritage and staying at arm's length from aspects of the black historical experience that might alienate white fans. As a *Newsday* article stated early in her career, "Though she makes race an undercurrent of her message, and it is part of her bearing, it does not define her following. She has what the business calls broad appeal" (Firstman 4). Winfrey's appeal rests on a careful balancing act whereby her proclaimed mission of "empowerment" emphasizes individual aspirations rather than collective political goals. As Quentin Fottrell has observed, "While embracing the philosophies of Eleanor Roosevelt and Martin Luther King," Winfrey "subtly distances herself from feminist politics and the radicalism of the Civil Rights movement" (Fottrell). Such strategies reflect an important change in the meaning of colorblindness that occurred in the aftermath of the civil rights movement when political progressives began rejecting the idea, calling instead for explicitly race-conscious political remedies such as affirmative action, while conservatives took up the cause of colorblind racial policy. As Ian Haney Lopez notes, "In that new context, colorblindness appealed to those opposing racial integration" and "provided cover for opposition to racial reform" (see also Kim "Racial Triangulation"; Bracey).

The new iteration of colorblind ideology found fertile ground in the 1980s as Ronald Reagan and the New Right backlash politics that buoyed him sought to "realign the electorate along racial, rather than class, lines" (Reeves and Campbell 157; also Macek). It played a central role in the Democratic Party's rightward reconfiguration in the late 1980s, which involved exorcising its historical identification with black voters and black issues. It figured in the emergence of the theory of the "underclass" that achieved bipartisan hegemony by the early 1990s. And it is deeply implicated in Oprah Winfrey's purported "transcendence of race" and appeal to a majority white audience, which rest on the seductions of "virtual integration" made possible by TV (Steinhorn and Diggs-Brown) and her own rejection of black political stances that might put off white followers. This chapter will consider these interlocking developments with the goal of demonstrating the complex political-economic and cultural foundations—and limits—of the ideology of colorblindness and of Winfrey's cross-racial appeal.

Neoliberalism, Colorblindness, and the
Redefinition of the Problem of Race

Writing in 2003, sociologist Douglas Massey observed, "One of the pleasant fictions that helps justify the Bush administration's opposition to affirmative action is the pretense that America has left behind the evils of segregation and achieved something approaching a race-blind society" (22). For Massey, the pretense stems from the fact that in contemporary U.S. society, severe racial segregation in housing and schools persists (Massey; Massey and Fischer, Kozol; Dillahunt et al.) and the racial wealth gap "remains huge" (Shapiro, Meschede, and Sullivan). The idea of a colorblind "post-racial" America draws its power not so much from facts, however, as from years of successful ideological combat that began during the period of "great racial transformation" of the late 1960s and 1970s in conjunction with powerful economic developments that would facilitate the rise of an organized New Right. Lyndon Johnson famously predicted in the mid-1960s that the passage of the Civil Rights Act and the Voting Act would ultimately "cost Democrats the south" (Toner). In 1968, Richard Nixon's political strategist Kevin Phillips capitalized on the opportunity to weaken the Democratic Party's historical advantage in southern states by painting it as the "Negro party" (Greenberg). Johnson's prophecy proved correct; in 1968, four out of five white southerners voted for Nixon or for segregationist independent candidate George Wallace (108). A victorious Republican Party would refine this racialized campaign strategy in a quest to deny Democrat Jimmy Carter a second presidential term in 1981.

Fueled by bitterness over Supreme Court rulings on school prayer (1962, 1963) and abortion (*Roe v. Wade*, 1973), opposition to Johnson's Great Society federal programs (e.g., civil rights, War on Poverty), and discomfort with social and cultural changes wrought by 1960s political movements, the Republican New Right emerged as a political force in the 1970s amid a crisis in U.S. capitalism that saw the end of the post–World War II economic boom. From 1945 to the early 1970s, the United States experienced an extended period of economic growth driven by Keynesian policies, including the development of the welfare state as a safeguard against economic crises, a commitment to full employment through government spending, and state regulation of sectors of the economy. The postwar boom began to falter by the late 1960s and early

1970s as both unemployment and inflation increased. Confronted with mounting debt from the Vietnam War, competition from the recovered economies of Europe and Japan, and political challenges from Third World national liberation movements, the United States began losing its grip on the competitive advantage it had enjoyed for more than two decades. The post-Vietnam shift to a peacetime economy, the 1973 oil crisis, and the global recession in 1973–74 marked the end of the twenty-five-year boom and launched the beginning of what Robert Brenner terms the "long downturn" (xix).

The end of the boom created divisions and polarization "not only between classes, but *within* classes" (Davis, *Prisoners* 178). The New Right's political strategy was to fashion an explanation for the economic downturn that would appeal to middle-class professionals and entrepreneurs while exploiting divisions within the working class to siphon off a bloc of Democratic support. That explanation targeted three causes of national decline: "big government" excesses (e.g., high taxes, unrestrained spending, overregulation); privileging of "special interests" at the expense of "average" Americans; and loss of "traditional values" of hard work, individual initiative, and self-sufficiency. Weaving together these elements, New Right leaders and candidate Reagan crafted a narrative in which hardworking Americans were being victimized by a voracious government that took their money, delivered it to undeserving social groups, and undermined the work ethic by punishing the diligent and rewarding the lazy. The proposed solution lay in reversing this unfairness, restoring economic growth, and reviving appropriate values. The "racialization" (Miles 76) of this narrative by which people of color were designated "special interests" and "traditional" values were associated with whites was a vital part of its ideological and political power.

Joining the emerging religious Right and coordinating an array of conservative single-issue campaigns—antibusing, anti–affirmative action, anti–gun control, anticommunism, anti–property taxes—New Right leaders "mobilized widespread support from classical New Deal, blue-collar constituencies, thus demonstrating that social conservatism, racism, and patriotism provided powerful entrees for New Right politics" (Davis, *Prisoners* 170; Wuthnow and Liebman; Perlstein; George). These forces swept Reagan into office in 1980 and provided support for a dramatic restructuring of U.S. economic policy, including cutbacks to social programs, increased military expenditures, aggressive deregulation (e.g., airlines, utilities, telecommunications, finance), major tax cuts for corporations and the wealthy, and high interest rates benefiting banks and speculators. Organized under the banner of "Reaganomics," these policies accelerated trends that had started in the late 1970s: the export of jobs in search of cheap labor from the unionized "Frostbelt" to the union-weak "Sunbelt" and to developing nations with low-cost, nonunionized labor and minimal regulation; a shift from relatively high-wage factory work in heavy industry to low-wage service occupations; growing dependence on part-time and temporary employment; and a large-scale movement of women into the workforce to offset declining household incomes.

The tensions generated by this climate of scarcity provided a rich medium for backlash politics. Mike Davis notes that skilled workers and the lower ranges of the white-collar middle class—"faced with a genuinely collapsing standard of living"—increasingly saw themselves "as locked into a desperate zero-sum rivalry with equality-seeking minorities and women" (*Prisoners* 228). Meanwhile, thanks to deindustrialization, the decimation of the urban manufacturing base, middle-class and white flight, dwindling property taxes, and the growth of a drug economy in income-starved neighborhoods, black rates of unemployment, poverty, homelessness, incarceration, and addiction climbed. The fallout of the political-economic policies of Reaganomics could thus be presented as evidence of cultural pathology among black Americans, who purportedly had been made dependent and irresponsible by overindulgent government policies and/or misguided beliefs about their own victimization.

These economic changes and the anxieties they stoked provided an apt setting for the rise of "underclass ideology," which was promulgated by books such as Ken Auletta's *The Underclass,* Charles Murray's *Losing Ground: American Social Policy 1950–1980,* and Michael Novak's *The New Consensus on Family and Welfare: A Community of Self-Reliance.* Based on the argument that poverty and dependence are effects of defective cultural attitudes and weak "family values," the "theory of the underclass emerged in the early 1980s with a surprisingly wide spectrum of liberal support—the first sign of changing times," according to Ann Withorn (501). Embraced by both conservative and liberal journalists and social scientists, underclass ideology focused on a specific sector of the poor: people living in core urban areas marked by high rates of poverty, crime, drugs, joblessness, and school dropouts and high rates of female-headed households, teenage pregnancy, out-of-wedlock births, and use of welfare.

Underclass theory rests on implicit racial and gender premises by identifying the underclass with central city neighborhoods and female-headed households. The supposedly self-reproducing nature of the underclass was attributed to women failing to instill responsibility and morality in their offspring; thanks to this "feminization" of the underclass, Withorn argues, "welfare mothers were discussed in the same breath as drug users, criminals and other antisocial groups" (502). The image of the "crack mother," for example, dominated 1980s media portrayals of drug problems in poor urban neighborhoods, becoming a potent symbol in Reagan's "war on drugs" and contributing to the demonization of poor—especially minority—women (Reeves and Campbell 207–16; also Macek 161–64). As Charles Mills notes, the notion of the underclass was also "racially coded" in that it provided a "way of talking about blacks (and, increasingly, Latinos) without talking about blacks" (859). By the beginning of the 1990s, according to Adolph Reed Jr., such conceptions of the underclass had "taken hold of the public imagination" and acquired the status of "deeply entrenched common sense"—a legacy of the long rightward shift in "public debate about social welfare" that began under Reagan (*Stirrings*, 179; also Kim "Racial Triangulation").

At the same time, the 1980s witnessed the rise of hugely popular black TV stars—Winfrey, Bill Cosby, Arsenio Hall—whose appeal was hailed as proof they transcended race, and whose success could be framed as an argument against the existence of structural racial discrimination. Jimmie Reeves and Richard Campbell argue that the "right-wing appropriation of the celebrated mainstream media achievements of a handful of prominent African-American 'individuals'" served as evidence to support its claim that any lingering problems of black Americans were the result of cultural or individual pathology (100). Indeed, Winfrey has consistently framed her life story in these terms.

By denying the existence of institutionalized racism, attributing black failure to lack of initiative or faulty values, and adulating black stars as proof that racial barriers to success had evaporated, the Reagan Revolution could tap historical undercurrents of racism in American culture while absolving whites of implication in that history. In the process, it "facilitated the upward redistribution of wealth in the 1980s by releasing people in the suburbs from any responsibility for—or identification with—the economic distress in the inner city" (Reeves and Campbell 157). Recasting poverty as the distinct sphere of "black Americans living in ghettoized neighborhoods" (J. Smith 179), underclass ideology helped deflect attention from the general effects of deregulated markets and the redistribution of wealth and turned it into the pathology of a specific segment of the population.[1] Using economic scarcity to drive a wedge between the upper and lower sectors of the working class, between the working class and the poor, between suburbanites and inner-city residents, and between whites and racial minorities, the Reagan administration reconfigured class alliances through a "divide-and-conquer/unite-and-mobilize" strategy" (Reeves and Campbell 157).

Witnessing the success of that strategy, the Democrats would seek to recapture the White House by emulating it. In 1985, after Reagan's second victory, a group of predominantly southern conservative Democrats, including Bill Clinton and Al Gore, formed the Democratic Leadership Council (DLC) with two aims: first, to move the Democratic Party to the right by weakening its historical identification with FDR's New Deal and Johnson's Great Society programs; and second, to counter the party's identification with black interests and the growing influence of African Americans in Democratic politics (Davis, *Dead Cities;* Hale; Henwood; Klinkner; Reed, "Introduction"; Roediger). Hoping to win back white Democrats who had voted for Reagan, the DLC took a page from the Republican playbook by capitalizing on racial divisions and anxieties. According to Kim, the DLC started from the assumption that because of Republicans' "indifference or outright hostility," black Americans had effectively been "captured" by the Democratic Party, which meant they were "unable to make a threat of defection and thus unable to exercise influence over the party's policies" ("Managing the Racial Breach" 57, 60). With black loyalty to the party guaranteed, there was little risk in emulating the GOP's track record in using race as a "wedge issue to draw whites" (60).

Clinton's electoral strategy was organized around the assumption that white voters were "'fed up' with race- and gender-specific policies"—an assumption central as well to the redefinition of the race problem and rise of colorblind ideology (Roediger 56). In contrast to Republicans, who had consistently handled the racial breach by openly embracing white demands and repudiating blacks, Clinton needed to please whites without alienating blacks—one of his party's "core constituencies" (Kim "Managing the Racial Breach" 60). Banking on the Democratic Party's capture of the black vote freed him to engage in "racial breach management" strategies consisting in "first, an initial electoral strategy of courting white support, in part through symbolic rejection of blacks; and second, an adjusted governing/reelection strategy of pleasing whites with substantive action on racial policy issues and placating blacks with largely symbolic gestures of support" (57). To maintain and maximize her market reach—and in particular to please her majority white audience without radically alienating black fans—Oprah Winfrey has also had to navigate the black/white racial divide with practices that bear resemblance to Clinton's racial breach management strategies.

Oprah Winfrey Manages the Racial Breach

Winfrey has made it clear she has limited patience for people who exhibit an "I am a victim" mentality. In 1989, asked by *Omni* magazine to share her vision of Utopia, Winfrey replied, "The thing that works so powerfully in holding Utopias back from coming into being is a failure—or a refusal—by some members of society to take responsibility for their own actions. If people want to solve their problems they must sooner or later reach inward to bring about a positive difference in their lives" (Long 106). This mantra of "personal responsibility" takes on particular salience in Winfrey's views of race and racism.

While on one hand Winfrey denies the significance of race—being black, she insists, has had no effect on her accomplishments—she also acknowledges its role in the success of her enterprise:

> I hear this a lot. I hear that I don't hug the black people the way I hug the white people, that I go to the white people in the audience first. First of all, there are *more* white people. There just are more! I could not survive with this show if I only catered to black people. I just could not. I couldn't be where I am if I did. (Mair 174)

In fact, Winfrey has cultivated her appeal to whites in part by reassuring them she does not "cater" to blacks and is willing even to publicly criticize African Americans. In 1990 she appeared on the syndicated national TV program *Ebony/Jet Showcase* and took aim at "Blacks who bash other Blacks in public." Such behavior, she suggested, was evidence of a "slave mentality" ("Oprah Winfrey Tells Why" 60). Evoking "the ancestors," who "don't deserve" descendants who "sit and try and tear each other apart," Winfrey said the antidote to the "slave mentality" was the "freedom to believe that you can really do anything that your mind can conceive" (61). Rather than criticizing each other, she said, blacks needed to take responsibility for their own shortcomings. "I see us as a people doing things to ourselves and our children. I see the drug problems. I see abusiveness toward ourselves" (62). A major impediment to blacks' advancement was "self-hatred" and failure to recognize that "the only thing that can free you is the belief that you can be free" (62, 61).

Winfrey's diagnosis helps deflect criticism from fellow African Americans, underscores her image as a champion of empowerment, and serves as an explanation for her white audience of blacks' purported unwillingness to overcome the victim stance and take personal responsibility. As she has stated:

A small but vocal group of black people fear me. Slavery taught us to hate ourselves. I mean, Jane Pauley doesn't have to deal with this. It all comes out of self-hatred. A black person has to ask herself, "If Oprah Winfrey can make it, what does it say about me?" They no longer have any excuse. (Mair 183)

This statement, I propose, goes to the heart of Winfrey's racial breach management strategy, which involves courting white favor with a substantive action and symbolic rejection of selected black individuals and groups, and placating African Americans with largely symbolic gestures. Among her breach management tactics are:

- avoiding or eschewing potentially controversial black political issues (i.e., those that propose institutional, rather than individual, diagnoses of race and class inequality) and figures (e.g., Malcolm X, Kweisi Mfune) that might threaten whites;
- embracing long-dead and/or depoliticized black heroes (e.g., Frederick Douglass, Sojourner Truth, the mythological Martin Luther King Jr.) and

cultural practices (styles of talk, tastes in music, dance and food, hair anxieties, and so on);

- appropriating underclass ideology, castigating blacks who embrace the "cult of victimization" and adopting conservative positions on racially coded issues (e.g., welfare, crime, public housing, affirmative action);
- portraying herself as a self-made role model (indeed, Winfrey was the 1993 recipient of the annual Horatio Alger Award);
- identifying with other exemplars of black success and racial transcendence (e.g., Bill Cosby, Chris Rock, Barack Obama);
- holding up her own success as evidence that white racism is largely a thing of the past.

Through such practices, Winfrey embodies and validates the new consensus on the problem of race and its accompanying colorblind ideology.

Given the endurance of black/white inequities in wealth, the unresolved issue of housing and educational segregation, and the residual tensions and injuries of a national history grounded in slavery, Winfrey's "transcendence of race" requires great sensitivity to the potential for alienating her predominantly white audience. Maintaining a reputation as a comforting, nonthreatening bridge between black and white cultures involves avoiding, minimizing, and/or depoliticizing race, while also presenting herself as an exemplary American success. Such breach management strategies are especially delicate in cases where Winfrey addresses race directly, as she did in a thirteen-episode series titled "Racism in 1992" that included the two installments of the "Rodney King Verdict" mentioned earlier. In keeping with the ideology of colorblindness, many of the white participants in the series equated not being racist with "not seeing color." Also in keeping with colorblind ideology's tendency to obscure "institutional arrangements reproducing structural inequalities . . . in a way that justifies and defends the racial status quo" (Rodriquez 645), the series constructed an understanding of race and racism organized within a liberal politics, a therapeutic view of human relationships, and a generic civil religiosity, all of which treat racism as the result of individual defects rather than the outcome of institutionalized practices or structural imperatives (Peck, "Talk about Racism").

When the problem of racism is cast in these terms, solutions also remain at the level of changes in individual perceptions and behavior, such as "not seeing color," which fit nicely with the therapeutic ethos that defines the daytime talk show genre (Peck, "TV Talk Shows"; Shattuc). Edward Sampson argues that thanks to its dominant cognitive orientation, psychology privileges the "primacy of inner events and transformations over external events and transformations," and in so doing, implicitly endorses the social status quo: "Existing arrangements of power and domination are served within a society when people accept a change in their subjective experience as a substitute for changes in their objective reality" (735–36). This preference for subjective/psychological explanations over objective/structural analysis dominated the "Racism in 1992" series, as seen in this exchange from the second "Rodney King Verdict" episode, when actor Lou Gossett raised questions about the connection between race and political-economic oppression:

> GOSSETT: Racism and violence is [sic] but a mere symbol of a deeper disease in this country and in this world and I think we have to attack the deeper [problem] and it's not racism. It's economics and power and opportunity. So we need to distribute power in some positive way.
>
> WINFREY: I too am here to try to find some solutions and I think the problem goes even deeper than economics. I think that we are in a moral and spiritual deficit in this country.

Winfrey's response deftly blends colorblind and underclass ideologies, whereby inequities of race and class fade from view and the political bases of the uprising (high unemployment and poverty rates, hyper-policing, segregated schools and housing) are transformed into moral failings and thereby depoliticized (Peck, "Talk about Racism"; Davis, "Urban America"). It is here, in the subordination of social structures and institutionalized practices to individual choice and perception, that inferential racism is sustained, even as participants denounce racial prejudice and embrace the idea of colorblindness.

Six months after this broadcast, Bill Clinton won the presidency with a campaign whose praise for a virtuous middle class, emphasis on "personal responsibility," and interpretation of equality as "equality of opportunity, not of results" (Baer 265) capitalized on the supposed "common sense" of underclass ideology and tapped into white voters' sense of racial victimization. In his zeal to woo Reagan Democrats, Clinton cut a wide path around urban issues and race to "reassure white suburbanites at every opportunity that he was not soft on crime, friendly with the under-class, or tolerant of big city welfare expenditures" (Davis, *Dead Cities* 257).

Political scientist Martin Gilens contends that crime and welfare reform are "widely viewed as 'coded' issues that play upon race (or, more specifi-cally, upon white Americans' negative views of blacks) without explicitly raising the 'race card'" ("Race Coding'" 593). In his study of welfare and race, Gilens found that whites significantly overestimate the percentage of African Americans who are poor and on welfare, and that negative per-ceptions of blacks—in particular the view that blacks are "lazy"—were the strongest predictor of opposition to welfare among whites. For Gilens, "the white public's thinking about welfare is inordinately shaped by highly salient negative perceptions of blacks" (593). In his view, "race-coded" issues, such as welfare, possess "symbolic value" because they afford poli-ticians an opportunity to "exploit the power of racial suspicion and ani-mosity while insulating themselves from charges of race-baiting" (602).

Welfare and crime functioned in precisely this way in Clinton's breach management strategy. The Clinton crime bill, signed into law on August 11, 1994, expanded the list of federal crimes to draw the death penalty, cre-ated harsher sentencing guidelines and mandatory sentencing for repeat offenders (the "three strikes and you're out" stipulation), provided for adult prosecution for children as young as thirteen for some offenses, and included money to hire 100,000 more police officers and vastly expand the prison system. Given that welfare is "one of the least popular compo-nents of the U.S. welfare state," and that "racial considerations are the sin-gle most important factor shaping whites' views of welfare," Clinton's 1992 campaign promise to "end welfare as we know it" was a key element of his racial breach management strategy to appeal to white voters (Gilens, "Race Coding" 594, 601). After Republicans gained control of both houses of Congress in 1994, Clinton made welfare reform a centerpiece of his quest to win a second term, signing into law the Personal Responsibil-ity and Work Opportunity Reconciliation Act in August 1996.

The media has played a substantial role in shaping public opinions about welfare and poverty through its habitual linkage of "homeless-ness, destitute urban neighborhoods, poverty, public housing, and wel-fare reform" with "deviance, dangers, and moral deficits of inner-city communities" (Macek 170; also Clawson and Trice; Entman and Rojecki; Gans; Gilens, *Why Americans Hate Welfare;* Gilliam; Gray; Reeves and Campbell; Rivers). In their study of television news coverage of the "war on drugs" under Reagan, Reeves and Campbell show how the "moral framing of economic distress" linked crime, domestic conflict, and the growth of a drug-based economy in impoverished inner cities with cultural deficiencies, rather than with political-economic policies (103). Steve Macek's *Urban Nightmares* found that television's treatment of poverty, welfare, and the underclass escalated during the welfare reform debate in the Clinton era. Further, just as "urban" acquired "semantic identity" with black/Latino in the 1980s (Davis, *Dead Cities* 255), poverty was similarly racialized by being "disproportionately portrayed as a 'black' problem" in the media (Clawson and Trice 54).

Winfrey participated in this process of public opinion formation with her talk show, as racially coded issues offered opportunities to curry support with white followers and distance herself from troubled/troubling sectors of black America. From her first episode on welfare in 1986 ("Pros and Cons of Welfare"), Winfrey's handling of this and other poverty-related issues was consistent. The underclass was portrayed as a parasitic burden on responsible citizens in "Three Generations of Underclass" (1989) and "Angry Taxpayers/Angry Tenants: Public Housing Controversy" (1991). She opened the first episode as follows:

> We have all heard stories of how being on welfare takes a hold of some families, about two and three generations of mothers and daughters and sons that get stuck in a cycle of poverty that provides little inspiration to the next generation to do better. People who work and pay taxes have a lot of big gripes about those who spend decades and generations on welfare. ("Three Generations")

In the "Public Housing" episode she cited the "psychological programming" that afflicts residents of government-funded housing: "How do you even pull yourself up when your mother had lived there and her mother had lived there? It's what we now refer to as, you know, the underclass system." When a panelist raised the question of the legacy of slavery, Winfrey asserted: "I think a lot of people still use the slavery experience as an excuse."

Between 1994 and 1996, as Clinton honed his own racial breach management strategy, several episodes of *The Oprah Winfrey Show* focused on racially coded topics ("I Kicked Welfare, You Can Too," "Violent Children: Detroit," "Is Affirmative Action Outdated?," "Should Welfare Pay for Her Kids?"), all framed through the lens of underclass ideology. Success and failure were the consequence of individual attitudes and behavior. The poor were responsible for their fate and, with the exception of needy children, were not deserving of public assistance or compassion. Those receiving public aid were legitimate targets of resentment from taxpaying citizens. Political/structural explanations of poverty (and wealth) were minimal, and the preferred solution to poverty was self-help and "personal responsibility" in most instances, or private charity in the case of the deserving few.

Two months after the signing of the Clinton crime bill, Winfrey broadcast live, back-to-back episodes from a Detroit theater titled "Violent Children: Detroit" (1994). By setting the show in Detroit—one of the most racially segregated cities in the United States—and calling the city "paralyzed by the crimes of violent children," Winfrey reinforced the semantic unity of urban, black, and criminality. During the broadcast, she described child crime as a "national crisis," suggested the juvenile justice system was "antiquated" because it had not been created for "child murderers," cited a Gallup poll that said "60 percent of the people surveyed think a teenager convicted of murder should get the death penalty," and quizzed the featured child offenders and their families about their "values." She thus implicitly endorsed the necessity of a Clintonesque crackdown because, as she stated near the end of the second installment, "these children have not been raised up in the way they should go."

Yet another important tool in Winfrey's racial breach management arsenal is her status as a "role model"—a notion deeply embedded in the history of black/white relations in the United States. Preston Smith notes that the idea of role modeling, which has long been central to black conservative self-help ideology, "confers moral superiority on those who have economic resources" and entitles them to "mentor" those of "lower status" (264). As an enthusiastic practitioner of this "elite-led moral uplift" (260), Winfrey epitomizes the "role model"—a female Horatio Alger who began at the bottom and achieved phenomenal success. In her widely publicized biographical narrative, Winfrey is portrayed as having overcome the obstacles of race, gender, and class entirely through self-determination and individual "bootstrap" activities. Since the early days of her career, she has been fond of quoting Jesse Jackson's statement that "excellence is the best deterrent to racism" (R. C. Smith 30) and opined in a 1988 interview, "The greatest contribution you can make to women's rights, to civil rights, is to be the absolute best at what you do" (Mosle 20).

The rhetoric of self-help and self-empowerment defines Winfrey's enterprise. Not only does her multimedia empire aim to "empower people" and be a "catalyst for people beginning to think more insightfully about themselves and their lives" (Adler 62), but she herself is also empowerment personified. Thus, her wealth and fame are the fruits of throwing off the "slave mentality," rejecting victimhood, and taking responsibility for her life. She is living proof of her claim that "you can be poor and black and female and make it to the top" (278). By implication, all those other poor black females (and males) could, if they were willing to take "personal responsibility," make it to the top too. And if they do not, as Winfrey says, she is a constant reminder that "they no longer have any excuse" (Mair 183).

Bill Cosby, another black role model credited with transcending race, delivered a similar message at the May 2004 commemoration of the fiftieth anniversary of the *Brown v. Board of Education* decision, where he accused "lower economic and lower middle economic people" for "not holding their end in this deal" thanks to defective parenting of offspring who are "going nowhere" (Cosby; also Lee). Articulating key tenets of underclass ideology, Cosby chastised blacks for their poor parenting, deficient moral values, criminal inclinations, and victim mentality, while rejecting the notion that blacks' problems lay in structural inequities of class and race: "We can't blame white people," Cosby asserted (Bracey 178). During the 2008 campaign, Barack Obama also took the role model position with a speech to a black audience, which he counseled to do a better job instilling the right values in their children (Sweet). The speech was widely hailed as groundbreaking by the mainstream (white) media. *Newsweek* columnist Mickey Kaus proclaimed it a sign that Obama might "guide white Americans toward a better racial future," but even more important, that the candidate's "most exciting potential for moral leadership could be in the African-American community." Such comments by prominent black role models reinforce the claim that integration and racial equality are accomplished realities and the socioeconomic gap between blacks and whites is the result of moral or behavioral failure.

In being beacons of moral uplift, Winfrey, Cosby, Obama, and other exemplars of "stratospheric black success" (Cashin xii) serve an important ideological function, according to Paul Street: "The majority of whites love to see black middle- and upper-class authority figures blame non-affluent blacks for their own problems" ("The Full Blown 'Oprah Effect'"). In the era of colorblindness, this is another means by which Winfrey courts white support. Sociologist Eva Illouz paints Winfrey's "transcendence of race" as a signal advance in the history of American race relations:

> To the extent that Oprah symbolizes the very values that are promoted in the white middle class to account for success (hard work, self-help, endurance, altruism, more self-improvement), she not only offers a powerful alternative to the stereotypical images of black women but also has become a symbol of power and moral strength for all women. That a black woman would become a model and a guide for mainstream white women is . . . unprecedented in American history. (228)

This helps explain the degree to which Winfrey is described as a personal friend by her predominantly white followers, most of whom can probably claim no other black friendships. As Winfrey explains this phenomenon:

> I transcend race, really. I believe I have a higher calling. What I do goes beyond the realm of everyday parameters. I am profoundly effective. I know people really, really, really *love* me, *love* me, *love* me. A bonding of the human spirit takes place. (Zehme 32)

Like *The Cosby Show*, which was crafted to supply "positive images" of African Americans through the lovable Huxtable family and was scoured of anything that conveyed what Cosby termed "downtrodden, negative, I-can't-do-I-won't-do" (Miller 73), Winfrey's enterprise—from her talk show debut in the 1980s to the creation of the Oprah Winfrey Network (OWN) in 2011—has been driven by an upbeat message of personal empowerment. Further, the very fact that these black celebrities have attracted a majority white audience is interpreted as a major advance in American race relations. Just as Cosby sought to instill good feelings in his audience, Winfrey's viewers, readers, and seminar attendees are meant to feel enlightened, uplifted, and empowered. What her followers are not asked to do is to consider how they might be implicated in (and even benefit from) the suffering of others, or to take responsibility for this possibility. They are not, in other words, ever made to feel *uncomfortable*. And this, I propose, is an important basis of Winfrey's "transcendence of race." This is what allows them to imagine that racism has been vanquished, or is about to be, because they invite a black woman into their homes and really love her.

Perhaps whites' embrace of black celebrities reveals more about the power of television than about the actual state of American race relations, however. Because the United States remains highly racially segregated, many whites' primary encounter with African Americans comes through television—a medium, Street argues, that "presents a dangerously schizophrenic image of black America split between super-successful and largely admirable (not-all-that) black superstars (Oprah being the best of all) and dangerous (all-too) black perpetrators" ("The Full Blown 'Oprah Effect'"). According to Leonard Steinhorn and Barbara Diggs-Brown, the repetitive character of TV programming and its domestic context of reception give "white Americans the sensation of having meaningful, repeated contact with blacks without actually having it"—a phenomenon they term "virtual integration" (146). In their view, "Virtual integration enables whites to live in a world with blacks without having to do so in fact. It provides a form of safe intimacy without any of the risks. It offers a clean and easy way for whites to establish and nourish what they see as their bona fide commitment to fairness, tolerance, and color blindness" (157). If through virtual integration "whites have made room in their lives for black celebrities" and take their affection for figures such as Winfrey and Cosby "as evidence of their own open-mindedness and as proof that the nation isn't so hard on blacks after all," Steinhorn and Diggs-Brown point out that this same colorblindness is "almost unattainable for blacks in the real world" (157).

The ideology of colorblindness—like the reformulation of the problem of race in which it had flourished—has played an important role in deflecting attention from powerful structural inequities of material resources and political power. Street makes a useful distinction between "level one (state-of-mind)" and "level two (state-of-being)" forms of racism (*Barack Obama* 171). The former, a problem of individual attitudes, is easily corrected at that level; the latter is societal and institutional, and thus irresolvable without fundamental structural and political change. As the idea of colorblindness was gradually stripped of its critical, emancipatory power and appropriated by conservatives for the end of "preserving, rather than challenging, the racial status quo" (Haney Lopez), it has become increasingly harmonious with neoliberalism's regressive redistribution of wealth and its "conventional wisdom" that "ascribes people's status and wealth to purely private and personal success or failure in adapting to the permanent, inherently human realities of inequality in a 'free market' system" (Street, *Barack Obama* 100).

This is the context of Oprah Winfrey's ascent to mainstream cultural icon, including her "transcendence of race." The political sea change that transpired over the last quarter of the twentieth century reflects the bipartisan consensus around the notion of the "underclass" and the nature of the "race problem" in the United States within which colorblind ideology has flourished. The fusion of underclass theory and self-help ideology that began with Reagan, continued under Clinton, and persists with Obama provides a rationale for black poverty, an alibi for the continued contraction of the state, and a scapegoat for working- and middle-class whites also caught in the juggernaut of neoliberal restructuring. But if whites' embrace of black "role models" such as Barack Obama and Oprah Winfrey seems to validate the ideology of colorblindness and reinforce the notion that racism is obsolete, such mainstream acceptance is not without limits. Winfrey's endorsement of Obama in 2008 triggered substantial criticism from her fans—some of whom accused her of supporting him only because he is black, and therefore betraying her claims to colorblindness—and contributed to a drop in her own popularity and declining ratings for her show and magazine (Panagopoulos). Faced with blowback from straying a little too far into the black/white racial breach, Winfrey quietly stepped back from the campaign to tend to her empire. Declarations that the United States is now a colorblind, post-racial society notwithstanding, it appears that the "transcendence of race"—be it Winfrey's or Cosby's or Obama's—is a necessarily fragile accomplishment, resting as it does on the denial of institutionalized inequality and the illusions of "virtual integration."

Notes

1. In 1965, a report written by Daniel Patrick Moynihan was issued by the Office of Policy Planning and Research of the Department of Labor. Titled *The Negro Family: The Case for National Action*, the Moynihan report characterized the black family as a "tangled web of pathology." The report was a significant new twist in the ethnicity paradigm, for it blamed the victims of a long history of systematic racial oppression, economic exploitation, and social exclusion for their own misery, supposedly caused by their failure to "assimilate" as individuals into an "accommodative" and increasingly "color blind" society" (Reeves 103).

WORKS CITED

Adelman, Robert M., and James Clarke Gocker. "Racial Residential Segregation in Urban America." *Sociology Compass* 1.1 (2007): 404–23. Web. 25 Jan. 2010.

Adler, Bill, ed. *The Uncommon Wisdom of Oprah Winfrey.* Secaucus, NJ: Birch Lane Press, 1997. Print.

"Angry Taxpayers/Angry Tenants: The Public Housing Controversy." *Oprah Winfrey Show.* 18 June 1991. Television.

Auletta, Ken. *The Underclass.* New York: Random House, 1982. Print.

Baer, Kenneth. S. *Reinventing Democrats.* Lawrence: University Press of Kansas, 2000. Print.

Bobo, Lawrence D., and Camille Z. Charles. "Race in the American Mind: From the Moynihan Report to the Obama Candidacy." *Annals of the American Academy of Political and Social Science* 621.1 (2009): 243–59. Print.

Bobo, Lawrence D., and Ryan A. Smith. "From Jim Crow Racism to Laissez-Faire Racism: The Transformation of Racial Attitudes." *Beyond Pluralism: The Conception of Groups and Group Identities in America.* Ed. Wendy F. Katkin and Ned Landsman. Champaign: University of Illinois Press, 1998. 185–220. Print.

Bonilla-Silva, Eduardo. "The Linguistics of Color Blind Racism: How to Talk Nasty about Black without Sounding 'Racist.'" *Critical Sociology* 28.1–2 (2002): 41–64. Print.

Bracey, Christopher Allen. *Saviors or Sellouts: The Promise and Peril of Black Conservatism, from Booker T. Washington to Condoleezza Rice.* Boston: Beacon Press, 2008. Print.

Brenner, Robert. *The Economics of Global Turbulence.* London: Verso, 2006. Print.

Brown, Elaine. *The Condemnation of Little B.* Boston: Beacon Press, 2002. Print.

Carr, David. "A Triumph of Avoiding the Traps." *New York Times* 22 Nov. 2009. Web. 22 Nov. 2009.

Cashin, Sheryll. *The Failures of Integration.* New York: Public Affairs, 2004. Print

Clawson, Rosalee A., and Rakuya Trice. "Poverty as We Know It: Media Portrayals of the Poor." *Public Opinion Quarterly* 64.1 (2000): 53–64. Print.

Cosby, Bill. "Dr. Bill Cosby Speaks at the 50th Anniversary Commemoration of the Brown v. Topeka Board of Education Supreme Court Decision" (transcript of speech). N.d. Web. 2 Jan. 2012.

Davis, Mike. *Dead Cities*. New York: New Press, 2002. Print.

——. *Prisoners of the American Dream*. London: Verso, 1986. Print.

——. "Urban America Sees its Future: In L.A., Burning All Illusions." *Nation* June 1992: 743–46. Print.

Dillahunt, Ajamu, Brian Miller, Mike Prokosch, Jeannette Huezom, and Dedrick Muhammad. "State of the Dream 2010: Drained." *United for a Fair Economy* 13 Jan. 2010. Web. 30 July 2010.

Entman, Robert. M., and Andrew Rojecki. *The Black Image in the White Mind: Media and Race in America*. Chicago: University of Chicago Press, 2000. Print.

Firstman, Richard. "Oprah Power." *Newsday* 1 Nov. 1989: Sec. II, 4. Print.

Fottrell, Quentin. "The Cult of Oprah Inc." *Irish Times* 5 Aug. 2000. Web. 2 Mar. 2001.

Gans, Herbert. *The War against the Poor: The Underclass and Anti-poverty Policy*. New York: Basic Books, 1995. Print.

George, Susan. *Hijacking America: How the Secular and Religious Right Changed What Americans Think*. Cambridge: Polity Press, 2008. Print.

Gilens, Martin. "'Race Coding' and White Opposition to Welfare." *American Political Science Review* 90.3 (1996): 593–604. Print.

——. *Why Americans Hate Welfare: Race, Media, and the Politics of Antipoverty Policy*. Chicago: University of Chicago Press. 1999. Print.

Gilliam, Franklin D., Jr. "The 'Welfare Queen' Experiment: How Viewers React to Images of African-American Mothers on Welfare." *Nieman Reports* 53.2 (1999). Web. 19 Nov. 2010.

Gray, Herman. "Television, Black Americans, and the American Dream." *Critical Studies in Mass Communication* 6.4 (1989): 376–86. Print.

Greenberg, Stanley B. "Private Heroism and Public Purpose." *American Prospect Online* 1 Sept. 1996. Web. 5 July 2004.

Hale, Jon F. "The Making of the New Democrats." *Political Science Quarterly* 110.2 (1995): 207–33. Print.

Haney Lopez, Ian F. "Colorblind to the Reality of Race in America." *Chronicle of Higher Education* 3 Nov. 2006. Web. 27 Dec. 2011.

Henwood, Doug. "Clinton's Liberalism: No Model for the Left." *The Socialist Register 1997*. Ed. Leo Panitch. London: Merlin Press. 159–75. Print.

Horton, Donald, and R. Richard Wohl. "Mass Communication as Para-social Interaction: Observations on Intimacy at a Distance." *Drama in Life: The Uses of Communication in Society*. Ed. James E. Combs and Michael W. Mansfield. New York: Hastings House, 1976. 212–28. Print.

"I Kicked Welfare, You Can Too." *Oprah Winfrey Show*. 19 Jan. 1994. Television.

Illouz, Eva. *Oprah Winfrey and the Glamour of Misery*. New York: Columbia University Press, 2003. Print.

"Is Affirmative Action Outdated?" *Oprah Winfrey Show*. 11 Apr. 1995. Television.

Jhally, Sut, and Justin Lewis. *Enlightened Racism*. Boulder, CO: Westview Press, 1992. Print.

Kaus, Mickey. "The Obama Dividend." *Newsweek* 22 Mar. 2008. Web. 1 Jan. 2011.

Kim, Claire Jean. "Managing the Racial Breach: Clinton, Black-White Polarization, and the Race Initiative." *Political Science Quarterly* 117.1 (2002): 55–79. Print.

———. "The Racial Triangulation of Asian Americans." *Politics and Society* 27.1 (1999): 105–38. Print.

Klein, Joel. "The Fresh Face." *Time* 15 Oct. 2006. Web. 15 Dec. 2011.

Klinkner, Philip A. "Bill Clinton and the Politics of the New Liberalism." *Without Justice for All.* Ed. Adolph Reed Jr. Boulder, CO: Westview Press, 1999. 11–28. Print

Kozol, Jonathan. *The Shame of the Nation: The Restoration of Apartheid Schooling in America.* New York: Crown, 2006. Print.

Lee, Felicia R. "Cosby Defends His Remarks about Poor Blacks' Values." *New York Times* 22 May 2004. Web. 2 Jan. 2012.

Long, Marion. "Paradise Tossed." *Omni* April 1988: 36–39, 42, 96, 98–102, 106, 108. Print.

Macek, Steve. *Urban Nightmares: The Media, the Right, and the Moral Panic over the City.* Minneapolis: University of Minnesota Press, 2006. Print.

Mair, George. *Oprah Winfrey: The Real Story.* Secaucus, NJ: Carol Publishing Group, 1998. Print.

Massey, Douglas S. "The Race Case." *American Prospect* 13 Feb. 2003. Web. 18 Dec. 2004.

Massey, Douglas S., and M. J. Fischer. "How Segregation Concentrates Poverty." *Ethnic and Racial Studies* 23.4 (2000): 670–91. Print.

Mead, Lawrence. *Beyond Entitlement.* New York: Basic Books, 1986. Print.

Mediamark Research, Inc. *Oprah Winfrey Show* and *O, The Oprah Magazine.* Fall, 2003. Print.

Miles, Robert. *Racism.* London: Routledge, 1989. Print.

Miller, Mark Crispin. *Boxed In: The Culture of TV.* Evanston, IL: Northwestern University Press, 1988. Print.

Mills, Charles. "Under Class Under Standings." *Ethics* 104 (1994): 855–81. Print.

Mosle, Sara. "Grand New Oprah." *Savvy* Aug. 1988: 20. Print.

Murray, Charles A. *Losing Ground: American Social Policy, 1950–1980.* New York: Basic Books. 1984. Print.

Novak, Michael. *The New Consensus on Family and Welfare: A Community of Self-Reliance.* Washington, DC: American Enterprise Institute for Public Policy Research, 1987. Print.

"Oprah.com Traffic and Demographic Statistics." *Quantcast* 2 Jan. 2012–2 Feb. 2012. Web. 3 Feb. 2012.

"Oprah Winfrey Tells Why Blacks Who Bash Blacks Tick Her Off." *Jet* 17 Sept. 1990: 60–62. Print.

Paget, Karen. "Can Cities Escape Political Isolation?" *American Prospect* 9.36 (1998): 54–62. Web. 28 Nov. 2010.

Panogopoulos, Costas. "Obama Supporter Oprah Takes a Big Dive." *Politico* 7 Apr. 2008. Web. 25 June 2009.

Peck, Janice. "Talk about Racism: Framing a Popular Discourse of Race in Oprah Winfrey." *Cultural Critique* 27 (1994): 89–126. Print.

———. "TV Talk Shows as Therapeutic Discourse: The Ideological Labor of the Televised Talking Cure." *Communication Theory* 5.1 (1995): 58–81. Print.

Perlstein, Rick. *Before the Storm: Barry Goldwater and the Unmaking of the American Consensus.* New York: Nation Books, 2009. Print.

"Pros and Cons of Welfare." *Oprah Winfrey Show.* 17 Nov. 1986. Television.

Reed, Adolph., Jr. "Introduction: The New Liberal Orthodoxy on Race and Inequality." *Without Justice for All.* Ed. Adolph Reed Jr. Boulder, CO: Westview Press, 1999. 1–10. Print.

———. *Stirrings in the Jug: Black Politics in the Post-segregation Era.* Minneapolis: University of Minnesota Press, 1999. Print.

———. "Where Obamaism Seems to Be Going." *Black Agenda Report* 15 July 2008. Web. 25 May 2010.

Reeves, Jimmie L. "Re-covering Racism: Crack Mothers, Reaganism, and the Network News." *Living Color: Race and Television in the United States.* Ed. Sasha Torres. Durham, NC: Duke University Press, 1998. 97–117. Print.

Reeves, Jimmie L., and Richard Campbell. *Cracked Coverage.* Durham, NC: Duke University Press, 1994. Print.

Richman, Alan. "Oprah." *People Weekly* 12 Jan. 1987: 52–55, 58. Print.

Rivers, Caryl. *Slick Spins and Fractured Facts.* New York: Columbia University Press, 1996. Print.

"Rodney King Verdict: The Aftermath and the Anger, Parts 1 and 2." *Oprah Winfrey Show.* 5 and 6 May 1992. Television.

Rodriquez, Jason. "Color-Blind Ideology and the Cultural Appropriation of Hip-Hop." *Journal of Contemporary Ethnography* 35.6 (2006): 645–68. Print.

Roediger, David. *Colored White: Transcending the Racial Past.* Berkeley: University of California Press, 2002. Print.

Sampson, Edward E. "Cognitive Psychology as Ideology." *American Psychologist* 36.7 (1981): 730–43. Print.

Schorr, Daniel. "A New, 'Post-Racial' Political Era in America." *All Things Considered.* NPR. 28 Jan. 2008. Web. 3 Jan. 2012.

Shapiro, Thomas M., Tatjana Meschede, and Laura Sullivan. "The Racial Wealth Gap Increases Fourfold." *Institute on Assets and Social Policy.* May 2010. Web. 20 Sept. 2010.

Shattuc, Jane. *The Talking Cure.* New York: Routledge, 1997. Print.

"Should Welfare Pay for Her Kids?" *Oprah Winfrey Show.* 19 Apr. 1995. Television.

Smith, Joan. "The Ideology of 'Family and Community': New Labour Abandons the Welfare State." *Socialist Register 1997.* Ed. Leo Panitch. London: Merlin Press, 1997. 176–96. Print.

Smith, Preston H. "'Self-Help,' Black Conservatives, and the Reemergence of Black Privatism." *Without Justice for All.* Ed. Adolph Reed Jr. Boulder, CO: Westview Press, 1999. 257–90. Print.

Smith, R. C. "She Once Trashed Her Apartment to Make a Point." *TV Guide* 30 Aug. 1986: 30–31. Print.

Steinhorn, Leonard, and Barbara Diggs-Brown. *By the Color of Our Skin.* New York: Dutton, 1999. Print.

Street, Paul. *Barack Obama and the Future of American Politics.* Boulder, CO: Paradigm, 2009. Print.

——. "The Full Blown 'Oprah Effect': Reflections on Color, Class, and New Age Racism." *Black Commentator* 24 Feb 2005: 127. Web. 20 July 2005.

Sweet, Lynn. "'Y'all Have Popeyes Out in Beaumont?' Obama on the Bully Pulpit." *Chicago Sun-Times* 29 Feb. 2008. Web. 2 Jan. 2012.

"Television." *Ebony* Aug. 1991: 50, 52. Print.

"Three Generations of Underclass." *Oprah Winfrey Show.* 22 Mar. 1989. Television.

Toner, Robin. "Southern Democrats' Decline Is Eroding the Political Center." *New York Times* 15 Nov. 2004: A1, A14. Web. 30 May 2007.

"Violent Children: Detroit." *Oprah Winfrey Show.* 3 & 4 Oct. 1994. Television.

Will, George F. "Misreading Obama's Identity." *Washington Post* 30 Dec. 2007. Web. 27 Dec. 2011.

Withorn, Ann. "'Why Do They Hate Me So Much?' A History of Welfare and Its Abandonment in the United States." *American Journal of Orthopsychiatry* 66.4 (1996): 496–509. Print.

Wuthnow, Robert, and Robert C. Liebman. *The New Christian Right.* Hawthorne, NY: Aldine, 1983. Print.

Zehme, Bill. "It Came from Chicago." *Spy Magazine* Dec. 1986: 30–32. Web. 10 Dec. 2011.

Zoglin, Richard. "Oprah Winfrey: Lady with a Calling." *Time* 8 Aug. 1988. Web. 4 Mar. 2006.

5

The Race Denial Card

The NBA Lockout, LeBron James, and the Politics of New Racism

DAVID J. LEONARD AND BRUCE LEE HAZELWOOD

In what has become a clichéd and commonplace facet of post–civil rights America, contemporary racial discourse follows a distinct path: accusations of individualized racism, denials that usually focus on intent, all followed by counteraccusations centering on claims about the race card. In a 2011 episode of *Real Time with Bill Maher*, Touré, an African American commentator, and white political comedian Bill Maher identified the shift in racial rhetoric that has resulted in the denial of racism becoming the new form of racism.[1] In their estimation, the race denial card is the most powerful and widely circulated in the deck, evident by its ubiquity and the constant demonization of those who "introduce" race into the discussion. Henry Giroux writes against the prevailing assessments of the declining or diminishing significance of race, highlighting the fluidity, contradictions, metamorphosis, and ubiquity of denials of the importance of race beginning in the 1970s:

> The importance of race and the enduring fact of racism are relegated to the dustbin of history at a time in American life when the discourses of race and the spectacle of racial representation saturate the dominant media and public life. . . . The politics of the color line and representations of race have become far more subtle and complicated than they were in the Jim Crow era. Unlike the old racism, which defined racial difference in terms of fixed biological categories organized hierarchically, the new

racism operates in various guises proclaiming among other things race neutrality, asserting culture as a marker of racial difference, or marking race as a private matter. Unlike the crude racism with its biological referents and pseudoscientific legitimizations, buttressing its appeal to white racial superiority, the new racism cynically recodes itself within the vocabulary of the civil rights movement. (2003, 198)

Eduardo Bonilla-Silva, in his examination of commonplace race rhetorical phrases, describes the process of racial denial in the following way: "Phrases such as 'I am not a racist' or 'some of my best friends are black' have become standard fare of post–Civil Rights racial discourse." Acting "as discursive buffers before or after someone states something that is or could be interpreted as racist,"[2] these rhetorical utterances serve to erase race from public discourse. Similarly, Allen Johnson argues how dominant ideologies, frames, and cultural practices contribute to a process whereby race is "denied and minimized." The race denial card and efforts to silence racial intrusion legitimize the status quo, thereby conferring the privileges derived through hegemony.[3] As Johnson comments, "When women and people of color are accused of 'whining,' for example, they're essentially being told that whatever they have to deal with isn't that bad and they should 'just get on with it.'" He notes further that "when you deny the reality of oppression, you can also deny the reality of privilege that underlies it, which is just what it takes to get off the hook."[4]

"Racism" functioning as the denial of racism is nothing new and so often works in conjunction with cultural racism. Whether manifesting as an individual deflection or a societal one, the "I am not a racist, but" frame defines post–civil rights racial discussions. Eduardo Bonilla-Silva and Tyrone Forman make this clear in their article, arguing as follows:

Since the civil rights period it has become common for Whites to use phrases such as "I am not a racist, but . . . " as shields to avoid being labeled as "racist" when expressing racial ideas (VanDijk, 1984:120). These discursive maneuvers or semantic moves are usually followed by negative statements on the general character of minorities (e.g. "they are lazy," "they have too many babies") or on government-sponsored policies and programs that promote racial equality (e.g. "affirmative action is reverse discrimination," "no-one should be forced to integrate").[5]

Evident here is not only the centrality of race denial and claims of colorblindness but also the ways in which culture and other rhetoric centering the "character of minorities" operates alongside of the hegemony of race denial. According to Bonilla-Silva, "Cultural racism is a frame that relies on culturally-based arguments."[6] Ben Carrington and Mary McDonald also argue, "Cultural racism posits that although different ethnic groups or 'races' may not exist in a hierarchical biological relationship, they are nevertheless culturally distinct, each group having their own incompatible lifestyles, customs and ways of seeing the world."[7] These discursive articulations are evident in a myriad of spaces from education and the political sphere to popular media and popular culture. Sport, because of its level of diversity, particularly the numbers of African Americans within sports like football and basketball, because of the increasing power of sports media, and because of the core ideologies that guide American sports culture, has shown a great propensity to foster discussions of race. Bill Rhoden, a sports columnist with the *New York Times,* in describing a phone conversation between a caller and a radio host about the possibility of the Chicago Bulls retaining a few white players in an effort to please its white fan base, offered the following:

> After a back and forth, the host politely, but firmly, said, "I don't want to sit here on this topic because I disagree with you." His point was that fans are largely colorblind: They want to see winning basketball. This is typical of recent conversations about the impact of racism on sports. The spreading attitude is that racism is something for the archives, especially in professional athletics, where so many black and brown athletes are richly compensated. In fact, racism is a constant, irritating hum in contemporary American life—too distracting, too draining, too time-consuming to constantly deal with. Ignore the hum and pick your spots. Sometimes the spots pick you.[8]

To acknowledge that race matters in a sports world is to deny that wins and losses are settled on the field; to acknowledge that race matters to fans is to deny the core narrative of what drives fans to the stadiums and arenas and onto their couches: love of team and pride in victory. The diversity of the sports world and the allegiance to narratives of the

American Dream, meritocracy, and integration have contributed to a culture where race and race denial are as important as the box scores, wins/losses, and the on-the-field happenings. While we can see both the "denial of racism" and the dismissal of the significance of race and cultural racism in how this denial operates, we also see the powerful ways the biological notions of difference continue to operate within this context.

With this in mind, this chapter examines the ways in which racial denial, or, better said, the race denial card, is ubiquitously played within the sports world, pointing to the efforts to silence, minimize, and erase race from public discourse. The erasure of race and the explicit denials of racial significance represent central tenets of a racist project. Focusing on the 2011 NBA lockout and recent controversies surrounding LeBron James, this chapter highlights the ways that racial language and narratives, as well as the desire to deny and dismiss efforts to reflect on race, are evidence of the continued significance of race. Examining the ways in which race—racial talk, the white racial frame[9]—is central to contemporary sporting discourses, the chapter explores the ways in which these sites exist as contested spaces of racial meaning. From the ways in which race penetrated and defined the 2011 NBA lockout to the ways in which race played out during LeBron James's 2010–11 season, this chapter highlights the powerful ways that race operates as a pivot within both the media and fan debates.

More illustratively, the hegemony of the race denial card, and the negative response to any efforts to interpret and analyze through a lens of racism and racial heresy, represent a fundamental element of new racism. In this regard, this chapter focuses on how efforts to reflect on race during the 2011 lockout were met with swift denials and condemnation, just as with LeBron James. In each case, readers will see how race and racial assumptions overdetermine the interpretations and understanding of the specific instances and larger issues of class, work conditions, and power. The chapter concludes that contemporary NBA culture, like other modern institutions, is littered with racial frames and rhetorics. While the diversity of the sports world and the popularity of athletes of color have led to societal celebration and claims that sports is a post-racial panacea,[10] sport reflects mainstream culture and its racial moment.

What's Race Got to Do with It? The NBA Lockout

The 2011 NBA lockout revealed the powerful ways that race operates within the context of the NBA. Shortly after the 1998 lockout, Todd Boyd argued that the NBA "remains one of the few places in American society where there is a consistent racial discourse," where race, whether directly or indirectly, is the subject of conversation at all times.[11] Little has changed since then, although systemic denials of racial importance and accusations regarding the "race card" have increased in the wake of Michael Jordan's retirement, the Palace Brawl,[12] and countless other issues. The 2011 lockout demonstrates the power in this discourse, and the stakes within the NBA's racial war. It revealed the ways in which race functions as a contested idea whereupon the proponents of color-blindness, those who deny the continued significance of race, balk at any and all questions about the impact of racial meanings, even as race continues to saturate the individual commentaries, discursive articulations, and institutional operations of the contemporary NBA.

Like many sportswriters, Bill Simmons, a former ESPN columnist and editor in chief of Grantland, a sport-related website, focused almost exclusively on the NBA's players during the lockout, ostensibly blaming them for the cancellation of games. While acknowledging the responsibility of owners, he invariably positioned the players at the center of the discussion. In one such column, he focused on the players' intellectual preparedness and the problems resulting from their limited skill sets. He noted:

> Should someone who's earned over $300 million (including endorsements) and has deferred paychecks coming really be telling guys who have made 1/100th as much as him to fight the fight and stand strong and not care about getting paid? And what are Garnett's credentials, exactly? During one of the single biggest meetings (last week, on Tuesday), Hunter had Kobe Bryant, Paul Pierce and Garnett (combined years spent in college: three) negotiate directly with Stern in some sort of misguided "Look how resolved we are, you're not gonna intimidate us!" ploy that backfired so badly that one of their teams' owners was summoned into the meeting specifically to calm his player down and undo some of the damage. (I'll let you guess the player. It's not hard.) And this helped the situation . . . how? And we thought this was going to work . . . why?

Congratulations, players—you showed solidarity! You showed you wouldn't back down! You made things worse, and you wasted a day, but dammit, you didn't back down! Just make sure you tell that to every team employee who gets fired over these next few weeks, as well as to all the restaurant and bar owners near NBA arenas.[13]

Beyond trotting out the "angry black man" trope, which was commonplace among the NBA punditry, and blaming the players for the forthcoming unemployment facing many employees within the NBA, Simmons hinges his evidence about the incompetence of the players by citing the amount of formal college education of Pierce, Bryant, and Garnett. In other words, people are losing jobs and fans are losing games because the NBA is at the mercy of its stupid/uneducated black players. And, Simmons wasn't done here, offering additional clarity about his comments. Explaining his growing affection for the NHL, Simmons ironically bemoans the absence of an NBA season, arguing that the lockout is the result of the "limited intellectual capital" of the players and the failure of the owners and agents to compensate for their deficiencies:

Where's the big-picture leadership here? What's the right number of franchises? Where should those franchises play? What's worse, losing three franchises or losing an entire season of basketball? What's really important here? I don't trust the players' side to make the right choices, because they are saddled with limited intellectual capital. (Sorry, it's true.) The owners' side can't say the same; they should be ashamed. Same for the agents. And collectively, they should all be mortified that a 16-hour negotiating session, this late in the game, was cause for any celebration or optimism. In my mind, it was more of a cry for help.[14]

Unusually, Simmons offers some blame for the owners. As the intelligent ones, they have an obligation to fix the situation. Although they have the intelligence, they allow the players, who lack intelligence, to have input into the situation. To Simmons, this is the source of the NBA's problem.

The racial paternalism here is as striking as his efforts to resuscitate the bell curve, a race-based theory that linked intelligence to race. Relying on this problematic and outdated theory, Simmons claims the players' lack of the requisite intelligence is widespread within sporting discourses.

As such, the underlying theme throughout the media reporting on the NBA lockout was that the players' lack of intelligence, knowledge, and sophistication was leading them to make poor decisions. Michael Eric Dyson, in describing Donald Trump's consistent questioning of President Barack Obama's academic record, identified the questioning of African American intelligence as central to the larger history of American white supremacy: "Skepticism about black intelligence and suspicion about black humanity have gone hand in hand throughout the history of this country in feeding the perception that black people don't quite measure up."[15] Building upon the work of Frantz Fanon, whose *Black Skin, White Masks* explores the incompatibility of blackness and intelligence within the white imagination, Ben Carrington highlights the dialectics between representations of black male athletes and the conception of body/mind. Carrington notes Fanon's exploration of the ways in which blackness was conceptualized and envisioned through white supremacy:

> When Fanon gives his white patients a word association test, it is significant to note how often his respondents mention either sports, or prominent black athletes of the period. Fanon informs us that the word "Negro brought forth biology, penis, strong, athletic, potent, boxer, Joe Louis, Jesse Owens, Senegalese troops, savage, animal, devil, sin." For Fanon, the black male was the repository of white fears, fantasies and desires, and of all of these constructions, there was one figure above all others that held a central place within the colonial imaginary: "There is one expression that through time has become singularly eroticized: the black athlete."

The efforts to depict NBA players as requiring help, as lacking the intelligence or leadership skills to make the proper decisions, are emblematic of "the colonial imaginary." Evident in the NBA's dress code, the requirement that NBA players attend college, and the overall paternalistic tone of the media, the racial discourse surrounding the NBA embodies a longer history of white paternalism.[16]

Yet more striking were the efforts to deny the racial implications here and elsewhere. Focusing on intent and the efforts of others to insert race into the NBA lockout, Simmons and others quickly denied the racial context here. In response to public discussion about his rhetorical devices, his deployment of the language of cultural racism, and the tone of his piece embodying the "white man's burden," Simmons scoffed at the racial implications with the proverbial denials: "some 'scholar' playing the race card."

Public support of Simmons's rhetoric took multiple forms, such as the assertion that Simmons was talking about all NBA players, not just those who are black. On one blog, fairweatherfan denies the racial implications of Simmons's comments, focusing instead on his generalization about all athletes: "Simmons seemed pretty clearly to be using a 'dumb athlete' stereotype, not a 'dumb black people' one. Whether or not it's appropriate to use that stereotype is debatable but I really don't think it's racially based."[17] Similarly, angryguy77 saw the comments as nonracial, arguing: "There are white guys who play in all major sports. It's not like he singled out a particular race in his statement. He's making a point that it's the guys who have experience in how to run a business [who] are more qualified to make the business decisions. I don't believe there should be an issue especially since he clarified what he meant. But it won't be enough, the pc crowd [sic] will bang his doors down anyway."

Several people also deployed colorblind rhetoric in an effort to discount claims about the racial implications evident in Simmons's commentary along with the significance of race within the NBA and society at large:[18]

ANDREW PAIK: Come on man. Isn't the point of racism to be "colorblind." Why are you so narrow-minded to think everything in terms of "it's because these guys are black." ALL ATHLETES HAVE NO COLLEGE EDUCATION (NOT JUST BLACK PEOPLE). Why do you use the race card and promote DISCRIMINATION among whites and blacks. Should journalists [be] prevented from speaking their minds because that group happens to be predominantly black? Do you have any idea how many times Bill Simmons has ripped David Stern? If he was black, then "O MY GOD SIMMONS IS A RACIST" but nah . . . he's an old white guy. Really? You think that's the world Dr. King envisioned? COLORBLIND. Simmons did not think anything about race when he posted this and it offends me when you accuse perfectly colorblind people and force them to start discriminating between races. Please, go pick on guys like Rick Perry and those Southern guys. This guy is just speaking his mind and it has NOTHING to do with race. Sick of this.

SCOTTBEN: Bottom line is these players don't have a negotiating background, or a law degree or any economic experience other than a few college

classes. They are basketball players. The same could be said for the
NFL, MLB, NHL, writers guild (as referenced in Simmons' article).
This has no racial component, these are facts. There is no embarrassment in one man, who has a year or 2 of college under his belt, not
being as versed in economics or negotiations than a man who graduated from law school with the express focus on labor laws, negotiating
tactics, etc. Pres Obama plays basketball, but I sure as hell wouldn't
start him at the point for LA, and I'd just as soon not ask Kobe to go
and speak at the joint sessions on a new jobs bill. Nor would I want
Aaron Rodgers negotiating a deal between Israel and Palastine [*sic*].

The level of animosity toward arguments that reflect on race and racism
demonstrates the appeal of sports as a post-racial fantasy. Reflecting
widespread belief in the declining significance of race, the forcefulness
of the responses embodies the power of the narrative of sports as pure
meritocracy and sports as colorblind because of the popularity of athletes. Focusing on race undermines the fundamental appeal of sports
as a post-racial playground. Writing about Tiger Woods, C. L. Cole and
David Andrews argue:

It is our contention that Tiger Woods is an extraordinary exemplar of the
new American logic. That is, Woods is the masculine extension of the
already familiar hybridized American [feminine] face invested in white
American culture. As such, he is the latest (but perhaps the first mas-
culinized) rendition of the American supericon: a commercial emblem
who makes visible and concrete late modern America's narrative of itself
as a post-historical nation of immigrants. Woods thus embodies the
imagined ideal of being and *becoming* American which, in its contemporary form, requires proper familial affiliations and becoming the global-
American. As a figure embedded in and who renders multiple national
narratives comprehensible, it is no wonder Woods appears to be a "universally celebrated" example of "America's son."[19]

While Woods was the most extreme manifestation of this process,
sports in general builds upon the appeal of "late modern America's narrative of itself as a post-historical nation of immigrants" and the corre-
sponding place of race.

Given the racial demographics of the league and the racial signifiers associated with basketball,[20] "NBA player" often functions as a code or stand-in for blackness within the dominant imagination. In other words, blackness and basketball become inextricably connected within the dominant imagination, akin to Kathryn Russell's idea of the "criminalblackman."[21] Just as the "criminalblackman" exists as a contained identity within the dominant white imagination, the black baller functions in similar ways. For example, while the NBA dress code did not specifically target clothing worn by African American players, its emphasis on clothing assumed to be worn by young black players—that associated with hip-hop—reflects the ways in which the words "blackness" and "basketball player" are interchangeable. This association and the negative associations are part of the NBA's larger history. When David Stern took over as commissioner in 1984, the league suffered because of its perceived blackness. According to Stern, "Sponsors were flocking out of the NBA because it was perceived as a bunch of high-salaried, drug-sniffing black guys" in Hughes 164). A *Boston Globe* reporter told Stern, "Nobody wants to watch ten black guys in short pants running up and down the court."[22] Little changed in the ensuing twenty years. In the aftermath of the Palace Brawl, media commentators lamented the blackness of the league. In their minds, fans identified the NBA as "too Black":[23] it was "too black, too angry, too paid, too unapologetic."[24] Indeed, the league had become "too edgy, too young and culturally black";[25] it was too "tattooed and bejeweled in the minds of many fans."[26]

The process of both essentializing and bifurcating the black baller is evident in the very distinct ways that the white racial frame conceives of both white and black players, which plays upon ideas of intelligence and athleticism. Whereas the black baller is imagined as athletic, naturally gifted, and physically superior, white basketball players are celebrated for their intelligence, work ethic, and team orientation. In *Am I Black Enough for You?*, Todd Boyd identifies a dialectical relationship between racialization and styles of play where whiteness represents a "textbook or formal" style of basketball, which operates in opposition to "street or vernacular" styles of hooping that are connected to blackness within the collective consciousness. As such, he describes a hegemonic narrative where "white basketball" players describe individuals for whom "adherence to a specific set of rules determines one's ability to play successfully and 'correctly.'"[27]

White players are seen as associated with intelligence, mental toughness, and mental agility, whereas the black baller is imagined through physical attributes—strength, toughness—and aggressiveness. Intelligence, orientation toward team play, and stick-to-itiveness preclude blackness.

A second and widely circulated denunciation against inserting or introducing race into discussions of sport centers on the idea of fairness or the double standard. Whereas critics denounced Simmons for his comments, little has been made about those of Jason Whitlock, a black commentator who similarly invoked rhetoric, language, and racial narratives in explaining the NBA lockout. Looking at his comments alongside those of Simmons further illustrates the ways in which ideologies are circulated, and how commentaries such of these cannot be understood outside of these larger contexts.

A belief in the superiority of white intelligence has been commonplace within American history. This remains the case today. In one study from the 1990s about the persistence of racial stereotypes, the author found the following:

> More than half the survey respondents rated African Americans as less intelligent than whites. Fifty-seven percent of non–African Americans rated African Americans as less intelligent than whites and thirty percent of African Americans themselves rated African Americans as less intelligent than whites. Sixty-two percent of the entire sample rated African Americans as lazier than whites and more than three out of four survey respondents said that African Americans are more inclined than whites to prefer welfare over work.[28]

In a 2010 study about race and politics, researchers at the University of Washington found that stereotypes about blacks as they relate to intelligence, work ethic, and trustworthiness remain prominent. Another recent study about race, politics, and stereotypes found that while there has been slight progress in terms of the rejection of long-standing prejudices, they remain constant within the national discourse.

These studies point to the power of the white racial frame and the persistence of racial realist arguments. At the foundation of racial realists is the idea that race is a biological category that is both meaningful and determinant, especially as it relates to temperament and intelligence.

Tim Wise describes "the primary arguments made by the so-called racial realist" as follows:

Racial "realists" argue that social policy should take these "truths" into account. This means that we should cease all efforts to create greater social or economic equity between the races, since they are inherently unequal in their abilities. It also means that personal biases on the basis of these truths—even those that perpetuate deep racial inequities in the society—are not unfair or unjust but rational. It is rational, for instance, for employers to favor white job applicants for high-level jobs, since they are more likely to possess the talents necessary to do those jobs well. So, in this sense, discrimination should not be prohibited. It should be toler-ated, and seen as a logical choice given the science of racial difference. And certainly we should not take racial disparities in income, wealth, occupational status, or educational outcomes to suggest the presence of racism; rather, these gaps merely reflect the persistent human inequali-ties that cluster along racial lines.[29]

The comments of Simmons, Whitlock, and countless others illustrate the powerful ways that colorblind racism operates within the sports world. The larger discourse exists inside the words, in the interpretations, the meaning, the reception, and the larger ramifications. Jason Whitlock, a nationally known sports columnist, highlights the ways in which racial talk, rhetoric, and narratives dominate the sporting landscape.

Referring to the "foolishness of basketball players" and players as "a group of spoiled, entitled, delusional kids who learned boardroom man-ners from watching episodes of *The Apprentice*," Whitlock concludes that the players are out of their league. Arguing that they are not victims of racism or of David Stern's "plantation mentality" (a reference to Bry-ant Gumbel's recent comments, discussed later), he offers the following:[30]

But these NBA players are not victims during this lockout. Not of David Stern.

They're victims of their own immaturity, stupidity and delusion. They have the wherewithal and resources to stand toe to toe with commis-sioner Stern, but they are improperly using and undermining their power. Gumbel's commentary on HBO's "Real Sports" won't help them realize and effectively utilize their power. It will assist the players in curling up in a fetal position and playing the victim.

That's what we, African-Americans, do all too often in the aftermath of the civil-rights movement. We have no real understanding of the effort, courage and disciplined strategy Martin Luther King Jr., Rosa Parks and their supporters used to win the freedoms we now take for granted.

Here we see that Whitlock's criticism of these "silly players," "a bunch of kids with sycophant publicists and groupies," who are acting "stupid," is rooted in criticism of African American youths. By contextualizing the NBA lockout within a larger discourse of the hip-hop generation, Whitlock links it to a wider discussion. Playing upon hegemonic ideas regarding the American Dream, hard work, and disciplinarity, Whitlock's comments also resonate with larger narratives about meritocracy and bootstraps ideology. Writing about sports as a powerful institution for mythmaking about the American Dream, C. Richard King and Charles Springwood argue:

> The commonsense notions of the self-made man and the American Dream work against personal and collective engagement with the materiality of racial difference. Individuals, effort, and ability to obscure the conditions and effects of racial hierarchy. . . . These life histories map out opposite itineraries, success, superstardom, and the American Dream juxtaposed with failure, obscurity, and a societal nightmare. The individual, they assert, makes his or her fortune based on his or her effort and ability. The system is open, fostering upward mobility for individuals with talent, character, and *discipline*. (my emphasis)[31]

In other words, the riches, the fame, and "the game" itself of the NBA are available to the players, even during this lockout. What precludes the fulfillment of the American Dream is the "character" and lack of "discipline" of the players during the labor negotiations. Whitlock, unlike many media pundits, offers a level of honestly here, making clear that public discussion of NBA players or the NBA is indeed a public debate about blackness.

Another striking aspect of Whitlock's column rests with his effort to invoke the metaphor of the "animal kingdom," describing the NBA lockout as a battle between two distinct species. He writes:

We ignore the laws of the jungle that we live in. Racism, classism, sexism, power imbalances, etc. aren't going away. They've been here since the beginning of time. They're part of our flawed nature. No different from a lion's nature to prey upon zebras, buffalos and wildebeest.

Have you ever seen zebras hold a news conference on "Animal Kingdom" demanding that lions quit attacking zebras? No. Zebras train their young in ways to avoid lions and other predators.

According to Whitlock, NBA players are conceived as zebras governed by rules of nature. As the lion, David Stern will be the aggressor with the players. Rather than "complain" and try to battle the lion (Stern), the zebras (the players) need to realize that they are incapable of defeating the more powerful, fierce, and fit king of the NBA jungle.

This rhetoric is striking in its imagination of the players and the commissioner as two distinct species with predetermined qualities, characteristics, and skills. Zebras and lions do not acquire their skills and place in the jungle hierarchy because of their own actions or training but because of nature. It is difficult to ignore the large racial implications of Whitlock's discussion of the "animal kingdom" given the ways in which biology and differences-grounded-in-nature have been central to racial discourse through American racial history.

The lockout illustrates the powerful ways that the black NBA player is conceptualized, imagined, and represented as a "bad boy Black athlete,"[32] defined by being "overly physical, out of control, prone to violence, driven by instinct, and hypersexual." The white racial frame ubiquitously imagines NBA black ballers as "unruly and disrespectful," "inherently dangerous," and "in need of civilizing."[33] Whether focusing on "intelligence," "levels of education," "maturity," or "disciplinarity," the NBA lockout discourse is a reminder of the powerful ways that the white "gaze" subjects blackness to "the prison of prior expectation."[34] Whitlock's blackness does not preclude his dissemination of a white racial gaze grounded by racial realist arguments and the white racial frame.

What's in a Name? The "Plantation" Metaphor and the NBA

In October 2011, at the conclusion of an episode of HBO's *Real Sports,* Bryant Gumbel took David Stern, the commissioner of the NBA, to task for his arrogance, "ego-centric approach," and eagerness "to be viewed as some kind of modern plantation overseer, treating NBA men, as if they were his boys." Highlighting the power imbalances and the systematic effort to treat the greatest basketball players on earth as little more than "the help,"[35] Gumbel invoked a historic frame to illustrate his argument:

> If the NBA lockout is going to be resolved anytime soon, it seems likely to be done in spite of David Stern, not because of him. I say that because the NBA's infamously ego-centric commissioner seems more hell-bent lately on demeaning the players than resolving his league's labor impasse. How else to explain Stern's rants in recent days? To any and everyone who would listen, he has alternately knocked union leader Billy Hunter, said the players were getting inaccurate information, and started sounding Chicken Little claims about what games might be lost, if players didn't soon see things his way. Stern's version of what's been going on behind closed doors has of course been disputed. But his efforts were typical of a commissioner that has always seemed eager to be viewed as some kind of modern plantation overseer, treating NBA men, as if they were his boys.
>
> It's part of Stern's M.O. Like his past self-serving edicts on dress code or the questioning of officials, his moves were intended to do little more than show how he's the one keeping the hired hands in place. Some will of course cringe at that characterization, but Stern's disdain for the players is as palpable and pathetic as his motives are transparent. Yes the NBA's business model is broken. But to fix it, maybe the league's commissioner should concern himself most with a solution, and stop being part of the problem.[36]

Not surprisingly, these comments have evoked widespread criticism and scorn that emphasized the unnecessary introduction of race into the NBA lockout. In his AOL-Fanhouse column, David Whitley denounced Gumbel for his "80-second rant against David Stern, 'the NBA's famously egocentric commissioner.'"[37] Worse yet, "he played the old 'Plantation Overseer' card, invoking the usual slavery images. . . . Gumbel's race baiting hurt the group he was trying to help."

Likewise, Bob Raissman, a sports columnist for the *New York Daily News,* deploys similar rhetoric:

> The underground nature of the NBA story changed Tuesday night when Bryant Gumbel injected race into the equation. He called David Stern a "modern plantation overseer" who treats "NBA men as if they were his boys." Gumbel voiced his opinion during his closing commentary on HBO's "Real Sports with Bryant Gumbel," where he has total editorial control of his commentaries. No one at HBO Sports can veto his scripts. . . . Yet when Gumbel, a well-known black commentator, calls Stern, the white commissioner of a league with predominantly black players, a racist, everyone suddenly has a perverse reason—the wrong reason—to become interested in the NBA story. The case Gumbel tried to make against Stern was beyond weak. The only legs he had to stand on were his own perceptions. Our perception is this: Gumbel's central mission here was to highlight Stern's patronizing, condescending style over the course of these negotiations. Among other things, Gumbel was offended by Stern saying union boss Billy Hunter was providing players with "inaccurate information." . . .
>
> Since Gumbel has no problems making grand leaps, we'll make one, too. During his contract negotiations it's not a reach to suggest he instructed his agent to be as tough as possible. And if that meant lying or being belligerent, or even condescending, so be it. That didn't make Gumbel a bad guy. Or a racist.[38]

Charles Barkley, a former NBA player turned TNT basketball analyst, agreed, referring to Gumbel's comments as "stupid" and "disrespectful to black people who went through slavery. When (you're talking about) guys who make $5 million a year."[39] Likewise, Scott Reid, a columnist at the blog Thyblackman.com, questioned the use of such an analogy given history: "The point is that too many people inappropriately use slavery and enslaved people to make points about things that are nowhere close to comparison. All of these casual slavery analogies do nothing but diminish one of the worst crimes against humanity in human history. Comparing enslaved Africans, or anyone else for that matter since slavery still exists for many enslaved people, is not only absurd, it is just plain disrespectful to the memory of the millions who perished under the worst kind of injustice."[40]

While seemingly representing a different set of politics, blogger David Friedman also noted the historic disrespect in Gumbel's comments:

> Bryant Gumbel's ludicrous, poorly thought-out (and anti-Semitic) rant against Stern: comparing Stern to a "plantation overseer" is offensive, a falsehood that simultaneously diminishes the true suffering of Black slaves in the American South while also slurring a Commissioner whose league has consistently been at the forefront in terms of hiring Black executives and coaches. Gumbel's attack against Stern comes straight out of the Louis Farrakhan playbook—portraying Jews as exploiters of Blacks—and Gumbel's consistent track record of expressing such bigoted attitudes would have terminated his career a long time ago if his chosen target were any group other than Jews (just imagine a White commentator speaking similarly about a Black person or anyone saying anything remotely derogatory regarding homosexuals).[41]

Sports commentators online and on television chastised Gumbel for inserting race into the discussions. As evidence, the response to Gumbel and the ubiquitous efforts to blame the lockout and the labor situation on the players through racialized language, illustrate the ways in which race and hegemonic ideas of blackness operate in this context.

Also revealing has been the response to Jeffrey Kessler, a lawyer for the National Basketball Players Association, who similarly described David Stern's treatment of the players. He told the *Washington Post:* "To present that in the context of 'take it or leave it,' in our view, that is not good faith. Instead of treating the players like partners, they're treating them like plantation workers."[42] While his comment elicited some backlash along with an apology, the vitriol and the level of indignation did not match the reaction to Gumbel. While reflecting their very different positions—sports commentator versus lawyer—and their very different public histories, the backlash directed at Gumbel reflects the commonplace backlash against people of color for "playing the race card."

Yet, his comments elicited some ire from NBA pundits and online commentators, who used them to lament yet another racial intrusion. Ray McNulty, a national sports columnist, utilized Eduardo

Bonilla-Silva's racial frame minimization amid denial and accusations regarding the race card:

> I'm especially done with the NBA players, who, despite receiving average annual salaries in excess of $5 million, continue to whine publicly about not being offered a fair deal. Truth is, the players lost me last week, when their union lawyer tried to play the race card. "Instead of treating the players like partners," Jeffrey Kessler said after the owners presented one final, take-it-or-leave-it offer, "they're treating them like plantation workers." You know, like slaves. In the Old South. Presumably, before they unionized. I'm not sure, exactly, how many of those Old South slaves were paid millions of dollars for their work. Or how their pain and suffering compared to the grueling, day-to-day hardships endured by today's overburdened and under-compensated NBA players. Frankly, I wanted to hear Kessler's history lesson. But before he could explain his inflammatory comparison, he apologized and said the words he chose were "inappropriate."
>
> Yes, they were. They were as insanely inappropriate as Bryant Gumbel's similarly ridiculous remarks on his HBO show a couple of weeks back. But, hey, the overwhelming majority of NBA owners are white. The overwhelming majority of NBA players are black. So, obviously, the owners' refusal to continue to give the players a majority of the profits must be rooted in racism, right? I'm sick of it. All of it.[43]

The power of the race denial card is in full effect here, reflective of a belief that diversity equals colorblindness and that racism comes from the constant playing of the race card rather than institutional organization or ideological configuration.

Similarly, Magic Johnson denied the racial issues here, citing Stern's history of racial benevolence as evidence of the insignificance of race: "This league is more diverse than any other league and has more minorities in powerful positions than any other league. That's all about David Stern and his vision and what he wanted to do. He made sure minorities had high-ranking positions from the league office all the way down to coaches and front office people."[44] Focusing on diversity and inclusion over justice, Johnson's comments are emblematic of the neoliberalist logic of new racism that measures race by examining the demographics of particular institutions. Failing to reflect on ideologies and other forms of demonization, Johnson's argument reflects the ideology of colorblind racism that if you see diversity, you cannot see racism.

LeBron James: Bad Decisions, Not Racial Implications

In what was probably the most talked about sports moment of 2010, LeBron James announced his intention to leave the Cleveland Cavaliers and sign with the Miami Heat. Broadcast live on ESPN, "The Decision" prompted anger and outrage, including fans taking to the streets to burn his jersey in effigy, widespread commentary, and a level of demonization unseen within the sports world. Leading the charge was Cavs owner, Dan Gilbert, who penned a diatribe against James in the wake of his announcement. Addressing the fans, he wrote:

> You simply don't deserve this kind of cowardly betrayal. You have given so much and deserve so much more. . . . If you thought we were motivated before tonight to bring the hardware to Cleveland, I can tell you that this shameful display of selfishness and betrayal by one of our very own has shifted our "motivation" to previously unknown and previously never experienced levels.
>
> Some people think they should go to heaven but NOT have to die to get there. Sorry, but that's simply not how it works. This shocking act of disloyalty from our home grown "chosen one" sends the exact opposite lesson of what we would want our children to learn. And "who" we would want them to grow-up to become.[45]

His comments, and the overall reaction from fans and media alike, prompted questions, accusations, and overall debate about the ways in which race colored the larger discourse. It led to debates and discussions about race not only between sports pundits but also among activists, nonsports pundits, and political figures.

In response, Jesse Jackson questioned Gilbert's motives, elucidating the racial overtones in his comments. Referring to the comments as "mean, arrogant and presumptuous," Jackson argued: "He speaks as an owner of LeBron and not the owner of the Cleveland Cavaliers. His feelings of betrayal personify a slave master mentality. He sees LeBron as a runaway slave. This is an owner employee relationship—between business partners—and LeBron honored his contract."[46] The slavery metaphor is certainly not new, having been used by Curt Flood,[47] Larry Johnson,[48] Rasheed Wallace,[49] and countless other black athletes. Philip Lamar Cunningham identifies the complexity of this metaphor: "That said, today's NBA player's situation is not wholly unlike that of the post–Civil War freedman. Free of literal shackles, the former slave is free to fend for himself now that he is no longer bound to the plantation. While he was free to go anywhere he chose, he faced the choice of living in a volatile South or a disdainful North that merited him no semblance of equality. Some fled North and carved something out of nothing; many stayed behind as sharecroppers."[50] Whether a player is seen as a "slave," a "plantation" worker, or a freedman, these analogies seek to emphasize not only the power differentials and the issues of labor but also the ways in which black bodies are controlled and put on display within professional sports.

Arguing that Gilbert's comments did not pass the "racism smell test," Michael Wilson offered a similar assessment, wondering if "one of [Gilbert's] cotton-pickers" got "away?"[51] Not surprisingly, these comments elicited widespread reactions, with the proverbial denials, accusations of playing the race card, and an overall focus on the intent and meaning rather than the broader significance of race.

Noting that Jesse Jackson was "saying something important about the paternalism that is the owner-player relationship in sports (could we finally desist with calling every owner "mister"?) and the childish nature in which Dan Gilbert reacted to a business deal that didn't go his way," Howard Bryant highlighted how "The Decision" and its aftermath reeked of racial meaning:

> Race is the third rail of America, class the light-socket you should not touch with wet hands. Jackson rightfully saw both in Gilbert's tone, racially insensitive in its insinuation that he "owned" James, class-ignorant in his confidence that his position of being "Mister Gilbert" allowed him to move both his—and LeBron James'—chess pieces when the time came. Marvin Miller should be smiling the biggest smile these days, Curt Flood a posthumous second, because in flustering the pompous ruling class enough that one would make such an ass of himself, the player, at

long last, after decades of being released, traded, demoted to the minors without recourse, finally got to say "checkmate."[52]

Similarly, Bomani Jones, a national sports commentator who frequently appears on ESPN, highlighted the significant ways that race operated through "The Decision" and its aftermath, moving the discussion beyond intent, beyond "is this racist or not," and beyond the hegemonic binaries associated with racial discourse, to reflect on the how race impacted the overall reaction:

> Was anything more predictably explosive than the combination of Jesse Jackson and slavery? Jesse's been talking for a living too long to not know what the response would be. But even if Jackson aimed to shock—and if so, he was clearly effective—his underlying point was correct, even if semantically clumsy.
>
> Bottom line: LeBron James took control of his financial existence in a way no athlete has before, with his friends in charge, treating the powers that be like powers that were. To discount the role that played in the tone and text of Dan Gilbert's foolishly ironic manifesto, which accused an independent contractor of betrayal, is naive. And while Jesse's credibility is shaky, his point is solid.[53]

The reaction to LeBron's decision to leave the Cavs, the ensuing debate about the significance or insignificance of race, LeBron's efforts to point to the racial subtext, and the overall contempt that resulted from his free agency have overdetermined his meaning since then. Like his blackness, his purported betrayal overdetermines his place within the sporting and cultural landscapes.

For example, as game 4 of the 2011 NBA Finals came to a close on another last-second shot, Dwyane Wade, of the Miami Heat, and Dirk Nowitzki, from the Dallas Mavericks, were praised for carrying their respective teams. The celebration of Nowitzki has been especially robust given his reported illness, a fact that has been used to celebrate his performance as heroic, as a sign of his toughness, and as evidence of his talents as a leader. "The truth hurts when it is spelled out in the composite box score of a championship series," wrote Harvey Araton in the *New York Times*. Wade has his ring, but James is exactly where Nowitzki was five years ago, entering midcareer and needing to look hard in the mirror—and less at a sneering news media—to acknowledge his stunning personal shortcomings in the finals."[54]

LeBron James, on the other hand, endured another bout of criticism from fans, media, and players alike. After game 3, in which LeBron had a stat line that included seventeen points, nine assists, and three rebounds, Gregg Doyel asked LeBron about his "shrinking" in the fourth quarter. Notwithstanding LeBron's dismissal of the question, Doyel maintained this line of criticism in his CBS Sports column the following day, writing:

> When someone makes a movie of the fourth quarter, they can cast Rick Moranis as LeBron James and call it Honey, I Shrunk the Superstar. That's what I'll remember about James from Game 3. His shrinkage, and how it continued a series of shrinkages. I asked him about that after Game 3. I asked him, pretty much word-for-word, how come he hasn't been playing like a superstar in the fourth quarter? What's going on with that? James played the defensive-stopper card. That's why he's out there, you know. For his defense. He's not a latter-day Michael Jordan. He's a latter-day Dudley Bradley.[55]

Doyel proceeds to criticize James for "complaining" to referees, whining, and otherwise having a "bitter-beer face" when he doesn't get his way on the court, only to conclude his article by highlighting an instance where James didn't get a foul call not because there was a foul but because he isn't a superstar: "Maybe the officials are onto something. Maybe LeBron James isn't a superstar. If the 2011 NBA Finals were the only games I had seen him play, that would be my conclusion." Doyel, especially after Game 4, is not alone in his criticism. Jordan Schultz identifies James's game 4 struggles not as an aberration but as evidence of his ineptitude and shortcomings as a player: "Wade is in essence, everything James is not. He has the will, the fire and the assassin's nature that LeBron lacks."[56]

Since joining the Heat, James has faced criticism at both ends of the spectrum: go for 35-12-10 and he's hogging the ball, but go 15-9-8 and he isn't doing enough. With Wade and Chris Bosh on the team, he either doesn't involve the other two superstars enough or defers to them too much. He is the walking embodiment of the long-standing criticism that has always plagued black athletes living amid American racism: too selfish and unable to be a leader. This highlights the power of the white racial frame, one that renders black bodies as undesirable and suspect, with the impossibility of redemption. In that James will face criticism irrespective of his on-the-court performance—if he shoots the last shot and misses, he lacks the "killer instinct"/he is selfish and should have passed the ball to Wade (this was a criticism after game 2, where James was questioned for not deferring to Wade, who had it going); if he passes the ball, he is depicted as mentally weak, scared, and otherwise unable to lead.

What is underlying much of this criticism is a false comparison to a reimagined Jordan. The nostalgia for Jordan as post-racial, as team player, as unselfish, and as godlike illustrates the impossibility of James meeting these expectations. While the nostalgia for Jordan emanates from his greatness on the floor, it is more reflective of the power of Jordan as a signifier of racial transcendence. Whereas Jordan in retirement has been reconstituted as a leader, as a fundamentally perfect player who was driven by team success and not individual accomplishment, James, as an embodiment of Thabiti Lewis's "baller of new school,"[57] has no possibility of becoming the next Michael Jordan. Given the ways in which black players are scolded and demonized for ego, James, despite his unselfishness, despite his willingness to defer to Wade, pass to Chris Bosh, and set up Mario Chalmers, is confined by the stains of blackness. His tattoos, his style, his swagger, his blackness, and his decision to control his own "brand" and "take his talents to Miami" made it impossible for him to become the next Michael Jordan.[58]

Conclusion

Evident in the demonization of LeBron James since "The Decision" and the denunciation of the players during the lockout, it is clear they cannot win because they are not Michael Jordan—they are unable to fulfill the post-racial fantasies provided by Jordan. LeBron, Kobe Bryant, and the other ballers of the new school do not embody what David Falk celebrated in Michael Jordan:

> When players of color become stars they are no longer perceived as being of color. The color sort of vanishes. I don't think people look at

Michael Jordan anymore and say he's a black superstar. They say he's a superstar. They totally accepted him into the mainstream. Before he got there he might have been African American, but once he arrived, he had such a high level of acceptance that I think that description goes away.[59]

The tattoos, the connection to hip-hop, the willingness to talk about race, to invoke the "plantation metaphor," to refuse to play racially constructed roles, James's decision to hire his long-standing friends to guide his career, "The Decision"—all contribute to a path not paved by Jordan toward racial redemption but one more traveled by many black athletes: one of derision, contempt, criticism, and scrutiny. "The irony of the connection between Willie Horton, O. J. Simpson, and Tookie Williams, and Michael Jordan, LeBron James, Allen Iverson, and Latrell Sprewell, along with most of the black NBA superstars of today is that, as easily as the first three, like so many countless criminalized black male bodies in the United States are denied social and moral redemption because of their race, their presumed inherent transgression, and the need of the American public to reify much of its racist (il)logic," writes Lisa Guerrero. While LeBron as a member of the Cavs, as a potential savior (of the NBA; of the Jordan legacy; of Cleveland) had the potential to "redeem *us,* to maintain our sense of ourselves as a nation that is righteous, equal, and free, and to allow us to continue dreaming the American Dream," that potential is gone.[60] The narrative of LeBron and other black players' "failure" redeems us; the hegemonic claims about the righteousness of others and the steps today's NBA player must take to be saved is a celebration of the system, not its black players. The post-racial fantasy remains intact, even amid denials of race, as the black baller's failure to become the next Jordan (a black basketball player loved by white America) is the result of his shortcomings, leaving intact the possibility of the post-racial imaginary.

Notes

This chapter constitutes an expansion of three articles that appeared at http://newblackman.blogspot.com. Thanks to Mark Anthony Neal. David J. Leonard and Bruce Lee Hazelwood, "LeBron James and the Redemptive Path to Nowhere," June 10, 2011 <http://newblackman.blogspot.com/2011/06/lebron-james-and-redemptive-path-to.html>; David J. Leonard, "Bill Simmons and the

Bell Curve: The 'Limited Intellectual Capital' of the NBA's Players," October 20, 2011 <http://newblackman.blogspot.com/2011/10/bill-simmons-and-bell-curve-limited.html>; David J. Leonard, "What's in a Name? The 'Plantation' Metaphor and the NBA," December 25, 2011 <http://newblackman.blogspot.com/2011/12/whats-in-name-plantation-metaphor-and.html>.

1. Bill Maher, "In Modern Republican Party 'Denying Racism Is the New Racism,'" October 7, 2011 <http://www.mediaite.com/tv/bill-maher-in-modern-republican-party-denying-racism-is-the-new-racism/>.

2. Eduardo Bonilla-Silva, *Racism without Racists: Color-Blind Racism and the Persistence of Racial Inequality in the United States* (New York: Rowman and Littlefield, 2003), 57.

3. Allen Johnson, *Privilege, Power, and Difference* (New York: McGraw-Hill, 2006), 108–9.

4. Ibid., 109.

5. Eduardo Bonilla-Silva and Tyrone Foreman, "'I Am Not a Racist But . . . ': Mapping White College Students' Racial Ideology in the USA," *Discourse and Society* 1.1 (2000): 50–85.

6. Bonilla-Silva, *Racism without Racists*, 28.

7. Ben Carrington and Mary McDonald, *"Race," Sport and British Society* (London: Routledge, 2001), 1.

8. William C. Rhoden, "Addressing Racism's Constant Hum in U.S. Sports," May 25, 2008 <http://www.nytimes.com/2008/05/25/sports/25iht-VANTAGE.1.13188102.html>.

9. According to Joe Feagin, "The socially inherited racial frame is a comprehensive orienting structure, a 'tool kit' that whites and others have long used to understand, interpret, and act in social settings" (*The White Racial Frame: Centuries of Racial Framing and Counter-framing* [New York: Routledge, 2010], 13).

10. See here for evidence of this phenomenon: Ryan O'Hanlon, "Breaking Down ESPN's Race and Sports Survey," January 12, 2011 <http://goodmenproject.com/newsroom/breaking-down-espns-race-and-sports-survey/>.

11. Todd Boyd, "Mo' Money, Mo' Problems: Keepin It Real in the Post Jordan Era," *Basketball Jones: America above the Rim,* ed. Todd Boyd and Kenneth L. Shropshire (New York: NYU Press, 2000), 60.

12. On November 19, 2004, a fight between members of the Indiana Pacers and the Detroit Pistons spilled over into the crowd, resulting in a brawl between various members of the Pacers and fans. The event led to suspensions and ample commentary about the state of the game. For a lengthy discussion, see David Leonard, *After Artest: The NBA and the Assault on Blackness* (Albany: SUNY Press, 2012).

13. Bill Simmons, "Avoiding the Lockout and the Red Sox," October 14, 2011 <http://www.grantland.com/story/_/id/7100999/avoiding-lockout-red-sox>.

14. Bill Simmons, "Behind the Pipes: Into the arms of the NHL," October 19, 2011 <http://www.grantland.com/story/_/id/7123705/arms-nhl>.

15. Qtd. in Kim Hutcherson, "Donald Trump Rejects Allegations of Racism," May 1, 2011 <http://articles.cnn.com/2011-05-01/politics/trump.racism. allegations_1_donald-trump-racism-comments?_s=PM:POLITICS>.

16. See Leonard, *After Artest*.

17. http://forums.celticsblog.com/index.php?topic=50116.0.

18. http://newblackman.blogspot.com/2011/10/bill-simmons-and-bell-curve-limited.html.

19. C. L. Cole and David L. Andrews, "America's New Son: Tiger Woods and America's Multiculturalism," *Commodified and Criminalized: New Racism and African Americans in Contemporary Sports*, ed. David J. Leonard and C. Richard King (Lanham, MD: Rowman and Littlefield, 2011), 26.

20. Leonard, *After Artest*; Todd Boyd, *Young, Black, Rich, and Famous: The Rise of the NBA, the Hip Hop Invasion and the Transformation of American Culture* (New York: Doubleday, 2003).

21. Kathryn K. Russell, *The Color of Crime: Racial Hoaxes, White Fear, Black Protectionism, Police Harassment, and Other Macroaggressions* (New York: NYU Press, 1998).

22. Qtd. in Leonard Wynter, *American Skin: Popular Culture, Big Business and the End of White America* (New York: Random House, 2002), 99.

23. Tim Hammer, "Interview: Bill Simmons, ESPN's 'The Sports Guy'/Author of The Book of Basketball," October 30, 2009 <http://bostonist.com/2009/10/30/ interview_bill_simmons_espns_the_sp.php>.

24. Scoop Jackson, "The Gilbert Arenas Comeback Template," January 29, 2010 <http://sports.espn.go.com/espn/commentary/news/ story?page=jackson/100129>.

25. Harvey Araton, "Brawl Evokes Real Story of N.B.A. and Its Fans," *New York Times*, November 23, 2004, D1.

26. Steve Wilstein, "Growing Disconnect between Fans, Players," November 23, 2004 <http://nbcsports.msnbc.com/id/6561841-nba/>.

27. Todd Boyd, *Am I Black Enough for You? Popular Culture from the 'Hood and Beyond* (Bloomington: University of Indiana Press, 1997), 115.

28. "How Do Americans View One Another? The Persistence of Racial/Ethnic Stereotypes," *DiversityWeb—A Resource Hub for Higher Education* <www.diversityweb.org/digest/w98/research2.html>.

29. Tim Wise, "Race, Intelligence and the Limits of Science: Reflections on the Moral Absurdity of 'Racial Realism,'" August 27, 2011 <http://www.timwise.org/2011/08/race-intelligence-and-the-limits-of-science-reflections-on-the-moral-absurdity-of-racial-realism/>.

30. Jason Whitlock, "Players Need to Stick to Their Day Jobs," October 20, 2011 <http://msn.foxsports.com/nba/story/NBA-David-Stern-Bryant-Gumbel-players-derek-fisher-dwyane-wade-kevin-garnett-can%2527t-hang-with-commissioner-in-boardroom-101811>.

31. C. Richard King and Charles F. Springwood, *Beyond the Cheers: Race as Spectacle in College Sport* (Albany: SUNY Press, 2001), 31–32, 34.

32. Patricia Hill Collins, *Black Sexual Politics* (London: Routledge, 2005), 153.

33. Abby Ferber, "The Construction of Black Masculinity: White Supremacy Now and Then," *Journal of Sport and Social Issues* 31.1 (2007): 20.

34. Patricia J. Williams, *Seeing a Color-Blind Future: The Paradox of Race* (New York: Farrar, Straus and Giroux, 1998), 74.

35. Marc Lamont Hill, "NBA Impasse: Owners and the 'Help,'" November 16, 2011 <http://articles.philly.com/2011-11-16/news/30406106_1_nba-owners-lockout-nba -impasse>.

36. "Bryant Gumbel Invokes Slavery in Editorial on NBA Commissioner David Stern," October 18, 2011 <http://www.youtube.com/watch?v=lTXI-ivWEdo>.

37. David Whitley, "Gumbel's Race-Baiting Comments about Stern Won't Help Players' Cause," October 19, 2011 <http://aol.sportingnews.com/nba/story/2011-10-19/ gumbels-race-baiting-comments-about-stern-wont-help-players-cause>.

38. Bob Raissman, "HBO's Bryant Gumbel Drops Bomb, Race Card in Calculated Move to Turn Heads during Stale NBA Lock-out," October 20, 2011 <articles.nydailynews.com/2011-10-20/ sports/30318137_1_billy-hunter-lockout-nba-story>.

39. Reid Cherner, "Barkley Calls Gumbel's Comments 'Stupid,'" October 20, 2001 <http://content.usatoday.com/communities/gameon/post/2011/10/ barkley-calls-gumbels-comments-stupid/1>.

40. Scott Reid, "Bryant Gumbel, Alan West, and Others, Please Stop with the Slavery Analogies," October 20, 2011 <http://thyblackman.com/2011/10/20/ bryant-gumbel-alan-west-and-others-please-stop-with-the-slavery-analogies/>.

41. David Friedman, "NBA Lockout: Three D's," October 29, 2011 <20secondtime-out.blogspot.com/2011/10/nba-lockout-three-ds.html>.

42. ESPN.com News Services, "Jeffrey Kessler Apologizes for Remarks," November 9, 2011 <http://espn.go.com/nba/story/_/id/7211447/ nba-lockout-jeffrey-kessler-apologizes-plantation-workers-comment>.

43. Ray McNulty, "No NBA, No Season, No Problem," November 16, 2011, <http:// www.tcpalm.com/news/2011/nov/16/no-nba-no-season-no-problem/>. Eduardo Bonilla-Silva's minimization frame suggests that discrimination is no longer a central factor affecting minorities' life choices. *Racism without Racists: Color-Blind Racism and the Persistence of Racial Inequality in the United States,* 3rd ed. (Lanham, MD: Rowman and Littlefield, 2010), 29.

44. Brian Mahoney, "Magic Johnson Backs Stern after Racial Suggestion," November 9, 2011 <http://www.huffingtonpost.com/2011/11/09/magic-johnson-david-stern-racial-suggestion_n_1083712.html>.

45. "Dan Gilbert's Open Letter," December 13, 2010 <http://sports.espn.go.com/ nba/news/story?id=5365704>.

46. "Jackson Rips Gilbert's LeBron Comments," July 20, 2011 <http://sports.espn. go.com/nba/news/story?id=5372266>.

47. Flood, a baseball player, once said that a "a well-paid slave is nonetheless a slave."

48. While a member of the New York Knicks, Johnson described his teammates as a group of "rebellious slaves."

49. Wallace, a former NBA player, described the league's draconian discipline policy as follows: "I know they're going to have to do something about this crazy zero tolerance law. That's retarded. In my mind, it's kind of like a slave and master or father and son. You've got your little son and (you say) don't say nothing back to me—and to me, that's totally wrong. It ain't like that in any other sport."

50. Philip Lamar Cunningham, "Toward an Appropriate Analogy," November 5, 2011 <http://resistingspectator.wordpress.com/2011/11/05/toward-an-appropriate-analogy/>.

51. Qtd. in Bill Simmons, "Business vs. Personal," November 18, 2011 <http://www.grantland.com/story/_/id/7250994/business-vs-personal>.

52. Qtd. in Joan Walsh, "Is LeBron James a 'Runaway Slave'?" July 12, 2010, <http://www.salon.com/2010/07/12/jesse_jackson_v_dan_gilbert/>.

53. Ibid.

54. Qtd. in Harvey Araton, "James Can Learn from Nowitzki," June 13, 2011 <http://www.nytimes.com/2011/06/14/sports/lebron-james-can-learn-from-dirk-nowitzkis-lessons.html>.

55. Gregg Doyel, "LeBron James: Story of an Incredibly Shrinking Superstar," June 6, 2011 <http://www.cbssports.com/nba/story/15202274/lebron-james-story-of-an-incredibly-shrinking-superstar>.

56. Jordan Schultz, "NBA Finals: LeBron James Shows True Colors in Game 4 Disappearance," June 8, 2011 <http://www.huffingtonpost.com/2011/06/08/nba-finals-lebron-james-shows-true-colors-in-game-4-disappearance_n_873255.html>.

57. Thabiti Lewis, *Ballers of the New School: Race and Sports in America* (Chicago: Third World Press, 2010).

58. "LeBron James: Race Played Role in 'Decision' Backlash," September 30, 2010 <http://www.huffingtonpost.com/2010/09/30/lebron-james-race-racism_n_745186.html>.

59. Qtd. in William C. Rhoden, *Forty Million Dollar Slaves: The Rise, Fall, and Redemption of the Black Athlete* (New York: Crown, 2006), 204.

60. Lisa Guerrero, "One Nation under a Hoop: Race, Meritocracy, and Messiahs in the NBA. *Commodified and Criminalized: New Racism and African Americans in Contemporary Sports,* ed. David J. Leonard and C. Richard King (Lanham, MD: Rowman and Littlefield, 2011).

WORKS CITED

Araton, Harvey. "Brawl Evokes Real Story of N.B.A. and Its Fans." *New York Times* 23 Nov. 2004: D1. Print.

———. "James Can Learn from Nowitzki." *Nytimes.com*. 13 June 2011. Web. <http://www.nytimes.com/2011/06/14/sports/lebron-james-can-learn-from-dirk-nowitzkis-lessons.html>.

Bedard, Paul. "Obama Is Changing America's View of Blacks." *Usnews.com*. 28 Mar. 2011. Web. <http://www.usnews.com/news/blogs/washington-whispers/2011/03/28/obama-is-changing-americas-view-of-blacks>.

Bonilla-Silva, Eduardo. *Racism without Racists: Color-Blind Racism and the Persistence of Racial Inequality in the United States*. New York: Rowman and Littlefield, 2003. Print.

———. *Racism without Racists: Color-Blind Racism and the Persistence of Racial Inequality in the United States*. 3rd ed. Lanham, MD: Rowman and Littlefield, 2010. Print.

Bonilla-Silva, Eduardo, and Tyrone Foreman. "'I Am Not a Racist But . . .': Mapping White College Students' Racial Ideology in the USA." *Discourse and Society* 1.1 (1990): 50–85. Print.

Boyd, Todd. *Am I Black Enough for You? Popular Culture from the 'Hood and Beyond*. Bloomington: Indiana University Press, 1997. Print.

———. "Mo' Money, Mo' Problems: Keepin' It Real in the Post Jordan Era." *Basketball Jones: America above the Rim*. Ed. Todd Boyd and Kenneth L. Shropshire. New York: NYU Press, 2000. 59–67. Print.

———. *Young, Black, Rich, and Famous: The Rise of the NBA, the Hip-Hop Invasion and the Transformation of American Culture*. New York: Doubleday, 2003. Print.

"Bryant Gumbel Invokes Slavery in Editorial on NBA Commissioner David Stern." *Youtube.com*. 18 Oct. 2011. Web. <http://www.youtube.com/watch?v=lTXI-ivWEdo>.

Carrington, Ben, and Mary McDonald. *"Race," Sport and British Society*. London: Routledge, 2001. Print.

Cherner, Reid. "Barkley Calls Gumbel's Comments 'Stupid.'" *Usatoday.com*. 20 Oct. 2011. Web. <http://content.usatoday.com/communities/gameon/post/2011/10/barkley-calls-gumbels-comments-stupid/1>.

Cole, C. L., and David L. Andrews. "America's New Son: Tiger Woods and America's Multiculturalism." *Commodified and Criminalized: New Racism and African Americans in Contemporary Sports*. Ed. David J. Leonard and C. Richard King. Lanham, MD: Rowman and Littlefield, 2011. 23–40. Print.

Collins, Patricia Hill. *Black Sexual Politics*. London: Routledge, 2005. Print.

Cunningham, Lamar Philip. "Toward an Appropriate Analogy." *Wordpress.com*. 5 Nov. 2011. Web. <http://resistingspectator.wordpress.com/2011/11/05/toward-an-appropriate-analogy/>.

"Dan Gilbert's Open Letter." *Sports.espn.go.com*. 13 Dec. 2010. Web. <http://sports.espn.go.com/nba/news/story?id=5365704>.

Doyel, Gregg. "LeBron James: Story of an Incredibly Shrinking Superstar." *CBSsports.com*. 6 June 2011. Web. <http://www.cbssports.com/nba/story/15202274/lebron-james-story-of-an-incredibly-shrinking-superstar>.

ESPN.com News Services. "Jeffrey Kessler Apologizes for Remarks." *ESPN.com*. 9 Nov. 2011. Web. <http://espn.go.com/nba/story/_/id/7211447/nba-lockout-jeffrey-kessler-apologizes-plantation-workers-comment>.

Feagin, Joe. *The White Racial Frame: Centuries of Racial Framing and Counter-framing.* New York: Routledge, 2010. Print.

Ferber, Abby. "The Construction of Black Masculinity: White Supremacy Now and Then." *Journal of Sport and Social Issues* 31.1 (2007): 11–24. Print. http://forums.celticsblog.com/index.php?topic=50116.0

Friedman, David. "NBA Lockout: Three D's." *20secondtimeout.com.* 29 Oct. 2011. Web. <20secondtimeout.blogspot.com/2011/10/nba-lockout-three-ds.html>.

Giroux, Henry. "Spectacles of Race and Pedagogies of Denial: Anti-black Racist Pedagogy under the Reign of Neoliberalism." *Communication Education* 52.3–4 (2003): 191–211. Print.

Guerrero, Lisa. "One Nation under a Hoop: Race, Meritocracy, and Messiahs in the NBA." *Commodified and Criminalized: New Racism and African Americans in Contemporary Sports.* Ed. David Leonard and C. Richard King. Lanham, MD: Rowman and Littlefield, 2011. 121–46. Print.

Hammer, Tim. "Interview: Bill Simmons, ESPN's 'The Sports Guy'/Author of *The Book of Basketball.*" *Bostonist.com.* 30 Oct. 2009. Web. <http://bostonist.com/2009/10/30/interview_bill_simmons_espns_the_sp.php>.

Hill, Marc Lamont. "NBA Impasse: Owners and the 'Help.'" *Philly.com.* 16 Nov. 2011. Web. <http://articles.philly.com/2011-11-16/news/30406106_1_nba-owners-lockout-nba-impasse>.

"How Do Americans View One Another? The Persistence of Racial/Ethnic Stereotypes." *DiversityWeb—A Resource Hub for Higher Education.* <www.diversityweb.org/digest/w98/research2.html>.

Hughes, Glyn. "Managing Black Guys: Representation, Corporate Culture, and the NBA." *Sociology of Sport Journal* 21 (2004): 163–84.

Hutcherson, Kim. "Donald Trump Rejects Allegations of Racism." *CNN.com.* 1 May 2011. Web. <http://articles.cnn.com/2011-05-01/politics/trump.racism.allegations_1_donald-trump-racism-comments?_s=PM:POLITICS>.

"Jackson Rips Gilbert's LeBron Comments." *Sports.espn.go.com.* 20 July 2011. Web. <http://sports.espn.go.com/nba/news/story?id=5372266>.

Jackson, Scoop. "The Gilbert Arenas Comeback Template." *Sports.espn.go.com.* 29 Jan. 2010. Web. <http://sports.espn.go.com/espn/commentary/news/story?page=jackson/100129>.

Johnson, Allen. *Privilege, Power, and Difference.* New York: McGraw-Hill, 2006. Print.

King, C. Richard, and Charles F. Springwood. *Beyond the Cheers: Race as Spectacle in College Sport.* Albany: SUNY Press, 2001. Print.

"LeBron James: Race Played Role in 'Decision' Backlash." *Huffingtonpost.com.* 30 Sept. 2010. Web. <http://www.huffingtonpost.com/2010/09/30/lebron-james-race-racism_n_745186.html>.

Leonard, David J. *After Artest: The NBA and the Assault on Blackness.* Albany: SUNY Press, 2012.

———. "Bill Simmons and the Bell Curve: The 'Limited Intellectual Capital' of the NBA's Players." *Newblackman.blogspot.com*. 20 Oct. 2011. Web. <http://newblackman.blogspot.com/2011/10/bill-simmons-and-bell-curve-limited.html>.

Leonard, David J., and Bruce Lee Hazelwood, "LeBron James and the Redemptive Path to Nowhere." June 10, 2011. Web. <http://newblackman.blogspot.com/2011/06/lebron-james-and-redemptive-path-to.html>.

Leonard, David J., and C. Richard King. *Commodified and Criminalized: New Racism and African Americans in Contemporary Sports*. Lanham, MD: Rowman and Littlefield, 2011. Print.

Lewis, Thabiti. *Ballers of the New School: Essays on Race and Sports in America*. Chicago: Third World Press, 2010. Print.

Maher, Bill. "In Modern Republican Party 'Denying Racism Is the New Racism.'" HBO. 7 Oct. 2011. Web. <http://www.mediaite.com/tv/bill-maher-in-modern-republican-party-denying-racism-is-the-new-racism/>.

Mahoney, Brian. "Magic Johnson Backs Stern after Racial Suggestion." *Huffingtonpost.com*. 9 Nov. 2011. Web. <http://www.huffingtonpost.com/2011/11/09/magic-johnson-david-stern-racial-suggestion_n_1083712.html>.

McNulty, Ray. "No NBA, No Season, No Problem." *Tcpalm.com*. 16 Nov. 2011. Web. <http://www.tcpalm.com/news/2011/nov/16/no-nba-no-season-no-problem/>.

"Nike Basketball: LeBron RISE." (2010). *Youtube.com*.

O'Hanlon, Ryan. 'Breaking Down ESPN's Race and Sports Survey." *Good Men Project*. 12 Jan. 2011. Web. <http://goodmenproject.com/newsroom/breaking-down-espns-race-and-sports-survey/>.

Raissman, Bob. "HBO's Bryant Gumbel Drops Bomb, Race Card in Calculated Move to Turn Heads during Stale NBA Lockout." *Nydailynews.com*. 20 Oct. 2011. Web. <articles.nydailynews.com/2011-10-20/sports/30318137_1_billy-hunter-lockout-nba-story>.

Reid, Scott. "Bryant Gumbel, Alan West, and Others, Please Stop with the Slavery Analogies." *Thyblackman.com*. 20 Oct. 2011. Web. <http://thyblackman.com/2011/10/20/bryant-gumbel-alan-west-and-others-please-stop-with-the-slavery-analogies/>.

Rhoden, William C. "Addressing Racism's Constant Hum in U.S. Sports." *New York Times* 25 May 2008. Web. <http://www.nytimes.com/2008/05/25/sports/25iht-VANTAGE.1.13188102.html>.

———. *Forty Million Dollar Slaves: The Rise, Fall, and Redemption of the Black Athlete*. New York: Crown, 2006. Print.

Russell, Kathryn K. *The Color of Crime: Racial Hoaxes, White Fear, Black Protectionism, Police Harassment, and Other Macroaggressions*. New York: NYU Press, 1998. Print.

Schultz, Jordan. "NBA Finals: LeBron James Shows True Colors in Game 4 Disappearance." *Huffingtonpost.com*. 8 June 2011. Web. <http://www.huffingtonpost.com/2011/06/08/nba-finals-lebron-james-shows-true-colors-in-game-4-disappearance_n_873255.html>.

Simmons, Bill. "Avoiding the Lockout and the Red Sox." *Grandland.com.* 14 Oct. 2011. Web. <http://www.grantland.com/story/_/id/7100999/avoiding-lockout-red-sox>.

———. "Behind the Pipes: Into the Arms of the NHL." *Grantland.com.* 19 Oct. 2011. Web. <http://www.grantland.com/story/_/id/7123705/arms-nhl>.

———. "Business vs. Personal." *Grantland.com.* 18 Nov. 2011. Web. <http://www.grantland.com/story/_/id/7250994/business-vs-personal>.

———. "Proactively Mourning the NBA." *Grantland.com.* 21 Oct. 2011. Web. <http://www.grantland.com/story/_/id/7131896/proactively-mourning-nba>.

Spencer, N. 2005 "Sister Act VI: Venus and Serena Williams at Indian Wells: 'Sincere Fictions' and White Racism." *Journal of Sport and Social Issues* 28.2 (2004): 115–35. Print.

Walsh, Joan. "Is LeBron James a 'Runaway Slave'?" *salon.com.* 12 July 2010. Web. <http://www.salon.com/2010/07/12/jesse_jackson_v_dan_gilbert/>.

Whitley, David. "Gumbel's Race-Baiting Comments about Stern Won't Help Players' Cause." *Sportingnews.com.* 19 Oct. 2011. Web. <http://aol.sportingnews.com/nba/story/2011-10-19/gumbels-race-baiting-comments-about-stern-wont-help-players-cause>.

Whitlock, Jason. "Players Need to Stick to Their Day Jobs." *Msn.foxsports.com.* 20 Oct. 2011. Web. <http://msn.foxsports.com/nba/story/NBA-David-Stern-Bryant-Gumbel-players-derek-fisher-dwyane-wade-kevin-garnett-can%2527t-hang-with-commissioner-in-boardroom-101811>.

Williams, Patricia J. *Seeing a Color-Blind Future: The Paradox of Race.* New York: Farrar, Straus and Giroux, 1998. Print.

Wilstein, Steve. "Growing Disconnect between Fans, Players." *Nbcsports.msnbc.com.* 23 Nov. 2004. Web. <http://nbcsports.msnbc.com/id/6561841-nba/>.

Wise, Tim. "Race, Intelligence and the Limits of Science: Reflections on the Moral Absurdity of 'Racial Realism'." *Timwise.org.* 27 Aug. 2011. Web. <http://www.timwise.org/2011/08/race-intelligence-and-the-limits-of-science-reflections-on-the-moral-absurdity-of-racial-realism/>.

Wojnarowski, Adrian. "NBA Winning Public Fight with Players." *Sports.yahoo.com.* 17 Oct. 2011. Web.<http://sports.yahoo.com/nba/news?slug=aw-wojnarowski_nba_labor_stars_union_101711>.

Wynter, Leonard. *American Skin: Popular Culture, Big Business and the End of White America.* New York: Random House, 2002. Print.

Young, Cathy. "Tea Partiers Racist? Not So Fast." *Realclearpolitics.com.* 25 Apr. 2010. Web. <http://www.realclearpolitics.com/articles/2010/04/25/tea_partiers_racist_not_so_fast_105309.html>.

Zaldivar, Gabe. "LeBron James: The NBA Needs Him to Be This Evil." *Bleacherreport.com.* 1 Feb. 2011. Web. <http://bleacherreport.com/articles/592841-national-signing-day-2011-wwe-lebron-james-and-tuesday-afternoons-sports-buzz/entry/46113-lebron-james-the-nba-needs-him-to-be-this-evil>.

Zirin, Dave. "LeBron's Jordan Problem." *Newyorker.com.* 7 June 2011. Web. <http://www.newyorker.com/online/blogs/sportingscene/2011/06/lebrons-jordan-problem.html>.

6

Representations of Arabs and Muslims in Post-9/11 Television Dramas

EVELYN ALSULTANY

In 2004, the Council on American-Islamic Relations (CAIR) accused the television drama 24 of perpetuating stereotypes of Arabs and Muslims ("Fox TV Accused of Stereotyping American Muslims"). CAIR objected to the persistent portrayal of Arabs and Muslims within the context of terrorism, stating that the "repeated association of acts of terrorism with Islam will only serve to increase anti-Muslim prejudice" ("24 under Fire from Muslim Groups"). CAIR's critics have retorted that programs like 24 are cutting-edge, reflecting one of the most pressing social and political issues of the moment: the War on Terror. Some critics further contend that CAIR is trying to deflect the reality of Muslim terrorism by confining television writers to politically correct themes.[1]

The writers and producers of 24 have responded to CAIR's concerns in a number of ways. For one, the show often includes sympathetic portrayals of Arabs and Muslims, in which they are the "good guys," or in some way on the side of the United States. A letter from the FOX Entertainment Group to CAIR states that the show has "made a concerted effort to show ethnic, religious and political groups as multidimensional, and political issues are debated from multiple viewpoints" ("24 Comes under Muslim Fire"). The villains on the eight seasons of 24 come from around the globe and include Russians, Germans, Latinos, Arabs/Muslims, Euro-Americans, Africans, and even the fictional president of the United States. Rotating the identity of the "bad guy" is one of the many strategies used by television dramas to avoid reproducing the Arab/Muslim terrorist stereotype (or any other stereotypes, for that matter).[2] The show's responsiveness to such criticism even extended to creating a public service announcement (PSA) that was broadcast in February 2005, during one of the program's commercial breaks. The PSA featured the lead actor Kiefer Sutherland, who plays Jack Bauer, staring deadpan into the camera, reminding viewers that "the American Muslim community stands firmly beside their fellow Americans in denouncing and resisting all forms of terrorism," and urging us to "please, bear that in mind" while watching the program.[3]

Throughout the presidency of George W. Bush, television shows became a crucial way that Americans saw, thought about, and talked about the United States in a state of emergency after 9/11. After September 11, 2001, a slew of television dramas were created with the War on Terror as their central theme. Dramas such as *The Grid* (2004), *Sleeper Cell* (2005–6), *Threat Matrix* (2003–4), *24* (2001–10), and *The Wanted* (2009) depict U.S. government agencies and officials heroically working to make the nation safe by battling terrorism.[4] A prominent feature of these television shows is Arab and Muslim characters, most of whom are portrayed as grave threats to U.S. national security. But in response to increased popular awareness of ethnic stereotyping, and the active monitoring of Arab and Muslim watchdog groups, television writers have had to adjust their storylines to avoid blatant, crude stereotyping.

The programs *24* and *Sleeper Cell* were among the most popular examples of the fast-emerging post-9/11 genre of terrorism dramas. The show *24*, broadcast on FOX from 2001 to 2010, was an action drama centered on Jack Bauer, a brooding and embattled agent of the government's Counter Terrorist Unit (CTU), who raced a ticking clock to subvert impending terrorist attacks on the United States. The title refers to a twenty-four-hour state of emergency, and each of a given season's twenty-four episodes represented one hour of "real" time. *Sleeper Cell* was not as popular as *24*, partly because it was broadcast on the cable network Showtime, and therefore had a much smaller audience; *24* had an average audience of 12 million viewers while *Sleeper Cell* had an average of 600,000. While *24* lasted for eight seasons, *Sleeper Cell* lasted only two. *Sleeper Cell*'s storyline revolved around an undercover African American Muslim FBI agent who infiltrates a group of homegrown terrorists (the "cell" of the show's title), in order to subvert their planned attack on the United States.[5]

The creation of these representations of Arabs and Muslims has worked to conflate and racialize Arab ethnicity and the religion of Islam as a potential threat to the United States. The racialization of Arabs and Muslims did not begin on 9/11. Rather, it was made possible through a history of government and media narratives that constructed Arabs and Muslims as outside of the purview of Americanness. Before 9/11, scholars of Arab American studies described Arab Americans in relation to the United States racial terrain as located within a racial paradox, in which they were simultaneously racialized as white and nonwhite. Not legally recognized by the U.S. government as a minority group, and unable to fit into the racial and ethnic categories used by the U.S. census (black, white, Asian, Native, and Latino), Arabs have not been legally "raced" and are therefore "outside of the boxes" and presumably white.[6] Nonetheless, as Nadine Naber writes, the Arab American racial paradox before 9/11 was constructed through a distinct process of racialization in which Arab Americans were racialized primarily according to religion (vis-à-vis Islam) and politics (vis-à-vis the Israeli-Palestinian conflict), as opposed to phenotype. After 9/11, Naber argues that "the post-9/11 backlash has been constituted by an interplay between two racial logics, cultural racism and nation-based racism" ("Look, Mohammed" 279). Naber defined cultural racism as "a process of othering that constructs perceived cultural (e.g. Arab), religious (e.g. Muslim), or civilizational (e.g. Arab and/or Muslim) differences as natural and insurmountable." In other words, justifications for discrimination and violence come to be based in culture, religion, or notions of civilization, as opposed to biology or phenotype. Naber defines nation-based racism as a process of othering based on notions of citizens versus foreigners, where foreignness is inscribed with criminality and therefore marked for abjection. Naber states that the convergence of cultural racism and nation-based racism has enabled the resurgence of domestic policies targeting immigrant exclusion and foreign policies involving military deployment and war ("Look, Mohammed" 280–81).

Despite this ambiguous racialization in the legal-political realm, Arabs and Muslims have long been racialized and phenotyped by American mass media and particularly through Hollywood films. Ella Shohat's work demonstrates that the racialization of Arabs relies on Eurocentric narratives in terms of imaging, troping, and narrative positioning, and Jack G. Shaheen's work demonstrates that Hollywood has created an Arab phenotype over the last century.[7] The Arab on-screen has dark features (skin, hair, eyes) and a distinctive hook nose and is further visually distinguished by clothing (veil, belly-dancing outfits, and so on) and various cultural characteristics (greedy, rich, corrupt oil sheik, fanatical, violent, religious terrorist, etc.). Even though Arab and Muslim "looks" span the racial spectrum, a conflated Arab/Muslim "look" has been defined by the American media—one that hate crimes during the Gulf War and after 9/11 demonstrate is often confused with Indians, Pakistani, and Iranians.

Arab and Muslim casting contributes to this conflation and racialization of Arab and Muslim identities by portraying a particular "look." Television dramas perpetuate the fiction of an Arab or Muslim "race" by projecting a phenotype and hence the notion that Arabs and Muslims can be racially profiled. In *Sleeper Cell*, the lead terrorist is Arab/Muslim but portrayed by an Israeli Jewish actor, Oded Fehr, who has played Arab roles before, most notably in *The Mummy* films (1999, 2001). In season 2 of *24*, the Arab terrorist is played by Francesco Quinn, who is Mexican American (his father, Anthony Quinn, has often played Arab characters). During the fourth season of *24*, Marwan Habib, the Arab/Muslim terrorist, is played by Arnold Vosloo, a South African actor who was also featured (as an ancient Egyptian) in *The Mummy* films. Nestor Serrano, who is Latino, Shoreh Aghdashloo, who is Iranian, and Jonathan Adhout, who is Iranian American, play the terrorist sleeper cell family—mother, father, and teenage son. The other terrorists include Tony Plana, who is Cuban American, and Anil Kumar, who is South Asian. In the sixth season of *24*, Alexander Siddig, who is Sudanese British, plays Hamri Al-Assad, the reformed terrorist who helps CTU in its investigation. The "good Arab American" CTU agent, Nadia Yassir, is played by Marisol Nichols, who is Mexican-Hungarian-Romanian. The villains are played by Kal Penn, Shaun Majumder, and Adonis Maropis, South Asian Americans and a Greek American, respectively. Most of the actors who play Arab/Muslim terrorists, at least in the past decade, are Latinos, South Asians, and Greeks.[8] The point here is not only that Arabs should portray Arab characters but rather that casting lends itself to the visual construction of an Arab/Muslim race that supports the conflation of Arab and Muslim identities. This construction of a conflated Arab/Muslim "look" inadvertently supports policies like racial profiling; it does the ideological work of making racial profiling seem like an effective tool when it is in fact an unrealistic endeavor.

The first section of this chapter maps the representational strategies used by writers and producers of television dramas in representing Arabs/Muslims as terrorists and also in seeking not to reproduce the Arab/Muslim terrorist stereotype. It identifies a list of representational strategies used in television dramas to illustrate how schematized they have become, and it discusses the ideological work performed by them through "simplified complex representations"—the appearance of seemingly complex images and storylines that are in fact quite predictable and formulaic. Simplified complex representations are composed of strategies used by television producers, writers, and directors to give the impression that the representations they are producing, in terms of both image and storyline, are complex. Though the focus here is on television, film also employs these strategies. While some of these strategies are used more frequently (and to greater narrative success) than others, they all help to shape the many layers of simplified complexity. Simplified complex representations are the representational mode of the so-called post-race era, signifying a new era of racial representation. These representations appear to challenge or complicate former stereotypes and contribute to a multicultural or post-race illusion. Yet at the same time, most of the programs that employ simplified complex representational strategies can promote logics that legitimize racist policies and practices. The following description of some of these strategies outlines the parameters of simplified complex representations and facilitates ways to identify such strategies.

Representational Strategies
Strategy 1: Inserting Patriotic Arab or Muslim Americans

Watching dozens of television shows between 2001 and 2009, it becomes evident that writers have increasingly created "positive" Arab and Muslim characters to show that they are sensitive to negative stereotyping. This character most commonly takes the form of a patriotic Arab or Muslim American who assists the U.S. government in its fight against Arab/Muslim terrorism, as either a government agent or a civilian. Some examples of this strategy include Mohammad "Mo" Hassain, an Arab American Muslim character who is part of the USA Homeland Security Force on the show *Threat Matrix*. On season 6 of *24*, Nadia Yassir is a dedicated member of the Counter Terrorist Unit.[9] In *Sleeper Cell*, the "good" Muslim is the lead African American character, Darwyn Al-Sayeed, an undercover FBI agent who proclaims to his colleagues that terrorists have nothing to do with his faith and cautions them not to confuse the two ("Al-Fatiha"). In a fourth-season episode of *24*, two Arab American brothers reveal that they are tired of being unjustly blamed for the terrorist attacks and insist on helping to fight terrorism alongside Jack Bauer, the lead character who saves the United States from danger each season ("Day 4: 7pm–8pm"). In such cases, Islam is often portrayed as inspiring American patriotism as opposed to inspiring terrorism.[10] This bevy of characters makes up the most common group of post-9/11 Arab/Muslim depictions. This strategy challenges the notion that Arabs and Muslims are not American and/or un-American. Judging from the sheer number of these patriots, it appears that writers have embraced this strategy as the most direct method to counteract potential charges of stereotyping.

Strategy 2: Sympathizing with the Plight of Arab and Muslim Americans after 9/11

Multiple stories appeared on television dramas with Arab/Muslim Americans as the unjust targets of hate—as victims of violence and harassment (Alsultany, "Prime-Time Plight"). The viewer is nearly always positioned so as to sympathize with their plight. In an episode of *The Practice*, the government detains an innocent Arab American without due process or explanation, and an attorney steps in to defend his rights ("Inter Arma Silent Leges").[11] On *7th Heaven*, Ruthie's Muslim friend Yasmine is harassed on her way to school, prompting the Camden family and their larger neighborhood to stand together to fight discrimination ("Suspicion"). This emphasis on victimization and sympathy challenges long-standing representations of Arabs and Muslims as terrorists that had previously inspired in audiences a lack of sympathy and even a sense of celebration when Arab/Muslim characters were killed.[12]

*Strategy 3: Challenging the Arab/Muslim
Conflation with Diverse Muslim Identities*

Sleeper Cell prides itself on being unique among the television dramas
that deal with the topic of terrorism because of its diverse cast of Muslim terrorists. *Sleeper Cell* challenges the common conflation between
Arab and Muslim identities. While the ringleader of the sleeper cell,
Faris al-Farik, is an Arab, the other members of this Los Angeles group
are not: they are Bosnian, French, Euro-American, Western European,
and Latino, and even include a gay Iraqi Brit. Portraying diverse sleeper
cell members strategically challenges how Arab and Muslim identities
are often conflated by government discourses and media representations by demonstrating that not all Arabs are Muslim and not all Muslims are Arab—and, even further, that not all Arabs and Muslims are
heterosexual. In addition, *Sleeper Cell* highlights a struggle within Islam
over who will define the religion, thus demonstrating that not all Muslims advocate terrorism. For example, in one episode, a Yemeni imam,
or religious leader, comes to Los Angeles in order to deprogram Muslim extremists and plans to issue a fatwa (religious ruling) against terrorism ("Scholar"). These diverse characters, and their heated debates
for and against terrorism, indeed distinguish *Sleeper Cell* from the rest
of its genre. But this strategy of challenging the Arab/Muslim conflation
is remarkable in part because of its infrequency.

Strategy 4: Flipping the Enemy

"Flipping the enemy" involves leading the viewer to believe that Muslim terrorists are plotting to destroy the United States and then revealing that those Muslims are merely pawns or a front for Euro-American
or European terrorists. The identity of the enemy is thus flipped: viewers discover that the terrorist is not Arab, or they find that the Arab or
Muslim terrorist is part of a larger network of international terrorists.
In *24*, Bauer spends the first half of the second season tracking down
a Middle Eastern terrorist cell, ultimately subverting a nuclear attack.
In the second half of the season, we discover that European and Euro-
American businessmen are behind the attack, goading the United States
to declare war on the Middle East in order to benefit from the increase

in oil prices. Related to this subversion of expectations, *24* does not glorify America; in numerous ways the show dismantles the notion that the United States is perfect and the rest of the world flawed: FBI and CIA agents are incompetent; other government agents conspire with the terrorists; the terrorists (Arab and Muslim alike) are portrayed as very intelligent. Flipping the enemy demonstrates that terrorism is not an Arab or Muslim monopoly.

Strategy 5: Humanizing the Terrorist

Most Arab and Muslim terrorists in films or television shows before 9/11 were stock villains, one-dimensional bad guys who were presumably bad because of their ethnic background or religious beliefs (Shaheen). In contrast, post-9/11 terrorist characters are humanized in a variety of ways. We see them in a familial context, as loving fathers and husbands; we come to learn their backstory and glimpse into the moments that have brought them to the precipice of terror. In 2005, *24* introduced viewers to a Middle Eastern family for the first time on American network television (in a recurring role for most of the season as opposed to a onetime appearance). In their first scene, they seem like an "ordinary" family preparing breakfast—mother, father, and a teenage son. It is soon revealed, however, that they are a sleeper cell; in the episodes to come, each family member's relationship to terrorism is explored. The father is willing to kill his wife and son in order to complete his mission; the mother will reconsider her involvement with terrorism only to protect her son; and the teenage son, raised in the United States, is portrayed with an evolving sense of humanity that ultimately prevents him from becoming a terrorist. This strategy of humanizing the terrorists by focusing on their interpersonal relationships, motives, and backstories is also central to *Sleeper Cell.* Each member of the sleeper cell has his or her own motivation for joining the cell: from rebelling against a leftist liberal parent (a professor at the University of California at Berkeley) to seeking revenge on the United States for the death of family members (one character's husband was killed by U.S. forces in Iraq). Adding multiple dimensions to the formerly one-dimensional bad guy has become increasingly common since 9/11.

Strategy 6: Projecting a Multicultural U.S. Society

Projecting a multicultural U.S. society is another strategy to circumvent accusations of racism while representing Arabs and Muslims as terrorists. In *Sleeper Cell*, the terrorists are of diverse ethnic backgrounds, and Darwyn, the African American FBI agent, is in an interracial relationship with Gail, a white woman. For several seasons of *24*, the U.S. president was African American, his press secretary Asian American; the Counter Terrorist Unit is equally diverse, peppered with Latinos and African Americans throughout the show's eight seasons. The sum total of these casting decisions creates the impression of a United States in which multiculturalism abounds. The projected society is one in which people of different racial backgrounds work together, and racism is socially unacceptable.

Strategy 7: Fictionalizing the Middle Eastern or Muslim Country

It has become increasingly common for the country of the terrorist characters in television dramas to go unnamed. This strategy rests on the assumption that leaving the nationality of the villain blank eliminates potential offensiveness; if no particular country or ethnicity is named, then there is less reason for any particular group to be offended by the portrayal. In season 4 of *24*, the terrorist family is from an unnamed Middle Eastern country. They are possibly from Turkey, but where exactly is never stated; it is, we assume, intentionally left ambiguous. In *The West Wing*, the fictional country of "Qumar" is the source of terrorist plots; in season 8 of *24*, it is "Kamistan." This is also done with other ethnic groups. For example, in season 7 of *24*, the African country "Sangala" is an important source. Fictionalizing the country of the terrorist can give a show more latitude in creating salacious storylines that might be criticized if identified with an actual country or nationality.

Simplified Complex Representations

These seven representational strategies are not exhaustive, nor are they all new to our post-9/11 world. Rather, these strategies collectively outline some of the ways in which writers and producers of television (and film) have sought to improve representations of Arabs (and other racial and ethnic groups). These strategies are an astounding shift in the mass entertainment landscape. They present an important departure from stereotypes into more challenging stories and characters. This new breed of terrorism programming reflects a growing sensitivity to the potential negative impact of stereotyping. These new representational strategies seek to make the point, and indeed, often with strenuous effort, that not all Arabs are terrorists, and not all terrorists are Arabs. However, for all their innovations, these shows remain wedded to a script that represents Arabs and Muslims only in the context of terrorism, and therefore they do not effectively challenge the stereotypical representations of Arabs and Muslims.

Stuart Hall has claimed that even those with the best of intentions, liberal writers and producers who seek to subvert racial hierarchies, can inadvertently participate in inferential racism. Hall defines inferential racism as "apparently naturalized representations of events and situations relating to race, whether 'factual' or 'fictional,' which have racist premises and propositions inscribed in them as a set of unquestioned assumptions" ("Racist Ideologies" 273). The persistent unquestioned assumption in these television dramas is that Arabs and Muslims are terrorists, despite writers' efforts to create a wider range of Arab and Muslim characters. The primary objective of commercial television networks is not education, social justice, or social change. Rather, the goal is financial: to keep as many viewers watching for as long as possible. Television must therefore strike a balance between keeping its products as engaging as possible and not offending potential viewers. Writers thus seem to be constrained and influenced by two factors: viewers have been primed to assume that Arabs/Muslims are terrorists, and therefore writers create what viewers expect and what will sell. At the same time, some viewers are particularly sensitive to and resistant to stereotyping, and therefore writers are faced with creating a more diverse world of characters. The results are some modifications to avoid being offensive while perpetuating core stereotypes that continue to have cultural capital.[13] Post-9/11 television dramas are a testimony to the fact that the stereotypes that held sway for much of the twentieth century are no longer socially acceptable—at least in their most blatant forms. But this does not mean that such stereotypes (and viewers' taste for them) have actually gone away; they have only become covert.

These strategies result in simplified complex representations, which produce the illusion of complexity and sensitivity while continuing to perpetuate stereotypes. They attempt to make representations complex yet do so in a simplified way; they are predictable strategies that can be relied on if the plot involves an Arab or Muslim terrorist, but are a new standard alternative to (and seem a great improvement upon) the stock ethnic villains of the past. Under the guise of complexity, these representational strategies construct a binary between "good" and "bad" Arabs and Muslims, reinforcing a narrow conception of what constitutes a "good" Arab or Muslim. As Mahmood Mamdani has written, the post-9/11 public debate has centered on this binary, and all Muslims are assumed to be bad until they perform and prove their allegiance to the United States. In television dramas, this framework is similarly relentless. "Bad" Arabs or Muslims are the terrorists, and their "good" counterparts are those who help the U.S. government fight terrorism. Despite the shift away from the more blatant stereotypes of previous decades, Arab and Muslim identities are still understood and evaluated primarily in relation to terrorism. This binary focus, in turn, overpowers the above strategies. Though some television writers might certainly have humane motives, and though some producers might honestly desire to create innovative shows that are devoid of stereotypes, any such efforts are overwhelmed by the sheer momentum of our current representational scheme. Thus, representations of Arab and Muslim identities in contexts that have nothing to do with terrorism remain strikingly unusual in American commercial media.[14] Arab and Muslim identities are rehabilitated as legitimate through rigid notions of either patriotism or victimization.

These complex characters and storylines fall short of subverting stereotypes. Fictionalizing Arab and Muslim countries, for example, tends to add to the conflation and generalization of Arab and Muslim identities by implying that terrorism originates from a fictional country that could be any of a number of Arab/Muslim countries. The specificity of the context becomes irrelevant. As a viewer, it is not a stretch to assume that the fictionalized country is supposed to be Arab or Muslim. These fictionalized countries operate as allegories that stand in as doubles for the "real" and in turn illustrate how the real sites in which the United States is waging its War on Terror (Iraq and Afghanistan) often feel like abstract or even fictional locations for viewers.

This fictionalizing strategy has many precedents. Fictional Latin American countries, with locations such as San Pasquale in *Commander in Chief* (2005), Tecala in *Proof of Life* (2000), and Curaguay in *The A-Team* (1983–86), have been a staple of mainstream film and television for decades. Similarly, fictional "Arabia" is not a new representational strategy; rather, it is a strategy that is making a comeback. The Hollywood film *Harum Scarum* (1965), starring Elvis Presley, for example, takes place in "Abulstan" and "Lunacan." Disney's *Aladdin* (1992) takes place in "Agrabah." It originally was set in Baghdad, but the location was changed to avoid associating this fairy tale with the Gulf War (Patrizio). These films seek to trade on the West's long-standing and carefully cultivated notions of an imaginary, fantastical, and exoticized East (Said). Recent films and television shows emphasize their portrayal of actual locations, in order to heighten the sense of place and create presumably realistic depictions of current and historical events. Post-9/11 television dramas have merely conflated their methods, emphasizing their "realistic" storylines—"ripped from the headlines," as *Law and Order* and others advertise—in the ideological safety of fictionalized locations.

Inserting a patriotic Arab or Muslim American and fictionalizing Middle Eastern countries are ineffectual devices if Arabs, Muslims, Arab Americans, and Muslim Americans continue to be portrayed through the narrow lens of good or bad in the fight against terrorism. Casting actors of color to give the impression of a "post-race" society propagates the comforting notion of an enlightened society that has resolved all of its racial problems. The various strategies used in the first decade of the War on Terror are akin to a Band-Aid over a still-festering wound. They give the impression of comfort, perhaps even of cure, but the fundamental problem remains.

Simplified complex representational strategies reflect the commodification of the civil rights and multiculturalist movements. The commodification of multiculturalism, while reflecting the sensibilities of some viewers, is submerged under the more prominent consumable message that Arabs and Muslims pose a terrorist threat to American life and freedom. This move toward advancing a post-race ideology is linked to a co-optation of movements for racial equality. The civil rights movement led to a shift in the U.S. government's approach to race and racism, from institutionalized white supremacy to recognition of racial inequality as a problem and to institutionalizing antiracist policies (Winant xiii). Howard Winant argues that while on the surface institutions implemented policies that advocated racial equality, in practice a repackaged version of white supremacy in the guise of colorblindness was produced. In this notion of colorblindness, racial inequality persists by "still resorting to exclusionism and scapegoating when politically necessary, still invoking the supposed superiority of 'mainstream' (aka white) values, and cheerfully maintaining that equality has been largely achieved" (xiii–xiv). Within this new racial formation that Jodi Melamed calls "neoliberal multiculturalism" and that Eduardo Bonilla-Silva calls "color-blind racism," "racism constantly appears as disappearing according to conventional race categories, even as it takes on new forms that can signify as nonracial or even antiracist" (Melamed 18). These new antiracist forms are aptly apparent when Guantánamo Bay prisoners are provided with copies of the Qur'an and time to pray as evidence of the cultural sensitivity of their captors; or when the USA PATRIOT Act contains a section that condemns discrimination against Arab and Muslim Americans. Such gestures attempt to subvert the focus from the violation of civil and human rights in favor of highlighting multiculturalism and racial sensitivity (Melamed). The emergence of sympathetic representations of Arabs, Muslims, Arab Americans, and Muslim Americans similarly deflects attention from the persistence of racist policies and practices after 9/11.

While these representational strategies that challenged the stereotyping of Arabs and Muslims were being broadcast, circulated, and consumed, real Arabs and Muslims were being detained, deported, held without due process, and tortured. In the weeks and months after 9/11, hate crimes, workplace discrimination, bias incidents, and airline discrimination targeting Arab and Muslim Americans increased exponentially. According to the FBI, hate crimes against Arabs and Muslims increased by 1,600 percent from 2000 to 2001. In just the first weeks and months after 9/11, Amnesty International, the Council on American-Islamic Relations, the American-Arab Anti-Discrimination Committee, and other organizations documented hundreds of violent incidents experienced by Arab and Muslim Americans and people mistaken for being Arabs or Muslim Americans, including several murders. Dozens of airline passengers perceived to be Arab or Muslim were removed from flights. Hundreds of Arab and Muslim Americans reported discrimination at work, received hate mail, or were physically assaulted, and their property, mosques, and community centers were vandalized or set on fire (American-Arab Anti-Discrimination Committee). Throughout the decade after 9/11, such racist acts have persisted. In addition, the U.S. government passed legislation that targeted Arabs and Muslims (both inside and outside the United States) and legalized the suspension of constitutional rights. The USA PATRIOT Act, passed by Congress in October 2001 and renewed in 2006 and 2011, legalized the following (previously illegal) acts and thus enabled anti-Arab and Muslim racism: monitoring Arab and Muslim groups; granting the U.S. attorney general the right to indefinitely detain noncitizens whom he suspects might have ties to terrorism; searching and wiretapping secretly, without probable cause; arresting and holding a person as a "material witness" whose testimony might assist in a case; using secret evidence, without granting the accused access to that evidence; trying those designated as "enemy combatants" in military tribunals (as opposed to civilian courts); and deportation based on guilt by association (not on what someone has done). Other measures included the Absconder Apprehension Initiative that tracked down and deported 6,000 men from unnamed Middle Eastern countries, in most cases for overstaying a visa. In the weeks after 9/11 at least 1,200 Muslim men were rounded up and detained without criminal charges.[15]

Certainly not all Arabs and Muslims were subject to post-9/11 harassment. Nonetheless, the argument here is that simplified complex racial representations, the new representational mode collectively constructed by these multiple representational strategies, perform the ideological work of producing a post-race moment in which denying the severity of the persistence of institutionalized racism becomes possible. These television dramas produce the reassurance that racial sensitivity is the norm in American society while simultaneously perpetuating the dominant perception of Arabs and Muslims as threats to U.S. national security.

Simplified complex representations are also deceptive: they offer a limited field of explanation on the War on Terror under the guise of an expanded field of explanation. Audiences are given the impression that multiple positions and perspectives have been considered, for example, by exploring the motives of terrorists. Terrorism, according to *Sleeper Cell,* is caused by disaffected non-Arabs who turn to fundamentalist Islam, and Arabs who embrace fundamentalist ideologies. Consistent with what Mamdani calls "culture talk," the notion that terrorism can be explained merely by examining Arab or Muslim "culture," the series perpetuates the idea that Arabs and Muslims have a monopoly on terrorism (Mamdani). This idea has been circulating in popular culture since a series of political events (the Arab-Israeli War in 1967, the Munich Olympics in 1972, the Arab oil embargo in 1973, the Iran hostage crisis in 1979–80, and airplane hijackings in the 1970s and 1980s) through which the news media played a crucial role in making the Middle East, and Islam in particular, meaningful to Americans as a place that breeds terrorism (McAlister). The motives for terrorism that are presented often lack real depth or exploration. These plotlines are, however, gripping and make it is easy to ignore all that remains unchanged and how these shows maintain the dominant discourse of the United States as an innocent victim of the War on Terror.

Simplified complex representational strategies attempt to challenge the Arab/Muslim terrorist stereotype by making concessions to how violence, sympathy, and context are framed. The Arab terrorist stereotype has emerged not only through repeating this one-dimensional character in films, news reports, and government speeches but also through its particular framing. The Arab terrorist stereotype has been birthed out of a fundamental distinction: violence perpetrated by Arabs and Muslims is framed as illegitimate, while violence committed by the United States is legitimate and necessary to democracy, freedom, and peace. What makes a terrorist a "terrorist" (a pejorative term, in comparison to "freedom fighter") is that the violence is illegitimate because it targets innocents and is senseless or without a moral outcome. "Arab/ Muslim terrorists" in the U.S. media have historically been portrayed as seeking power or chaos; the U.S. government, in contrast, is consistently portrayed as fighting to preserve equality. Recent television dramas seem to challenge this basic distinction. Behind the grim certainty of Jack Bauer's fatalism, *24* seems to relish its portrayals of the U.S. government as flawed, and at moments even morally bankrupt. Similarly, *Sleeper Cell* provides its terrorist characters ample opportunity to state their grievances; their evolved backstories appear to lend a degree of legitimacy to their violence. However, in the broader arc of these shows, and their eventual, if tortured, triumph against evil, such grievances are ultimately framed as illegitimate. The complexities of history and religion are eventually boiled down to Arab/Muslim individuals spewing nonsensical, hateful rhetoric toward the United States or Israel. Furthermore, the portrayal of Arab/Muslim terrorists as well organized and intelligent, while a departure from previous representations of incompetent Arab/Muslim terrorists, conveys the idea that the threat is "real" and that the U.S. government is still smarter since the terrorists are inevitably outwitted in these television dramas.

As with all instances of framing, what is not shown is as important as what viewers do see.[16] While it has become increasingly common to show the verbal tirades of Arab terrorists, and violent promises to free their country from U.S. foreign policies, it is uncommon for the context of such references to be adequately addressed. The concept of freeing an Arab country from the negative impacts of U.S. foreign policies remains abstract, since viewers do not see the daily realities of those countries. Both the suffering of Palestinians living under Israeli military occupation that is supported by U.S. policies, and the suffering of Iraqi people as a result of a decade of U.S. sanctions are absent from the storyline. This absence operates to ensure that any consideration of their violence as legitimate remains taboo. Thus, while simplified complex representational strategies make concessions to complexity by giving voice to the grievances of terrorist characters, and allowing us to see them in the context of their families, "their" violence remains incomprehensible, beyond reason, and in the service of hatred.

How violence is framed, including what parts of the story are intentionally omitted, is intimately connected to how sympathy is framed and who is represented as deserving or undeserving of audience sympathies. Because terrorists commit senseless acts of violence, because they are the "bad" guys, they are not deserving of sympathy. By contrast, the "good" Arab/Muslim characters, including patriotic Americans and innocent victims of post-9/11 hate crimes, are positioned as worthy of sympathy. These dramas are remarkable in that they encourage a post-9/11 audience to root for certain Arab and Muslim characters, and to feel sadness and even outrage when those characters are unfairly attacked. But such sympathy, it becomes clear, is only possible because of the basic binary between good and bad. We root for these unlikely good guys because they challenge (though they do not overturn) our deeply laden cultural assumption that the Arab/Muslim character is the bad guy. These particular concessions are reflective of the "post-race" moment. Herman Gray states that representations of blackness in the 1980s and 1990s rewrote "a strife-ridden past into a harmonized vision of possibility" and in so doing made it difficult to differentiate between "progressive political possibilities" and "neoliberal and conservative rewrites of the same old racial narratives" (*Watching Race* 163). Similarly, post-9/11 television dramas, through multidimensional characters and storylines, construct an internal logic of racial sensitivity and diversity that makes it increasingly difficult to differentiate between new Arab and Muslim representations and the reinscription of long-standing terrorist stereotypes.

The television landscape shifted on 9/11 as a vague, ominous threat to U.S. national security took center stage. The story lines in television dramas such as *24* and *Sleeper Cell* reinforce the government's need for a War on Terror; these shows have, in numerous guises, replayed the tragedy of 9/11 weekly to American audiences, keeping the trauma fresh in the collective memory. These cultural productions, despite employing a range of strategies to avoid reproducing stereotypes, offer a very specific story that keeps viewer-citizens living and reliving the War on Terror. There is a fundamental contradiction between representational strategies that project an enlightened, postracial culture yet maintain the relevance of the threat. So long as Arabs and Muslims are represented primarily in the context of terrorism, our current crop of representational strategies, for all their apparent innovations, will have a minimal impact on viewers' perceptions of Arabs and Muslims and, far worse, will perpetuate a simplistic vision of good and evil under the guise of complexity and sensitivity.

What is most strongly conveyed by these post-9/11 television dramas is that Arabs and Muslims pose a threat to U.S. peace and security. The articulated fear, similar to that during the Cold War, is that the enemy is among "us," so that we must live in a state of constant fear and vigilance. According to Douglas L. Howard, "For all we know, our neighborhoods, our businesses, and our highways have been or are being targeted even as we speak, but we are (and we must feel) powerless to protect ourselves from what we cannot see and what we do not know. . . . *24*, in all its violent glory, makes us believe that, if the terrorists are out here, something, everything, in fact, is being done to stop them and to keep us safe" (142). The programs 24 and *Sleeper Cell,* despite their representational strategies, do the ideological work of perpetually reenacting the Arab/Muslim threat.

Above all, what is depicted in these television dramas is a nation in perpetual danger. As McAlister has written, "The continuing sense of threat provides support for the power of the state, but it also provides the groundwork for securing 'the nation' as a cultural and social entity. The 'imagined community' of the nation finds continuing rearticulation in the rhetoric of danger" (6). Writers and producers create an "imagined community" of virtual viewer-citizens,[17] many of whom are interpellated into a sense of impending threat that supports the state.[18] Television is the fundamental way such a threat can be conveyed to a nation. In addition to being the disseminator of this threat, television capitalizes on it, keeping viewers both fearful and captivated.

Challenging Simplified Complex Representations

If the representational strategies identified here fail at humanizing Arabs and Muslims, then what strategies might prove more successful? The contention here is not that these simplified strategies such as flipping the enemy, diversifying Muslim identities, and sympathizing with the plight of Arab Americans are simply useless. Rather, the problem is that these representations are chained to the War on Terror, thereby associating Arab and Muslim identities indelibly with terrorism, extremism, and oppression. What would make a difference is to see Arab and Muslim characters in contexts that have little to do with terrorism, or extremism, or oppression; characters that break out of the good/bad Muslim dichotomy; and characters in more leading and recurring roles. In digging through the mire of 9/11 popular culture, we actually find a few mainstream productions that have been trying all three of these things. Interestingly, four of these shows, *Whoopi, Aliens in America, Community,* and *Little Mosque on the Prairie,* are sitcoms. One, the most recent, *All-American Muslim,* is a reality show. While these five shows refer to the context of the War on Terror, they do not take it as their central subject.

Whoopi Goldberg's sitcom *Whoopi* (2003–4) premiered two years after 9/11 and centered on Mavis Rae, a former singer and one-hit wonder who opens a small hotel in New York City. Much of the humor centers on her interaction with her Iranian handyman, Nasim, played by Omid Djalili (the first Iranian in a recurring role on U.S. television). Nasim is the butt of jokes about terrorism, his experiences with racial profiling are highlighted, and he is fearful of deportation. In one scene, Mavis complains that her unemployed brother is driving her crazy and jokes that if he does not find a job soon, she will kill him. Nasim replies, "It's a shame you live in America. You don't have a secret service where they can just come in, bash him on the head, put a hood over it, take him away and then get him in a cell and place two electrodes . . . " ("Pilot"). Nasim is a humorous and likable character whose life as a handyman is impacted by 9/11 in ridiculous ways. *Whoopi* favors a representational strategy that challenges stereotypes and diffuses racial tension by using humor to accentuate stereotypes in order to demonstrate their absurdity. Though nominated for an Emmy Award, the show lasted for only one season on NBC.

Aliens in America (2007–8) also lasted only one season, this one on the CW network. It was about the Tolchucks, a middle-class, white American family in Wisconsin with two children in high school: a daughter who is popular and an awkward son who is not. The mother comes up with a scheme to popularize her son by signing up for a foreign exchange student from Norway. She assumes that he will be blond and gorgeous, and therefore make her son immediately popular. Instead, they receive a Pakistani Muslim named Raja Musharaff who they initially try to get rid of, since his presence would ruin the popularity plan. However, the Tolchucks end up raising Raja as their own after they discover that his parents have died. Raja is an offensively one-dimensional character: he speaks with an accent, wears traditional Pakistani clothing, has strange customs, and is very naive and square. He is a caricature. Upon first meeting the Tolchucks, he says, "You are such good people to open your home to me. Thank you Allah for the Tolchucks" ("Pilot"). He believes in dating only if chaperoned, will not kiss until married, does not lie, and is extremely honest and giving of himself. In one episode, he works at a convenience store and refuses to sell alcohol to his classmates with fake IDs ("Help Wanted"). His host brother pleads with him to sell them alcohol so that they could have a chance at becoming popular, but Raja is unyielding; he does not care about being cool and subscribes to higher principals. Raja is not alone in being stereotyped: Americans are depicted as ignorant and racist, but the Tolchuck family tries to rise above their surroundings.

Despite the stereotype, the sitcom is notable for having this character in a leading role, and the focus of the show is ultimately about two misfits—the white American boy who does not fit in at school and the Pakistani Muslim who does not fit into suburban American culture. The representational strategy is to parallel these two outcasts to accentuate their similarities, while still exploring cultural and religious differences. Like *Whoopi,* the show tries to diffuse post-9/11 tension about Muslims through humor, reveling in the ordinariness of daily life, reminding viewers of how much of life is *not* about terrorism, or September 11, but rather about petty squabbles, social anxieties, and the other mundane dilemmas of being human.

Community (2009–present), is a sitcom on NBC about students at a community college who form a study group. Danny Pudi plays Abed Nadir, a Palestinian American student who is obsessed with popular culture and socially awkward. Abed is a weird guy, but his weirdness has nothing to do with his ethnic or religious identity. Despite references to his obligation to take over the family falafel business and a stereotypical appearance by his father, Abed is a refreshingly original character unlike any other portrayal of Arab Americans on network television to date.

Little Mosque on the Prairie (2007–12), winner of numerous awards, has been broadcast for five seasons on the Canadian Broadcasting Corporation and is slated for a sixth and final season. Created by Zarqa Nawaz, a Muslim Canadian woman of Pakistani descent, it is about Muslims in a small Canadian town who start a mosque and community center. Nawaz began the sitcom with an explicit teaching mission: to bring the lives of ordinary Muslims to North American viewers and to educate viewers about who ordinary Muslims are. Beneath the laughs, it is about two communities colliding and learning to live together and also about the internal dynamics and struggles within the Muslim community. In an interview, Nawaz states:

> I think people are assuming because of the title and the subject matter that it's going to be really controversial and political. But it's just a comedy that happens to have Muslim people in it, and it's meant to make people laugh. It's about relationships and human interactions and life in

a rural setting. But it's really the first comedy of its kind in North America, and that's why it's so intriguing. ("Camels on Hand to Celebrate Premier of 'Little Mosque on the Prairie'")

The uniqueness of the show is evident throughout. As a sitcom, it is successful because it is at heart about what all good comedy is about: "relationships and human interactions"—universal conditions that are explored through a very particular, and often revelatory, situation. The show thus immerses us in the specifics of observant Islamic life and focuses on internal debates between conservative and liberal Muslims. This results in discussions that are both hilarious and unprecedented, including how to determine when Ramadan officially begins (does one spot the new moon with a telescope or with one's eyes, or follow what is determined in Saudi Arabia?); whether there should be a barrier between men and women at the mosque; whether Muslims can celebrate Halloween; what a Muslim-compliant bachelor party should look like; and whether Muslim women can take a swimming class if the instructor is a gay man. Nawaz says, "We try to find the hilarity in every scenario. . . . Muslim women cover their hair because they're worried men will be attracted to it. But what if the guy is gay and isn't attracted to it? Does that count?" (Intini). In addition to internal debates, the series also addresses issues external to the community, such as racial profiling and assumptions by the public that Muslims are terrorists. The representational strategies used include humanizing Muslims by featuring them as lead characters and depicting the differences among them, showing that Muslims are not monolithic but have diverse perspectives and varying degrees of religiosity. What is particularly notable about *Whoopi, Aliens in America, Community,* and *Little Mosque on the Prairie* is that the storylines do not revolve around terrorism or homeland security. They portray a boutique hotel, a high school, a community college, and a community center. Not only do the storylines represent a departure from prior tropes, but the characters also deviate from the standard patriot and victim molds. What makes these programs notable in challenging simplified complex representational strategies is that characters are not measured in relation to terrorism; they are people with varied lives. These shows at times contain elements of the stereotyping and simplified representations common to television dramas.

But at other moments they also utilize this common reference point to push it to its extreme, creating characters and situations so absurd that they in turn highlight the problem of racism itself.

Finally, and most important, *All-American Muslim,* a reality show that follows five Muslim families in Dearborn, Michigan, premiered on the TLC network in November 2011 to an average of 900,000 viewers. The show was met with protest from the Florida Family Association (run by David Caton and known for its antigay activism), which accused it of hiding the danger that Islam poses to America and pressured advertisers to pull their commercials. In other words, because there are no terrorists in the show and Muslims are depicted as ordinary people, these right-wing activists see *All-American Muslim* as deceptive propaganda "attempting to manipulate Americans into ignoring the threat of jihad." Lowe's Home Improvement and Kayak.com subsequently pulled their commercials, leading to much controversy.

All-American Muslim is unprecedented in its focus on Muslim Americans on U.S. television and in deviating from stereotypical representations of Muslims as terrorists. At the same time, however, *All-American Muslim* conforms to some of the new representations of Muslims that have become standard since 9/11, namely, the Muslim or Arab American "patriot" and/or the "victim" to post-9/11 hate crimes. The cast members of *All-American Muslim* include a police officer, a football coach, a county clerk, and a federal agent, thus fulfilling the requisite "patriotic" American representations on U.S. television. And the cast members are not immune to discriminatory experiences. One of the married couples leaves Dearborn to have breakfast in a neighboring town, only to be ignored while other customers are offered seating. Students at Fordson High School recount how they are called cameljockeys when playing football with other schools.

These representations of "patriot" and "victim" are undoubtedly improvements over past representations as terrorists, oil sheiks, belly dancers, and oppressed veiled women, and *All-American Muslim* conforms to these two new standard representations. However, the show also deviates from them in two fundamental ways: by not representing terrorists and by including and moving beyond these standard Muslim characters. Many shows that portray a patriotic or victimized Arab/ Muslim American do so in the context of Muslims as terrorist threats.

All-American Muslim is about the everyday lives of five families and has very little to do with terrorists. The events of 9/11 are relevant insofar as they have impacted the lives of the cast members who have to contend with stereotypes of Islam condoning violence.

Furthermore, the show includes cast members who break the mold of the "patriotic" and the "victimized," including a woman entrepreneur who wants to open a nightclub in Dearborn and a woman who marries an Irish Catholic American—neither of whom wear the hijab. *All-American Muslim,* in some ways, expands the field of representations of Muslim identities on U.S. television. Apparently, this expansion is of concern to the right-wing activists who believe that representing Muslims outside of the context of terrorism constitutes "deception and obfuscation." The backlash against the show demonstrates resistance to seeing Muslims outside the context of terrorism.

In response to Lowe's pulling its advertising, a grassroots movement, the National Lowe's Boycott Campaign, was launched, and hip-hop mogul Russell Simmons bought up the advertising space. The controversy around the reception of this reality show reveals that while some media producers and viewers are ready to see Muslims as human beings, a segment of the population remains resistant to nonstereotyped images of Muslims in the United States.

Television has participated in the co-optation of multiculturalism by portraying limited and acceptable versions of diversity, thus demonstrating again and again that an increase in diverse representations of Arab and Muslim identities does not in itself demonstrate a victory over racism. Gray has written that the evolving strategy of television networks since the 1980s, from containing the many difficult questions of race to a superficial support of liberal pluralism, has had a nasty side effect: the elimination, repression, or incorporation of difference as part of the co-optation mechanism (*Cultural Moves* 107–8). Similarly, Hall has written that the spaces "won" for difference are "very carefully policed and regulated . . . that what replaces invisibility is a kind of carefully regulated, segregated visibility" ("What Is This 'Black'?" 24).[19] This careful regulation can be seen with the limiting of representations to the patriotic and/or victimized Arab and Muslim Americans, and the carefully managed efforts to humanize terrorists and reference terrorist motives, while restricting audience sympathies or identification toward "the terrorists." These four sitcoms, however, offer an intriguing alternative. They incorporate some elements of media co-optation of difference by including elements of caricaturing yet at the same time offer possibilities for future diversions from representing all Arab and Muslim characters in contexts exclusively focused on terrorism, and solely in supporting or inconsequential roles. As Hall writes of black identities, "What is at issue here is the recognition of the extraordinary diversity of subject positions, social experiences and cultural identities which compose the category 'black'" ("New Ethnicities" 443). These sitcoms and reality show help construct a different field of representation that produces diverse meanings about Arabs and Muslims, and hints at the potential for a more varied field of representations in the future.

Notes

Portions of this chapter were previously published in Evelyn Alsutany, *Arabs and Muslims in the Media: Race and Representation after 9/11* (NYU Press, 2012).

1. Critics of CAIR include www.jihadwatch.org and www.frontpagemag.com.
2. I use "Arab/Muslim" not to denote that these identities are one and the same, but rather to point to how Arab and Muslim identities are portrayed as conflated.
3. This public service announcement (PSA) was broadcast during one of the program's commercial breaks on Monday, Feb. 7, 2005, FOX.
4. *24*, FOX, Nov. 2001–9; *Threat Matrix*, ABC, Sept. 2003–Jan. 2004; *The Grid*, TNT, July–Aug. 2004; *Sleeper Cell*, Showtime, Dec. 2005–Dec. 2006; *The Wanted*, NBC, July 2009.
5. This chapter draws from the many prime-time television dramas in the United States that either revolved around themes of terrorism or the War on Terror or included a few episodes on these themes, particularly *24* and *Sleeper Cell*.
6. See, for example, Naber, "Ambiguous Insiders," and Samhan, "Not Quite White."
7. See Shohat, "Gender and the Culture of Empire."
8. For more on racial casting during the War on Terror, see Rana, "When Pakistanis Became Middle Eastern."
9. *Threat Matrix*, ABC, Sept. 18, 2003–Jan. 29, 2004; *24*, FOX, season 6, Jan. 14–May 21, 2007.
10. Waleed Mahdi argues that Islam is portrayed as inspiring U.S. patriotism in Hollywood films after 9/11, for example, in the film *Traitor* (2008).
11. For an analysis of this episode and representations of Arab Americans as victims of post-9/11 hate crimes on television dramas, see Alsultany, "The Prime-Time Plight of Arab-Muslim-Americans after 9/11."
12. For more on the history of representations of Arabs, see Shaheen, *Reel Bad Arabs.*

13. My use of "cultural capital" comes from Bourdieu, *The Field of Cultural Production*.

14. Even recent films with positive representation of Arabs and Muslim characters, such as *The Visitor* (2007) and *Sorry, Haters* (2005), are framed in the context of 9/11. *Little Mosque on the Prairie* (2007–12), a sitcom on the Canadian Broadcasting Corporation, has not crossed over into the United States.

15. For a summary of government initiatives, see Cainkar, *Homeland Insecurity,* and Bakalian and Bozorgmehr, *Backlash 9/11,* 253–65.

16. For more on the significance of how the news media portrays Arab violence as terrorism through framing sympathy, violence, and context, see the documentary *Peace, Propaganda, and the Promised Land: U.S. Media and the Israeli-Palestinian Conflict*.

17. The term "imagined communities" originates with Anderson, *Imagined Communities*.

18. My use of "interpellation" comes from Althusser, *Lenin and Philosophy and Other Essays,* 85–126.

19. For an examination of minority self-representation, see, for example, Fregoso, *The Bronze Screen;* Noriega, *Shot in America;* See, *The Decolonized Eye;* and Feng, *Identities in Motion*.

WORKS CITED

<http://news.bbc.co.uk/2/hi/entertainment/6280315.stm>.

"Al-Fatiha." *Sleeper Cell*. Showtime. 4 Dec. 2005. Television.

Alsultany, Evelyn. "The Prime-Time Plight of Arab-Muslim-Americans after 9/11: Configurations of Race and Nation in TV Dramas." *Race and Arab Americans before and after 9/11: From Invisible Citizens to Visible Subjects*. Ed. Amaney Jamal and Nadine Naber. Syracuse, NY: Syracuse University Press, 2007. 204–28. Print.

———. "Selling American Diversity and Muslim American Identity through Non-profit Advertising Post-9/11." *American Quarterly* 59.3 (2007): 593–622. Print.

Althusser, Louis. *Lenin and Philosophy and Other Essays*. New York: Monthly Review Press, 2001. Print.

American-Arab Anti-Discrimination Committee. "Report on Hate Crimes and Discrimination against Arab Americans: The Post-September 11 Backlash." Washington, DC: American-Arab Anti-Discrimination Committee Research Institute, 2003.

Anderson, Benedict. *Imagined Communities: Reflections on the Origin and Spread of Nationalism*. New York: Verso, 1983. Print.

Andrejevic, Mark. "Watching Television without Pity: The Productivity of Online Fans." *Television and New Media* 9 (2008): 24–46. Print.

Bakalian, Anny, and Mehdi Bozorgmehr. *Backlash 9/11: Middle Eastern and Muslim Americans Respond*. Berkeley: University of California Press, 2009. Print.

Bonilla-Silva, Eduardo. *Racism without Racists: Color-Blind Racism and the Persistence of Racial Inequality in the United States.* 2nd ed. New York: Rowman and Littlefield, 2006. Print.

Bourdieu, Pierre. The Field of Cultural Production. New York: Columbia University Press, 1993. Print.

Cainkar, Louise. *Homeland Insecurity: The Arab American and Muslim American Experience after 9/11.* New York: Russell Sage Foundation, 2009. Print.

"Camels on Hand to Celebrate Premier of 'Little Mosque on the Prairie.'" *Yahoo! News.* 4 Jan. 2007. Web. 28 Jan. 2008. <http://ca.news.yahoo.com/s/capress/070104/entertainment/tv_little_mosque>.

"Day 4: 7pm–8pm." *24.* Fox. 14 Mar. 2005. Television.

Feng, Peter X. *Identities in Motion: Asian American Film and Video.* Durham, NC: Duke University Press, 2002. Print.

"Fox TV Accused of Stereotyping American Muslims." *Free Republic.* 13 Jan. 2005. Web. 16 May 2011. <http://www.freerepublic.com/focus/f-news/1320357/posts>.

Fregoso, Rosa Linda. *The Bronze Screen: Chicana and Chicano Film Culture.* Minneapolis: University of Minnesota Press, 1993. Print.

Gray, Herman S. *Cultural Moves.* Berkeley: University of California Press, 2005. Print.

———. *Watching Race: Television and the Struggle for Blackness.* Minneapolis: University of Minnesota Press, 1995. Print.

Hall, Stuart. "New Ethnicities." *Stuart Hall: Critical Dialogues in Cultural Studies.* Ed. David Morley and Kuan-Hsing Chen. New York: Routledge, 1996. 442–51. Print.

———. "Racist Ideologies and the Media." *Media Studies: A Reader.* 2nd ed. Ed. Paul Marris and Sue Thornham. New York: NYU Press, 2000. 271–82. Print.

———. "What Is This 'Black' in Black Popular Culture?" *Black Popular Culture.* Ed. Gina Dent. Seattle: Bay Press, 1992. 21–33. Print.

"Help Wanted." *Aliens in America.* CW. 29 Oct. 2007. Television.

Howard, Douglas L. "'You're Going to Tell Me Everything You Know': Torture and Morality in FOX's *24.*" *Reading 24: TV against the Clock.* Ed. Steven Peacock. New York: I. B. Tauris, 2007. 120–48. Print.

"Inter Arma Silent Leges." *The Practice.* ABC. 9 Dec. 2001. Television.

Intini, John. "Little Mosque on the Prairie: Recreate Small-Town Canada, Then Add Muslims—For Laughs." *Macleans.ca.* 11 Dec. 2006. Web. 24 July 2008. <http://www.macleans.ca/article.jsp?content=20061211_137752_137752>.

Mahdi, Waleed. "US vs. Arab/Muslim Trauma Unpacked: An Analysis of the Challenging Mode of Depiction in *Traitor.*" Paper presented at the annual conference of the Middle East Studies Association. Boston, MA. 2009.

Mamdani, Mahmood. *Good Muslim, Bad Muslim: America, the Cold War, and the Roots of Terror.* New York: Pantheon, 2004. Print.

McAlister, Melani. *Epic Encounters: Culture, Media, and U.S. Interests in the Middle East, 1945–2000.* Berkeley: University of California Press, 2001. Print.

Melamed, Jodi. "The Spirit of Neoliberalism: From Racial Liberalism to Neoliberal Multiculturalism." *Social Text* 89 (2006): 1–24. Print.

Naber, Nadine. "Ambiguous Insiders: An Investigation of Arab American Invisibility." *Ethnic and Racial Studies* 23.1 (2000): 37–61. Print.

———. "Introduction: Arab Americans and U.S. Racial Formations." *Race and Arab Americans before and after 9/11: From Invisible Citizens to Visible Subjects.* Ed. Amaney Jamal and Nadine Naber. Syracuse, NY: Syracuse University Press, 2007. 1–45. Print.

———. "Look, Mohammed the Terrorist Is Coming! Cultural Racism, Nation-Base Racism, and the Intersectionality of Oppressions after 9/11." *Race and Arab Americans before and after 9/11: From Invisible Citizens to Visible Subjects.* Ed. Amaney Jamal and Nadine Naber. Syracuse, NY: Syracuse University Press, 2007. 276–304. Print.

Nacos, Brigitte L., and Oscar Torres-Reyna. *Fueling Our Fears.* Lanham, MD: Rowman and Littlefield, 2007. Print.

Noriega, Chon. *Shot in America: Television, the State, and the Rise of Chicano Cinema.* Minneapolis: University of Minnesota Press, 2000. Print.

Patrizio, Andy. "Aladdin: Special Edition." *IGN.com.* IGN Entertainment, 17 Sept. 2004. Web. 14 May 2011. <http://dvd.ign.com/articles/549/549036p1.html>.

Peace, Propaganda, and the Promised Land: U.S. Media and the Israeli-Palestinian Conflict. Dir. Sut Jhally and Bathsheba Ratzkoff. Media Education Foundation, 2003. DVD.

"Pilot." *Aliens in America.* CW. 1 Oct. 2007. Television.

"Pilot." *Whoopi.* NBC. 9 Sept. 2003. Television.

Rana, Junaid. "When Pakistanis Became Middle Eastern: Visualizing Racial Targets in the Global War on Terror." *Between the Middle East and the Americas: The Cultural Politics of Diaspora.* Ed. Evelyn Alsultany and Ella Shohat. Ann Arbor: University of Michigan Press, 2013. 176–92. Print.

Said, Edward. *Orientalism.* New York: Vintage, 1979. Print.

Samhan, Helen Hatab. "Not Quite White: Race Classification and the Arab-American Experience." *Arabs in America: Building a New Future.* Ed. Michael W. Suleiman. Philadelphia: Temple University Press, 1999. 209–26. Print.

"Scholar." *Sleeper Cell.* Showtime. 7 Dec. 2005. Television.

See, Sarita. *The Decolonized Eye: Filipino American Art and Performance.* Minneapolis: University of Minnesota Press, 2009. Print.

Shaheen, Jack G. *Reel Bad Arabs: How Hollywood Vilifies a People.* Northampton, MA: Interlink, 2001. Print.

Shohat, Ella. "Gender and the Culture of Empire." *Visions of the East: Orientalism in Film.* Ed. Gaylyn Studlar and Matthew Bernstein. New Brunswick, NJ: Rutgers University Press, 1997. 19–68. Print.

"Suspicion." *7th Heaven.* WB. 21 Jan. 2002. Television.

"24 Comes under Muslim Fire." *Northern Territory News* [Australia]. 19 Jan. 2007: 23. Print.

"24 under Fire from Muslim Groups." *BBC News.* 19 Jan. 2007. 16 May 2011. Web.

Winant, Howard. *The New Politics of Race: Globalism, Difference, Justice.* Minneapolis: University of Minnesota Press, 2004. Print.

7

Maybe Brown People Aren't So Scary If They're Funny

Audience Readings of Arabs and Muslims on Cable Television Comedies

DINA IBRAHIM

This chapter contrasts the perceptions and reactions of non-Arab and non-Muslim audiences to those of Arab and Muslim audiences regarding the portrayal of Arabs and Muslims in a variety of contemporary cable television programming. The results of two focus groups are compared and analyzed for emerging themes. Examples of Arab and Muslim characters were provided to the groups in the form of episodes and segments from contemporary shows, and questions guided the discussions about how images and characters are interpreted by these disparate audiences. The study was conducted in San Francisco. The Northern California Bay Area is known for its ethnic and religious diversity and has a substantial population of Arabs and Muslims.

The terms "Arab" and "Muslim" are not necessarily comparable, as not all Muslims are Arab, and not all Arabs are Muslim. Neither Arab nor Muslim is a race or a culture. An Arab is a person whose national origin can be traced to an Arabic-speaking country. A Muslim is a person who identifies as adhering to the faith of Islam. Despite their U.S. census classification as white, Arabs come from a wide spectrum of racial and ethnic backgrounds. They can be white, brown, black, or Asian, or a combination of races and ethnicities. "If not white, what color are Arabs? Some respondents tried to place themselves on a color chart, citing olive, brown, gray, or black" (Cainkar 65). Muslims exist in every color of the ethnicity rainbow, and they take great offense at color distinctions as being colorblind is part of the Islamic faith, and Muslims do not conform to American mainstream politics of color (Shryock). In a post-racial landscape, Muslims and Arabs personify the blurring lines between race and culture as the common thread that unites these diverse people is language and/or faith, not culture, race, or color. Over ten years after 9/11, it remains problematic to describe the persistent marginalization and demonization as the "Other" of Arabs and Muslims as well as those who are perceived to be Arab and Muslim (e.g., South Asian Sikhs and Hindus) as racism, since there is no "Muslim race" or "Arab race." If anything, these groups are perceived to be part of an invented, imagined race of brown, swarthy terrorists whose men have consistently been portrayed by television dramas as inherently violent and whose women are either overly sexualized or oppressed and passive (Pitcherit-Duthler and Yunis).

Arabs and Muslims have been maligned in Hollywood ever since the earliest silent movies of the 1920s. Jack Shaheen's prolific research on stereotypes of Arabs and Muslims in Hollywood and television documents movies and TV shows produced in the twentieth and twenty-first centuries that contained derogatory portrayals (2001, 2008). Shaheen summarizes these stereotypes as the three "Bs": billionaires, bombers, and belly dancers. For his book *The TV Arab,* he conducted numerous interviews with television executives who said that reducing Arabs to stereotypes was the easiest and simplest way of conveying characters to audiences. But in his more recent research, Shaheen focuses on movies, and while the film industry remains significantly influential and worthy of continual study, the contemporary cable television landscape is a largely unexplored territory of Arab and Muslim stereotypes. Paid subscription cable channels such as HBO and Showtime have not been rigorously analyzed for their portrayal of Arabs or Muslims, or, as James Ryan puts it, "Scary Brown People," beyond cursory analysis of cable dramas such as HBO's *Game of Thrones* and Showtime's *Sleeper Cell.* While research shows that the network television dramas *24* and *The Practice* reflect a post-racial view of Arabs and Muslims by portraying them either as terrorists struggling to assimilate into American culture (Halse) or as victims of regrettable yet necessary discrimination in a post-9/11 landscape where public safety prevails over civil and constitutional rights (Alsultany), cable comedy shows have yet to be examined. Most research on Arab and Muslim representations in mass media prioritizes the examination of content as opposed to the audience reception of that content. In that regard, this chapter represents a methodological and subject departure from most literature on Arabs and Muslims on TV.

Theoretical Foundation

The central principle of cultivation theory is that people learn a lot of what they know from television; thus, the theory serves as a cornerstone of television audience reception studies even in a new media ecosystem. Electronic media sources, which now include the Internet and social networks, are where we get the information that shapes our social realities. If we take news sources as an example, even with the increasing popularity of the Internet as a news source (61 percent of Americans report accessing their news online), TV news reaches 78 percent of the American people and is still the primary source of news for the American public (Purcell et al.). The same principle applies to entertainment programming; despite an increasing proportion of young people accessing their television shows for free online as opposed to actually watching a physical television screen and paying for cable subscription services, currently more Americans as a whole are watching television than getting their shows online (Vasquez). In this context, television is considered to be a relatively ubiquitous environment for learning in American culture whether the programming is accessed online or on TV.

Cultivation theory explains how television impacts individuals and their understanding of the world around them. George Gerbner and his colleagues argue that television content plays a significant role in shaping viewers' social realities through a process of cultivation. Central to the cultivation perspective is the principle that dominant mass media serve as cultural levelers, uniting audiences into a common mainstream of thought. Television has a powerful impact within that cultural process. In 1990, Morgan and Signorielli argued that television is the "most common and constant learning environment" for individuals in our culture today (13). In 2012, while the Internet continued to gain mass popularity as an entertainment distribution medium, and a source of news and information, network and cable television companies remained the primary content providers. The media landscape is experiencing rapid changes as the Internet provides unlimited opportunities for new and original content creation, as well as the ability to access international television programming. However, traditional television is still the most popular source of entertainment ("Nielsen Cross Platform Report").

George Gerbner has extensively documented and argued that television's influence on attitudes and values is rooted in its ability to mass-produce a coherent structure of images and messages for a diverse audience. In other words, television reinforces its own version of the status quo, sustaining (rather than altering) the perceptions of the viewers. After long-term, constant exposure to repetitive images that permeate the culture as a whole, a "media mainstream" is created. Upon examining the influence of television on the formation of values and attitudes among viewers, researchers have repeatedly found a strong correlation between exposure to television messages and viewers' perceptions of reality (Gerbner et al. 1980; Greenwald; Hawkins and Pingree).

Cultivation theorists also suggest that the level of television viewing can serve as an indicator of the medium's influence on viewer attitudes and beliefs about the real world. Studies have supported the notion that television viewing exerts a significant influence on young viewers. Potter and Chang (1990), for example, found that television has a substantial impact on attitude formation and construction of reality among middle school students. Cultivation theory illuminates how fictional narratives on television have been shown to play a significant role in shaping audiences' political views (Mutz and Nir). Other researchers who study how television affects viewers' values and attitudes find a robust connection between exposure to television messages and the audiences' perceptions of reality (Greenwald; Hawkins and Pingree).

Thus television in particular shapes how people from diverse ethnic backgrounds are portrayed and perceived by society, supplementing the images we receive from other sources of popular culture such as movies, video games, books, comics, and the Internet. By watching television programming, whether on a TV or a computer, an act that seems inherently passive as we stare at the screen, we are in fact actively creating and interpreting meaning from the stories we see and hear. As generations increasingly drift away from print media and consume more video content, the impressions they have about people and places are often constructed using information from television. Although scriptwriters create the narratives, they do not actually control what those stories mean to the audience. It is the viewers who actively create meaning, and that interpretation can vary widely depending on their individual backgrounds (Hall).

Method

Two focus groups were conducted in June 2011 with men and women aged twenty to thirty-eight living in the San Francisco Bay Area. Subjects responded to flyers posted at local universities; recruiting e-mails were sent to student clubs, including Muslim and Arab student associations, and electronic flyers were distributed via local cultural centers. During the two-hour focus group meetings a set of predetermined questions was utilized, and respondents were also allowed to add topics of discussion. The participants in group 1 (G1) were Arab and/or Muslim, and those in group 2 (G2) were non-Arab, non-Muslims. All participants were American citizens.

There were nine participants in G1, who identified themselves as either Arab American or Muslim American. Among those nine, three were non-Arab American Muslims of South Asian origin, five were of Arab American Muslim origin, and one was an Arab American Christian. Of the nine participants in G1, seven were female and two were male. Group 2 consisted of ten participants; seven identified as Caucasian, two were Asian American, and one was African American. The religious affiliations of those in G2 were as follows: five were Christians, one was Jewish, and the other four participants listed "none" as their response to that questionnaire item. There were six men and four women in G2. The first seventy-five minutes of both focus groups were spent viewing "The Blind Date," episode 3 of the fourth season of *Curb Your Enthusiasm;* "Dearborn Again," episode 10 of the sixth season of *Weeds;* and two skits starring Aasif Mandvi of the *Daily Show with Jon Stewart,* "Allah in the Family" and "Tennessee No Evil."

After the viewing, responses from both focus groups were audio-taped, transcribed, and analyzed for patterns and trends. The focus group participants were asked to discuss their reactions to the shows, their impressions of the storyline, script, and characters related to Arabs and Muslims. Subjects were asked to think not only about these representations of Arabs and Islam and how they felt about them as manifested in these particular shows, but also in terms of their general television viewing and personal experiences.

The shows aired on HBO, Showtime, and Comedy Central respectively. Target demographics for all of the shows are primarily males aged eighteen to forty-nine. The comedy genre allows people who may think of themselves as post-racist to laugh at racist tropes because they find them funny in a way that either reinforces their own perceptions or is so contradictory to their reality that the comedy is recognized as ironic or satirical, absurd representation of harsh realities (Husband). The programs analyzed have received overwhelmingly positive critical acclaim by the television industry. *Curb Your Enthusiasm* won a Golden Globe and an Emmy. *Weeds* has won two Satellite Awards, a Golden Globe, an Emmy, and a Writers Guild of America award. *The Daily Show with Jon Stewart* is respected among television professionals and audiences, with sixteen Emmy Awards and two Peabody Awards. *The Daily Show* has become a prominent source of news and entertainment, and research indicates younger, college-age viewers "tune out" traditional news in favor of satirical news programming (Mindich).

Focus Group Responses
Curb Your Enthusiasm: "The Blind Date"
(Original Air Date: January 18, 2004)

Larry David sets up his blind friend Michael with a Muslim woman who wears the *niqab*, which is a full veil that covers her entire face except for her eyes. This is meant to be a fortuitous match, as the female character, Haboob, does not show her face; therefore, she would make a perfect date for a blind man. Haboob and Larry strike a friendship after she lets him in to her house to use her restroom. Haboob and Michael hit it off, but in the final scene of the episode, Larry *accidentally* pulls off her veil after fumbling with a faulty umbrella, and he is frightened and disgusted by her looks, which are not revealed on camera.

While both groups of study participants found Larry David funny as a character, the Arab American and Muslim group (G1) was by far more critical of the plot details of the *Curb Your Enthusiasm* episode than the non-Arab, non-Muslim group (G2). One participant from G1 pointed out that it is highly unlikely that a conservative Muslim woman wearing the *niqab* would ever let a man she had just met into her house. The participant stated, "There's no way a *monaqqaba* [a term used to describe a woman with a full face veil] would let a stranger inside her home to use the bathroom. And what's up with her name, Haboob, what is that? It's a made-up silly name that vaguely sounds Arabic but is really just jibberish."

Muslim and Arab participants pointed out the discrepancies of the plotlines and criticized the show for stretching fiction beyond what they perceived as reasonable limits. Even though these shows are works of fiction, participants stressed that the general public is not necessarily conscious of the nuances of Muslim American society beyond what it has already been conditioned to believe from movies and television dramas. Two G1 female participants were particularly concerned about the possibility that the general audience might think that all Muslim women are completely covered head to toe, and that this episode was a manifestation of that stereotype. They countered that women who wear the *niqab* are a minority among Muslims, and one participant said it did not really bother her that much that the face veil was an object of ridicule because she did not personally agree with that veiling method. She said, "It sucks that Muslim women happen to be the target of this episode, but hey, I'm not a fan of the *niqab* anyway as a Muslim, I mean, it's a personal choice, but it's more of a Saudi tradition than a religious requirement. I don't really care that it's being made fun of. I mean, yeah, it's ridiculous, but it's pretty funny." While there were dedicated fans of Larry David among the G1 participants, not everyone appreciated his brand of humor or his approach to women. The final scene was deemed particularly offensive when Larry and his friend Michael run away from Haboob after accidentally pulling off her veil. A participant observed, "Larry David is annoying. I just don't get his appeal. This episode just pisses me off. It's derogatory. At the end when they run off after seeing her face, that to me implies that she's covered up because she's ugly. That's just mean."

Participants in G2, the non-Muslims, were more likely to find the episode funny and contextualized the humor within the overall themes of the show. Larry David is offensive, they admitted, but he is equally insulting to Jewish stereotypes and Christian ones as well. No one was asked directly if they were regular viewers of the show *Curb Your Enthusiasm,* but the respondents in G2 seemed more comfortable and familiar with the format and humor than those in G1. One G2 participant said, "I can see how that would be totally offensive, but I just think it's hysterical. Larry David makes fun of his Jewishness all the time. His whole schtick is saying and doing things that are totally wrong. That's what makes the show funny." Another commented, "Larry David has done some pretty offensive episodes about Christianity too. Religion is great fodder for humor. It's like the more seriously people take this stuff, the funnier it gets."

There were moments in the episode when a non-Muslim participant felt that the show was trying to humanize veiled women. In her opinion, veiled women rarely have speaking roles on television, so even though the portrayal was problematic, it was a start:

> I think it's kinda sweet how Larry and Haboob strike a friendship and go out together in public to a restaurant. There's an underlying guilt about the stigma of wearing a veil and a lot of curiosity out there. On a weird level this character sort of outs veiled women, instead of being a voiceless, shapeless person you see them hanging out, eating together, and her expressing a desire to meet somebody special.

Another G2 participant expressed her dismay at the show's depiction of female characters, not only the Muslim or Arab ones. She lamented the poorly developed Jewish female characters on *Curb Your Enthusiasm* and drew attention to her interpretation of an overall trend of misogyny: "Larry David has a problem with his portrayal of women in general. Even the Jewish women on the show are shrill, pushy and generally unappealing. I'm not a huge fan." Participants in the non-Muslim group said *Curb Your Enthusiasm* was essentially a funny, albeit offensive, show. That point was not necessarily used to justify the negative stereotype of the veiled Muslim woman, which most if not all recognized as inappropriate, but to highlight the repeated use of stereotypes as a comedy mechanism throughout the show.

Weeds: "Dearborn Again" (Original Air Date: October 25, 2010)

The main character, Nancy Botwin, and her family are on the run from the police, so they decide to head to her childhood home in Dearborn,

Michigan, to buy fake passports to enable them to flee the country. They have drugs to sell to finance the passport purchase, and Nancy meets with an Arab club owner who buys drugs from her. Nancy's former brother-in-law, Andy, walks into a mosque during prayer in search of a Muslim who will sell him fake passports.

G1 participants tended to compare the episode's plot and characters to their own shared experiences of having traveled to Dearborn, Michigan, and personally interacted with the Arab American community there. Because of this personal experience, some participants were particularly disappointed with the show's fictionalized version of Arabs in America.

One asked, "Why do all the Arabs have weird accents? If you've actually been to Dearborn, you'd know that most Arabs there were born and raised there and sound totally American."

Another G1 participant expressed his admiration for the show; he admitted he was a regular viewer of *Weeds,* and even though he was unhappy with the mosque scene, he agreed with what some G2 participants said about the Arab club owner character, in terms of him being a departure from the typical stereotype: "I love this show. Yeah, ok, the Arab characters in this episode are mostly stereotypical—and I agree the mosque scene was a fail—but if you think about it, an Arab character that drinks and gets high is a refreshing change."

Most of the G1 group were not enthusiastic supporters of *Weeds,* and they had strong reactions against the Dearborn episode. One G1 participant was particularly frustrated after another participant said that at least the show's characters were different from other television depictions of Arabs. The participant stated, "I just want normal Arab and Muslim characters on TV shows. Is that too much to ask? If we're not terrorists plotting to blow up Americans, we're opportunistic shady drug dealers? Come on. That show sucks. I've never watched it and definitely won't start now."

Many of the comments from the non-Muslim group (G2) about the *Weeds* episode centered around the scene in which one of the characters walks into a mosque while people are praying and tries to ask if anyone knows where he can get a counterfeit passport. The group as a whole recognized that this act in itself was sacrilegious and offensive, but most of them were as entertained as they were horrified. Responses included "The mosque scene was awesome (laughs). He walks in with his yoga mat and tries to score a fake passport? So wrong. But I couldn't stop laughing," as well as, "I was groaning inside at the mosque scene. Awkward! Yes, it's horrible to assume that Muslims would have access to fake passports. But it's playing on what we already think of Muslims with the whole terrorism thing, especially the idea of the homegrown terrorist that's constantly pushed out there by right-wing crap like Fox News."

Another character in this *Weeds* episode who garnered significant attention from the G2 participants was an Arab drug dealer and nightclub owner. Several of the G2 participants commented on how, despite his shortcomings, this character was a clear departure from the depictions of Arabs that have become standard in television shows. One participant suggested that this character was closer to the reality of his own experience with members of the Arab community that he personally knows: "The club owner guy is kind of dumb. But at least he's not a terrorist, right? This show is about criminals and drug dealers, who probably exist in pretty much every ethnicity out there. I actually think the *Weeds* writers go beyond what we've been conditioned to expect from Arab characters on TV." He continued by saying, "OK, this is going to sound terrible, but I have Arab friends, and the guy who arranges the fake passports is more like regular Arabs than any other TV character I can think of. I mean, he's not religious, he obviously drinks and takes drugs and pretty much has nothing to do with religion."

On the other hand, the Arabs and Muslims in the G1 group were appalled by the mosque scene and were quick to point out the technical discrepancies within the scene, expressing indignation that the show's producers and writers had no knowledge of how Muslims actually pray. Cultivation theory works to shape audience's perceptions of the world around them, but those perceptions also intersect with personal experiences, and the difference between G1 and G2 was the level of personal connection to the material and the extent of cultural knowledge. G1 rejected the show's depiction of the mosque scene on the basis of cultural competency, while G2 "didn't know any better" and found the scene entertaining. A common G1 response, "Oh my God, the mosque scene was awful! First of all, they're not even praying correctly. Why don't they at least ask a Muslim person how they're supposed to do those scenes? The men are saying the wrong thing out of sequence."

The Daily Show with Jon Stewart: "Allah in the Family"
(Original Air Date: February 17, 2011)

Aasif Mandvi, a show "correspondent" (fake reporter) and, in this skit, an aspiring actor, stars in a pilot called "The Qu'osby Show," modeled after *The Cosby Show* but starring a Muslim family. The satirical skit is shot in the same style as *The Cosby Show* and raises the question of how Muslims can appeal to an American audience that is skeptical and suspicious of Muslims. In the lead-in to the pilot, Mandvi interviews a group of Americans who are not fans of Muslims or Islam, and they make suggestions about how the show should be done.

There was robust laughter among both groups during the Comedy Central skits starring Aasif Mandvi, an actor of South Asian Indian Muslim origin. The clips that were shown were played directly from Comedy Central's website and included an introductory skit by Jon Stewart. Participants from G2 were enthusiastic about the idea of watching a series like *The Cosby Show* that starred Muslim characters. Although not all the participants were familiar with *The Cosby Show* and its impact on race relations in the United States (Downing), they viewed the categorization of the "Other" as a distinction between urban and rural Americans; those who were exposed to diversity and others who were more insular in their personal experiences. Another show the participants were not likely to be familiar with was the Canadian comedy *Little Mosque on the Prairie,* which depicts a Muslim community trying to assimilate in rural Canada. One participant in the non-Muslim group (G2) stated:

> Actually, that would be a great idea, if that kind of show existed. I believe in the power of television to change our minds about minority groups in America. But it's going to be a tough sell for people like those white people who live in the middle of nowhere and aren't exposed to a multicultural side of the U.S. They are the ones who will always hate Muslims no matter what, and they are the same people who still hate black people, Mexicans, and Asians.

Most G2 participants reacted with praise for the use of comedy to break down barriers between Muslims and the rest of American society.

They recognized television's power to integrate immigrant communities and promote diversity, particularly with programming that appeals to a wide audience through the use of humor. This was the closest to a post-racial reading of comedy programming. However, G2 participants also acknowledged that the views expressed on *The Daily Show* are progressive and liberal and thus not representative of the entire American spectrum of political and social ideology. As one participant commented:

> That was an awesome spoof. The idea of using comedy to address bigotry is brilliant. This only goes to show that we want everybody to have the same shared American experience. There must be Muslims out there who are country music fans, right? I don't really remember watching *The Cosby Show*, but I know what it is and what it did to humanize the African American community to the rest of the country.

Other G2 participants were more cynical when it came to considering the idea of Muslims being generally as accepted as other ethnic groups. *The Cosby Show* depicted an African American family experiencing the trials and tribulations of raising children, dealing with issues that most Americans regardless of their color could relate to (Downing). But there was some doubt as to whether that level of identification could be achieved with a show starring Muslims, such as *All-American Muslim* on TLC:

> A lot of it is about outward appearance, you know? If folks look and talk like us, without an accent or a beard or a head cover, we tend to be more accepting. But what if the characters on that hypothetical show looked different? Would a network pick it up? Are we ready to fully accept Muslims and Arabs as "normal"? I don't know.

All of the G2 participants were avid fans of *The Daily Show* (target demographic, males aged eighteen to forty-nine) and commended its writers and producers for their inclusiveness and sharp, witty content. They were glad to see a Muslim comedian succeeding on television by making people laugh and exposing ugly stereotypes in a lighthearted, sarcastic context, thus exposing just how absurd those images are. "Too funny. I love how the writing refers to already existing stereotypes and has fun with them. Aasif Mandvi is hilarious. *The Daily Show* really scored big with him. A lot of other comedians have broken down the barrier with laughter, and I've seen him make fun of a lot of issues on the show. He's really good."

The Muslims and Arabs in G1 agreed that Mandvi was very funny, and there was no shortage of laughter among these participants when they watched the skit. However, the G1 group was far more critical of plot and writing details than the G2 group. The G1 participants were very proud of the fact that there is a prominent Muslim comedian as a primary correspondent on *The Daily Show* who gets significant airtime as current events frequently require a "Muslim perspective" (one that is expressed by a Muslim but likely manufactured by non-Muslim scriptwriters), but they acknowledged that as talented as he is, Mandvi is merely a performer and that the writing in the skit was borderline offensive.

> Pork juice? That's disgusting. The pilot show itself really wasn't that funny, but the segment leading up to it was great. I see what he's getting at, and it would be cool if there was a show on TV that starred Muslims as regular people, but this is obviously a caricature. I bet even if there was a show with Muslims, it would be just like this, a typical American's fantasy of what a Muslim is.

There was also general agreement among the G1 participants that there is a dire need for Muslim actors and comedians to break through to the general public to challenge and begin to eliminate stereotypes. Two G1 participants noted the impact that Mandvi had on changing popular perceptions of Muslims:

> I have so much respect for Aasif Mandvi and what he's trying to do for Muslims in the comedy world. Just the fact that he got those people to show their real prejudice against Muslims shows what kind of discrimination is out there and how bad we need Muslims to be represented on TV.

> Just the fact that he's bringing up Islamophobia in a pop culture context is huge. We do have a problem, and all joking aside, we need to do

something about it and be proactive like other ethnic groups have done, using music, TV, comedy, and film to get through to people.

Muslim and Arab depictions have evolved in cable television comedy programming such as *The Daily Show*; however, a G1 participant believes America is still not culturally aware enough to recognize the differences between a non-Arab (South Asian, for example) Muslim and a Muslim from an Arabic-speaking country. One G1 participant felt it was crucial to differentiate between South Asian Muslims and Arab Muslims, a distinction that most Americans may not make. Parallels were raised between the lack of knowledge and sophisticated understanding of African American and Hispanic subgroups:

> I wish he was Arab, but he's not Arab, and most Americans won't make that distinction. That's just too complicated, to try and distinguish between brown people. It's all the same. South Asian, Arab, whatever. It's all the "Middle East" even when it's not. OK, Aasif is Indian. But he's a funny Muslim, and we really need that right now.

The Daily Show with Jon Stewart: "Tennessee No Evil" (Original Air Date: August 25, 2010)

This segment aired during the controversy over building a Muslim community center in lower Manhattan near the World Trade Center site. Aasif Mandvi reported from Murfreesboro, Tennessee, where he interviewed Muslims and non-Muslims about public opposition to building an Islamic cultural center.

Participants in the G1 Arab and Muslim group seemed to appreciate the point that the skit was trying to make against bigotry, but a few of them thought the Aasif Mandvi had gone too far and made too much fun of Muslims. One of the G1 participants said, "I didn't appreciate the way he harassed the center's spokeswoman. I felt bad for her. The piece was kind of ruined by his ironic choice to adopt a fake terrorist attitude, pretending to be part of a sleeper cell, calling other terrorists on the phone, making fun of imams. Like the average American knows what an imam is." Overall, the G1 participants appreciated the skit, particularly the introductory material presented by Jon Stewart, in which he lampooned hysterical cable television coverage of the community center controversy. Another commented, "He basically admitted just how stupid and pointless it is to deny Muslims the right to build a mosque or a community center. I have mad respect for him and his writing team. They don't always get it right, but you can see that they're trying. This one was a gem. Comedy has come a long way, and *The Daily Show* is the most progressive one out there."

G1 participants felt that *The Daily Show* was an exception to the rule of TV shows that consistently degraded and vilified Arabs and Muslims. They recognized that the show was constantly trying to shed light on the hypocrisy of the media and politicians through the use of satire and irony:

> Community center of DEATH! (laughs) That whole issue was crazy. I'm glad it was dealt with that way by Comedy Central. I don't always like their humor, but their take on the mosque thing was admirable. They chose to stand up for the real American values of freedom of religion, when it is much easier to get more ratings by further insulting Muslims and Arabs and stereotyping them as terrorists, which is what most other comedians do.

A recognition and acknowledgment of the hegemonic influence of corporate media were common among participants in both groups, who did briefly bring up the commercial nature of television and its impact on the common use of stereotypes. Television is a business, and most audiences recognize that when they are prompted to think about the images they consume and grew up with. Many agreed that reducing ethnic groups to caricatures is a way of gaining popularity and garnering higher ratings. Participants in G2 also commended Jon Stewart for his emphasis on individual rights and freedom of worship:

> Stewart is right about this issue being one of personal freedom, and he's also right about not being able to please everybody. There will always be a certain number of people who are so upset about 9/11 and hate Islam and there will always be a group of Muslims who hate America. The majority are stuck dealing with the views of extremists, and that those views are the ones that make it on the news and on to cable news talk shows.

> There's a reason why *The Daily Show* is the best comedy news out there, and it has a lot to do with who they've chosen to contribute as correspondents. Stewart has done well with including a Middle Eastern guy and tackling issues from multiple perspectives.

Aasif Mandvi was well received by the non-Arab, non-Muslim group (G2), which found him entertaining and funny, and a welcome addition to *The Daily Show*. Participants in this group articulated a need for gifted Muslim comedians and actors who contribute more than just perpetuating stereotypes. As one of them elaborated:

> This guy [Mandvi] is really talented. I'm not aware of any other Muslim comedians, let alone anyone who's gone mainstream like on *The Daily Show*. I thought it was great how he confronted that lady who was telling him that Islam is basically a cult, and he's like, "You know I'm Muslim," and she goes, "Nobody's perfect." It's cool how he wears his faith on his sleeve openly, the way that Jon Stewart is open about being Jewish. It's really changing comedy and making it a whole lot more diverse.

Participants in both focus groups lived in either San Francisco or one of the many neighboring cities in the Northern California Bay Area, a diverse and cosmopolitan region of the United States. Races and religions of all kinds coexist in the Bay Area in a mostly peaceful manner, and there is a large Muslim population as well as a higher than average concentration of Asians. In general, inhabitants of the Bay Area pride themselves on their tolerance and acceptance of people with multicultural backgrounds. It is with this in mind that a few participants made it a point to set themselves apart from the prevalent mentality they perceive to exist in other regions of the United States, as this quotation from a G1 participant illustrates:

> It's scary that there are people out there who are so bigoted against Muslims. I guess it's hard not to be, given what we're exposed to in the media, and also what's been happening lately. But I really think it boils down to your personal experiences, and how open you really are to diversity. Here in the Bay Area, there are people from all races, faiths, and ethnicities,

and that's just the way it is. But out in Tennessee? That's some serious hick country.

Discussion

This research builds on the analyses of Arabs and Muslims on drama or crime-oriented television shows that consistently employ clichéd terrorist or potentially violent characters that fit the Bush era frame of "with us or against us." However, in the allegedly post-racial era of Barack Obama, discussions from these focus groups reveal an evolved level of cognizance of the stereotypes and a discernible discourse shift toward a less polarized and negative perception of Arabs and Muslims among an urban, West Coast audience. There is a proliferation of marginally more complex and nuanced portrayals of Arabs and Muslims on comedy programming, particularly on Jon Stewart's counterhegemonic political satire show. *The Daily Show* demonstrates a willingness to invite audiences to consider the irony of demonizing the "Other" and to be more open to considering different images of Arabs and Muslims. By placing a South Asian Muslim in a position of "correspondent," Aasif Mandvi is the face of *The Daily Show* satire that attempts to provide colorblind and post-racial interpretations of the evolved bigotry against Muslims in the United States after 9/11. G2 seems to buy into *The Daily Show*'s "abstract liberalism" frame (Bonilla-Silva), while G1 remains skeptical and rejects the naive contention that we are truly "over 9/11" and ready to fully embrace Arabs and Muslims as equals and nonthreatening members of American society.

The examples from *Curb Your Enthusiasm* and *Weeds* illustrate the continuation of gendered sexist representations of Muslim women and the reinforcement of Muslim Americans as sources of illegitimate behavior and conduct. This indicates that if we remove the intellectual political satire of Comedy Central from the equation, shows that perpetuate the ugly stereotypes of Arabs and Muslims that have prevailed throughout the history of American film and television continue to find ways to manifest their message that Arabs and Muslims are outliers, and their narratives are easier to digest when they are sugarcoated with comedy.

Both groups admitted that all the programming was intended to be funny; there was lots of laughter in both groups, but the G2 participants laughed harder and more frequently and were less analytical. They tended to enjoy the shows for the most part at face value. While the G1 laughed too, they were far more critical of details regarding plot and characters. Both groups agreed there were obvious problems with the portrayal of Arabs and Muslims, but G1 was more specific about how to fix them: for example, G1 participants recommended hiring consultants to ensure accurate portrayals. There is a sense among G2 participants that no input from Muslim and/or Arab communities was solicited by the shows' writers. However, there is no evidence that writers on any of these shows consult Arabs or Muslims. This is an important recommendation for future research.

Both groups thought *The Daily Show* was hilarious and strongly approved of Aasif Mandvi. G1 was particularly delighted that Mandvi was a prominent Muslim comedian who was not an Arab. The distinction between a non-Arab Muslim and an Arab Muslim was not clear to the non-Muslim, non-Arab G2 group. Groups such as non-Muslim South Asians or Arab Christians are invisible and lost in the wide sweep of the brown paint used to illustrate pictures of the "enemy" that was prevalent in the Bush era from 9/11 through the Iraq War and remains present in the Obama era.

The South Asian members of G1 said that the non-Arab diversity of Islam was rarely represented on television and that it was important for the American public to know that not all Muslims are Arab, and the majority of Muslims worldwide are non-Arab. The main differences in reception of content became more evident in discussions of the *Weeds* episode, which elicited more supportive responses from G2 than G1. Throughout the episode, the participants in G2 laughed much more openly than those in G1. Even though participants admitted it was funny, the scene in the mosque was deemed offensive by members of G1, who pointed out that the actors were reciting the wrong verses and the prayer scene was inaccurate.

There was significantly more cynicism from G1 and more optimism from G2 in terms of potentially positive developments like the presence of a prominent Muslim comedian on *The Daily Show*. G1 was far more defensive and quick to explain what was wrong with the content, while G2 knew that the content was probably offensive but was conditioned by the conventions of *The Daily Show* to expect and appreciate offensive humor that it also found funny when applied to parodies of other ethnicities and faiths. G2 also put the content within the larger context of other groups who are subjected to ridicule and stereotypes. The group equated Muslims with Jews and highlighted the fact that Jewish comedians make fun of Jews too, and Jewish women are not necessarily any better represented than Muslim women on television.

There is a clear need for further research on audience reception of television content. Examining content is illuminating, but it is only one part of the bigger picture of how that content shapes audience perceptions and attitudes toward a post-racial society. Investigating how audiences interpret the content provides for a more in-depth qualitative analysis of how images are perceived and contextualized within a larger framework of how we view and value diversity in media production and consumption. There are also several questions regarding the writing process that remain unanswered in light of the lack of research involving primary interviews with show content producers and show writers. At the time the focus groups were conducted, the show *All-American Muslim* on TLC was not yet on the air. The program premiered in November 2011 and featured the regular lives of several Muslim families in Dearborn, Michigan. The desire expressed by one of the Arab, Muslim G1 participants for a show that highlighted normal lives of American Muslims, without references to terrorism or drug dealing, seems to be on its way to being fulfilled. This may provide the illusion of optimism that the future of Muslim and Arab communities on television may be closer to an accurate depiction; however, that is not necessarily the case. The show did not receive high ratings partially because it portrayed no sensationalist conflict, and thus it did not live up to audience expectations regarding storylines about Muslims in America. The show was mired in conflict after major advertisers withdrew their funding following viewer complaints that it was promoting Islam as a normal religion (Chen). The controversy and spirited online debate that ensued between supporters and opponents of *All-American Muslim* illustrate the polarization in American society between the post-racial, colorblind discourse of civil rights advocates who thought the advertising boycott was outrageous and the persistent marginalization and vilification of Muslims who protested the very notion that Muslim Americans could be "just like us." This case study, which begs to be analyzed in a more structured manner in future research, illustrates that America has yet to become and may never attain the status of a truly post-racial society.

WORKS CITED

Alsultany, Evelyn. "The Prime-Time Plight of the Arab Muslim American after 9/11: Configurations of Race and Nation in TV Dramas." *Race and Arab Americans before and after 9/11*. Ed. Amaney Jamal and Nadine Naber. Syracuse, NY: Syracuse University Press, 2008. 204–28. Print.

Bonilla-Silva, Eduardo. *White Supremacy and Racism in the Post–Civil Rights Era*. London: Lynne Rienner, 2001. Print.

Cainkar, Louise. "Thinking outside the Box: Arabs and Race in the United States." *Race and Arab Americans before and after 9/11*. Ed. Amaney Jamal and Nadine Naber. Syracuse, NY: Syracuse University Press, 2008. 46–80. Print.

Chen, Michelle. "Lowe's *All-American Muslim* Fiasco and the Politics of Normalcy." *Huffingtonpost.com*. 25 Dec. 2011. Web. 22 Jan. 2012.

Dolliver, Mark. "A Split Verdict on Post-Racial." *Adweek* 50.5 (2009): 15. Print.

Downing, Jon H. "*The Cosby Show* and American Racial Discourse." *Discourse and Discrimination*. Ed. Teun Van Dijk and Geneva Smitharman. Detroit: Wayne State University Press, 1988. 46–73. Print.

Gerbner, George, L. Gross, M. Morgan, and N. Signorielli. "The 'Mainstreaming' of America: Violence Profile #11." *Journal of Communication* 30.3 (1980): 10–29. Print.

———. "Growing Up with Television: The Cultivation Perspective." *Media Effects: Advances in Theory and Research*. Ed. J. Bryant and D. Zillmann. Hillsdale, NJ: Erlbaum, 1994. 17–41. Print.

Gerbner, G., L. Gross, M. Morgan, N. Signorielli, and J. Shanahan. "Growing Up with Television: Cultivation Processes." *Media Effects: Advances in Theory and Research*. 2nd ed. Ed. J. Bryant and D. Zillmann. Mahwah, NJ: Erlbaum, 2002. 43–68. Print.

Gerbner, George, L. Gross, N. Signorielli, M. Morgan, and M. Jackson-Beeck. "The Demonstration of Power: Violence Profile no. 10." *Journal of Communication* 29.3 (1979): 177–96. Print.

Greenwald, Anthony. *Cognitive Learning: Psychological Foundations of Attitudes*. New York: Academic Press, 1968. Print.

Hall, Stuart. "What Is This 'Black' in Black Popular Culture?" *Stuart Hall: Critical Dialogues in Cultural Studies*. Ed. D. Morley and K.-H. Chen. New York: Routledge, 1996. 465–75. Print.

Halse, Rolf. "The Muslim-American Neighbour as Terrorist: The Representation of a Muslim Family in *24*." *Reconstruction: Studies in Contemporary Culture* 11.4 (2011): Web. 20 Jan. 2012.

Hawkins, Robert, and Suzanne Pingree. "Some Processes in the Cultivation Effect." *Communication Research* 7.2 (1980): 193–226. Print.

Husband, Charles, ed. *White Media, Black Britain*. London: Hutchinson, 1975. Print.

Mindich, David. *Tuned Out: Why Americans under 40 Don't Follow the News*. New York: Oxford University Press, 2005. Print.

Morgan, Michael, and Nancy Signorielli. "Cultivation Analysis: Conceptualization and Methodology." *Cultivation Analysis: New Directions in Media Effects Research.* Ed. N. Signorielli and M. Morgan. Newbury Park, CA: Sage, 1990. 13–34. Print.

Morley, David. *Family Television: Cultural Power and Domestic Leisure.* London: Comedia, 1986. Print.

Mutz, Diana C., and Lilach Nir. "Not Necessarily the News: Does Fictional Television Influence Real-World Policy Preferences?" *Mass Communication and Society* 13.2 (2010): 196–217. Print.

"Nielsen Cross Platform Report: Americans Watching More TV, Mobile and Web Video." *Blog.nielsen.com.* 15 June 2011. Web. 21 Jan. 2012.

Picherit-Duthler, Gaelle, and Alia Yunis. "Tramps vs. Sweethearts: Changing Images of Arab and American Women in Hollywood." *Middle East Journal of Culture and Communication* 4.2 (2011): 225–43. Print.

Potter, W. James, and Ik Chang. "Television Exposure Measures and the Cultivation Hypothesis." *Journal of Broadcasting and Electronic Media* 34.3 (1990): 313–33. Print.

Purcell, Kristen, et al. "Understanding the Participatory News Consumer: How Internet and Cell Phone Users Have Turned News into Social Experience." Pew Internet and American Life Project. Web. 2010.

Reddy, Mrinalini. "TV Muslims Get a Much-Needed Makeover." *News21.com.* 24 Aug. 2007. Web. 22 Jan. 2012.

Ryan, James B. "Does HBO's 'Game of Thrones' Have a Race Problem?" *Nerve.com.* 18 Apr. 2011 Web. 3 Dec. 2011.

Shaheen, Jack G. *Guilty: Hollywood's Verdict on Arabs after 9/11.* Northampton, MA: Olive Branch Press, 2008. Print.

———. *Reel Bad Arabs: How Hollywood Vilifies a People.* Northampton, MA: Olive Branch Press, 2001. Print.

———. *The TV Arab.* Bowling Green, OH: Bowling Green State University Press, 1984. Print.

Shryock, Andrew. "The Moral Analogies of Race: Arab-American Identity, Color, Politics, and the Limits of Racialized Citizenship." *Race and Arab Americans before and after 9/11.* Ed. Amaney Jamal and Nadine Naber. Syracuse, NY: Syracuse University Press, 2008. 81–113. Print.

Temple, Christel. "Communicating Race and Culture in the Twenty-First Century: Discourse and the Post-Racial/Post-Cultural Challenge." *Journal of Multicultural Discourses* 5.1 (2010): 45–63. Print.

Vasquez, Diego. "Assessing the Promise of Connected TV." *Medialifemagazine.com.* 30 Nov. 2010. Web. 29 Nov. 2011.

PART III

Reinscribing Whiteness

8

"Some People Just Hide in Plain Sight"

Historicizing Racism in Mad Men

SARAH NILSEN

Mad Men, the critically acclaimed AMC television series, created and produced by Matthew Weiner, has since its premiere on July 19, 2007, received widespread praise for its historical verisimilitude and "truth" about America in the 1960s. The show's creators utilize a fictional Madison Avenue advertising agency, Sterling Cooper, as the prism through which to appraise and evaluate retrospectively the United States at the cusp of a period of radical social and political transformations that would ultimately have lasting impact on American society today. *Mad Men* has garnered fifteen Emmys and four Golden Globes and is the first cable series to win an Emmy Award for Outstanding Drama Series, an award it has won for each of its first four seasons.

A part of the show's appeal can be explained in terms of a sentimental nostalgia for an era of uncontested white privilege, where the mechanisms of this power and privilege, in the form of either qualities of character (masculine power, feminine ingenue) or social status (white and wealthy)—and often illegitimately obtained (as in the case of Don Draper)—are the cause of much of the characters' semitragic flaws and dissatisfaction. The main characters seem to be battling constantly against a backdrop of social forces that will have a determinate effect on their future successes and failures. Much of the critical writing about the show focuses on the major discursive debates regarding social identity that defined the political battleground of the period: questions about race, gender, and sexuality. Notably, the most famous events of the modern civil rights movement serve as a narrative anchor throughout the first five seasons. This chapter analyzes the underlying racial discourse that serves as a part of the backdrop for the narrative action in *Mad Men*. Well-known and emblematic moments in the civil rights movement become one of the social forces that intersect with the action line in the narrative to provide a semblance of historical veracity that is recognizable and palatable to its audience. The representation of racism and the civil rights movement is presented in a way that denies audiences empathetic identification with these events, thus disassociating them from other social movements and the identity politics of the time. Furthermore, a politically correct mode of racial representation works to allay the anxieties of the predominantly white, liberal, and wealthy audience for *Mad Men,* offering viewers a "new race parable" that is not about the black struggle for civil rights and equal treatment, but as Richard Corliss writes, instead offers "fables of reassurance for white folk" that make "your parents" into the heroes who "dared to be tolerant."

Consistent with the current racial discourse in America, following the election of our first black president, *Mad Men,* despite being set in the sixties, imagines our nation as post-racial and having obtained the inevitable goals of the civil rights movement. As a major turning point in American race relations, the civil rights movement has served as a marker against which contemporary race relations and racial progress are judged. The history of the civil rights movement has become fully incorporated in the dominant racial narrative of today, in which a group of exceptional black male leaders, emblemized by Martin Luther King Jr., were able to eradicate the social and political injustices perpetrated by a virulently racist South during the middle of the twentieth century. This 'master narrative' has become so widely accepted and codified that it "prevents one of the most remarkable mass movements in American history from speaking effectively to the challenges of our times" (Hall 1234). Television has been a major discursive agent in securing and normalizing this dominant narrative, and *Mad Men* illustrates how, as Herman Gray has argued, "within the American discourse of race, the civil rights subject performs important cultural work since it helps construct the mythic terms through which many Americans can believe that our nation has transcended racism" (356).

The Dominant Narrative of the Civil Rights Movement

Popular media has played an important role in the writing of the widely accepted and dominant narrative of the civil rights movement. Media scholars have documented how television was a crucial medium for garnering national support for civil rights during the early years of the movement. Much of this coverage was sympathetic and constructed racism as a local, southern issue perpetuated by a select group of white, ignorant bigots. These widely circulated images of the early years of the civil rights movement served to establish the major archive of the movement that would provide the iconographic images for documentaries and museums on the history of civil rights. The national media coverage shifted radically in the mid-1960s with the emergence of the Black Power movements and black uprisings in the urban North. The passage of the Civil Rights Act of 1964 and the Voting Rights Act of 1965 marked for many whites the end of the movement, with the popular struggles of the seventies then seen as elitist battles over identity politics. The emergence of the New Right, following the election of Ronald Reagan, led to the rewriting of this narrative by insisting on colorblindness as central to the goals of the movement. By ignoring the main and original demands of the movement for the systemic dismantling of structural inequality, they reduced the complexity and dynamism of the movement to a central objective: "color blindness—defined as the elimination of racial classifications and the establishment of formal equality before the law" (Hall 1237). Within this narrative, racism became defined as an individual act perpetuated by an isolated bigot, typically from the South. Institutionalized racism, it was argued, had been remedied by the courts, and any racial inequalities that persisted were the product of individual social failings rather than systemic failures within the social structure.

The Reagan era ushered in a full-scale attack on and dismantling of the social programs implemented during the Johnson administration that had been created to remedy past racial inequities, including affirmative action and desegregation. At this same time, Martin Luther King Jr. became lionized as the iconic image of the modern civil rights movement. On November 2, 1983, after many failed attempts to establish a holiday honoring King, President Reagan was finally persuaded to sign the national holiday into the law. In his speech at the signing of the bill he stated that "Dr. King had awakened something strong and true, a sense that true justice must be colorblind." The destiny of black Americans, he explained, "is tied up with our destiny, and their freedom is inextricably bound to our freedom; we cannot walk alone." He directly discussed the impact of the passage of the civil rights legislation of the 1960s, arguing that, "most important, there was not just a change of law; there was a change of heart. The conscience of America had been touched. Across the land, people had begun to treat each other not as blacks and whites, but as fellow Americans" (Reagan 1529). Martin Luther King's "I Have a Dream" speech became central to establishing in popular memory the idea that the civil rights movement was colorblind in its goals. King's dream that all "children will one day live in a nation where they will not be judged by the color of their skin but by the content of their character" became a central tenet of the national civil rights narrative. According to colorblind neoconservatives, the original purpose of the civil rights laws was to prevent isolated acts of wrongdoing against individuals, not to redress present, institutionalized manifestations of historical injustices against blacks as a group (Hall 1238). Republican administrations were central to the establishment of civil rights memorials, including Ronald Reagan's creation of the Martin Luther King Jr. national holiday in 1983, and George W. Bush's involvement in the Martin Luther King Jr. memorial in Washington, DC, and the establishment of the National Museum of African American Art and Culture in 2003. As Jacquelyn Hall has argued, the civil rights movement circulates through American memory in "forms and channels that are at once powerful, dangerous and hotly contested" (1233). And this remembrance is always a "form of forgetting, and the dominant narrative of the civil rights movement . . . distorts and suppresses as much as it reveals" (Hall 1233).

The media has played a central role in representing the history of the civil rights movement and in the process has significantly shaped the popular memory of these events. These narratives, typically created by white producers, rely heavily on the same characters and narrative tropes to present an image of this period that is consistent with the colorblind rhetoric of the New Right. Virulent forms of racism and the struggles of the civil rights movement are confined to the rural South.

Typically the main characters are white men who overcame their racism through the intercession of noble black people (e.g., *The Crisis at Central High*, CBS, 1981; *Heart of Dixie*, 1989; *The Long Walk Home*, 1990; *I'll Fly Away*, NBC, 1991–93), or would operate as heroes of the civil rights movement who fight against uneducated, poor whites on behalf of helpless, black victims (e.g., *Mississippi Burning*, 1988; *Ghosts of Mississippi*, 1996), or are colorblind innocents thrown into a racist society (e.g., *Forrest Gump*, 1994; *American Dreams*, NBC, 2002–5) (Perlman 211). These narratives of the civil rights movement have persisted during the presidency of Barack Obama, and their continued popularity was evident in the awarding of the 2012 Academy Award for Best Supporting Actress to Octavia Spencer for her portrayal of a black domestic in the film *The Help*, which was also nominated for Best Picture, Best Actress (Viola Davis), and another Best Supporting Actress (Jessica Chastain). *The Help*, like *Mad Men*, focuses on the civil rights movement in the early 1960s in order to reinscribe its dominant narrative that constructs the current post-racial moment in contemporary race relations in the United States as the successful realization of the movement's goals. These films and television shows function to make white audiences experience the civil rights movement as a remnant of a regressive and violent past that no longer exists. They also appease white guilt and anxiety about current racial and social injustices by drawing on the American ideals of fairness and justice in the resolution of racial inequities.

Mad Men: The Television Series

The series *Mad Men* was created by and is produced by Matthew Weiner. In 2000, while working as a staff writer for the Ted Danson sitcom *Becker*, Weiner wrote a spec script for the pilot episode of *Mad Men*. David Chase, the producer of the HBO series *The Sopranos*, offered Weiner a writing position on *The Sopranos* after reading the spec script in 2002. "It was what you're always hoping to see," Chase recalled. "It was lively and it had something new to say. Here was someone who had written a story about advertising in the 1960s, and was looking at recent American history through that prism" (Steinberg). After *The Sopranos* went off the air, Weiner submitted his pilot for *Mad Men* to HBO, but the network executives not only turned down *Mad*

Men but never responded to Weiner's proposal. AMC gladly picked up the series as it was seeking out "quality programming" like *The Sopranos* that could compete with the other cable networks such as HBO, which had gained both prestige and audience viewership with shows such as *The Sopranos, Six Feet Under,* and *The Wire.* "The network was looking for distinction in launching its first original series," according to AMC Networks president Ed Carroll, "and we took a bet that quality would win out over formulaic mass appeal" (Witchel).[1]

Quality Television and Historical Verisimilitude

Much of the critical writing on *Mad Men* has noted the exceptional historical accuracy of the series, and in interviews Weiner frequently discusses his obsessive control over period details in the show. As Weiner explained in a *New Yorker* blog, "I deal with history in a realistic way and say, how do human beings experience history?" (Byock). The press makes frequent mention of the volumes of historical research that Weiner and his team of writers have accumulated in their drive to make most aspects of the series historically accurate. This emphasis on historical truth legitimates the behaviors of the characters in the narrative as authentic and correct for the time. It also brings to the series a sense of historical significance and "quality" that draws in an upscale white, liberal demographic. The audience for *Mad Men* occupies a very similar demographic to that of its creator, Matthew Weiner.[2]

Unlike much television writing, which tends to focus on the stars of a series, Weiner is the public face of *Mad Men.* He is continually celebrated and lauded as the authorial voice behind the series whose artistic control and vision place him in the role of an auteur. As the creator and showrunner for *Mad Men,* Weiner wrote the original pilot, he writes every episode (along with four other writers), is the executive producer, and approves every actor, costume, hairstyle, and prop. Weiner admits, "I do not feel any guilt about saying the show comes from my mind and that I'm a control freak. I love to be surrounded by perfectionists, and part of the problem with perfectionism is that by nature, you're always failing" (Witchel). He considers all the main characters in the series to be reflections of him. "There's no doppelganger there," he says. "I'm a mixture of Roger, Peggy, Don, Pete, Joan, Betty. . . . *Mad Men* is a constructed world for me to talk about how I feel about the world, for me to talk about my family, talk about my parents, talk about my fantasies, see my wish fulfillments, trash my enemies, vanquish my fears" (Konigsberg). A large part of the series' popularity results from Weiner's ability to cinematically capture for his audience the same level of personal experiential identification with his main characters that he enjoys.

Mad Men delivers for its advertisers a much desired audience demographic. In 2010, *Mad Men* viewers were one of the wealthiest audiences for all of television, with nearly half making more than $100,000 annually. This wealthy, white, and progressive audience has proved a marketing juggernaut, with licensed merchandise being sold at both Banana Republic and Brooks Brothers. The elite historical and cultural knowledge that Weiner brings to the production of *Mad Men* explains its appeal to a very specific audience demographic. Even though the show averaged far fewer viewers than other cable dramas like USA's *Burn Notice,* AMC fully endorses marquee shows such as *Mad Men* because they boost the network's "visibility, image and value" ("Cable Shows"). The widespread and extensive media coverage of the series is especially prevalent in the liberal media outlets that share a similar upper-class, highly educated audience demographic. The *New York Times* provides continual coverage of the show, frequently lauding its style and design along with its social significance. As Benjamin Schwarz reported in the *Atlantic,* "*Mad Men*'s affluent, with-it target audience are particularly susceptible to liking what *The New York Times*' Art and Styles sections tell them to like with thirty plus articles in two years alone." *Rolling Stone* has published several pieces on Weiner, including a special fashion issue with the show's stars. Weiner has also been interviewed on *Charlie Rose* and has appeared three times on Terry Gross's NPR show, *Fresh Air,* including a special show the day after the season 5 premiere.

Much of the prestige of the show depends on the audiences' historical knowledge, which provides moments of cultural awareness and recognition. The quality aspects of the series depend on this sense of a shared historical and cultural understanding. Since the majority of the audience are adults between nineteen and forty-nine, most of the show's fans are either younger adults, "to whom its world represents an alluring historical fantasy of a time before the present era's seemingly endless prohibition against pleasures once taken for granted; or younger baby boomers—people in their forties and early fifties who remember, barely, the show's 1960s setting, attitudes, and look. For either audience, then, the show's style is, essentially, symbolic: it represents fantasies, or memories, of significant potency" (Mendelsohn). The writers are so aware of audiences' investment in the pleasure of shared historical knowledge and cultural capital that they have intentionally written in misinformation that the audience can catch and discuss online.[3]

"Prosthetic Memories" in *Mad Men*

The dominant narrative line in *Mad Men* focuses on the personal and professional lives of the major characters within a Madison Avenue advertising agency. This narrative line is predominantly melodramatic, relying on the conventions of the soap opera, and centers on the interpersonal relationships between the main characters, Don, Roger, Peggy, Joan, and Pete, who are the primary sources of identification for the audience. As original characters whose history is unknown to the audience, narrative pleasure for the audience is provided through the unraveling of the enigma of these characters' lives. Because of the explicit historical time line that forms the show's backdrop, we know that these characters' lives will progress and be transformed by the turbulent cultural and social events of the period, and that these characters' options and choices are many and politically salient. We literally are invested in the growth and advancement of each of these character's lives. Since our identification is fully sutured, through the use of narrative structure, shooting, and editing, with these fictional characters, we experience history at the personal level, creating experiential memories of this period for the viewers. Memory describes an "individual relation to the past, a bodily, physical relation to an actual experience that is significant enough to inform and color the subjectivity of the rememberer. History, on the other hand, is traditionally conceived as impersonal, the realm of public events that have occurred outside the archive of personal experience" (Burgoyne). In contemporary media culture, historical events are frequently filmed, framed, and narrated in such a way as to encourage subjective experiences of historical events.

Alison Landsberg has described the media's capacity to generate the memories of events that spectators have never experienced as "prosthetic memories because they are not the product of lived

experience, but are derived from engagement with a mediated representation . . . and like an artificial limb, they are actually worn on the body;
these are sensuous memories produced by an experience of mass-medi-
ated representations" (222). Landsberg argues that media, because of its
technological ability to develop identification for the spectator through
the cinematic techniques of shooting and editing, creates the formation
of a memory of historical events that, "because they feel real, they help
condition how a person thinks about the world and might be instrumental in articulating an ethical relation to the other" by forcing the
viewer to engage on a personal level with historical events that might
be uncomfortable or radically different from their own lived experiences (222). As mentioned previously, the significant cultural cachet
that *Mad Men* enjoys with the mainstream liberal press and its fans is
dependent on the emotional and affective "truth" of America's historical
past the show creates in its cinematic rendering of the sixties that audiences can inhabit through identification with the major characters. The
series' success in creating sympathetic prosthetic memories for its audience can be evidenced in the very popular online game applications
"MadMenYourself," which allows you to construct a *Mad Men* avatar
of yourself, and "Which Mad Men Are You?," which uses a question
format to identify which character is most like yourself. Both of these
games open with images of the dominant white characters, including
the major women characters and Sal, the gay character. The only way
in which you can occupy a racialized position in the world of *Mad Men*
is through the "Choose Your Skin Color" section of the "MadMenY-
ourself" game, and this position is not even imagined or rendered anywhere in the presentation of the games.

The primary narrative line of the show creates for its audience the
emotional certitude we associate with memory, thus forming a basis for
mediated collective identification with the period. The dual nature of the
Mad Men plot, though, creates an opposition between prosthetic memory and history, which punctuates the somatic, melodramatic narrative
through the replaying of familiar and authentic documentary footage of
selective historical events of national significance from the period. As
actual and universally known events from our national memory of the
period, the historical time line structures the major experiential and
subjective narrative line. This time line is heavily mediated and depends

on the replaying of previously recorded television and radio broadcasts that are widely known and familiar to the audience. Unlike films such as *Forrest Gump*, which morphs the figure of Forrest Gump into the archival material from the period, allowing viewers to inhabit through identification key historical events, in *Mad Men* audiences are denied the same level of experiential identification with these events, which remain peripheral and technologically removed from the action of the primary narrative. These recorded events are demarcated as remnants of our national historical record that have entered into the realm of objective, public history occurring outside personal experience and memory. The major characters in the dominant narrative of *Mad Men*, all of whom are white, have active agency in the direction of their lives, but the historical narrative time line is predetermined and devoid of the opportunity for change through either surprise or suspense. The civil rights movement is codified as popular history and is conscribed by the conventions of the movement's dominant narrative. Audience investment in the historical time line becomes one of cultural knowledge, not personal identification, and yet the understood social importance and emotional resonances of these events are used to further legitimate the actions of the major white characters in *Mad Men* as historically accurate and socially significant. The narrative of *Mad Men* therefore depends on actual recorded historical events from the civil rights movement in order to legitimate the personal pleasures and indulgences of white privilege that are manifested in the primary narrative line.

Though a large percentage of viewers (and all the major creators) of *Mad Men* never personally participated in or were even alive at the time of these events, viewers can identify with the sympathetic white characters Weiner has created because their struggle is defined by the dominant ideology of the American Dream and traditional middle-class values of work, material success, and heterosexual marriage. We identify with these characters because sympathetic identification, as Landsberg explains, "assumes similarity, a pre-existing connection between sympathizer and sympathizee. In sympathy, one shares the feelings of another person. And most notably, when one sympathizes with another, one focuses on oneself, on how she would feel in the other's situation" (223). As Tim Goodman noted in the *Hollywood Reporter*, "Along that march of time, *Mad Men* has always used the turbulent social and political changes [the civil rights movement] in America as a 'B' storyline. If *Mad Men* focused only on those themes, it would be a boring and predictable drama. Instead, by centering on [white] people experiencing the changes indirectly, it became a character drama—a tapestry of personalities with Draper at the core, his existential crises of identity and lack of meaning in his life the catalyst of the series." Television shows like *Mad Men*, through the televisual technology of memory formation, play a crucial role in creating and generating public spheres of memory that, as Landsberg claims, "ha[ve] the capacity to bring us into intellectual and emotional contact with circumstances that lie well beyond our own lived experiences, and in the process can force us to confront, and enter into a relationship of responsibility and commitment toward 'others'" (225). But these prosthetic memories can also, as I argue occurs in *Mad Men*, function to reinscribe positions of dominance that depend on not seeing racialized others as subjects of identification. As Herman Gray has written, contemporary television is "very much engaged in a kind of recuperative work, a kind of retrospective production of black subjects whose cultural labor—for liberals and conservatives alike—is the social and cultural revitalization of a high moment of American power" (356) in which racism, through the power of the civil rights movement, was transcended by our nation and its universal values of equality and justice.

Even though most of the plot action in *Mad Men* is centered on the interpersonal relationships between the dominant white characters, much of the popular critical praise of the show has been for its explicit portrayal of sexism and racism. The narrative does contain multiple dominant female characters (in particular Joan, Betty, and Peggy) who must continually negotiate the gender codes and mores of this fictionalized rendering of the sixties. We as viewers are continually exposed to and meant to experience through our sympathetic identification with these women the impact of the sexual harassment and gender bias they must endure in the workplace and at home. The narrative, though, contains no major black characters through whom we can experience the racial biases of the public or private realms; therefore, the acts of racism within the narrative are always experienced through the actions of the dominant white characters and usually consist of snide comments, and insensitivity to racial issues and differences. Racism is primarily used narratively to illustrate individual character flaws within the white characters that the audience is cued to recognize immediately and understand as a form of socially unacceptable and politically incorrect racial intolerance. Racism in *Mad Men* is never ugly or violent, and the "N" word is never spoken. The rhetoric of political correctness is maintained throughout, and acts of racism themselves are treated with the upmost politeness and critical distance. As audience members we are always placed in a position of condemnation and are never asked to experience the actual psychic toil and emotional impact of systemic racism on any of the individual characters' lives, especially that of the victims of the racism, who are never permitted to exhibit any anger or aggression in response. Racism, then, becomes a spoken or public enunciation that is manifested externally through the dominant white characters, is based in language rather than action, and is immediately condemned by the audience, thus implying both their understanding of racism and their own nonracist identity. The audience's primary emotional investment and identification are with the major white characters, and yet since we as spectators are constantly asked to make politically correct judgments about these characters' actions, the narrative encourages a sense of personal investment in progressive, racial awareness. But in actuality not only are we consistently denied sympathetic identification with the black characters, but also the audience is more significantly disallowed the more radical and ethically important position of empathetic identification with them. "The experience of empathy requires an act of imagination—one must leave oneself and attempt to imagine what it was like for that other person given what he or she went through. . . . Empathy takes work and is much harder to achieve than sympathy. In part, empathy is about developing compassion not for our family or friends or community, but for others—others who have no relation to us, who resemble us not all, whose circumstances lie far outside of our own experiences" (Landsberg 223).

When asked directly in an interview with Dave Itzkoff why there are no major black characters in *Mad Men*, no characters of any kind of racial minority, Weiner asked in response if "Jews count as racial minorities? Because there have been lots of Jews on the show." And in fact there are multiple Jewish characters in the series with whom we do have strong sympathetic identification, especially Don's psychologist girlfriend, Dr. Faye Miller. Weiner further explained the absence of black characters was because "that is the world they move in. It's like saying, well, you're telling a story about baseball, where's Jackie Robinson? I'm like, Jackie Robinson is Jackie Robinson because he was one person, and this story in not taking place in that other universe" (Itzkoff). Thus this intentional drawing of a color line between dominant white culture and minority black culture denies the continual and systematic way in which racism continues to perpetuate white privilege and significant social and racial inequities. The Mad Men in New York City in the midsixties, like most of the United States, inhabited a world immersed in unprecedented racial strife that generated significant national anxieties, fears, and animosity within the dominant culture about the changing racial landscape. This fear was particularly felt in New York City with the rise of the Black Power movement and the widespread media coverage of Malcolm X. His assassination in Harlem on February 21, 1965, received international attention, including front-page coverage by the *New York Times*, and yet this event garners only a one-line mention by Peggy in which she asks, "Did you know Malcolm X was shot last Sunday?" ("The Rejected"). Throughout the series, well-known and traumatic national events are inserted into the narrative in order to enhance the impact of the primary melodramatic narrative line. This one-line reference to Malcolm X's killing is immediately followed by Peggy learning the devastating news that Pete's wife, Trudy, is pregnant. The Harlem riot of 1964 erupted in July, resulting in 465 men and women being arrested, 500 injured, and 1 killed. This event was followed by Malcolm X's assassination on February 21, 1965. And in August 1965, while Don was visiting Disneyland with his family and soon-to-be wife in the finale of season 4 ("Tomorrowland"), the Watts riots exploded in Los Angeles leading to thirty-four deaths and $40 million in property damage. Consistent with the dominant narrative of the civil rights movement, these violent, racialized events that served as powerful indicators of the urgent need for systemic social and economic investment in African American communities in the North are removed from the show's civil rights time line. By constructing these events as occurring in "another universe," both the characters and the audience are positioned as external to and in no way implicated in the institutions of privilege and entitlement they inhabit.

The televisual world of *Mad Men* is inhabited by several singular African American characters whose narrative function is fundamentally to provide encounters that will enhance the character development of the dominant white characters. This is particularly true of the young male elevator operator, Hollis (La Monde Byrd), who appears in six episodes of the show and stoically bears witness to clearly marked acts of racism that the audience is meant to immediately recognize as politically incorrect. He also exhibits remarkable self-awareness about his own marginalized status as a black male at the time. This again is meant to resonate with audience members' own presumed foreknowledge about the impact of racism on an individual and also an awareness that this type of behavior is a relic from the past. For example in the episode "Six-Month Leave" (season 2, episode 9), Hollis uses the news of the death of Marilyn Monroe in order to comment on his own invisibility as a black man in a white society. Peggy mentions in the elevator, in reference to Monroe's death, that "you just don't imagine her ever being alone. She was so famous." Hollis responds, discussing his own racial identity and social status, that "some people just hide in plain sight." The black characters are constructed to silently bear witness for the audience to the tribulations of racism that they must endure, but this suffering is framed in such a way to assure audiences that this intolerance will soon be ended. Since *Mad Men* is set in the sixties, "every action the character makes is not really a reflection of who they are: they're mostly a commentary on the era. . . . Characters can do and say whatever they want without remorse, because almost all their decisions can be excused (or at least explained) by the circumstances of the period. . . . The people on this show need to be irresponsible for the sake of plausibility, so we can't really hold them accountable for what they do" (Klosterman). We also are never allowed entrée into black characters' private lives or thoughts in order to create empathetic identification with them. Carla (Deborah Lacey), the domestic who works for the Draper family, appears in fifteen episodes and is provided with the most character development, but again her primary narrative function is to reveal Betty's racism and her greater lack of moral development or awareness. These singular black characters are constructed as functioning outside of the dominant and mainstream white society that is the subject of the show, and therefore racism is presented as a social burden suffered and endured solely by individual African Americans who are bereft of any identifiable community or social group.

The series bifurcates racism and the civil rights movement. The secondary fictionalized black characters who bear witness to acts of casual racism are never allowed to respond in any way that reveals anger, hostility, or resistance, while the civil rights movement is played out through the radio coverage of specific, selective events that are already familiar to the audience. Racism is silently endured by individual black characters in their public lives, while the battle for civil rights and justice is fought by Martin Luther King Jr. on the behalf of these individuals whose sole means of social engagement and participation in the movement is through the passive consumption of the media coverage of these events. By denying the audience identification with the African American characters, the series' writers create a racial ideology that makes racism in America not only consigned to the past but furthermore a minority issue that did not enter into mainstream discursive debates or discussions. By surrounding racism with a facade of ironic nostalgia, *Mad Men* adopts a colorblind ideology that makes the work of the civil rights movement appear to be relegated to a historicized past, and not applicable to today. Empathetic prosthetic memories of racism are elided by the narrative and also through the formal cinematic aspects employed by the show's creators. The dominant white characters narrate their story in a way that "emphasizes certain zones of social and cultural coherence within the deeply fractious, racial reality of the period. . . . Social memory [in *Mad Men*] is refunctioned in a way that allows it to be integrated into the traditional narrative of nation, producing an image of social consensus built around memory" (Burgoyne).

Political Correctness and Racism

As a melodrama about the personal and professional entanglements of a Madison Avenue advertising agency during the sixties, *Mad Men* is foremost a series about the privileges of white masculinity and the guilt with which it is associated. Even though many critics have challenged Weiner's decision to make Sterling Cooper an entirely white advertising agency, since there were already at that period well-known and well-established African American copywriters and advertising agencies, Weiner has insisted that the agency, in order to be historically correct, must remain white (Itzkoff). Many commentators have noted that much of the pleasure of watching *Mad Men* derives from simultaneously occupying a position of smug condemnation and gleeful indulgence—"A strange and lovely space between nostalgia and political correctness," as Mary McNamara wrote in the *Los Angeles Times*. Political correctness as a rhetorical political strategy arose during the Reagan years as a means by the Left to "change [racialized and gendered] discourses on the assumption that changing discourses will, or may, lead to changes in other elements of social practices through processes of dialectical internalization" (Fairclough 22). *Mad Men* presents social interactions and behaviors that the audience can immediately identify as politically incorrect. These sexist and racist encounters occur at the level of everyday interactions and encounters, making them a private individual act rather than a product of systemic and institutionalized structures of inequality. With its "cigarette-puffing, garter-snapping, five-martini-lunch vision . . . the idea of letting viewers revel in the thrill of 1960s-endorsed bad behavior, while also allowing them to keep the moral high ground of our relatively enlightened times, felt groundbreaking" (Maerz). Audiences are denied empathetic identification with the African American characters in *Mad Men*, and these characters are consistently presented within a politically correct representational mode that is overwhelmingly dependent on casting black female characters who are exceptionally articulate, self-aware, noble, and docile. So while a select group of the major white characters (in particular Betty and Roger) frequently express racist and politically incorrect views, the black characters are constructed in a politically correct mode that is one-dimensional and devoid of resistance or offense. In comparison, many of the major characters express overtly sexist and non–politically correct views, but many of the female characters are shown actively and aggressively resisting these comments. Because of the historical lens that *Mad Men* assumes, these acts of resistance to sexist discourse confirm liberal audiences' confidence that cultural interventions at the level of personal discourse have led to significant social and cultural changes in the status of women in the United States. But in the construction of the African American characters, the rhetoric of political correctness functions in the series to deny the black characters any possibility of collective resistance to the dominant white culture. Audience members are instead empowered on two levels: they are reassured by their ability to read acts of discursive intolerance that confirm their own racial sensitivity while reveling in the presentation of African American characters who appear contented, nonthreatening, and fully accepting of the white middle-class values of hard work, individual initiative, and strong moral values as the means for social integration.

White male privilege is divided according to the show's logic between the old-school WASP characters embodied in Roger Sterling (John Slattery) and Don Draper's first wife, Betty, and her family, who represent the traditional power structure that had historically dominated the American economy, and the self-created businessmen, like Don Draper, who are replacing the traditional power bloc. In his interview with Charlie Rose, Weiner describes how he admires the character Roger Sterling's "dry confidence. Guilelessness. If [Mad Men] is about white men there is a lot of guilt that goes with that power right now. And maybe there should be. But Roger is so confident in his standing in the world. How things work. What is right. What is fun. He's an Id. He's pure Id. It's part of what's fun" ("William J. Fallon/Mad Men"). The characters in the show are, as Weiner explains, "that idealized WASP family . . . the blonde model—they are aspirations. We have our royalty. We have our own thing to aspire to. And there is still the reality that you must become a WASP to succeed in this country. . . . Our aspirations are still connected to that person" (Byock). The most egregious acts of overt racism are perpetrated by the WASP characters, most strikingly seen in Roger's blackface performance in the episode "My Old Kentucky Home" and Betty's treatment and firing of her black domestic maid, Carla. Racist acts therefore become a tool used within the narrative to critique traditional white privilege that is understood as outdated and reactionary. As Witchel explains, "Knowing that these unsuspecting sexists and bigots sit on the brink of their doom is all part of the fun." In a time in which political correctness has significantly altered public behavior, the historical claims of the show allow audiences to simultaneously condemn the characters for their offensive behavior while also enjoying the "freedom" to offend that becomes a hallmark of the Mad Men style of social critique. It becomes a form of "perverse entertainment (Weiner calls it pornography)" in which the audience revels in the supposed reality of the racism and sexism of the period along with watching the characters "smoke like chimneys (including pregnant women), drink like extras from 'Lost Weekend' and eat steak, cheesecake and creamed corn without consequences" (Witchel). The show therefore permits audiences to "indulge in impulses that will soon be socially forbidden" (Packer), and these impulses, including racism, sexism, alcoholism, promiscuity, homophobia, and anti-Semitism, are presented as individual choices that can be and soon will be eradicated through the inevitable tide of social condemnation and progressive change instigated and supported by the dominant majority culture.

According to the historical logic of the narrative of *Mad Men*, the dominance of the WASP dynasties is being rapidly supplanted in the early 1960s by a new model of American male corporate titans like Don Draper. Weiner turned to the biographies of Bill Clinton and Sam Walton and his own life in order to create Draper ("William J. Fallon/Mad Men"). According to Weiner, Draper "does a lot of things I wish I could. But because I write about the consequences of those things, I really don't fantasize about being him. I'll say that there is a lot of Don in me, and all of the emotional issues in my life are in the show" (Lewine). As Weiner has revealed in multiple interviews, his original inspiration for creating the pilot *Mad Men* grew out of his own sense of white guilt. "I wanted to write the greatest pilot ever," he explained in an interview for *Rolling Stone*. "That was my ambition. I wanted it to be profound, and I wanted it to be true, and I wanted to be about a man my age and what I was interested in: Who do you look up to? Why am I still 18 inside? Why am I so ungrateful for everything I have? And who am I?" (Konigsberg).[4] Don, as a self-made man who came from extremely poor and destitute origins, possesses much greater tolerance for difference than the higher-status white characters. In the face of Roger's blackface performance ("My Old Kentucky Home"), Don turned away appalled while the rest of the country club set remains in on the joke. As the protagonist of the narrative, Don is shown to possess the prescience of historical hindsight, thus creating an image of tolerant progressive whiteness that is critical of the society that he meant to constitute. Yet, Don's inability to actually condemn the racism he witnesses is part of the role he must occupy, partly because of the literally false identity that he has to maintain. The majority of popular critical reviews of *Mad Men* applaud the show for its portrayal of racism, but not for its narrativization of the pleasures of white male privilege that dominates the series. As one of the show's producers explained, "On some level everyone dreams of being Don Draper. We haven't changed that much we're just better at being polite" ("The Making of *Mad Men*").

The history of the sixties as presented in *Mad Men* is heavily mediated, with the distillation of an entire decade into a series of traumatic, singular events that are widely known to audiences not through their actual experience of the events but rather through their enculturation. These events are looped by replaying again and again the broadcast coverage of these events in the style of "crisis coverage" that characterized the media at the time: coverage that, because of the technology, is grainy, black-and-white, and displayed on small television screens or via radio broadcasts. This selective replaying of these televisual reports focuses on national memorialized figures (John F. Kennedy, Martin Luther King Jr.) participating in singular "events" as constitutive of our own popular history. These recorded events are not narrativized and stand as historical place markers and metaphoric, interpretive cues for the narrative of the characters' private lives, which is rendered in an exceptionally rich and vivid cinematic palate. The series functions by "placing in abeyance . . . the distinction between the real and the imaginary. Everything is presented as if it were of the same ontological order, both real and imaginary—realistically imaginary or imaginarily real, with the result that the referential function of the images of the events is etiolated" (White 200). And in *Mad Men* the imaginary overwhelms the real because we as spectators are continually placed within the position of the imaginary characters and are denied empathetic identification with the real events contained on the television screen or radio. An extreme example of this occurs in "The Fog," an episode whose intention was, according to Weiner in his audio commentary for the episode, to show what the process of childbirth was like at the time. Heavily sedated while giving birth, Betty enters into a dream state and encounters her recently deceased father, her long-dead mother, and the recently killed civil rights activist Medgar Evers. The primary narrative drive of the episode is to represent Betty's subconscious guilt over her father's death and her anxieties about her mother's excessive criticism of her as a child. As Weiner notes in analyzing the scene, "I just love what you guys did here. I love the camerawork this is an expression of exactly what I wanted it to feel like. Her subconscious anxieties. The day residue[5] that Freud calls it of Medgar Evers." The historical rendering of the martyr Evers becomes the means through which we as an audience create sympathetic identification with Betty as she is forced to confront her stress and anxiety over her parents' deaths. Evers remains a phantom of her unconscious that we are never asked to identify with or understand, thus denying the audience the opportunity to engage both intellectually and emotionally with another who is radically different from oneself. Therefore, *Mad Men* disavows the difficult ethical work that is crucial in the development of empathy for the offer that would in turn enable the "larger political project of advancing egalitarian social goals through a more radical form of democracy" (Landsberg 222).

The Civil Rights Movement in *Mad Men*

The media plays a crucial role in the shaping of popular memory, since it "provide[s] the matrix that collects and circulates diverse memories in America, shaping them in various ways and keeping some alive while burying others" (Rosenberg 4). The public memory of the civil rights movement depends overwhelmingly on the stories, events, and personalities that had circulated in past media coverage. As Emily Rosenberg has written, "In America, there is increasingly no effective memory or history outside of the media" (4). Though a large majority of popular criticism of *Mad Men* makes frequent mention of the show's handling of racism as a particularly laudable aspect of the series, the actual direct mention of race relations is scant and strategically interjected into the narrative. Season 3 (2009) of *Mad Men* is set in 1963 and is the one most heavily dedicated to utilizing the civil rights movement to set up the historical time line of the series and to provide ironic counterpoint to the dominant narrative line. Besides the previously discussed episode that included the figure of the martyred Medgar Evers, in "We Small Hours" (episode 9) both Martin Luther King Jr.'s iconic "I Have a Dream" speech and his "Eulogy for the Martyred Children" speech at the funeral for the four girls killed at the Sixteenth Street Baptist Church in Birmingham are played over the radio. The Kennedy historical time line structured the first three seasons of *Mad Men,* and each ended on a national event or crisis (season 1: Nixon versus Kennedy television debate; season 2: Cuban missile crisis; season 3: assassination of President Kennedy). The series relies on the replaying of the televised broadcasts of these occurrences, which are presented as national events witnessed by the entire nation that had a significant social and cultural impact on American society. In contrast, the civil rights time line follows a teleological structure that begins with Paul's trip to Mississippi to register voters in 1962, includes Medgar Evers's death and King's speeches in 1963 and the killing of the civil rights activist Andrew

Goodman, in Mississippi, in 1964, and ends with the assassination of Malcolm X in 1965. None of the civil rights events are projected on television like the actual footage of the coverage of the Kennedy assassination, and therefore these events are framed as having minimal impact and relevance to the dominant characters in the series.

The penultimate episode in the treatment of the civil rights movement is "Wee Small Hours" (season 3, episode 9). Typical of the narrative structure of the series, this episode interweaves two actual speeches by King, including a short excerpt of his iconic "I Have a Dream" speech from August 28, 1963, into the dominant narrative line that focuses on Conrad Hilton's hiring of Don for his international advertising campaign and Betty's decision to pursue an extramarital affair. The episode explicitly interjects social relevance by conflating the battles of the civil rights movement with the gay rights movement through the outing and firing of the gay character, Sal. Similar to the audience's ability to develop sympathetic prosthetic memories through identification with the female characters in *Mad Men*, Sal is a fully developed character with a richly rendered private and work life whose emotional struggles with his gay identity and societal homophobia create immediate sympathy on the part of the audience. The audience is positioned to fully identify with Sal in this episode in order to experience the intolerance and devastating impact of homophobia on a complex and endearing character. In comparison, access to the civil rights movement is provided through the replaying of King's speeches on the radio. The audience is denied experiential access and the possibility of the formation of empathetic prosthetic memories of racial injustice. The "I Have a Dream" speech occurs in the midst of a scene where Don is driving around after receiving a late-night call from Conrad Hilton. Hilton tells Don, "I want Hiltons all over the world. . . . America is wherever we're going to be." While out contemplating how to orchestrate the most important advertising campaign in his career, one that will lead to the successful spread of American capitalism globally, Don passes by his young daughter's attractive, elementary school teacher, Suzanne, out jogging. After Don convinces her to join him in the car, we hear on the radio a commentator state that "more than 200,000 people demonstrated in the nation's capital for civil rights," and then King is heard saying, "I have a dream that my four little children will one day live in a nation where they will not be judged by the color of their skin but by the content of their character. I have a *dream* today!" In the audio commentary for the episode, Weiner, as in his discussion of Medgar Evers's assassination, relates it to the episode's opening scene in which Betty dreams of a sexual encounter with a stranger. "I have a dream." Weiner explained, "Betty had her dream at the beginning of this thing. . . . It was meant to be literal about the impulse to have change in your life and to get what you want and you felt you deserved. And, of course, the nobility of what Martin Luther King is asking for and the privacy of what Don is asking for." In a rhetorical move consistent with colorblindness, King's speech about racial inequities becomes a message about personal choice and individual freedom and, specifically within the context of the narrative, the freedom for Betty and Don to have extramarital affairs.

The latter half of this episode is devoted to Sal's sexual harassment at work by the company's Lucky Strike client, an incident that will lead to his dismissal from the agency and his removal from the series. Intercut with this narrative line is Betty's decision to pursue a relationship with Henry, a secret that her maid, Carla, unintentionally discovers. During a fundraiser for Henry's boss, Nelson Rockefeller, Betty's neighbors and friends chat conspicuously about southern racism and intolerance while showing utter indifference to Carla's presence and status. The racism theme culminates with Carla in the Draper kitchen listening to King's speech "Eulogy for the Martyred Children" after the Birmingham church bombing that killed four young girls. Again we hear a brief audio clip of the speech: "These children—unoffending, innocent, and beautiful—were the victims of one of the most vicious and tragic crimes ever perpetrated against humanity." Betty intercedes at this point, saying, "I hate to say this but it really makes me wonder about civil rights. Maybe it shouldn't happen right now." In his audio commentary about this scene, Weiner explained that "he wanted to show how depressing this was, this is the reaction to Martin Luther King. . . . Betty identifying with her own struggle to be with this guy, responding to her own need. This is not just white guilt. . . . I love the idea of just experiencing the history that way and not giving people a message about civil rights. It's so important to some people and it's going to be in their face the more martyrs there are. The harder it is for America to ignore it and not that a lot of white people didn't support it but it did change."

Even though *Mad Men* has been fully embraced by the liberal media outlets and has been lauded for its progressive treatment of significant social issues, the civil rights time line integrated into the narrative line of the show is consistent with the dominant narrative of the civil rights movement constructed by neoliberals and the New Right. This time line (Medgar Evers's assassination, King's two speeches) presents the civil rights movement as a southern phenomenon initiated by exceptional male individuals, the most important of whom is Martin Luther King Jr., who is presented as espousing a colorblind ideology about tolerance and individual freedom. These iconic leaders, according to the narrative logic, are necessarily martyred in order for white people to accept their demands for equality, thus erasing the long and brutal history of the hundreds of individuals involved in the battle for racial justice in America. The current dominant narrative of the civil rights movement, as manifest in *Mad Men,* "took root in the conservative soil of the 1980s and 1990s and had a clear political purpose: to discredit controversial race-conscious programs, including affirmative action, school desegregation, and minority voting districts, as a betrayal of 'the movement'" (Sugrue 70). Fittingly, in the premier episode of season 5 ("A Little Kiss"), Weiner has created yet another very articulate, self-aware, and passive black woman hired by the firm as the result of a protest by a group of matronly black women.[6]

According to Weiner's version of the racial politics of the time, by 1966 the actions of the civil rights leaders in the South, and in particular the nonviolent actions of Martin Luther King Jr., had succeeded in opening up the workplaces of the North. The civil rights time line in *Mad Men,* like the dominant narrative of the civil rights movement, ends with triumphant integration and equal treatment. This time line of race relations in America, combined with Weiner's decision to create singular black characters in *Mad Men* with whom the audience is denied empathetic identification and who stoically endure casual racist comments without complaint, consign racism and racial issues to a distant past. The series provides no uniquely racialized empathetic prosthetic memories for its audience of the virulent forms of institutionalized and systemic racism that permeated society at that time. Racism, then, becomes conflated with other forms of non–politically correct social behaviors that will be eradicated through the intervention of enlightened white Americans. The series reinforces the claim that the reality of civil rights activism was in its support for and defense of universal American values. This version of history fails to acknowledge that "for those marching for civil rights both

North and South—as well as their opponents—the civil rights struggle was dangerous, transgressive, and sometimes revolutionary" (Sugrue 72). Weiner's claim that a lot of white people did support the civil rights movement and that "it did change" implies that the civil rights movement made white people the agents of change who only needed their consciousness raised in order to support the goals of the movement. As Sugrue and other historians have extensively documented, the "assumption that an interracial working-class movement was just around the corner in 1968—or at any other point in the twentieth century, for the matter—is wishful thinking. The persistence of racial inequality . . . was the result of a long history of public policies, deindustrialization, and systemic disinvestment from black communities, persistent segregation in housing and education, discriminatory practices by employers and unions, and longstanding racial gaps in wealth, health, and income" (70).

Because *Mad Men* is a television show that enjoys extensive cultural cachet with its liberal, educated audience, one would imagine that its racial politics would challenge the dominant narrative of the civil rights movement that has been employed by the Right in order to justify post-racial and colorblind social policies. And yet the series' creators, through their deployment of a politically correct mode of representation and their inability and refusal to occupy the uncomfortable position of the racialized other, point to how these narratives "maintain a strong hold on the public imagination, in part, because they have been repeated so often and broadcast so widely, and in part because they avoid uncomfortable questions about the relationship between cumulative white advantage and present social ills" (Hall 1262).

Notes

1. The series is produced by Lionsgate Television and premiered on July 19, 2007. The fourth season was completed on October 17, 2010, and the fifth season premiered on March 25, 2012, with two more seasons planned. Since the first season premiere, ratings for the show have continued to grow steadily and significantly. The audience for the premiere at 10:00 p.m. on July 19, 2007, was larger than for any other AMC original series to date, with 900,000 viewers. The numbers for the first-season premiere were more than doubled for the heavily promoted second-season premiere. However, the second-season finale posted significantly higher numbers than the series' first-season finale and was up 20

percent over the second-season average. A total of 1.75 million viewers watched the second-season finale of *Mad Men*. The third-season premiere, which aired August 16, 2009, gained 2.8 million views on its first run. In 2009, *Mad Men* was second in Nielsen's list of top ten time-shifted prime-time TV programs, with a 57.7 percent gain in viewers, second only to the final season of *Battlestar Galactica*. The fourth-season premiere of *Mad Men* was the most watched episode in AMC history until the premiere of the AMC original series *The Walking Dead*, clocking in at 2.9 million viewers, up 5 percent from the ratings for season 3's debut and up 61 percent from the third-season average. However, the heavy and widespread media coverage of *Mad Men* belies the fact that much more popular cable shows like MTV's *Jersey Shore* have regular audience numbers of 8 million.

2. Weiner is the son of the acclaimed neuroscientist Leslie P. Weiner, who served as the neurologist for former president Ronald Reagan. The neurological care and research center at the University of Southern California is named for him. Matthew Weiner attended the prestigious Harvard Westlake School in Los Angeles and was by his own admission a mediocre student. He was still, though, able to gain admission to Wesleyan University, where he graduated with a nongraded major in philosophy, history, and literature. Not able to get into the University of Southern California School of Cinema-Television with his academic record, Matthew Weiner was admitted after his father personally interceded with the dean of the college.

3. For example, in the episode "The Chrysanthemum and the Sword" (season 4, episode 5), Roger Sterling asks, "Why don't we just bring Dr. Lyle Evans in here?" The name set up a frenzy of "little viral reindeer games." As vanityfair. com coverage of the 'mad meme' stated, "It appears that *Mad Men* script writers deliberately made up a fictional character named Dr. Lyle Evans to get people's attention, and it appears that their tactic has worked out really well" (Weiner).

4. He would reiterate on the National Public Radio program *Fresh Air with Terry Gross* how a personal crisis of his was the inspiration for his creation of *Mad Men* (2007). "My inspiration for writing this piece—the first moment of interaction with really where Don was—was: I was 35 years old; I had a job on a network sitcom; it was rated number nine (which means I was basically in Major League Baseball for my job—there's 300 people in the country that have this job, and I had one). I had three children, and I was like what—this incredible life—you know, I was like, 'What is wrong with me? Why am I unhappy? Why is there so much going on in my head that I can't express to other people because it's all awful? And what is enough? And I'm going to die one day.' And I'm looking at it and saying, 'This is it?' It could be an excuse to behave very badly."

5. Day residue, according to Freud, is "one or more seemingly innocent waking (conscious) trains of thought that stimulated preconscious associations to various themes and issues in one's life, beginning to arouse unconscious/repressed wishes."

6. The *New York Time*'s writer Michael Wilson triumphantly led his article of March 28, 2012, with the title "On 'Mad Men,' an Opening Scene Straight from Page 1." Weiner and other critics lauded the verbatim transcription of a "real" historical event to the

television screen. No commentators mentioned, though, that the protest staged in the opening of the episode was in response to cuts to the antipoverty programs being administered through the Office of Economic Opportunity (OEO). The OEO was created as part of Johnson's War on Poverty and was soon a ready target for critics on the left and right. In the *Mad Men* episode, the protesters lead Sterling Cooper Draper Pryce to place an ad claiming to be an "equal opportunity employer." The Equal Employment Opportunity Commission was created under Title VII of the Civil Rights Act of 1964 and, according to the agency's own history, was a "toothless tiger" until 1971. The series significantly alters the actual substance of the protest in order to better fit into the dominant narrative of the civil rights movement in which integration in the workplace is easily remedied by nonviolent protest and the easy acceptance by the company of a black employee. The much more difficult question of the lack of funding for antipoverty programs is simply ignored.

WORKS CITED

Ankersmit, F. R. "Historiography and Postmodernism." *History and Theory* 28.2 (1989): 137–53. Print.

Burgoyne, Robert. "Prosthetic Memory/Traumatic Memory: *Forrest Gump* (1994)." http://tlweb.latrobe.edu.au/humanities/screeningthepast/firstrelease/fr0499/rbfr6a.htm.

Byock, Lila. "Talking 'Mad Men' with Matthew Weiner." *New Yorker* 18 Oct. 2009. Web. 28 Dec. 2011.

"Cable Shows with the Wealthiest Viewers." *Hollywood Reporter* 25 July 2010. Web. 11 Jan. 2012. <http://www.hollywoodreporter.com/news/cable-shows-wealthiest-viewers-25905.>

Cardwell, Sarah. "Is Quality Television Any Good? Generic Distinctions, Evaluations and the Troubling Matter of Critical Judgment." *Quality TV: Contemporary American Television and Beyond*. Ed. Janet McCabe and Kim Akass. New York: I. B. Tauris, 2007. 19–34. Print.

Corliss, Richard. "Flashbacks in Black and White." *Time* 13 Jan. 2003. Web. 4 Mar. 2012. <http://www.time.com/time/magazine/article/0,9171,1004033,00.html>.

Fairclough, Norman. "'Political Correctness': The Politics of Culture and Language." *Discourse and Society* 14.17 (2003): 17–28. Print.

Feld, Rob, Jean Oppenheimer, and Ian Stasukevich. "Tantalizing Television." *American Cinematographer* Mar. 2008. Web. 23 Mar. 2012. <http://www.theasc.com/ac_magazine/March2008/Television/page1.php>.

Feuer, Jane. "HBO and the Concept of Quality TV." *Quality TV: Contemporary American Television and Beyond*. Ed. Janet McCabe and Kim Akass. New York: I. B. Tauris, 2007. 145–57. Print.

"The Fog." *Mad Men*. AMC. 13 Sept. 2009. Television.

Goodman, Tim. "Mad Men: TV Review." *HollywoodReporter* 14 Mar. 2012. Web. 30 Mar. 2012. <http://www.hollywoodreporter.com/review/mad-men-review-season-5-300109>.

Gray, Herman. "Remembering Civil Rights: Television, Memory, and the 1960s." *The Revolution Wasn't Televised: Television and Social Conflict*. Ed. Lynn Spigel and Michael Curtin. New York: Routledge, 1997. 349–58. Print.

Grief, Mark. "You'll Love the Way It Makes You Feel." *London Review of Books* Oct. 2008. Web. 4 Oct. 2011.

Gross, Terry. "For Mad Men It's All about the Hard Sell." NPR: *Fresh Air*. 9 Aug. 2007. Radio.

Hall, Jacquelyn Dowd. "The Long Civil Rights Movement and the Political Uses of the Past." *Journal of American History* 91.4 (2005): 1233–63. Print.

Itzkoff, Dave. "Matthew Weiner Closes the Book on Season 4 of 'Mad Men.'" *New York Times* 17. Oct. 2010. Web. 6 Oct. 2011.

Kifner, John. "Poverty Pickets Get Paper-Bag Dousing on Madison Avenue." *New York Times* 28 May 1966. Web. 2 May 2012. URL.

Klosterman, Chuck. "Bad Decisions." *Grantland*. 12 July 2011. Web. 26 Jan. 2012. <http://www.grantland.com/story/_/id/6763000/bad-decisions>.

Konigsberg, Eric. "A Fine Madness." *Rolling Stone* 1113 (2010): Web. 13 Mar. 2012.

Landsberg, Alison. "Memory, Empathy, and the Politics of Identification." *International Journal of Politics, Culture and Society* 22 (2009): 221–29. Print.

Lewine, Edward. "Matthew Weiner's 'Mad' House." *New York Times Magazine* 29 Sept. 2007. Web. 6 Oct. 2011.

"A Little Kiss." *Mad Men*. AMC. 25 Mar. 2012. Television.

Maerz, Melissa. "Longing for a Time When Bad Was Good." *Los Angeles Times* 22 May 2011. Web. 4 Oct. 2011.

"The Making of *Mad Men*." *Amctv*. N.d. Web. 16 Mar. 2012. <www.amctv.com/mad-men/videos/the-making-of-mad-men-part-1>.

McNamara, Mary, "Back When Men Were Mad Men." *Los Angeles Times* 19 July 2007. Web. 4 Oct. 2011.

Mendelsohn, Daniel. "The Mad Men Account." *New York Review of Books* 24 Feb. 2011. Web. 4 Oct. 2011.

"Milestones in the History of the U.S. Equal Employment Opportunity Commission." EEOC. N.d. Web. 2 May 2012. <http://www.eeoc.gov/eeoc/history/35th/milestones/index.html>.

"My Old Kentucky Home." *Mad Men*. AMC. 30 Aug. 2009. Television.

Newman, Michael. "'Turning Creative Success into Business Is Your Work!'" *zigzagger*. 26 July 2010. Retrieved 22 Mar. 2012.

Ono, Kent. "Postracism: A Theory of the 'Post-'as Political Strategy." *Journal of Communication Inquiry* 34:3 (July 2010): 227–33. Print.

Packer, George. "What's So Good about 'Mad Men'? *New Yorker* 2 Nov. 2009. Web. 28 Dec. 2012.

Perlman, Allison. "The Strange Career of Mad Men: Race, Paratexts and Civil Rights Memory." *Mad Men*. Ed. Gary R. Edgerton. New York: I. B. Tauris, 2011. 209–25. Print.

Reagan, Ronald. "Remarks on Signing the Bill Making the Birthday of Martin Luther King, Jr. a National Holiday," Nov. 2, 1983. *Public Papers of the Presidents of the United States, 1983.* Washington, DC: U.S. Government Printing Office, 1985. 1529–30.

"The Rejected." *Mad Men.* AMC. 15 Aug. 2010. Television.

Rosenberg, Emily. *A Date Which Will Live: Pearl Harbor in American Memory.* Durham, NC: Duke University Press, 2003. Print.

Schwarz, Benjamin. "Mad about *Mad Men.*" *Atlantic* November 2009. Web. Retrieved 28 Dec. 2012.

"Six Month Leave." *Mad Men.* AMC. 28 Sept. 2008. Television.

Steinberg, Jacques. "In Act 2, the TV Hit Man Becomes a Pitch Man." *New York Times* 18 July 2007. Web. 12 Mar. 2012.

Sugrue, Thomas. "Racial Romanticism." *Democracyjournal.org.* Summer 2009: 69–73. Web. 8 Apr. 2012.

"Tomorrowland." *Mad Men.* AMC. 17 Oct. 2010. Television.

"Wee Small Hours." *Mad Men.* AMC. 11 Oct. 2009. Television.

Weiner, Juli. "Dr. Lyle Evans, We Presume?" *Vanityfair* 23 Aug. 2010. Web. 9 Mar. 2012.

White, Hayden. *Figural Realism: Studies in the Mimesis Effect.* Baltimore: John Hopkins University Press, 1999. Print.

"William J. Fallon/Mad Men." *Charlie Rose.* 28 July 2008. Television.

Wilson, Michael. "On 'Mad Men,' an Opening Scene Straight from Page 1." *New York Times* 28 Mar. 2012. Web. 2 May 2012.

Witchel, Alex. "'Mad Men' Has Its Moment." *New York Times* 22 June 2008. Web. 13 Mar. 2012.

9

Watching TV with White Supremacists

A More Complex View of the Colorblind Screen

C. RICHARD KING

Few of us knowingly watch television with individuals who advocate white power. We do, however, have increasing opportunities to view storylines featuring prominent characters who express overtly racist and white supremacist attitudes, including the Aryan Brotherhood prison gang on *Oz*, the Klan on *Boardwalk Empire*, neo-Nazis on *Sons of Anarchy*, and more recently the racist brothers of *The Walking Dead*. They have emerged as something of a meme, a preferred trope for putting drama in motion and establishing a moral arc for the televisual narrative. Even in these more complex and celebrated cable shows, which pride themselves on character development and nuance, they emerge as transgressive, perverse, violent, antisocial, and often hypocritical adversaries. Importantly, they always remain at a remove from their target audience, even though many self-described white nationalists and white separatists take pleasure in them. They are outcasts, for instance, in prison or outlaw biker gangs; they are set in another time, namely, after a future zombie apocalypse or during Prohibition; or, they are confined to a specific geography, such as the Deep South. All of these features surely comfort viewers (not unlike the fantasy world of the wildly popular *Mad Men*): white racism where it exists is extreme, excessive, and marginal; white racists dwell elsewhere; white racists and, hence, white racism are bad. In a real sense, in a sociohistorical moment committed to the entangled ideologies of colorblindness and multiculturalism, such messages reassure as they trace the limits of race and power and let white audiences off the hook.

One testament to the power of contemporary framings of racism can be found in a recent interview of Walton Goggins, who plays a white supremacist on *Justified* convicted of plotting to bomb a black church, later born again in prison, who then denounces his past. Asked by Terry Gross, host of *Fresh Air*, what it was like to play this character, Goggins replied:

> I never believed that Boyd Crowder was a white supremacist, to be quite honest with you. . . . . It was very important for me as an actor not to play this guy as a white supremacist but to play him as a bit of a Svengali: a person who doesn't necessarily believe all that he espouses. . . . [In one episode] Tim says, "Boyd, I don't think you believe everything that you're saying. I think you just like to blow stuff up." And that was very important to me.

Nevertheless, as Crowder, Goggins had a swastika emblazoned on his arm and made racist remarks, an experience he described in some detail:

> Honestly, it was awful. . . . We did a table reading of this script, and . . . immediately after, I felt like I had to say "I'm sorry. I don't believe any of this. A lot of my best friends are Jewish." It's difficult, and it's difficult to have a swastika on your arm. And I actually wore it home. I didn't let them take it off. I kept it with me during the process of filming the pilot episode. . . . You're certainly affected by ink on your body, and something as powerful as a swastika and the negative connotations that come along with that. I definitely wanted to feel that, and there were times during the day when I wasn't working and I was out at dinner, that I would roll up my T-shirt and I would leave the swastika there just to see people's reactions. And there was one time when I was with Tim, when I had rolled my shirt up just to see what would happen, and Tim [Oliphant] didn't notice it for about five minutes until there were tourists walking through the lobby of the hotel who almost gasped—like, you could hear it, you could hear them step back with their Starbucks coffee in their hands. And Tim said, "Please, please roll down your shirt. Please. Or I'm gonna have to leave you here alone."

Goggins's experience is instructive on a number of levels. In this "time after race," as Herman Gray calls it, overt racism is taboo, and even playacting it is transgressive: no one wants to be a racist. Enlightened whites, who naturally have friends who are Jewish (or black or Latina/o), cannot reconcile such ideologies with their own identities. They pull back aghast like the tourists when confronted with illicit symbols or, like Goggins, explain away the values and practices of white power when forced to embody them: this cannot be serious; it must a ploy; it cannot be internalized. And yet, it can be fun, a provocation, a means of getting a rise from an audience. Indeed, white supremacists allow for the creation of fantasies, which remain safe and ultimately reaffirm the settled and silent operations of race and power today—inequalities persist, frequently in more pernicious and problematic forms.[1]

In other words, characters emblematic of white power not only allow some audience members to indulge in the pleasures of representations that openly speak the language of white supremacy and overtly tie whiteness to (antiquated) vestiges of superiority, but also, for many more viewers, render white racism outdated, antisocial, and disturbing, affirming their enlightenment and taste. As both an iteration of retrograde racial discourse and confirmation of acceptable subject positions, then, such characters and stories distance viewers from and allow them to deny prevailing racial conditions, which overt white supremacy effectively effaces. Such disengagements anchor post-racial worldviews, nurturing racial power and its reproduction, precisely because they prompt (predominantly white) audiences not to see race and racism or discern their lasting significance. As comforting as these uses and understandings may be, they allow us to forget that while few of us knowingly watch television with advocates of white power, many of them do watch television. Their interests and interpretations undermine an easy assertion of colorblindness and encourage a more complex rendering of the racial landscape.

Much of the study of colorblindness and racism has untangled the ways in which it fosters more covert reiterations of racial ideologies, thus reinforcing racial hierarchies in softer, less visible terms (Bonilla-Silva). Less discussed are the ways in which colorblindness, as a hegemonic formation, nurtures the articulation of latent and emergent ideologies. The persistence and growing popularity of white power as an interpretive frame offer a unique occasion to explore these understudied elements. This chapter examines online discussions among, and historical documents by, advocates of white power—here understood as a broad discursive

field that encompasses perspectives typically identified as white supremacist and white nationalist—with two objectives. First, it seeks to tease out
the preoccupations the advocates of white power bring to television and
how these shape the dominant themes in their accounts of the medium.
Second, it works to make sense of the relationship between the interpretive frame of white power and colorblindness, arguing the latter dominant form clears a space for emergent and latent ideologies, while offering them a target to spread their messages and broaden their audiences.

In exploring these themes, I advance the following arguments. Many,
if not most, white supremacists see television as a powerful threat. From
their perspective, both the medium and its messages imperil whiteness,
posing an existential threat. Indeed, television endangers whites because
of who they believe controls it (Jews), what they assert it communicates
(messages that denigrate whites while celebrating blacks), and what they
identify as guiding ideologies (multiculturalism and race mixing). Of
particular concern within this racist subculture is the impact of television on children and youth. While speaking from the margins and in
terms many would reject as extreme or inappropriate, their concerns
with corruption, breakdown, and peril resonate with more normative
and accepted interpretations of the ills of television today.

Watching White Supremacists Watch TV

A note on terminology: Throughout this chapter, I describe the diverse
ideologies of those who advocate white power as "white supremacist." I
have opted for this phrase because it is succinct and familiar, capturing
many of the core elements of the subculture. The reader should keep in
mind two caveats. First, many advocates of white power bristle at the
label, arguing they are about loving the white race, not hating others,
and do not (necessarily) assert that whites are superior. These rhetorical counterpoints are meant to reframe and normalize, allowing white
power discourse to thrive in a colorblind, multicultural milieu. Second,
there is a danger in dubbing one set of people white supremacist in
the United States because it threatens to communicate a false image of
the nation and its history. That is, I understand that the United States
has always been anchored in white supremacy, and my usage should
not be taken as a denial of this foundational feature of the American

experience. More space for the presentation of the nuances of the movement and the contextualization of it more fully in the history of white racism would allow more exacting language.

And a word on method: In researching this chapter, I did not knowingly watch television with individuals who advocate white power. Instead, I watched them talking about watching television. More specifically, I read online forums at a leading white nationalist website, stormfront.org. Here, I reviewed and coded comments posted in discussions threads, identified by browsing the forum devoted to popular culture and through keyword searches for specific television programs. These were supplemented with reviews of shows located at other white power websites and texts published by individuals and organizations affiliated with the subculture.

The Problem with Pop Culture

Popular culture poses fundamental problems for many advocates of white power (Leonard and King). And television is no exception. The media, including television, is biased, hinging on what David Duke, former Grand Wizard of the Ku Klux Klan and Louisiana state representative, describes as "a double standard," rooted in a "very anti-white racist attitude" (Swain and Nieli 172). Don Black, founder of stormfront. org, underscores and expands this position:

> The bias is certainly directed against the white majority in this country and toward white culture throughout the world, where white people are typically characterized as being oppressors and exploiters of other races. . . . nonwhites are typically portrayed as being intelligent, sensitive, and often the victims. . . . So there is a liberal bias . . . the disproportionate Jewish influence. (Swain and Nieli 155)

Indeed, for many advocates of white power, Jews control television and use it to orchestrate their diabolic plans, communicating antiwhite messages while championing blacks and racial mixing. Or, as one discussant in a thread on the most offensive television programs in history put it, "I've certainly just about had it with *Glee*. Gays, Jews, and race-mixing with some teen pregnancy (a Christian White girl, naturally) thrown in for good measure."[2]

Television troubles, then, because it has visible impacts; far from self-contained stories or flat images, its messages reshape social subjects and structure their worldviews. "Television IS A JEWISH MEDIUM," exclaims one poster, putnamvt. "They have control of it from the start. It ossifies people, passifies [*sic*] them, hypnotizes them, transforms them from humans into consumers, marching idiot-like to the Jew-advertising drumbeat."[3] Alienated, emptied, inhuman, viewers become zombies or puppets. Or as Fritzie Weiss would prefer, "The Jewtube comes up with some of the most despicable propaganda. . . . I can't even watch the Jewtube anymore as I get sick. . . . But sometimes will watch the thing to see the mindset and subliminal messages."[4] Such propaganda, often described as the active process of brainwashing, conjures for many white supremacists images from Orwell's *1984* or Stalin's Soviet Union. It distorts the world, distracting whites from their interests as a race and from the immanent dangers threatening them. For Holocaust denier Ernest Zündel, Jewish control of the media "is truth. A lethally dangerous truth" (17). Hence, watching television is never mere entertainment; it is always about racial politics in an overdetermined context in which far from privileged whites find themselves besieged and endangered. In large part, this is why watching television with white supremacists matters so much.

Kill Your TV

Not surprisingly, in light of this larger frame, some white supremacists do not watch television, and call for others in the subculture to follow their lead. Discussion threads with titles like "TV Kills Society So Will Society Kill TV" and "Happiness Is Life Free from Television" speak to the virtues of turning off or away from the television:

> Kill the TV, throw it out the window. . . . We need to engage socially, not atomize. We need to be action-oriented rather than passive mass media consumers and sockpuppets [*sic*]. TV is the Jew-run state social control mechanism par excellence [*sic*].[5]

Killing one's TV promises escape and emancipation. Several discussants at stormfront.org propose a rather simple equation: freedom from television equals freedom. After he stopped watching television, Geborenzuschaukein detailed the life-changing transformation:

> I have since enriched my life with education and real people. I learn what I want to know, when I want to learn it, not when the media tells me to. Free from TV means that you choose: You choose whether or not you want to expose yourself to the propaganda, the lies, and the filth . . . and my critical thinking skills have greatly improved without the MSM [mainstream media] influence.[6]

Without television, then, one is a free agent, empowered for self-improvement. To get to this juncture requires an awakening or a breaking of a biochemical addiction that few white supremacists have yet to achieve.[7]

What (Not) to Watch

Despite these protestations, many advocates of white power watch television. This raises an important problem: What should a white supremacist watch? It is perhaps easier to highlight what not to watch on television. In part, this is because, according to swimmingly (qtd. in Venus-16's post), "TV is nothing but a bunch of kikes, coons, perverts, and race mixers."[8] More than the characters, for many white supremacists, the messages put them off. For instance, black comedies are bad, but not simply because blacks have prominent roles. To make this point, one discussant contrasted *The Jeffersons* and *Good Times:*

> *The Jeffersons,* besides being uppity negroes with a particularly obnoxious paternal figure, was chosen mainly for its hard push of race mixing. While *Good Times* was about a struggling black family, the jewish writers just had to push their own agendas such as gun control, "black is good, Whitey is bad," etc. [9]

Even shows focused almost exclusively on a white family can prove problematic, as the same commentator continued: "As for *Roseanne,* it might ostensibly be about a White working class family, it openly mocked White people/values by praising homosexuals, jews, 'affirmative action,' etc."[10] Similarly, according to Blue Eyes, *L.A. Law* was little more than antiwhite propaganda:

> It was a real jewfest promoting multi-culturalism and race mixing. The lawyers were a mix of jews, mestizo, negro, and females. One of the few white lawyers in the law firm had a blonde, attractive ex-wife who fell in love with the firm's negro attorney. This same negro attorney had nailed one of the white female attorneys in an earlier episode. It showed scenes of them in bed together, snuggling, kissing, hugging, etc. There was also a jew divorce attorney who would end up bedding his female clients. Of course his female clients were all white. Pretty disgusting.[11]

Not surprisingly, groundbreaking programs like *Roots* and *The Cosby Show* take on a whole new meaning at stormfront.org. While the former was intended to rewrite the past and brainwash Americans, and the latter projected upper-class white mannerisms onto blacks, "dress[ing] up chimps as humans," neither presented the world as it is but offered a fantasy to assuage discontent and push multiculturalism.[12]

Antiwhite/pro-black messages combined with race mixing and Jewish control render much of television programming offensive; however, it is not just about race. Sexuality also proves pivotal for many discussants. The sociologists Abby Ferber (1999) and Jessie Daniels (1997) have clearly demonstrated the ways in which race, gender, and sexuality anchor and animate white supremacist discourse.[13] I offer but one list of offensive shows (from whiteworkingclasswoman) as a means of quickly showing the centrality of intersectionality:

"Jewy" Springer Show (obvious)
Flavor of Love Charm School (a group of nigresses fighting all day)
Degrassi Jr High (racial mixing and homosexuality about 13 year olds)
King of the Hill (I take special exception to that one since I am a Texan)
Chapelle Show (nig filth)
Queer as Folk and its dyke counterpart the L Word
The Simpsons
Rosanne (disgusting jewess)
MTV (the whole network)
Nickelodeon (whole network)

Ellen Degenerate
John Stewart Show and the Colbert Report[14]

Here, the author includes shows celebrating race mixing and centering on African Americans, networks with multicultural programming, and shows hosted by or about gays and lesbians. Race, gender, and heterosexuality together determine deviance, abjection, and impropriety. To offer two further examples, *Sex and the City* was called out as "Whores and their fag friends. Why else would there be a Jewish actress in it?"[15] And the management and transformation of white masculinity made *Queer Eye for the Straight Guy* especially problematic for many discussants. Thus, while race might matter most or most obviously, it takes on greater significance for white supremacist viewers in conjunction with, and as set in motion by, gender and sexuality.[16]

If little contemporary television recommends itself, that does not mean there are no "Good TV Shows for White Folks." In fact, an entire discussion thread exists at stormfront.org to list and debate those programs "worth watching for WNs [white nationalists] and their families." One thing is immediately clear from this forum: it is like stepping into a time warp or creating a nostalgic playlist of old-time television. That is, earlier shows from a bygone era do have a certain appeal for white supremacists, including comedies, like *Gilligan's Island* and *The Honeymooners,* Westerns, such as *Gunsmoke* and *Bonanza,* and children's programs, like *The Adventures of Johnny Quest* and *The Wonderful World of Disney.* These shows not only center exclusively on whites but also celebrate a vision of the heterosexual nuclear family with marked gender roles and a clear sexual hierarchy, glossed on this forum as white values. Importantly, almost all good or pro-white shows were in production before the reverberations of the freedom struggles impacted the culture industries: before the end of the Vietnam War, before feminism and gay rights, before the culture wars and multiculturalism, and before globalization. In other words, they come from an era when whiteness, masculinity and femininity, and heterosexuality were largely uncontested, from an era before the fall. Or, as one discussant put it, "When CBS did their 'purge' of 'country' shows in the early '70s that was the point at which TV went anti-White."[17]

Not all shows worth watching are now off the air or relegated to the TV Land network. Reality and "fact-based" programs have clear appeal.

Part of the attraction appears to be the sense that such shows lack bias or ideological framing. DanJunior, for instance, likes National Geographic programming because "they simply show the facts, and are devoid of liberal political agendas."[18] The praise for *Cops* seems to fit with this description as well: an authentic glimpse of the mean streets and the police officers who patrol them. It likely does not hurt that the show focuses obsessively on urban dysfunction and transgression, confirming existing stereotypes. Another set of shows in this category deserves mention: work or, better, dangerous work reality shows, like *Ice Road Truckers, Deadliest Catch*, and *Ax Men*. Not only real or factual, these shows focus exclusively on white protagonists battling nature, exerting their manhood, and proving themselves through their labor and their bodily exploits. Or, to borrow from one discussant, "It should be noted that both of these professions [timber harvesting and fishing] are among the most dangerous in the world, and that in both shows the work crews . . . are noticeably WHITE."[19] Again, gender and race form a potent narrative core that resonates with the discussants.[20]

Identification with particular characters sparked a key debate in this thread. Specifically, discussants sparred over how to regard Archie Bunker and *All in the Family*. Some of them championed the character as working-class hero who speaks truths now unspeakable, while others chastised their peers for taking text out of context, for *All in the Family* challenged social norms, parodied racially conscious whites, and worse, from their reading, was produced by Jewish communists. Thus, a positive white character with which one can identify is not enough to make a show pro-white or good for whites to watch. A similar debate broke out over *Sons of Anarchy,* in another forum, with some discussants finding the show "bad-ass" for its inclusion of white supremacist characters and others dismissing easy identification with caricatures that malign the movement and mock its principles.[21]

Open to Interpretation

While white supremacists who watch television find little to praise and much to condemn in contemporary programming, they find deep meaning and satisfying allegories in select shows. One recent example is the program *V.*[22]

Opening a discussion thread on the show, -Chaos- remarked, "I find amusing the parallels between the V's and Jews, and how things work in the real world,"[23] and then offered a two-page summary of the show. Screaming_In_Digital echoed his conclusion, asserting, "It IS about (Zionism) the Jews!."[24] Others thought it less about "Zionist occupation government" and more a critical commentary on current politics. Whiterider pronounced it decidely "anti-leftist" and an indication of "growing discontent with the Magic Negroe's [sic] regime,"[25] finding eerie similarities with ongoing events, including the use of health care "to dupe the masses," manipulation by the media, and "fake Hate Crimes."

Discussants, of course, pictured white supremacists as the freedom fighters, struggling against the oppressive oligarchs and alien invaders. Whether wrapped in a conspiracy theory or not, they draw particular attention to a world turned upside down in the show and every day. Importantly, "political correctness" constrains free thought and public discourse. On the show, Father Jack delivers a sermon that reveals deep truths about the invaders and the world they have wrought, and the powers label it hate: "The ones preaching 'hate' are actually the good guys." The analogy is plain: in a colorblind, multicultural society, "we" speak the truth about race, and it is labeled hate.

Apparently, not everyone at stormfront.org tuned in to *V* for the storyline or the politics. The actresses sparked interest and dialogue as well. At least one poster watched it for "the athletic blonde girl,"[26] while another was originally put off by the "mulatto V leader."[27] The latter comment caused something of a stir, pushing the conversation in a predictably sideways direction—as is all too common on the site. Where MisanthroPunk disputed the claim,[28] Whiterider indicated she was Brazilian actress Morena Baccarin,[29] and PhoenixHawk interjected she was "probably mostly Spanish [sic]. . . . Not a typical mestizo, as . . . the short brown trolls with the dull eyes that infest my state."[30] Even where race seems irrelevant, it becomes a defining feature, key to making sense of the show and establishing correlations with everyday life. Fixing the racial identity of the actress is no small matter because beauty, value, and goodness follow from category and placement. And yet, it does not matter that Brazil was a former Portuguese, not Spanish, colony, but only that the actress can be typed as white, salvaged as distinct from the abject racial Other encountered daily. Indeed, exceptions and things out of place pose problems that disrupt narratives and must be explain away for the resolution of apparent contradictions. In much the same way, discussants puzzle over how a show exposing Zionist conspiracies could be written and produced by Jews.

While *V* and any other of number of programs are open to interpretation at stromfront.org, not all participants embrace allegorical readings and conspiratorial thinking. As one commentator said, "I think it's all reading too much into a sci-fi show about alien invaders."

Save the Children

Even though white supremacists watching television may find solace in select shows, the medium remains dangerous. Nowhere is the threat more clearly pronounced than in discussions of children and television. While programming generally troubles them, television shows directed at children are found to be especially problematic. Moreover, because of these dangers, they often outline rules or strategies to guard against the ills of television.

Nickelodeon and PBS come under steady assault for their programming, which discussants read as endorsing multiculturalism and corrupting children. *Sesame Street,* for instance, is often singled out for its inclusion of diversity and what is read as an open endorsement of race mixing. In a discussion of the most offensive shows in the history of television, one participant opined:

> I remember watching that as a small child, and seeing chinese [*sic*] and Mexican kids playing with white kids. That was something I never seen in my small north Florida town in 1987. I remember thinking, "did they go to another country to film this?" Looking back, I never seen all white kids or all black kids together, there was all races playing together. Subtle brainwash [*sic*], but effective.[31]

Similarly, according to 88aussie, *Dora the Explorer* "encourages the one race theory."[32] That is, its characters, imagery, and narrative have an agenda to convince viewers—here, innocent children—that "the world would be a better place if we morphed into a single race, its a jewish thing [*sic*]."[33] Other discussants lamented her poor English and wondered if a show titled "Jamal" featuring "ebonics" could be far off. Whatever the precise reason, the discussion of *Dora the Explorer* suggests a consensus that it is "filth" or "garbage" that few "on this forum would let their child(ren) watch."[34]

Responsible parents, committed to what they might view as raising racially conscious children, have not only reacted to the content of specific shows but proactively detailed how to protect their children. A 2002 speech by Jan Cartwright[35] broadcast on the Aryan Nations' program *American Dissident Voices,* lectured listeners on the best practices for "raising white children in a multicultural society." Cartwright identifies television as one of many dangers, including public education, children's books, and video games:

> My children do not watch television. Upon occasion we do view the news. . . . We discuss what we've seen, and they know to read between the lines. We can't even trust the educational channels. . . . Children are too young to split apart the truth from the "glitz and glimmer" on television, to read between the lines and look behind everything. If they just sat in front of the Almighty Television they're lost.

While difficult, these measures put children on the right path, "the true path our race must take."[36]

Rachel Pendergraft, in an undated commentary at the self-proclaimed official website of the Knights Party, USA, a re-creation of the Ku Klux Klan led by Thomas Robb, who also serves as a pastor at the Christian Revival Center, reiterates and extends the position laid out by Cartwright:

> As Christian racialists we must continually stay on guard in our homes— where the enemy most often attacks. They are looking for new recruits into their new multi-racial, bi-sexual, plastic monetary one world system. . . .
>
> Those in the racialist movement should continually strive to monitor their home's television viewing. America's future lies in our children and it is our responsibility as parents or future parents to safeguard our children's mind before ideas of abortion, homosexuality, racemixing, globalism, or euthanasia take root.

She proceeds to enumerate a set of "guidelines for safe TV watching," including knowing what your children watch, watching television with them, discussing its messages, and using offensive shows to highlight the antiwhite, anti-Christian agenda.

Pendergraft and Cartwright emphasize responsibility, vigilance, and future focus. They position children as vulnerable and in need of protection. Both endorse cultivating a racially conscious, white supremacist, and critical literacy. Where Cartwright discourages television viewing, Pendergraft, perhaps more of a pragmatist, encourages using programming to unmask biases she perceives in the media. Both aim to protect the white race by protecting its future, echoing one of the key refrains of the white power movement today, the 14 Words, initially coined by David Lane, a leading figure in the white nationalist movement and founding member of the Aryan-inspired organization the Order: "We must secure the existence of our people and a future for White Children." The focus on the family and the protection of progeny underscores the entanglements of race, gender, and sexuality in the white power subculture today, an intersection Pendergraft makes much more explicit in her linkage of "abortion, homosexuality, racemixing, globalization, [and] euthanasia." Again, television matters because it presents an ever-present existential threat, one that white (supremacist) parents must actively defend against at the peril of their children and the future of their race.

Conclusions

Rarely do many television viewers stop to think about how a white nationalist or white supremacist might interpret the medium and its messages. Listening to the accounts of white supremacists offers a stark counterpoint to the purported colorblindness of the contemporary moment. They remind us of the ways in which racial rhetorics reinvent themselves, taking on novel appearances to communicate seemingly antiquated ideologies. These latent and resurgent forms of white supremacy speak less and less in the language of hate, and more and more in terms familiar from multiculturalism (heritage, racial uplift, diversity). Nevertheless, when applied to television, white supremacist frames continue to emphasize theories of Jewish control, the overt antiwhite/pro-black biases of the medium, the fundamental dangers of race mixing, the breakdown of tradition, and the corruption of youth, reading in the medium and its messages an existential threat of grave importance.

It would be comforting if we could separate these views in a discrete domain, set apart from how other critics talk about television and its impacts; however, it is only false comfort. On the one hand, liberal media bias and the elite agenda of Hollywood regularly surface in neoconservative commentaries on the state of American culture, which read popular culture generally and television specifically as denigrating tradition, family, and propriety in favor of transgressive celebrations of hedonism, promiscuity, drug use, and homosexuality. On the other hand, the culture wars that have raged for the better part of three decades have routinely targeted diversity and multiculturalism, actively defending white perspectives and privileges in an ongoing, if little-recognized, race war. In keeping with the decorum of the day, few of these voices speak of a Jewish conspiracy, but they do fret about corruption, damage to youth, and the future of (white) America. Homologous projects, marked by distinct rhetorics and styles, directed at a common end: maintaining differences that make a difference (race, gender, sexuality) in a context that denies that difference can have any significance because, to turn a phrase, we all are colorblind here now.

Importantly, it is precisely the predominance of post-racial framings, typified by the ideology of colorblindness, that anchors resurgent formulations of white supremacy today, energizing their interpretations of television. On the one hand, the success of the civil rights movement and derivative projects like multiculturalism has brought an end to overt racism, encouraged the celebration of attributes that make ethnic groups unique (culture, heritage, identity, and the like), and established the importance of the recognition and respect of differences. These cultural changes have led many advocates of white power to recast their rhetoric and revisit their strategies. As multiculturalism and colorblindness drain power, violence, and history out of white racism, whites reimagine themselves as one more racial or ethnic group, a unique people. For white supremacists, or, in this softer reworking, for white nationalists, one of the key problems with television, as outlined in this chapter, is that it threatens whites as a distinct people, who possess a unique culture and whose traditions warrant defense. On the other hand, the very dominance of a post-racial worldview opens an oppositional space within which to formulate cultural criticism and present an alternative social vision. The colorblind screen, because of its pervasiveness and popularity, in turn, becomes a primary site to interrogate racial common sense, illustrate what they understand to be its ill effects, and defend white power.

Notes

1. http://www.npr.org/2012/01/13/145159926/walton-goggins-playing-bad-boy -boyd-on-justified.

2. Shenanigans RE: The Most Offensive Shows in TV History. Post #512. Posted 6/18/2011. Retrieved 9 Dec. 2011 from http://www.stormfront.org/forum/t311123/.

3. putnamvt RE: The Most Offensive Shows in TV History. Post #534. Posted 6/23/11. Retrieved 9 Dec. 2011 from http://www.stormfront.org/forum/t311123/.

4. Fritzie Weiss 7/31/2006 RE: The Most Offensive Shows in TV History. Post #94. Posted 7/31/06. Retrieved 9 Dec. 2011 from http://www.stormfront.org/forum/t311123/.

5. putnamvt 6/23/2011 RE: The Most Offensive Shows in TV History. Post #534. Posted 6/23/11. Retrieved 9 Dec. 2011 from http://www.stormfront.org/forum/t311123/.

6. Geborenzuschaukein 10/31/2010 RE: Happiness Is Life Free from Television. Post #40. Posted 10/31/10. Retrieved 10 Oct. 2010 from http://www.stormfront.org/forum/t752887/.

7. Happiness Is Life Free from Television. Retrieved 10 Oct. 2010 from http://www.stormfront.org/forum/t752887/; TV Kills Society So Will Society Kill TV? Retrieved 9 Dec. 2011 from http://www.stormfront.org/forum/t825568/.

8. swimmingly [qtd. in Venus-16's post] RE: The Most Offensive Shows in TV History. Post #4. Posted 7/18/2006 on stormfront.org.

9. Knightrider1961 RE: The Most Offensive Shows in TV History. Post #8. Posted 7/19/2006 on stormfront.org.

10. Knightrider1961 RE: The Most Offensive Shows in TV History. Post #8. Posted 7/19/2006 on stormfront.org.

11. Blue Eyes RE: The Most Offensive Shows in TV History. Post #299. Posted 7/27/2007 on stormfront.org.

12. All quotations in this paragraph from The Most Offensive Shows in TV History. Retrieved 9 Dec. 2011 from http://www.stormfront.org/forum/t311123/.

13. Abby L. Ferber is professor of sociology and director of the Matrix Center for the Advancement of Social Equity and Inclusion at the University of Colorado at Colorado Springs. Her research and scholarly work center around issues of race, ethnicity, and white privilege. Jessie Daniels is associate professor of urban public health at CUNY. A large part of her research also focuses on issues of race and racism, particularly in contemporary media.

14. whiteworkingclasswoman RE: The Most Offensive Shows in TV History. Post #164. Posted 5/31/2007 on stormfront.org.

15. AMericanREnaissance RE: The Most Offensive Shows in TV History. Post #13. Posted 7/19/2006 on stormfront.org.

16. All quotations in this paragraph from The Most Offensive Shows in TV History. Retrieved 9 Dec. 2011 from http://www.stormfront.com/forum/t311123/.

17. All quotations in this paragraph from Good TV Shows for White Folks. Retrieved 9 Dec. 2011 from http://www.stormfront.org/forum/t233328/.

18. DanJunior RE: Good TV Shows for White Folks. Post #102. Posted 8/2/2007 on stormfront.org.

19. Knightrider1961 RE: Good TV Shows for White Folks. Post #215. Posted 3/23/2009 on stormfront.org.

20. All quotations in this paragraph from Good TV Shows for White Folks. Retrieved 9 Dec. 2011 from http://www.stormfront.org/forum/t233328/.

21. Discussion of Archie Bunker in the thread Good TV Shows for White Folks. Retrieved 9 Dec. 2011 from http://www.stormfront.org/forum/t233328/; discussion of Sons of Anarchy can be found at the Sons of Anarchy online forum. Retrieved 12 Oct. 2011 from http://www.stormfront.org/forum/t829667/.

22. All quotations in this section refer to the following discussion thread on V (2009) (TV series). Retrieved 9 Dec. 2011 from http://www.stormfront.org/forum/t688621/.

23. -Chaos- V (2009) (TV series). Post #1. Posted 3/7/2010 on stormfront.org.

24. Screaming_In_Digital Re: V (2009) (TV series). Post #2. Posted 3/7/2010 on stormfront.org.

25. Whiterider RE: V (2009) (TV series). Post #16. Posted 5/21/2010 on stormfront.org.

26. Stormbear Re: V (2009) (TV series). Post #19. Posted 5/22/2010 on stormfront.org.

27. White Pride We Must Unite Re: V (2009) (TV series). Post #17. Posted 5/21/2010 on stormfront.org.

28. MisanthroPunk Re: V (2009 (TV series). Post #20. Posted on 5/24/2010 on stormfront.org.

29. Whiterider RE: V (2009) (TV series). Post #21. Posted 5/25/2010 on stormfront.org.

30. PhoenixHawk RE: V (2009) (TV series). Post #22. Posted 5/25/2010 on stormfront.org.

31. jasonhowello3 [qtd. in post by RM-33] RE: The Most Offensive Shows in TV History. Post #116. Posted 8/2/2006. Retrieved on 9 Dec. 2011 from http://www.stormfront.org/forum/t311123/.

32. 88aussie Dora the Explorer. Post #1. Posted 8/24/2011 on stormfront.org.

33. 88aussie RE: Dora the Explorer. Post #6. Posted 8/25/2011 on stormfront.org.

34. Dora the Explorer. Retrieved 9 Dec. 2011 from http://www.stormfront.org/forum/t826749/.

35. Jan Cartwright is a vocal member of the National Alliance, a white supremacist and white nationalist political organization.

36. Robert Griffin (137–43) offers a portrait of a family that embodies these principles and is, in his words, "raising honorable white children."

WORKS CITED

Bonilla-Silva, Eduardo. *Racism without Racists: Color-Blind Racism and the Persistence of Racial Inequality in the United States.* Lanham, MD: Rowman and Littlefield, 2003. Print.

Cartwright, Jan. "Raising White Children in a Multicultural Society." *Free Speech* 8, 11 (Nov). Retrieved 18 Mar. 2004 from http://www.thirdworldplanet.com/adv/fso211c.htm.

Daniels, Jessie. *White Lies: Race, Class, Gender and Sexuality in White Supremacist Discourse.* New York: Routledge, 1997. Print.

Ferber, Abby. *White Man Falling: Race, Gender, and White Supremacy.* Lanham, MD: Rowman and Littlefield, 1999. Print.

Gray, Herman. "Culture, Masculinity, and the Time after Race." *Toward a Sociology of the Trace.* Ed. Herman Gray and Macarena Gomez-Barris. Minneapolis: University of Minnesota Press, 2010. 87–108. Print.

Griffin, Robert S. *One Sheaf, One Vine: Racially Conscious White Americans Talk about Race.* Bloomington, IN: Author House, 2004. Print.

Gross, Terry, "Walter Goggins: Getting 'Justified' with Brother Boyd." *Fresh Air,* National Public Radio. <http://www.npr.org/templates/story/story.php?storyId=126889536>

Leonard, David J., and C. Richard King. *Commodified and Criminalized: New Racism and African Americans in Contemporary Sports.* Lanham, MD: Rowman and Littlefield, 2012. Print.

Pendergraft, Rachel. "Television and Your Kids." kkk.bz. n.d. Web. 11 Jan. 2012. <http://www.kkk.bz/weekly10.htm>.

Stormfront.org. Web. http://www.stormfront.org/forum/.

Swain, Carol M., and Russ Nieli. *Contemporary Voices of White Nationalism in America.* Cambridge: Cambridge University Press, 2003. Print.

Zündel, Ernest. "Media Control." *Calling Our Nation* 82 (1991): 17–18. Print.

10

BBFFs

Interracial Friendships in a Post-Racial World

SARAH E. TURNER

A Complex Cultural Moment

America is embroiled in a complex cultural moment in terms of race, and one seminal locus where that complexity is being explored is television.[1] Jim Crow laws, white-only signs, and the civil rights movement are safely in the past, historical moments now, not day-to-day markers of racial struggle. The country has elected its first biracial president, and one-third of African Americans have entered the middle class. And yet, race still matters. When news of black Republican presidential hopeful Herman Cain's infidelity surfaced in the fall of 2011, he responded by accusing the media of a "high tech lynching."[2] When then presidential hopeful Barack Obama won the Democratic nomination in 2008, he was accused of being both too black and not black enough. Television, as Herman Gray argues, "remains a decisive arena in which struggles for representation, or more significantly, struggles over the *meanings* of representation, continue to be waged at various levels of national politics, expressive culture, and moral authority" (xvii). If, as Gray posits, television is a discursive site where struggles over the complex question of racial representation occur, reading that struggle through the lens of Stuart Hall's theories of encoding and decoding provides a necessary framework through which to consider the possible meanings of race as represented on and through television today. Hall characterizes television as a discourse that encompasses the messages "encoded" by and through the production of a show and the messages "decoded" by those watching the show; however, while both the production and the reception of the messages rely on shared frameworks of knowledge, Hall's theories acknowledge that "distortion" or a "misunderstanding" frequently occurs during the moment of decoding.

Ten years ago, in 2002, the National Association for the Advancement of Colored People (NAACP) released the first of a series of reports documenting the state of racial representation on major American television networks. *Out of Focus—Out of Sync Take 1* reported that of the twenty-six new shows that debuted in the fall 1999–2000 season, not one featured an actor of color in a lead role. The fall 2011–12 lineup on the major networks has twenty-seven new shows, and despite the fact that most white Americans espouse a colorblind ideology, the belief that race no longer plays a central or significant role, there are no black female leads in any of the prime-time network shows, and nearly all the male leads are white.[3]

This is not to say, however, that there are no black or minority roles on television; there are, but instead of being cast in the lead or starring role, black female actors are being cast more and more in the role of best friend to the white lead.[4] Drawing heavily on the legacy of interracial "buddy" films—originating as a male-dominated movie paradigm linking white and black men together in interracial friendships—contemporary programming links a white female lead with a supporting and supportive black woman who is "wise, loyal, and sassy," but always secondary, often sublimating her needs to those of the white lead (Braxton 29).

What is especially interesting about this moment is that it represents a shift from the traditional male genre of interracial buddy films (think of *48 Hours* [1982], *Beverly Hills Cop* [1984], *Lethal Weapon* [1987], *The Fast and the Furious* [2001]) to female-centred interracial relationships in both television and movies. For the purpose of this study, the focus will be on television, namely, the Disney Channel;[5] however, this new paradigm is not solely the purview of Disney or television. A recent *Los Angeles Times* article outlines the prevalence of this pairing on television and in movies, citing, for example Merrin Dungey's character in *Alias* (2003) and the pilot for *Grey's Anatomy* spin-off *Private Practice* (2007); Wanda Sykes in *The New Adventures of Old Christine* (2005); Brandy in *I Still Know What You Did Last Summer* (1998); Amerie in *First Daughter* (2004); Regina King in *A Cinderella Story* (2004), *Miss*

Congeniality 2: Armed and Fabulous (2005), and *Legally Blonde 2: Red, White and Blonde* (2003); Alicia Keys in *The Nanny Diaries* (2007); Kellee Stewart in *My Boys* (2007); Stacey Dash in *Clueless* (1995); Cress Williams in *Hart of Dixie* (2011); Maya Rudolph in *Up All Night* (2011); and Aisha Tyler in *Ghost Whisperer.*[6]

Two current Disney Channel shows, *Shake It Up* (2010–) and *Good Luck Charlie* (2010–), feature white female leads and black females in the buddy or best friend position (BBFF: black best friend forever).[7] Keeping in mind the fact that television, as the major discursive medium today, plays a central role in the articulation and construction of racialized identities in the United States, this study will explore the impact of Disney's representational strategy on its children and tween viewing audience through Hall's theories of encoding and decoding. While previous studies of race/racism and/in Disney do exist,[8] studies of Disney's role in the perpetuation of the politics and ideology of colorblindness, especially in the twenty-first century, are lacking. This study does not seek to vilify Disney; rather, it is an examination of the complexity of representational choices Disney writers, producers, and executives, and other channels, face in America's "Obama moment."

Disney Does Race

At first glance, twenty-first-century Disney and its multiracial casts seem to embody the move toward inclusiveness and diverse representation on its cable network, Disney Channel. And yet, a closer examination of the most popular shows on Disney Channel over the past decade suggests that the channel's diversity is in fact representative of this new colorblind racism, presenting diversity in such a way as to reify the position and privilege of white culture and the white cast members. While appearing to foreground race through racially diverse casts, Disney Channel exemplifies one of the tenets of colorblindness that suggests it is not necessary to see race because in fact America has moved "beyond color or race [and instead is able to] focus on the content of a person's character" (Neville et al. 29). Not seeing race effectively erases race and suggests that "we are all the same," and yet this seemingly liberal viewpoint works to deny the existence of social, cultural, economic, and/or political disenfranchisement that is the result of institutionalized racism. In this way, colorblindness serves to legitimize racism and certain racial (read white) privileges. Thus audiences can see and celebrate multicultural assimilation while disregarding existing racial hierarchies. As Angharad N. Valdivia argues, "To be sure, Disney does not pursue new representational strategies unless it is certain that profits will increase without alienating the bulk of its audience" (286). If that audience exists in a colorblind world, then Disney's representational strategies work to reify that ideology.

Disney's racial representational strategies have shifted or evolved over time; the result is that contemporary Disney is seemingly no longer open to charges of overt racism or overreliance on stereotypes. Instead, the new Disney, in both television and film, reflects a shift to the politics of colorblindness—an evolution from the "presence of absence" (*Lizzie McGuire* [2001–4], *Hannah Montana* [2006–11]) through a targeted race-specific format (*That's So Raven* [2003–7], *Corey in the House* [2007–8], *The Cheetah Girls* [2003]) to the new black best friend format.[9] While many Disney Channel shows are notable for their inclusion of main or supporting characters of color, this chapter will argue that such representation, idealized as colorblind, instead works to locate those characters in stereotypical roles that disenfranchise, not empower, the groups represented. A close examination of Disney's twenty-first-century representational strategies suggests that many shows at one level actually work to erase difference and imply that the characters are the same, no matter what they look like, and that they share the same social experience. That these shows are geared toward younger viewers suggests that Disney is exposing these viewers to what Eduardo Bonilla-Silva calls "racism without racists," outwardly presenting an ideology of "we are all the same" (4) while at the same time subtly adhering to a post-racial doctrine that undermines while it represents.

Twentieth-century Disney clearly imagined an audience that was white and that shared the ideologies of the hegemonic culture; films such as *The Jungle Book* (1967), *The Lion King* (1994), *Song of the South* (1946), and *Aladdin* (1992), for example, all illustrate Disney's recognition of the social and racial positioning of its audience, a positioning that would recognize tropes of blackness or racial representation but that would not problematize the use of those tropes in any way. However, more recent Disney films and, more important for this study, television shows have attempted to widen that audience base, but in such a way as to not alienate the core audience that is white.[10] The success of this strategy is evident in the May 2010 Nielsen ratings that saw Disney Channel hold onto the number one spot for the sixty-third consecutive month in the Kids 6–11 demographic and for the sixty-second straight month among Tweens 9–14.[11] A quick glance at the recent Disney Channel lineup suggests that diversity is indeed central to its mandate; yet, upon closer examination, Disney's racial representation is both promising and problematic in the same moment. While tweens and younger girls are presented with characters of color with whom they might identify, the race of the nonwhite characters is encoded in such a way as to make it seem negligible, as if it does not matter. Viewers are thus able to decode the characters as essentially raceless, as "just girls" and not Asian, Latina, or black girls. Selena Gomez, who played Alex Russo in all four seasons of Disney's *The Wizards of Waverly Place* (2007–12), is herself Mexican and Italian American. On the show, which revolves around the three Russo children who are wizards like their father, Gomez plays the daughter of an Italian father and a Mexican mother. While her mother, Theresa, is clearly marked as Mexican American through her accent and her references to Latina culture, Alex is given no cultural or racial markers; in fact, in one episode, she is shown as being completely unaware of the importance of her mother's *quinceañeras* celebration.[12] The only marker of difference between Alex and her best friend, Harper, who is white, is that Alex is a wizard.

Brenda Song, herself half Hmong Chinese and half Thai American, plays London Tipton, a wealthy teen who is the daughter of a hotel owner, on one of Disney Channel's longest-running contemporary series, *The Suite Life of Zack and Cody* (2005–8), and its spin-off, *The Suite Life on Deck* (2008–11). Instead of relying on the stereotype of the cerebral and hardworking Asian, Song's character is constructed in such a way as to destabilize that image: she is wealthy, spoiled, and vacuous, concerned only with her clothes and shopping. In fact, viewers are told that it took London fourteen years to learn the alphabet. This representational strategy is problematic in that Song is one of the only Asian actors on the Disney Channel, and yet in no way can she be read as a role model or positive representation by the viewing audience. Her Asian heritage is never foregrounded, as made apparent from the moment she is introduced as

London Tipton, and viewers are shown her adult-free penthouse full of markers of consumerism as if these markers of excess are what define her, not her ethnic or racial background. The backstory to her character reveals that she has a Thai mother now divorced from her white father, who is almost entirely absent from the show and her life. And yet, while Tipton does appear in contrast with the other main female character, Maddie Fitzpatrick, played by blond Ashley Tisdale, herself famous for her role as spoiled Sharpay Evans in the *High School Musical* franchise (2006, 2007, 2008), the obvious racial differences are never acknowledged, suggesting again that Disney has chosen to adhere to a colorblind "we are all the same" approach in its representational strategies.

Interracial Buddies and Black Best Friends

It is possible to argue, superficially at least, that the Disney Channel's shift from a historical and overt reliance on stereotypes to a colorblind "we are all the same" approach to race is both necessary and positive. But, as this chapter argues, a colorblind representational strategy is dangerous and open to multiple interpretations. Interracial buddy films seem to epitomize the polysemic position of Hall's theories of encoding and decoding through the presentation and celebration of interracial friendships and often interdependent partnerships. Traditionally, interracial buddy films involve two men, one white and the other black, who are thrown together by circumstance and are forced to form a partnership in order to succeed or survive; often there is an initial reluctance on the part of the white man to engage with or befriend the black man, who, however, is often shown as willing to help the white man for reasons often not fully explained. In what is often considered the first of the interracial buddy films, *The Defiant Ones* (1958), black Sidney Poitier is handcuffed to white Tony Curtis; both men are escaped cons on the run, and ultimately Poitier allows himself to be recaptured in order to save Curtis's character. Donald Bogle's comprehensive study *Toms, Coons, Mulattoes, Mammies, and Bucks: An Interpretive History of Blacks in American Films* describes the appeal of Sidney Poitier (and by extension buddy films) to Hollywood and audiences: he was the black man who had met [the] standards of the mass white audience—he dressed well, spoke "proper English," and had the best table manners (175). He was a Christlike figure in many of his roles, extending his hand to help the white man (*Edge of the City* [1957] and *The Blackboard Jungle* [1955]), and he was sexless. The success of the buddy film formula is encapsulated in the list of adjectives Bogle accords to Poitier: well-dressed, well-spoken, "civilized," and sexless—one might also add cultureless (175). Encoded in interracial buddy films is hegemonic America's response to the racial tensions of first the civil rights years, and then the post–civil rights years: the black man's willingness to befriend and assist the white man, often at great personal cost, reifies the viewing audience's sense of race relations.

In one of the seminal studies of interracial buddy films, B. Lee Artz analyzes the connection between the appeal of buddy films and the American racial maelstrom the country found itself in after the civil rights movement:[13]

> Through the production, distribution, and consumption of fictions that include entertaining, innocuous interracial narratives, Blacks appear to be "movin' on up." Pleasing to Blacks and comforting to Whites, the fictions of interracial buddy movies simplify race relations, reassuring America of its continuing goodness. Viewed by millions of Americans, cultural vehicles such as interracial buddy movies help negotiate popular consent for the "new" racism—touting equality while ignoring the actual condition of race relations. (68)

Although Artz's study was concerned with the rise of buddy films in the 1980s, his use of the term "new racism" is, unfortunately, still relevant; in this case, however, the new racism is the ideology of colorblind racism that is so ubiquitous in America today. On one level, Guerrero's sense that buddy films were a form of "Reaganite entertainment" can be repositioned as "Obama entertainment" to reflect the rise of contemporary television shows that rely on the buddy formula to still "negotiat[e], contain, and fantastically resolv[e] the tangled and socially charged issue of race relations on the [television] screen" (240).

Through this lens of "Obama entertainment," Disney's utilization of the buddy film formula, repackaged as the black best friend, is further complicated. Pragmatically, creating shows with diverse casts broadens the appeal and potential audience segment for Disney; politically, if those shows also work to assuage the racial concerns and ambivalence of that audience (or their parents), the status quo remains unchanged. Disney's *Shake It Up*, which premiered on 7 November 2010, exemplifies the black best friend formula. The show is set in Chicago and centers around two high school students, white CeCe Jones (Bella Thorne) and black Rocky Blue (Zendaya Coleman), best friends who, at CeCe's urging, audition for a new live television show *Shake It Up, Chicago*, a youth-oriented dance program designed to showcase new talent. Created by Chris Thomson, in the pilot "Start It Up," the two main characters, CeCe and Rocky, are shown busking unsuccessfully on a Chicago subway platform; after demonstrating their dancing prowess, and seemingly entertaining the commuters and others on the platform, the girls pass the hat, hoping for donations, but receive none. Thus viewers are informed from the outset that the girls are entrepreneurial and self-confident, but, unlike other Disney characters such as London Tipton, Sharpay Evans, or Hannah Montana, not wealthy.[14] One theme of the show, as suggested by the title and the formulaic use of three-word titles ending in "It Up" for each of the episodes as well as the series itself, is access to the American Dream and upward mobility. While the girls are not impoverished, they belong to a working middle-class America and share the dream of social and financial mobility, which explains the busking as well as the desire to audition for the show.[15] What seems to bond them together, then, is their desire to succeed, and that desire works to negate any differences based on race; instead of being seen as two friends, one of whom is black and the other white, they are seen as the personification of the American Dream's melting pot, where everyone has the ability to better herself.

After the opening scene, the credits roll and the show switches to one of its main locales: CeCe's apartment, which she shares with her mother, a police officer, and her younger brother, Flynn. Although a far cry from Lorraine Hansberry's Broadway play *A Raisin in the Sun* (1959), which centered around the cramped Chicago apartment of the Younger family, intergenerational working-class blacks determined to move up and out of the neighbourhood, CeCe and her family also live in an apartment, not a house in the suburbs with a lawn and a garage. Again, the audience is reminded that this is not a story of privilege; instead, it is about the "99 percent"—regular working Americans.[16] The choice of Chicago for the show's setting is fascinating because of Chicago's problematic history of race-based housing discrimination, neighborhood covenants that barred black families from purchasing homes, and overcrowded slum tenements. In the background, a television is tuned to the *Shake It Up, Chicago* show and announces the upcoming auditions. CeCe hears the call for dancers and turns from the kitchen to one of the open windows of the apartment, sticks her head out of the window, and yells to Rocky, who subsequently appears, climbing into the apartment through the open window. While viewers are not explicitly told that Rocky lives in the same building, or that their respective apartments are connected by the fire escape, the implication is clear: the girls and their families live in an apartment building, complete with fire escapes, instead of houses in the suburbs that act as markers of middle-class status and often racial and economic segregation. Rocky is rarely shown entering the apartment through the front door; the window seems to be her choice, but the reverse is not shown. Never (at least in season 1) do viewers see Rocky's apartment or see CeCe entering (or exiting) through the same window. At one level, the window entrance is meant to suggest the close relationship of the girls (Rocky has unimpeded access to CeCe and her home through the always open window).[17] However, despite Disney Channel's reliance on an encoded politics of colorblindness, the fact that it is black Rocky who enters through the window can be decoded as connecting her blackness to a sense of Otherness reminiscent of segregation or the kitchen door rather than the front door of the "big house." The potential for the audience to misunderstand the image of Rocky and the window undermines the "we are all the same" tenet of colorblind racism.

The next scene serves to introduce the central recurring cast members, namely, Rocky's brother, Ty Blue, played by Roshon Fegan, and his best friend, Deuce Martinez, played by Adam Irogoyen. Black Ty and Rocky engage in a dance-off, while white CeCe and Flynn, and Latino Deuce sit on the steps of the apartment building and watch, vicariously enjoying the dancing prowess of the siblings but unable to join in. Having established, through this scene, Rocky's dancing abilities, the scene shifts to the actual audition, where CeCe is clearly in charge; she literally drags Rocky toward the center stage and the host of the show, holding on tightly to Rocky, who appears poised to flee. After the large group audition, the remaining dancers, CeCe and Rocky included, are given individual auditions—a chance to demonstrate original choreography and moves. Rocky, after a shaky start, does well and makes the cut; CeCe, on the other hand, gets stage fright and freezes up, thus ruining her chances of also making the show despite Rocky's attempts to help by standing behind her and manipulating her, puppetlike. CeCe's robot-like movements stand in stark contrast to Rocky's dancing abilities—the first time in the show that there is any suggestion of difference between the girls. Rocky pledges her allegiance to CeCe as her BFF (best friend forever [read BBF: black best friend]) and refuses to do the show without CeCe. Here, Disney draws from the historical legacy of buddy films, as discussed earlier; black Rocky is willing to forgo her chance at stardom as a means to help salvage white CeCe's ego and her embarrassment at freezing while onstage. However, the show then flips the usual buddy film formula when CeCe is shown forcing Rocky to attend the first taping.

In an intriguing, yet unrecognized by young Disney viewers, homage to *The Defiant Ones,* at the *Shake It Up, Chicago* taping, Rocky reveals the handcuffs she has "borrowed" from CeCe's police officer mother and cuffs the two girls together, forcing CeCe to go onstage with her and dance. Thus linked, the two girls dance, mimicking and mirroring each other's moves, literally because of the handcuffs but also symbolically because, once again, they are the same. When the host of the show approaches them, both girls expect him to be angry because of CeCe's presence; however, it is Rocky who offers to take the blame, explaining that it was her fault CeCe was even present at the audition. Ironically, the host likes what he assumes is choreographed dancing and offers CeCe a spot on the show as well. While ultimately CeCe is also asked to join the cast of *Shake It Up, Chicago,* having failed on her own, one possibly unintended reading or decoding of this pairing suggests that white CeCe can only dance by imitating black Rocky, thus appropriating one aspect of her blackness for herself.

Good Luck Charlie, another Disney Channel hit show to utilize the black best friend formula, debuted on 4 April 2010, garnering 4.6 million viewers and earning the show the week's highest rating for cable programs.[18] Starring white, blond Bridgit Mendler as Teddy, the lead, the show focuses on Teddy and her family, with each episode ending

with Teddy shooting a video diary full of big-sister advice for baby sister, Charlie. Raven Goodwin plays Teddy's BBF, Ivy Renee Wentz, and,
interestingly, Micah Williams plays the BBF to Teddy's older brother,
PJ, played by Jason Dolley, although neither appears in every episode,
unlike Rocky in *Shake It Up*.

Although Ivy, black best friend to Teddy, appears sporadically, when
viewers do see her, her sole function is to assist Teddy. Episode 24 of the
first season, "Snow Show," is a two-part episode based around a vaca-
tion Teddy and her family take at a nearby ski resort. In the lobby of
Mount Bliss, Teddy encounters a psychic who offers to give her a free
reading; although initially suspicious of the woman's abilities, Teddy is
convinced that she will "come face to face with the love of her life" at the
ski lodge as predicted by the psychic. Inevitably, Teddy encounters not
one but three possible "loves," including her former boyfriend, Spencer,
with whom she has recently broken up. Confused by the three possibilities and awakened after a dream in which she has married all three,
Teddy calls Ivy to ask for her help. Viewers are shown a bedside clock
that reads 2:25 a.m.—despite the late hour, Teddy offers no apologies for
the late night call—and, the next morning, Ivy is shown walking into
the ski lodge. She wears so many layers of clothing that she can barely
move, and in response to Teddy's queries regarding the ensemble, Ivy
replies, "Ivy doesn't do cold." Despite her personal discomfort, and the
four-hour bus ride she has endured, Ivy's first action upon arriving is to
immediately confront one of the three young men, Justin, who is black.
After asking him if he is a skier, she then asks somewhat antagonisti-
cally, "Does your family have money?" He is dismissed after the two
girls hear him laugh, and then Ivy questions the second young man,
Brandon, who is summarily dismissed as well after he is shown to be
overly dependent on his mother. When Teddy refuses to even consider that her true love might be her former boyfriend, Ivy responds
by questioning her own role in the scenario as well as Teddy's desire for
Ivy's presence. However, instead of responding to Ivy, Teddy continues
to focus on her own conundrum, and Ivy is heard muttering: "I come
all the way up here for nothing, but yeah, let's keep it on you." Teddy's
solipsistic self-absorption leaves no room for empathy or gratitude for
her friend, who has seemingly dropped everything to join Teddy at the
lodge. At the end of the show, after Teddy bumps into yet another young

man, she turns to Ivy and says, "Go get his number." Ivy's response is simply "I'm on it," as if this is a well-rehearsed role and, by extension, relationship.

In season 2, episode 24 ("Alley Oops") of *Good Luck Charlie,* Teddy convinces Ivy that they should both send in videos of themselves singing in order to win a car through a contest sponsored by Denver's professional basketball team. However, Ivy's mom, Mary Lou Wentz, wins the contest instead and gets the chance to sing the national anthem at a Denver Nuggets basketball game. Ivy's mother gets stage fright when they arrive at the arena and refuses to sing; Teddy offers to take her place in the spotlight and arranges for a microphone that will allow Ivy's mom to sing offstage while Teddy lip syncs. The audiences, both at the game and those watching the show, see Teddy perform "black voice"—viewers see Teddy, a white, blond teenager, sing with a voice reminiscent of Aretha Franklin or Bessie Smith. It is a totally incongruous scene, with Teddy awkwardly trying to anticipate when Mary Lou will finish, and Mary Lou drawing out the last notes and adding an obvious blues (and black) inflection to the song and performance.[19] This episode is intriguing in that it is a radical shift from the black best friend format of the other episodes in which Teddy and Ivy are depicted as best friends from similar backgrounds: both live in freestanding one-family homes in nice neighborhoods in Denver; both have two parents, although Ivy is an only child while Teddy is one of four; both have strong mother characters in their lives; and, both often conspire together to fool their parents into letting them stay out late or attend parties they are too young to attend. The two-family structure, one black and one white, of *Good Luck Charlie* stands in marked contrast to CeCe's single-parent family and Rocky's almost entirely absent family on *Shake It Up.* Herman Gray argues that the success of the long-running *The Cosby Show* (1984–92) has made the depiction of "black upper-middle class families a safe, banal and routine staple of television fare . . . engaging and attractive, these familiar tropes of the (black) television family are the perfect barometers of black visibility and recognition in television's national imagination" (xxii). Audiences are shown families that are "just like us"; therefore, while Teddy and Ivy coexist in the asymmetry that the black best friend role demands, the families are depicted as parallel and sharing similar concerns and aspirations.

Reading Disney's Racial Representations

While no one is suggesting that television does or should present a completely accurate picture of life in this country, given the role that television plays in the articulation of racialized identities, a colorblind, "we
are all the same" approach works to deny the existence of racialized economic realities and disadvantages. In film and television studies, representation is defined as being either mimetic or simulacral, the former
referring to representations that reflect a cultural or social reality (i.e.,
life as it is) and the latter referring to representations that create an inaccurate portrayal that can be seen to effect change or improve conditions
but can also be seen as having the ability to displace the actual reality. At
one level, Disney's use of the black best friend formula in its tween offerings must be seen as simulacral, echoing this warning by Artz:

> Undoubtedly, Hollywood has always constructed fantasy worlds for
> moviegoers, a primary function of the entertainment industry. But
> [four] decades after the civil rights movement, at a time when the United
> States remains severely racially divided, and while major policy ques-
> tions affecting race relations are being debated and decided, the singular
> big screen fantasy of interracial heroes triumphing over all is a danger-
> ous fantasy. (77)

The fantasy is all the more troubling when read through the lens of a
study undertaken by the Pew Center and National Public Radio one year
after the election of Barack Obama that found the "majority of black
Americans say they believe that the standard-of-living gap between
whites and blacks has narrowed" (Halloran). Recent Pew reports suggest that the income gap between whites and other minorities, instead
of decreasing, is in fact getting larger. The Pew Research Center reports
that, based on 2009 government data, the median wealth of white
households is twenty times that of black households and eighteen times
that of Hispanic households (Kochhar, Fry, and Taylor). Equally troubling is the September 2011 census report that finds nearly one in six
Americans live in poverty; while poverty rates rose across most races
save for Asians (whose rate stayed at 12.1 percent), the numbers reveal
a similar gap in the median wealth differences. The rate for whites in

poverty rose from 9.4 to 9.9 percent, while the rate for Hispanics rose from 25.3 to 26.6 percent, and for blacks it went from 25.8 to 27.4 percent (U.S. Census Bureau). Embracing a colorblind ideology is detrimental to all racial groups; for whites, it enables a denial of differences, which ultimately leads to racial intolerance and racism. For blacks and other minorities, being colorblind can "actually serve to work against one's individual and group interests" (Neville et al. 30). While cultural critics such as Cornel West object to the portrayal of black culture through the lens of welfare recipients, HIV, incest, and rape in films such as *Precious* or *For Colored Girls,* little has been said about the detrimental effects of contemporary children's television that suggest that no economic disparities or inequities exist.[20] Indeed, in her insightful study of Nickelodeon, Sarah Banet-Weiser argues that "the inclusion of explicitly racial images on Nickelodeon programming coincides with the exclusion of a specifically racial agenda, so that inclusion functions as a kind of exclusion" (171). The same can be said of Disney Channel; while viewers see diversity, it is superficial. In previous decades, sitcom writers attempted to present an authentic image of black culture. For example, the writers for the first season of the popular Fox Network show *The Fresh Prince of Bel Air* (1990–96), Andy and Susan Borowitz, frequently turned to the show's star, Will Smith, for insight into black culture in their attempt to create an "authentic" portrait of black life. Smith told journalists that "he often provided behind-the-scenes cultural tutoring for the couple [but] these white writers just didn't understand the concept" (Zook 18). Andy Borowitz himself acknowledged that at that cultural moment "black sitcom writing [was] largely 'guesswork' done by whites" (18). With the newest offerings on Disney Channel, the concern for authentic blackness or minority representation seems to have vanished.

Disney's choice to embrace the black best friend formula, especially the female-centered relationship, while not unique, can be read at one level as seemingly symptomatic of American culture's continuing unease with black masculinity. As made apparent by the dozen or more shows and movies mentioned at the beginning of this chapter, audiences are comfortable with black women on television and in the movies. But, as Edward Wyatt documents, in the 2008–9 season, right after the election of Barack Obama, shows that featured black men as hosts or leads did not fare well; shows such *Chocolate News* (2008), *D. L*

Hughley Breaks the News (2008–9), *Do Not Disturb* (2008), and *Everybody Hates Chris* (2005–9) were either canceled or not renewed because of low ratings. Even Disney's own *That's So Raven* spin-off, *Corey in the House*, which featured Kyle Massey as the black teen lead, lasted just one season, while the original show with its black-girl focus ran for four years and more than a hundred episodes.

Jeffery P. Dennis, in his qualitative study of racial representation and male character roles on children's television, found that while the racial distribution of characters on the three largest children's networks Nickelodeon, the Cartoon Network, and Disney Channel, did reflect American racial demographics, a "smaller proportion of black male characters were teenagers, especially when compared with black female characters, evidencing a preference for casting them as small, safe children rather than teenagers, as nearly adult" (182). Moreover, his study found that while white male characters were frequently cast as either leaders or bullies, black characters were never portrayed in either role and were more likely to be cast as computer nerds, tricksters, or background characters. While it is possible to argue that such demographically correct casting merely reflects previous ratings and audience preference, it is also possible to argue that limiting the roles and ages of specific minority groups is emblematic of the dangers of the "post-racial" moment in that, as Gabriel Gutiérrez argues, the "liberal multiculturalism espoused by Disney [among others] reflects a larger sociopolitical phenomenon that reclaims privilege for conservatives and liberals, who seek to 'win back' what they assume was lost during the Civil Rights era" (12).

Jennifer Fuller argues that "by the end of the twentieth century, the dominant understanding of 'racial progress' had shifted from creating social *equality* through policy to fostering racial *harmony* between individuals" (171, original emphasis). Through this lens, it is possible to read the twenty-first century's tendency to utilize and foreground female black best friends as indicative of this desire to foster racial harmony through media representations. The white and black pairings of female friends exemplify what Benjamin DeMott calls "the friendship orthodoxy," which posits that "the race situation in America is governed by the state of personal relations between blacks and whites" (7). Locating the race situation in the realm of the personal, rather than the political, absolves the country's policies (and by extension politicians) of any responsibility or call to action. Furthermore, the friendship orthodoxy suggests that if we "see" black and white friends, we will "believe" that all is right with the world. If, as theorist Anne McClintock argues, women are politically marginal yet central to the national imagination,[21] depicting friendships between black and white women, while not read as politically threatening, can be read as promising or fulfilling America's sense of racial harmony by, in Fuller's words, "leading the nation into a less racist future" (178).

Through this lens, it is possible to argue that female black best friends are safe and acceptable markers of racial representation; Disney's tween characters are too young and too naive to fall into the trope of the hypersexualized black woman.[22] Instead, black girls, cast in the best friend role, while often sassy and outspoken, draw heavily from the "Mammy as nurturer" as well as the Magical Negro stereotypes wherein they are apparently willing to sublimate their own desires in order to privilege the desires of their white friends.[23] Such nonthreatening strategies of racial representation allow Disney to access the tween market's $43 billion buying power by appealing to a multicultural viewing audience in such a way as to not disrupt America's racial status quo. Nielsen ratings demonstrate the success of Disney's strategic use of race: "First-run episodes of *Shake It Up*, *Wizards of Waverly Place* and *Good Luck Charlie* earned six of television's top 10 telecasts [in February 2011] in key child demographics."[24] The show's popularity resulted, not surprisingly, in Disney launching a line of CeCe- and Rocky-inspired clothing, footwear, and dolls in June 2011, hoping to further benefit from the show's popularity during the back-to-school shopping season.[25]

At one level, Disney's choice to increasingly utilize multicultural casts on its Disney Channel seems in direct response to the call by the NAACP's *Out of Focus—Out of Sync* reports to increase minority representation on the major networks. However, as this chapter has demonstrated, "showing" diversity without actually "doing" diversity is just as problematic as historical tendencies to whitewash television. Encoding black best friends through the idealized lens of colorblindness relies too heavily on the idealistic and problematic "we are all the same" approach to race without creating a space for a black lead and subsequently a black culture that is appealing to all audiences, color notwithstanding.

Notes

1. *New York Times* television critic Manohla Dargis argues that the election of President Obama has "inaugurated a new era of racial confusion—or perhaps a crisis in representation" in Hollywood that has resulted in what she calls a "whiteout" (Dargis and Scott, AR1).
2. Cain's reference point was the highly publicized 1991 Supreme Court nomination hearings for black Clarence Thomas, whose legal preparedness was overshadowed by accusations of sexual assault by black Anita Hill. Thomas referred to the hearings as a "high tech lynching" in which black sexuality, both masculine and feminine, was foregrounded.
3. See C. A. Gallagher (2003) and L. Bobo and C. Z. Charles (2009) for an analysis of recent Gallup polls and social indicators that support the view that color-blindness has become a normative ideology.
4. Rose Catherine Pinkney, executive vice president of programming and production for TV One, a cable network dedicated to black audiences, explains the BBF syndrome in this way: "It's wonderful that studios recognize great talent. And there's more diversity, so it looks like the world. But it's a shame that studios don't have the courage to put these [black] actresses in leads" (Braxton 2007: E29).
5. Founded initially in 1983, The Disney Channel changed its name to Disney Channel in 1997.
6. Patrick Day, *Los Angeles Times* 18 October 2011.
7. The Disney Channel Original Movie *High School Musical* (2006) and the second and third follow-up movies all relied on the black best friend formula with Zac Efron and Corbin Bleu playing interracial buddies Troy Bolton and Chad Danforth; Disney's *Starstruck* (2010), starring Sterling Knight as pop star Christopher Wilde and Brandon Mycal Smith as his black best friend "Stubby" Stubbins, had a premiere audience of 6 million viewers, which was second only to the audience for *High School Musical 2* (2007).
8. See, for example, Henry Giroux's *The Mouse That Roared* (2001).
9. See Phil Chidester's (2008) examination of whiteness on network television in "May the Circle Stay Unbroken: *Friends,* the Presence of Absence, and the Rhetorical Reinforcement of Whiteness."
10. One of Disney's longest-running and most popular shows, *Hannah Montana,* debuted on 24 March 2006 and ran through ninety-nine episodes, ending its run on 16 January 2011. The show was based on the main character Miley Stewart living a secret life as teen pop sensation Hannah Montana. While the show was undoubtedly successful, it was also almost completely devoid of diversity; the main characters, Miley, played by Miley Cyrus, her father Robby, played by her real-life father, Billy Ray Cyrus, her brother Jackson, played by Jason Earles, and her best friend, Lilly, played by Emily Osment, are white.

11. Disney Channel is ranked as the second-most-watched cable channel among total viewers during prime time, behind first-place USA Network, which has an average of 2.8 million viewers (http://en.wikipedia.org/wiki/Disney_Channel).

12. A *quinceañeras* celebration marks a Latin American girl's fifteenth birthday, which is considered the age at which she passes from childhood to adulthood.

13. Indeed, Guerrero characterizes this Hollywood moment as "Reaganite entertainment"—wherein "ideologically conservative Hollywood films reflect the tenure and tenor of the Reagan years" (Guerrero 1993: 239).

14. These characters appear in *The Suite Life of Zack and Cody,* and *The Suite Life on Deck, High School Musical,* and the *Hannah Montana* show, respectively.

15. In addition to highlighting the tantalizing promise of the American Dream, the show also imparts a much-needed warning about consumerism. In the second episode, "Meatball It Up," the girls receive their first paychecks and debit cards and immediately overspend their limit and their income.

16. The expression "we are the 99 percent" became a rallying cry for the Occupy Wall Street protests that took place in the fall of 2011 and that challenged the wealth disparities and economic power wielded by the richest 1 percent.

17. In an interesting second-season shift in the narrative, Rocky's home and family are foregrounded; viewers are told that her father has just returned from an eight-month tour with a group similar to Médecins sans Frontières, and the family is frequently shown holding "family meetings" to discuss issues or events related to Rocky and her brother.

18. http://en.wikipedia.org/wiki/Good_Luck_Charlie.

19. Shilpa Davé coins the term "brown voice" in her insightful study of Hank Azaria's role as the voice of the Indian shopkeeper Apu Nahasapeemapetilon on *The Simpsons.*

20. In Manohla Dargis and A. O. Scott's "Hollywood Whiteout," West is quoted as saying, "With all the richness in black life right now the only thing Hollywood gives us is black pathology" (AR1).

21. McClintock argues that "excluded from direct action as national citizens, women are subsumed symbolically into the national body politic as its boundary and metaphoric limit. . . . Women are typically constructed as the symbolic bearers of the nation but are denied any direct relation to national agency" (90).

22. Patricia Hill Collins explores this question of representation in *Black Sexual Politics.*

23. The term "Magical Negro" is often defined in relation to the books and films of Stephen King although the actual character of the Magical Negro can be traced back to Sydney Poitier's role in *The Defiant Ones;* in such texts, black men frequently appear as saviors for the white male leads.

24. http://en.wikipedia.org/wiki/Good_Luck_Charlie.

25. Disney earned $28.6 billion from licensed merchandise sales in 2010; by comparison, Warner earned "only" $6 billion in sales, even with the profitable Harry Potter franchise; http://www.thewrap.com/media/article/

report-disney-made-286b-2010-licensed-merchandise-27526 (accessed 17
October 2011).

WORKS CITED

Artz, B. Lee. "Hegemony in Black and White: Interracial Buddy Films and the New
Racism." *Cultural Diversity and the U.S. Media.* Ed. Yahya R. Kamalipour and Theresa Carilli. Albany: State University of New York Press, 1998. 67–78. Print.

Banet-Weiser, Sarah. *Kids Rule: Nickelodeon and Consumer Citizenship.* Durham, NC:
Duke University Press, 2007. Print.

Beltrán, Mary C. "The New Hollywood Racelessness: Only the Fast, Furious (and Multiracial) Will Survive." *Cinema Journal* 44.2 (2005): 50–67. Print.

Bobo, Lawrence D., and Camille Z. Charles. "Race in the American Mind: From the
Moynihan Report to the Obama Candidacy." *Annals of the American Academy of
Political and Social Science* 621.1 (2009): 243--59. Print.

Bogle, Donald. *Toms, Coons, Mulattoes, Mammies, and Bucks: An Interpretive History
of Blacks in American Films.* 4th ed. New York: Continuum, 2001. Print.

Bonilla-Silva, Eduardo. *Racism without Racists: Color-Blind Racism and the Persistence
of Racial Inequality in the United States.* 3rd ed. New York: Rowman and Littlefield,
2010. Print.

Bonilla-Silva, Eduardo, and David Dietrich. "The Sweet Enchantment of Color-Blind
Racism in Obamerica." *Annals of the American Academy of Political and Social Science* 634.190 (2011): 190–206. Print.

Bramlett-Solomon, Sharon, and Yvette Roeder. "Looking at Race in Children's Television: Analysis of Nickelodeon Commercials." *Journal of Children and Media* 2.1
(2008): 56–66. Print.

Braxton, Greg. "Buddy System." *Los Angeles Times* 29 Aug. 2007: E29. Print.

Chidester, Phil. "May the Circle Stay Unbroken: Friends, the Presence of Absence, and
the Rhetorical Reinforcement of Whiteness." *Critical Studies in Media Communication* 25.2 (2008): 157–74. Print.

Collins, Patricia Hill. *Black Sexual Politics: African Americans, Gender, and the New
Racism.* New York: Routledge, 2004. Print.

Dargis, Manohla, and A. O. Scott. "Hollywood's Whiteout." *New York Times* 11 Feb.
2011: AR1. Print.

Davé, Shilpa. "Apu's Brown Voice: Cultural Inflection and South Asian Accents." *East
Asian Main Street.* Ed. Shilpa Davé, Leilani Nishime, and Tasha G. Oren. New York:
NYU Press, 2005. 313–36. Print.

DeMott, Benajmin. *The Trouble with Friendship: Why Americans Can't Think Straight
about Race.* New York: Atlantic Monthly Press, 1995. Print.

Dennis, Jeffery P. "Gazing at the Black Teen: Con Artists, Cyborgs and Sycophants."
Media, Culture and Society 31.179 (2009): 179–95. Print.

Fuller, Jennifer. "Debating the Present through the Past: Representations of the Civil
Rights Movement in the 1990s." *The Civil Rights Movement in American Memory.*

Ed. Renee C. Ramano and Leigh Raiford. Athens: University of Georgia Press, 2006. 167–96. Print.

Gallagher, Charles A. "Color-Blind Privilege: The Social and Political Functions of Erasing the Color Line in Post Race America." *Race, Gender and Class* 10.4 (2003): 22–37. Print.

Gates, Philippa. "Always a Partner in Crime: Black Masculinity in the Hollywood Detective Film." *Journal of Popular Film and Television* 32.1 (2004): 20–29. Print.

Gillan, Jennifer. "No One Knows You're Black: 'Six Degrees of Separation' and the Buddy Formula." *Cinema Journal* 40.3 (2001): 47–68. Print.

Gray, Herman. *Watching Race: Television and the Struggle for Blackness.* 1995. Minneapolis: University of Minnesota, 2004. Print.

Guerrero, Ed. "The Black Image in Protective Custody: Hollywood's Biracial Buddy Films of the Eighties." *Black American Cinema.* Ed. Manthia Diawara. New York: Routledge, 1993. 237–46. Print.

Gutiérrez, Gabriel. "Deconstructing Disney: Chicano/a Children and Critical Race Theory." *Aztlán* 25.1 (2000): 7–46. Print.

Hall, Stuart. "Encoding and Decoding in the Television Discourse." *Channeling Blackness: Studies on Television and Race in America.* Ed. Darnell M. Hunt. New York: Oxford University Press, 2005. 46–59. Print.

Halloran, Liz. "Study Shows Blacks Optimistic in Obama Era." NPR interview. 12 Jan. 2010. Radio.

http://en.wikipedia.org/wiki/Disney_Channel (accessed 14 October 2011)

http://en.wikipedia.org/wiki/Good_Luck_Charlie (accessed 17 October 2011).

http://www.thewrap.com/media/article/report-disney-made-286b-2010-licensed-merchandise-27526 (accessed 17 October 2011).

Kochhar, Rakesh, Richard Fry, and Paul Taylor. "Wealth Gaps Rise to Record Highs between Whites, Blacks and Hispanics Twenty-to-One." *Pew Research Center Publications* 26 July 2011. Web. 5 Oct. 2011. < http://pewresearch.org/pubs/2069/housing-bubble-subprime-mortgages-hispanics-blacks-household-wealth-disparity>.

McClintock, Anne. "'No Longer in a Future Heaven': Gender, Race and Nationalism." *Dangerous Liaisons: Gender Nation, and Postcolonial Perspectives.* Ed. Anne McClintock, Aamir Mufti, and Ella Shohat. Minneapolis: University of Minnesota Press, 1997. 89–112. Print.

Neville, Helen A., Georgia Duran, Richard M. Lee, and LaVonne Browne. "Color-Blind Racial Ideology and Psychological False Consciousness among African Americans." *Journal of Black Psychology* 31.27 (2005): 27–45. Print.

Out of Focus—Out of Sync Take 1: A Report on the Television Industry. NAACP. Nov. 2002. Print.

Out of Focus—Out of Sync Take 4: A Report on the Television Industry. NAACP. Dec. 2008. Print.

Seiter, Ellen, and Vicki Mayer. "Diversifying Representation in Children's TV: Nickelodeon's Model." *Nickelodeon Nation.* Ed. Heather Hendershot. New York: NYU Press, 2004. 120–33. Print.

Sexton, Jared. "The Ruse of Engagement: Black Masculinity and the Cinema of Policing." *American Quarterly* 61.1 (2009): 39–63. Print.

U.S. Census Bureau. Annual Report. Sept. 2011. Web. 14 Sept. 2011. <www.census.gov/ newsroom/releases/archives/ . . . /cb11-157.html>.

Valdivia, Angharad N. "Mixed Race on the Disney Channel: From *Johnnie Tsunami* through *Lizzie McGuire* and Ending with *The Cheetah Girls*." *Mixed Race Hollywood*. Ed. Mary Beltrán and Camilla Fojas. New York: NYU Press, 2008. 269–89. Print.

Watkins, Mel. *On the Real Side: A History of African American Comedy from Slavery to Chris Rock*. Chicago: Lawrence Hill Books, 1999. Print.

Wyatt, Edward. "No Smooth Ride on TV Networks' Road to Diversity." *New York Times* 18 Mar. 2009: C1. Print.

Zook, Kristal Brent. *Color by Fox: The Fox Network and the Revolution in Black Television*. New York: Oxford University Press, 2009. Print.

PART IV

Post-Racial Relationships

11

Matchmakers and Cultural Compatibility

Arranged Marriage, South Asians, and Racial
Narratives on American Television

SHILPA DAVÉ

South Asian Americans and the racial space they occupy in the United States in popular culture have often vacillated between the material definition of where South Asians fit in the racial and ethnic hierarchy in the United States and the highly commercialized "model minority" immigrant. South Asians are racial anomalies in the black-white racial paradigms of the United States. Unlike other ethnic and racial minority groups, South Asian Americans do not have a history inflected with war or colonialism in relation to the United States but instead are linked to the United States economically and politically by the ties of capitalism and a British-based democracy; India, for example, is represented as an Asian country with Western (if not American) values. Early Hollywood portrayals emphasized Indians in the context of British history rather than part of U.S. history. Many Hollywood images of South Asians were confined to British tales of adventure or spiritual discovery set in colonial India from films such as *Gunga Din* (1939) to *Indiana Jones and the Temple of Doom* (1984) or resistance to British rule such as the film *Gandhi* (1982). After the 1965 U.S. Immigration Act, the dominant representations of South Asians in film and television were Indians and featured stories of Indian immigration and assimilation in the United States, including religious practices adopted by American youth in the counterculture movement of the 1960s and 1970s. By the 1980s, the representations of Indians were similar to general depictions of Asian Americans as new immigrants with foreign accents or model minority sidekicks. White or non-Indian actors played most of the Indian roles. One of the most famous Indian American figures on U.S. television is the animated character Apu Nahaseemapetilon (voiced by white actor Hank Azaria), the proprietor of the Springfield Kwik-E-Mart on the longest-running television show *The Simpsons* (1989–). Network television shows such as *The Simpsons* and *Seinfeld* (1989–98) to *The Big Bang Theory* (2007–), as well as the USA Network comedy *Royal Pains* (2009–), have storylines that feature Indian and Indian American characters and Indian (primarily Hindu) arranged marriages.[1]

In U.S. history, South Asians have been racially categorized as Caucasian, nonwhite, other, and finally as an Asian American minority group. These multiple designations have led to a racial identity that is not easily explained or understood by dominant culture, by American racial and ethnic minorities, or even by South Asian Americans. The ambiguous nature of South Asian American identity challenges American paradigms of racial categorization. One of the main critiques of a post-racial era, according to Eduardo Bonilla-Silva, is that racial difference and racial language are relegated to the past as if they are no longer present when, in fact, racial difference does exist but is gestured to in alternative ways.[2] In a post-racial narrative, racial difference still exists, but it is expressed in different terms. The representation of South Asian Americans as foreign immigrants with distinctive cultural practices and characteristics is an example of how race is discussed in a supposed post-race world—cultural difference is emphasized over racial difference. The proliferation of stereotypical representations of arranged marriage (as opposed to Western ideals of a love marriage) in mainstream American television recur and present Indians as culturally and racially foreign to the United States. This chapter discusses how the narratives of arranged marriage on American television become a trope for racializing South Asians; in addition, I also offer an alternative to post-racial models that discusses and incorporates the ideas of racial and cultural difference through the re-creation of the use of the term "compatibility."

Critical race studies scholars such as Bonilla-Silva have discussed how the conversation around and expression of racism have evolved from open verbal slurs and visual cues such as the practice of blackface to more subtle cues with phrases such as "unwed mothers" or "illegal immigrant."[3] Additionally, the idea of "post" in "post-racial" implies that racism was in an American past that was addressed in the civil rights era and that racial difference no longer signifies in current times. However, the denial of the consequences and effects of racial difference is just another means of solidifying a racial hierarchy where dominant culture and white privilege are the normative standard by which every other group is judged.

While South Asians hail from a diverse geography (Afghanistan, Bangladesh, Bhutan, India, the Maldives, Nepal, Pakistan, and Sri Lanka), the majority of images in popular culture tend to focus on Indian immigrants. Oftentimes characterizations associated with Indian immigrants are extended to all South Asian groups, even though the nationalities and ethnicities have different historical, social, and cultural practices. In contemporary times, the term "South Asian American," like "Asian American," is a political identity that is composed of several ethnic, religious, linguistic, and national identities.

The racial position of South Asians in the U.S. racial stratification has been in flux since the beginning of the twentieth century. South Asians have been classified in the U.S. census as "White," "Hindoo," "Other," and Asian American. The discussion around racial categories that occurred in the early twentieth century put Indian Americans in the middle of the legal controversy about how to define "whiteness." Indian Americans were the only Asian group to be granted naturalization on the basis of "being white," and then were subsequently stripped of citizenship rights by the U.S. Supreme Court in 1923 and relegated to a nonwhite position.[4] The current legal language of the U.S. federal government classifies South Asian identity as a minority under the racial category of Asian Pacific American.

In American television and film, South Asians are not so ambiguous and are racialized by cultural characteristics associated with their national origin. For example, South Asians are visually marked as brown and dressed in foreign clothing (e.g., a sari) or found in exotic landscapes. In addition, cultural practices such as religious ceremonies, elaborate weddings, and the practice of arranged marriage supplement the visual cues.[5] In a post-racial world, the phrase "arranged marriage" is a racial and cultural marker of South Asian and particularly Indian culture, which makes it an appropriate and provocative topic of discussion. An examination of how racial narratives operate in a supposed post-racial world highlights the intersection of racial and gendered narratives about romance and marriage.

After beginning with a discussion of marriage narratives and the representation of South Asian arranged marriages in the United States, this chapter follows with a close reading of episodes from television shows that feature Indian weddings, such as *The Simpsons, The Office* (2005–13), and *Miss Match* (2003–4), and presents a side-by-side comparison of familiar American notions of dating and matchmaking with what seem like the strange and foreign traditions of Indian matrimonial practices. American practices are normalized in relation to Indian customs, and yet also exposed as being in a mode of crisis. The portrayal of marriage becomes a manifestation of a national expression of American and Indian cultural relations.[6] It is the process and production of the arrangement of marriage that I am interested in exploring as opposed to the institution of arranged marriage. Although the idea of arranged marriage is often used to designate differences between American and Indian American cultural values, I am instead arguing that the twenty-first-century arranged marriage also provides a narrative that dissolves the foreign nature of the arrangement process in American culture and instead shows a compatibility between American and Indian ideas of matchmaking.

Arranged Marriage, Romantic Love, and National Values

Although the practice of arranged marriage has roots in many cultures, the actual term "arranged marriage" is popularly associated with South Asian, and more specifically Indian, matrimonial customs. South Asians view marriage as an essential institution and the defining marker (regardless of career or profession) of a woman's social status.[7] Marriage, in South Asia, is seen as a relationship between families that can take into account individual preferences, but ultimately the duty to family outweighs individual desires. This cultural and social pressure applies to first-generation immigrants as well as second- or third-generation Indian Americans. For many immigrant Indians, regardless of class, arranged introductions and arranged marriages are the primary means through which men and women meet and marry. The adherence to Indian family values and cultural norms is often expressed through marriage.

The American ideal of romance in marriage promises the act of individual choice of one's partner. Although matchmakers are a tried and tested method of bringing a couple together for lifelong relationships,

American depictions of marriage privilege love as the key ingredient for a happy relationship. Historian Nancy Cott argues that because the state has long dictated the terms of marriage through laws (antimiscegenation laws, immigration policy, gender qualifications), marriage becomes an important means to express freedom of choice outside the sphere of government influence.[8] Class, religion, race, age, geography, or the law, for example, should not be a barrier to getting married to the person you love. American romance narratives, including Disney's *Cinderella* (1950), *Beauty and the Beast* (1991), *The Princess and the Frog* (2009), *Sex and the City* (2010), and *Avatar* (2009), emphasize the expectation that true love involves the promise of marriage (or long-term relationship) that defies every obstacle. Hence the depiction of the quest for true love is tied to contemporary American democratic ideals of freedom of choice and equal opportunity. The practical concerns of compatibility are at odds with the idealization of true love. And yet in her study of marriage, historian Stephanie Coontz points out in the last thirty years of the twentieth century, marriage was no longer the image of stability and commitment, and all the rights associated with marriage (bank account, owning property, having children, tax benefits) were available to single and solitary adults.[9] The rights of being an adult, which used to be gained only by getting married (especially for women), are now available without marriage.[10] So if marriage is no longer the principal means of achieving economic stability or raising children, the qualifications for marriage change to fit a population looking for love and long-term relationships and partners. Marriage becomes associated with "choice" rather than necessity and also bears the burden of being the most important site for emotional and physical intimacy for men and women.

For Asian American groups in general, American marriage practices have varied depending on a community's social history in the United States. In the nineteenth and twentieth centuries, "picture brides" were representative of a common form of arranged marriage for Chinese, Japanese, and Korean immigrants.[11] Karen Leonard chronicles the history of Punjabi Sikhs who immigrated in the early part of the twentieth century and intermarried with Mexican Americans when they were unable (due to antimiscegenation laws) to marry Indian women.[12] Popular depictions of ethnic groups in relation to marriage often focus on the clash of immigrant and American culture. For Asian Americans marriage is often associated with the retention of culture. The old-world traditions versus modern traditions that are often translated as the East-West clash in Asian American communities represent a resistance to marriage customs of the ethnic community by the second generation and marrying outside the community by the first generation. Issues such as language, food, cultural traditions, and relationship to your ethnic and racial heritage influence marriage considerations.

The word "compatibility" enters the vocabulary associated with marriage matches in the "Who's Sari Now?" episode of *Miss Match* when the protagonist asserts that she is trying to find her client (an Indian American woman) a compatible match.[13] This term provides an alternative spin on the idea of arranged marriage. It is more broadly associated with a partnership that allows the melding of two separate entities to create something larger, be it in computer technology, biological organ transplant, or cross-pollination. Technologically speaking, the notion of compatibility often relates to software working with different models: the idea that even though the hardware or outer shell is different, the software can be made to work (sometimes with minor fixes) in multiple models. For organ transplants, compatibility means having nonnative organisms inserted without being rejected by the host. Both these meanings have resonance for ethnic and cultural practices in that immigrant cultures, for example, can practice their traditional customs (language, religion, clothing, eating habits) without facing rejection from the dominant culture and retaining some cultural specificity. Compatibility means acquiring a sense of understanding and communication with your partner in a social partnership. With regard to immigration narratives, the metaphor of compatibility works in concert with the depictions of South Asians in the United States. In the television narrative of *The Simpsons*, Indian Americans such as Apu have the ability to fit in within the existing system in America despite and sometimes because of their differences. As a racialized group, Indians and Indian Americans are compatible and can be culturally assimilated into U.S. culture but still are depicted as colorfully exotic immigrants. Throughout the chapter, I use the term "compatibility" to gesture to an alternative of representing Indian American and American cultural practices at odds with each other in order to highlight the convergence and exchange of cultural norms that are possible in television narratives.

Arranged Marriage and Media

Arranged marriage carries the connotation of an Indian marrying an Indian whereas a love marriage is often but not always associated with individualistic act of marrying outside of the racial and ethnic group. Fiction by South Asian writers often focuses on relationships and arranged marriage, such as Chitra Bannerjee Divakaruni's short-story collection *Arranged Marriage* and Jhumpa Lahiri's short-story collections and her novel *The Namesake*. Romantic and marriage expectations are at the center of both popular and independent films that feature Indian Americans or Indians in America. Popular films among the Indian diasporic population that have marriage as a central component include most Hindi films produced in India (Bollywood), as well as English-language films such as *Chutney Popcorn* (1999), *Monsoon Wedding* (2001), *Bend It Like Beckham* (2002), *Bride and Prejudice* (2003), and *The Namesake* (2006). Each of these films features a debate about life partners and romance and also often includes a vibrant set that showcases Indian culture through marriage.

American television is one of the most powerful mediums to discuss the representation of American norms such as marriage. Although many television shows exaggerate the strangeness of Indian cultural ceremonies, there are modern narrative moments that characterize Indian traditions as compatible with an American identity predicated on inclusiveness and adaptability. In film, for example, South Asian directors such as Mira Nair and Gurinder Chadha have tackled the changing idea of arranged marriage in popular crossover English-language independent films such as *Monsoon Wedding* (Nair, 2001), *Bride and Prejudice* (Chadha, 2004), and *The Namesake* (Nair, 2006).

American television has more structural and budget limitations than film, but it can reach and influence a wider American audience. Television programming, according to Bonnie Dow, is a complex entity that can be seen as "simultaneously, a commodity, an art form, and an important ideological forum for public discourse about social issues and social change."[14] The rituals associated with Indian marriages accentuate how we think about American family values through an exaggeration of the representation of Indian marriage practices in U.S. television.

Most American popular television programs (even in satire) continue to depict South Asians as foreign and strange despite their status as an immigrant or second-generation or multiracial individual. The romance narrative and the wedding ceremony are visually etched in popular culture from Disney's fairy tales to advertisements and reality television. Indian ceremonies are not Christian white weddings but instead are exotic, colorful, and full of strange rituals. We see how "Indianness" is identified and racialized through the spectacle of arranged marriage narratives and wedding stories.[15] In television shows such as *The Simpsons,* the Indian ceremony is reduced to silliness and satire, with consumable icons of "Indian-ness" peppered throughout the ceremony, such as the presence of an elephant, representations of Indian gods, Hindi pop music, and extravagant Indian clothing.

When arranged marriage appears on American television, it is also represented as a practice that is antithetical to romantic love in the United States. Situation comedies such as *The Office* emphasize the foreign nature of a practice associated with Indians. There are variations in the expression of arranged marriage, but most television narratives (as I will discuss in detail in my readings) tend to focus on three aspects. The common belief is that (1) an arranged marriage is forced because the individual has no choice about the marriage partner, (2) there is no love or deep feelings involved, and (3) the individuals barely know their future spouse and are marrying a virtual stranger.

Love marriages, in contrast, are viewed as an individual choice, and there is usually no indication that there might be a more complex system that influences U.S. ideals about the institution of marriage. As Dow asserts in her work on television culture, "Television implicitly supports a view of the world that discounts the ways in which cultural norms and values affect people's lives. The medium's individualistic view of the world implies that most problems can be solved by hard work, good will, and a supportive family."[16] This includes a heteronormative assumption about marriage or romantic love as a basis for a long-term relationship. In a television narrative there is no overt threat or danger to American cultural norms or the institution of marriage because the premise is that our individual choices are an anomaly that are not necessarily influenced by dominant social or cultural traditions. And yet despite these portrayals, the proliferation of reality shows challenges some of the traditional narratives because they show that individuals do not make their choices by themselves.

In the 1990s and after 2000, reality shows became the most prominent examples of matches and arranged meetings, including *The Bachelor* (2002 debut), which is now in its fifteenth cycle, and *The Bachelorette* (January 2003 debut). Reality television shows also have started to stress the opinions of family and friends in dating arrangements and make them part of the decision-making process for the individuals. In these reality television shows, non–South Asians are exposing themselves to highly choreographed meetings with their future partner. *The Bachelor* and *The Bachelorette* include the family in the show and televise their input in the individual choices involved in selecting a partner. As a result, these shows gesture toward a convergence of Indian American and American cultural practices in relation to marriage because the depiction of Indian families who are concerned for their children and see marriage as an alliance of families can be compatible with parents and families on the reality shows who also want the best for their children.

In contemporary times, the attitude toward arranged marriage in Indian immigrant communities in the United States has been modified to keep up with the changing nature of the community but "the abiding principles behind an arranged marriage still remain strong—lust does not a lasting marriage make and family knows best."[17] During the 2006 episode of *The Office* entitled "Diwali," the company's regional manager, Michael (Steve Carrell), highlights the importance of arranged marriage when he teaches his employees about Indian culture.[18] While his presentation is a satire of what white middle-class middle management knows about Indian culture, the tutorial also reflects the most popular images of Indians in America. Other aspects of his presentation include pictures of the fictional cartoon character Apu, Gandhi, and the Kama Sutra. But despite the comic implications in television, there is a recognition in the South Asian diaspora that if an Indian immigrant wants his or her son or daughter to marry another Indian, there needs to be some flexibility on the idea of what an arrangement entails. So currently an arranged marriage can mean anything from a family-facilitated first meeting/date for compatibility to a marriage match set up solely by the family without input from the bride or the groom.[19] Popular depictions of arranged marriages in films produced by Indians or independent Indian Americans or British Indians often feature both individual and family approval of the match.[20]

Two dramatic television programs that focused on issues related to marriage and matches on American television were *Cupid* (1998–99, 2009) and *Miss Match* (2003).[21] Dramatic roles and plotlines, while often limited by a strict sixty-minute commercial television format, allow for the representation of conflict and discomfort that is not always resolved by humor. While *Cupid* was more related to personal counseling and single life, *Miss Match* attempted to meld divorce law and family stories with personal stories of love and romance. Arranged marriage brings into focus the distinction between the ideas of a match versus an arrangement. A match implies a certain degree of compatibility that is based on individual characteristics, whereas an arrangement can be done without the consent or knowledge of the individuals. However, the meeting is one of strangers, and the intent is to enter into a long-term relationship. The idea of a match fits in with American notions of dating and dating services and also into the more formal arena of the matchmaker. The inherent values underlying the match still align with freedom of choice and individualism. Love, however, is an elusive factor in both matches and arrangements. Kate, the matchmaker in the 2003 *Miss Match* episode "Who's Sari Now?," tells her client Rashmi, "I can't find you love in 10 days."[22] And yet, the show is titled *Miss Match*, not Miss Love or even Miss Cupid. The emphasis on the idea of a match and the plot of the show featured a variation of an arranged marriage/meeting on a weekly basis.

In *The Simpsons* episode "The Two Mrs. Nahaseemapetilons" (1997), the second and third aspects of arranged marriage appear when we discover that Apu has been engaged since he was eight years old and has not seen his future wife for more than ten years.[23] Apu and Manjula are strangers to each other, and their engagement is depicted as an exchange of goods (rather than romantic love) between the adults in the family combined with the proper matching astrological horoscopes. Although *The Simpsons* episode is older, similar scenarios in other television shows follow the pattern that the episode sets forth in shows where Indian Americans are significant characters such as the physician assistant Divya Katdare (Reshma Shetty) in the series *Royal Pains*.[24] In this case, she has been engaged for many years to a family friend, but when she breaks it off because she is not in love with him, her parents disown her, and she is forced to pay off a wedding debt to her once future in-laws. Her entanglement with an arranged marriage influences all the decisions she makes in the first three seasons of the series. Thus *The Simpsons* episode becomes an important basis of comparison as representative of the most stereotypical images of arranged marriage. In *Miss Match*, these aspects ("forced" marriage, no love, and marrying of strangers) of arranged marriage are the subjects of the episode "Who's Sari Now?"[25] Both of these shows are interesting case studies that illustrate how the portrayal of arranged marriage reflects generational and social change in American ideals of romance and marriage. While *The Simpsons* represents Indian American cultural traditions in opposition to American cultural norms of marriage, *Miss Match* portrays an alternative representation of arranged marriage that highlights the convergence of Indian American and American attitudes toward the idea of arranged marriage and reconfigures Indian practices as compatible with American cultural values.

The Swinging Single and the Dutiful Son: Apu and Arranged Marriage

In *The Simpsons* episode "The Two Mrs. Nahaseemapetilons," creator Matt Groening presents a side-by-side comparison of American and South Asian dating and marriage practices.[26] After being pressured to participate in the local bachelor auction, Apu describes himself as the following: "I have a doctorate in computer science. I run my own business. I do like to cook, I'm not much of a talker but I love to listen, and in my leisure time I like to build furniture and then have a discussion about where it could be placed in a room."

The practice of the bachelor auction illustrates how consumerism operates in the American context. While not paying for marriage, you are in fact buying a meeting or date for a possible match. Apu's self-presentation results in a fierce bidding war for his company by the single women of Springfield. Each of his descriptors (from having a doctorate to owning his own business to being a good listener), although humbly delivered, represents economic, cultural, and gendered traits associated with an idealized and romantic man who happens to be Indian. As a potential date, he demonstrates that he is smart and an entrepreneur but also is modest and sensitive to the needs of others. He is handy around the house but also has a sense of taste and aesthetics. He is also domestic and so appeals to the modern woman who does not feel pressured to put a meal on the table. He is someone who will listen (hence be appreciative—not selfish) and he is a carpenter/artist. He possesses the tropes of masculinity (education and business) but also appeals to women because he is not bound by traditional gender roles. Since the character speaking is Apu, we hear his difference in his accent, but his voice does not detract from his attractiveness to the women of Springfield.

Apu's appeal and markers of compatibility bear no trace of Apu's racial identity. Instead, he is shown as the heteronormative romantic idealized man for single women. It is only when he is faced with an arranged marriage to an Indian woman that his cultural background takes him off the singles market in the United States and separates him from the other residents of Springfield. The comic element of the episode "The Two Mrs. Nahaseemapetilons" centers on how he tries to avoid his cultural obligation but eventually embraces whom and what his Indian mother has chosen for him. In the end, arranged marriages are depicted as Indians marrying other Indians and do not include interracial weddings.

Apu's cultural traditions and relationship with his family are set in opposition to his single life in the United States, thereby setting up an East versus West dichotomy in attitudes toward dating and marriage. The core value at issue in Apu's marriage is that of freedom—the freedom to choose a spouse rather than having one chosen for you, and the freedom of the individual versus the duty of children to family. The classic binary setup in Asian American narratives often emphasizes the conflict of family duty versus individual desire and cloaks it in an Eastern versus Western cultural conflict. This episode goes one step further by characterizing Apu's choice as an indicator of his ability to be an American citizen—to exercise his individual rights as a citizen of the nation, or to "remember his past" and exist as the cultural repository of Indian culture and a representative of Indian arranged marriage.

The episode's flashback to the marriage negotiation illustrates how arranged marriage is also an economic transaction that is based on a bartering exchange involving goats and factories. The families make the final details of the arrangement across a table in a gazebo, and we are introduced to the idea that marriage is a serious business transaction that combines family intimacy with economics. The contract of marriage serves as a permanent arrangement, so as audience members, we tend to judge the agreement made on the couple's behalf as a practice that does not include Apu's or Manjula's desires or wishes. As a result, the context of his arranged marriage is much more foreign when juxtaposed with Apu's success with the American rituals of courtship and romance. Why would he follow an alienating custom when it is clear that he could be involved in a long-term relationship with a woman in Springfield?

When Apu lies to his mother that he is no longer an available bachelor, he evokes sympathy from Homer Simpson and his family because the alternative is a forced, arranged marriage. In the episode, he rejects his past and physically remakes himself (with a new hairstyle) to show that he has changed and assimilated the idea that marriage should include love and romance. His lie that he is already married "sets him free" until his mother (holder of family honor and cultural traditions) arrives in Springfield. Interestingly, no one on the show questions the fact that Apu should not marry his intended, Manjula. Eventually Apu consents to the wishes of his mother because he finds that Manjula is smart, possesses a sense of humor, and is just as nervous as he is about the idea of an arranged marriage. Neither Marge Simpson, who usually defends the right of individuals and particularly women in their choices, nor Lisa Simpson (her daughter), who is usually a crusader for justice, questions the manner of the marriage. They are only interested in making the ceremony culturally authentic. Their obeisance to Apu's mother depicts respect for another culture over any individual qualms they may have about the marriage. While Marge and Lisa may not want this type of marriage for themselves (they do not admit this one way or the other), they accept that the practice of arranged marriages exists, and they embrace the custom. The marriage is not about love. It is a contract of filial duty that Apu and Manjula fulfill, and while they joke about their situation, the unspoken message that is being sent is that Indian Americans on television must have Indian American marriages, with "strange" ceremonies that include elephants, fire, and colorful garments. Even though the scene is funny because it seems so unlikely, the fact is Apu has married Manjula.

The last part of the episode shows Apu's hesitancy, and he voices what many people think about arranged marriages: "Two people cannot fall in love sight unseen." But he goes through with the ceremony because the marriage becomes a matter of keeping a promise between two families. Manjula is never shown as having a choice, though she points out to Apu that "we can always get a divorce." Apu replies, "God Bless

America." Thus, it is not romance that sanctions this marriage but the promise that relationships can be broken easily and freedom restored if they do not work out. Although the show constantly satirizes American cultural practices, this is not necessarily a humorous moment. The ending redefines the marriage as a transaction that can be broken by a common American practice—divorce—and reiterates the contradictory meaning of the United States as a nation that espouses family values and also is a place where you can free yourself from the shackles of marriage. Part of the promise of being in America is the ability to release Apu and Manjula from traditional practices of Indian heterosexual marriage. The underlying message is that romantic love (this is shown in other *Simpsons* episodes) will determine whether or not Apu's marriage with Manjula will thrive.[27] While *The Simpsons* portrays a stereotypical representation of Indian arranged marriage, the series *Miss Match* offers a notion of marriage that combines aspects of Indian American cultural practices with American romance and a more viable representation of how racial difference can be represented in American culture.

New Traditions: *Miss Match* and the Arranged Marriage Debate

The television series *Miss Match,* written and created by Darren Star (who also created HBO's *Sex and the City* [1998–2004]) and Jeff Rake, premiered in the fall of 2003. Eighteen episodes were aired before the series was canceled by NBC because of low ratings. Critics described the show as "hovering between the sincere optimism of the *90210* kids and the wry cynicism of the *Sex and the City* ladies."[28] In other words, the formula of the week was to provide a guest star with a romantic match while empathizing with the trials and travails of the single matchmaker. In *Miss Match,* the South Asian marriage, although still culturally distinct, is one of many types of marriages that occur on the series and is one of the only ethnic matches that is featured. The premise of the program centers around the idea that finding "your soul mate" or the "one" is not working out for American women and men. While the hopes of romantic love still remain, the reality of the people in the drama is that they are breaking up and getting divorced. Enduring relationships and long-term marriage are in crisis, and so, in this series, the idea of being matched or having an arranged marriage is not depicted as strange and foreign but a solution to an American crisis. Kate Fox, aka Miss Match, works as a divorce lawyer in her father's firm. Her economic security rests on the fact that marriages do not last, but her emotional security relies on her belief in love and that there is someone for everyone. Jaded by the constant and often hostile breakups that she handles in the courtroom and the conference room, Kate (played by Alicia Silverstone) starts a side business as a matchmaker where most of her clients are friends or referrals.[29] For her character, pairing up two people for a long-term relationship is dependent upon chemistry and romance, but her role as a matchmaker affirms that romance needs some help from someone who can recognize compatible individuals. In consumer society, the contemporary matchmaker serves as a personal shopper, making it possible for men and women to meet a variety of people with a minimum investment of time.[30] The mediated and structured means of meeting is at odds with the romantic vision of seeing someone across a crowded room, but the supposed lack of feeling associated with the process of matching does not mean that there will not be an emotional connection.

Miss Match focuses on the connections between the acts of divorce, marriage, and arranged dates by setting the majority of the series in the offices of divorce lawyers. The monetary settlements and the consumer aspect of marriage and relationships are often the topic of the show, and yet the ideals professed by all the characters still subscribe to the dominant cultural message that love should conquer all. The show does not challenge the institution of marriage as archaic or problematic but rather suggests that divorces happen because you are not with the right person and the solution is to find love with the right person. The series operates as an advertisement for romantic love while recognizing the contemporary economic realities of the divorce industry. Matchmaking as a business of love can be compatible with the tenets of arranged marriage because both practices are interested in finding compatible partners. Matchmaking relies on setting up individuals in a relationship (which will hopefully lead to marriage), whereas arranged marriages are predicated on the idea that a permanent arrangement and relationship between individuals and families will happen through marriage. These two practices are not at odds with each other, and Kate comes to see the similarities between what she aspires to do as a matchmaker and the philosophy behind arranged Indian marriage.

The pun of the episode title "Who's Sari Now?" describes the plight of Kate and also the "friend" (or guest star of the week) that Kate is going to help during the program.[31] Besides referencing "Who's Sorry Now?" (1958), a popular song by Connie Francis, the title explicitly states that this is going to be an episode that features Indians. In describing one of the clothing styles associated with South Asians and Indian Americans, the title is asking what "sari" will be worn but, more important, what type of marriage, an arranged marriage or a love match, will occur for the protagonist. The opening of the episode sets up the cultural values of an American romantic love against the strict traditions of an Indian arranged marriage.

Rashmi Chopra (Sunita Puram) has asked Kate to find her alternatives to the match her parents have arranged for her in the hopes that Rashmi can find love again rather than participate in a businesslike arranged marriage. Kate agrees to help Rashmi but tells her that she "cannot find her love in ten days." Kate can only find her matches that may or may not lead to a compatible relationship. Rashmi tells Kate she is not interested in love; she wants to show her parents that she has other prospects besides the person they have chosen for her. She says, "I know what love is," and the prospect offered by her parents is not what she would like. In other words, Rashmi has been in love before and had her heart broken. The episode sets up the stereotypical feelings associated with arranged marriage. Rashmi, a second-generation Indian American, is being forced by her immigrant parents to quickly marry someone she does not love. There is a communication and generation gap between what Rashmi wants for herself (a love marriage) and what Mr. and Mrs. Chopra want for her (a stable and settled arranged marriage). Despite the fact that Rashmi is a college-educated working professional who may have many viable prospects, her individual desires are initially seen as unimportant in her parents' desire to get her married.

The tone of the episode changes and offers up arranged marriage as a practical and perhaps appealing alternative when Rashmi's family finds out that Kate has been setting up matches for their daughter. Mr. and Mrs. Chopra confront Kate in her office and insist that she does not understand their traditions. When Kate meets Rashmi's parents for the first time, her interaction with them addresses three different issues, but ultimately she hears a defense of arranged marriage that she finds convincing. The scene takes place in a mediation conference room at Kate's office. Kate and Rashmi sit on one side of the table, and the matchmaker and parents sit opposite them on the other side. Kate and Rashmi are cast as the Americans who doubt the practice of arranged marriage as one that is consistent with finding love. Mr. and Mrs. Chopra and their Indian matchmaker, Savita, are presented as middle-class immigrant Indian professionals. They speak with a slight accent, but their clothing and speech are not exaggerated; thus, they are presented not as alienated but as comfortable in the environment of the conference room. Later we see their beautiful home, which is another testimony to their financial success and professional class in the United States.

Mrs. Chopra's opening remark, "Who are you to question our traditions?," immediately suggests that Kate is attacking an Indian cultural tradition that she does not understand. The narrative thus sets up Kate as a representative of the opinion that arranged marriage may not work for the Americanized Rashmi when she says: "I don't mean to question anything [such as traditions]. I'm just trying to help your daughter find a *compatible* match" (my emphasis). Kate's desire to "find a compatible match" shows that she sees herself as aligned with tradition. Kate's choice of the word "compatibility" affects how she thinks about matches for others—that the process of matching is in fact more than just love but also about pleasing and reconciling all parties (including the families) to live and, hopefully, love without conflict. Her attitude reflects a change from classic assimilation narratives that separate American cultural practices from ethnic traditions. She offers an alternative that mirrors a pluralistic world where different practices of marriage can be compatible.

In the second exchange, Savita, the Indian matchmaker, points out that marriage is more than an individual choice. She says Rashmi's potential husband, Sanjay, is from a "good family, graduated from Yale, is a doctor." Settling an arranged marriage for Savita involves both families and individuals. A marriage is a community event that is not only about a single relationship but also highlights the compatibility of families. The qualities the matchmaker and the parents have sought in a potential match for their daughter include intelligence and education, financial security, and a good family environment. Couldn't these characteristics be the foundation for a long-term relationship? Kate cannot argue with the qualifications that the matchmaker and the parents have produced with their candidate and finally objects by saying that Rashmi wants love. Rashmi's father counters with his own example, saying, "Why do you assume

Rashmi will not have love? We married as strangers and love grew." He represents a generation of many Indian parents who had arranged marriages and are happy. In a world where young professionals are taught how to network, the idea of a matchmaker appeals to the business nature of setting meetings and the romantic nature of dating and marriage. The return to marriage as a business arrangement may not entirely resonate with a popular romantic ideal, but using the structure of a business in order to facilitate introductions to possible partners can be a prudent strategy because the idea of compatibility based on education, profession, and background is one with which most of the candidates are familiar and has been shown to be successful. In one sense arranged marriage is being portrayed as a very practical and measured process that makes the hierarchical nature of human relations visible, but it can also create a gap between the idea of feeling love and marrying for long-term relationships. Mr. Chopra uses his own experience to argue his point that he is looking out for the best interests of his daughter and that he believes romantic love will also eventually be a part of Rashmi's marriage.

This series of exchanges is fascinating because there is a serious attempt in the narrative to address many of the questions that popularly whirl around the idea of arranged marriage. The setting of the conference room plays as a mediation that is being performed with a businesslike aspect that perhaps offers some hope to both parties and also shows there is a convergence between Kate's and Savita's approaches to marriage. At the end of the scene Kate advises Rashmi to consider talking to the person her parents have selected for her: "[You] shouldn't be forced to do anything but try it." As with Apu, the key issue is one of choice. And so, although Kate says that Rashmi should not be "forced," she is open to the idea that arranged marriage might work as well as, if not better than, her own system of setting up matches.

At the end of the program Rashmi does marry an Indian American man acceptable to her parents, but she chooses the more assimilated and flexible Indian American brother that she had a relationship with and loved in the past rather than the brother with the accent, the medical degree, and the almost robotic commitment to success. The younger brother, Raj, is a professional in the music industry and clearly the black sheep in his family. His parents barely talk about him because his education and professional pedigree do not match those of his brother. Raj is shown as a man who respects his parents but also believes in individual choices. Rashmi and Raj met through their mutual interest in music and also fell in love. In this case their match is a combination of compatibility (education, family ties, and similar interests) and romantic chemistry. And yet neither brother is willing to discuss his interest or lack of interest (in the case of Sanjay) in marrying Rashmi because they are inhibited by the cultural traditions of their parents. Kate, as the matchmaker, has to intervene and facilitate communication between Rashmi and Raj in order for them to have a happily arranged match and marriage. In terms of compatibility, Rashmi finds romantic love; her individual situation is resolved and her parents are also pleased because she has married an Indian who is an educated man with a good family.

While the love marriage versus the arranged marriage is a traditional trope in Bollywood films, it plays out differently in this context because of the way cultural traditions are laid out along national lines as well as gendered ones. When hiring Kate, Rashmi indicates that her only condition for a mate is someone who likes music. Her match "doesn't have to be Indian but he should be a Vedic astrological match." She does qualify her statement by admitting her astrological signs also have to match her partner's. While she is supposedly asserting herself to look for love, she also puts forth a condition that exoticizes and trivializes her respect and love for her parents and their interest in her well-being. So while on the one hand arranged marriages are being treated as a respectable and viable outgrowth of Kate's own business of matchmaking, the drama still finds an aspect of Indian culture that has to be ridiculed and shown as strange and foreign.[32]

In *Miss Match*, although the Chopras express the idea that a non-American notion of family is not problematic for them, it is clearly an issue that the second-generation children cannot discuss with them. Although the plot is right out of a Bollywood film narrative, what this episode does is engage in a debate about how we think about marriage and partnership. Off the small screen, Indians in the United States are shifting arranged marriage to make it more compatible with contemporary American lifestyles (and Western ideals) through the establishment of marriage conventions and "assisted" arranged marriage practices.[33] The converging relationship between arranged marriage and matchmaking through the idea of compatibility provides a new line of discussion and inquiry into how we talk about portrayals of love, romance, and marriage in American popular culture. The proliferation of dating agencies and reality shows based on finding "the one" illustrates the inherent contradiction between the need for individual affection and compatibility and the emphasis on the institution of marriage to fulfill all feelings and needs. By focusing on the idea of compatibility, national and cultural identities are not the single determining factor in a relationship but instead become part of a larger conversation about the nature of marriage and long-term relationships.

Conclusion

The introduction of Indian arranged marriages as a viable strategy for long-term partnership for Americans provides an opportunity to represent South Asian American practices in American culture that do not depict Indians as foreign, strange, or distant but instead compatible with U.S. cultural practices. I theorize the term "compatibility" to show the blurring of racial, ethnic, and cultural boundaries in narratives of desire and marriage. Instead of the process of racial and cultural assimilation that requires Asian American and other immigrants to conform to white American dominant cultural norms, compatibility implies the ability to live together without conflict and to fit in while not exactly being the same. Compatibility as a factor in a potential relationship takes precedence over the "love at first sight" philosophy because it is focused on the long-term nature of a relationship rather than first impressions. In terms of South Asian American and non–South Asian American traditions related to marriage, compatibility is a concept that spans the gap between two traditionally divergent marriage philosophies. In addition, the concept provides an alternative means to discuss how racial and ethnic difference are embedded in American cultural assumptions about marriage and love. The primary association of Indians with arranged marriage racializes South Asians as the other without explicitly mentioning racial difference. In a post-racial narrative, racial difference still exists, but it is expressed in different terms. This chapter discusses how stereotypical representations of arranged marriage (as opposed to Western ideals of a love marriage) in mainstream American television reoccur and present Indians as culturally and racially foreign to the United States, but it also suggests an alternative reading of these stereotypes that promotes compatibility as a narrative that expands American cultural definitions and practices of marriage and partnership.

Notes

1. The TV series *Outsourced* (2010–) is set in India and in the early episodes shows how the American characters balk at the idea of an arranged marriage even though it is the custom and everyday reality of the Indian characters and culture around them.

2. See Eduardo Bonilla-Silva's *Racism without Racists: Color-Blind Racism and the Persistence of Racial Inequality in the United States* (Lanham, MD: Rowman and Littlefield, 2003).

3. See ibid.

4. See *U.S. v. Bhagat Singh Thind.* In this 1923 case, the Supreme Court ruled that the popular, or "the common man's," definition of racially identified language was instrumental in interpreting citizenship and naturalization law for both South Asians and Asian Americans, in general, for the United States. For more on this case, see Ian Haney Lopez's *White by Law: The Legal Construction of Race* (New York: NYU Press, 1997).

5. For more on accent as a racializing trope for South Asians, see Shilpa Davé's *Indian Accents: Brown Voice and Racial Performance in American Television and Film* (Champaign: University of Illinois Press, 2013) and "Apu's Brown Voice: Cultural Inflection and South Asian Accents," in *East Main Street: Asian American Popular Culture,* edited by Shilpa Davé, LeiLani Nishime, and Tasha Oren (New York: NYU Press, 2005), 313–36.

6. Although popular rhetoric has proclaimed the age of postnationalism in the 1990s and a post-racial society in the early twenty-first century, the concept of Indian American arranged marriages represents an alternative model of American culture that speaks to blurring of national and global trade and cultural boundaries of postnationalism and the negation of racial categories in post-racial moments. As many critics such as Dorrine Kondo, Aihwa Ong, Michael Omi, and Judith Halberstam have discussed, national and racial narratives have not disappeared but have been cloaked into other forms of expression.

7. For more information of South Asians and arranged marriage, see Shilpa Davé's "'No Life without Wife': Masculinity and Modern Arranged Meetings for Indian Americans," *Catamaran: South Asian American Writing* 5 (2006): 53–66; and Margaret Abraham's *Speaking the Unspeakable: Marital Violence among South Asian Immigrants in the United States* (New Brunswick, NJ: Rutgers University Press, 2000).

8. Nancy Cott, *Public Vows. A History of Marriage and the Nation* (Cambridge: Harvard University Press, 2002).

9. Stephanie Coontz, *Marriage, A History: From Obedience to Intimacy, or How Love Conquered Marriage* (New York: Viking, 2005), 276.

10. Ibid., 276–77.

11. See Yen Espiritu's *Asian American Women and Men* (Thousand Oaks, CA: Sage, 1992). *Picture Bride* and *The Joy Luck Club* are only a few of the films that portray arranged marriages in Asian American communities.

12. See Karen Leonard's history *Making Ethnic Choices* (Philadelphia: Temple University Press, 1994).

13. "Who's Sari Now?," *Miss Match*, season 1, episode 11, NBC, WVIT, Hartford, Dec. 15, 2003. Television.

14. Bonnie Dow, *Prime Time Feminism: Television, Media Culture, and the Women's Movement since 1970* (Philadelphia: University of Pennsylvania Press, 1996), xi.

15. The growing recognition of Bollywood films and themes televised in U.S. cable packages is a testimony to the power of performance (particularly dance, music, and fashion) and the spectacle of difference in ornate wedding dramas. Popular films among the Indian diasporic population in the United States include *American Desi* (2001), *Chutney Popcorn* (1999), *Monsoon Wedding* (2001), and *Bride and Prejudice* (2004). Each of these films features a debate about life partners and romance and also often includes a vibrant set that showcases Indian culture through marriage. Gurinder Chandra's Bollywood-influenced *Bride and Prejudice*, an updated version of Jane Austen's novel *Pride and Prejudice*, offers a contemporary discussion on arranged marriage, Indian immigration to the United States and the United Kingdom, and the expectations and approaches to marriage of Indian immigrant bachelors.

16. Dow, *Prime Time Feminism*, xxi.

17. Lizette Alvarez, "Arranged Marriages Get a Little Rearranging," *Nytimes.com*, June 22, 2003. This article discusses arranged marriages in the immigrant community in Britain.

18. "Diwali," *The Office* (2005–13), season 3, episode 6, NBC, WHGH, Boston, Nov. 2, 2006. Television.

19. See Davé, "'No Life without Wife.'"

20. There are many examples such as *Monsoon Wedding* and *Bride and Prejudice*. See Jigna Desai's work *Beyond Bollywood: The Cultural Politics of South Asian Diasporic Film* (Philadelphia: Temple University Press, 2004).

21. In the 1970s and 1980s, dramas such as *The Love Boat* (1977–86) and *Fantasy Island* (1978–84) depicted singles finding love or couples reuniting under the auspices of true love. In the 1990s and after 2000, there was a change in the dramas and situation comedies, which started to feature young people out on their own who were finding it difficult to meet people. Facilitated matches became more of a prime-time event as older single people found it more difficult to meet people after college. Also, *Love American Style* as well as the game shows *The Dating Game* and *The Newlywed Game* were part of the staples of 1960s television programming. The revival in the 1990s signaled a new adult population and interest in dating. Many reality shows, including *The Love Connection* (1983–99), tried to match people up by compatibility.

22. "Who's Sari Now?," *Miss Match*, season 1, episode 11.

23. "The Two Mrs. Nahaseemapetilons," *The Simpsons:* The Complete Ninth Season, episode 7, Fox, writ. Richard Appel, dir. Steven Dean Moore, 2006, DVD. Original airdate was November 16, 1997.

24. *Royal Pains* (2009–), USA Network. The first episode of season 1 aired June 4, 2009.

25. "Who's Sari Now?," *Miss Match*, season 1, episode 11.

26. "The Two Mrs. Nahaseemapetilons," *The Simpsons:* The Complete Ninth Season, episode 7.

27. In later episodes Apu does show how he falls in love with Manjula (he woos her with romantic Valentine's Day gifts), starts a family with her (they have octuplets), and also betrays his marriage vows by seeing another woman.

28. Cariana Chocano, "TV Review of *Miss Match*" (2003), *EW.com*, Oct. 10, 2003

29. She teams up with another single woman who works in a local bar that becomes the meeting place for the matched couples. Interspersed with the weekly storylines of the matchmaking business is Kate's own quest for love. Each match helps clarify her individual feelings about matches, relationships, and her search for a partner.

30. Ultimately the "lack of time" was the main reason people hired specific matchmakers. As one interviewee explained to Melanie Thernstrom in "The New Arranged Marriage," "He didn't like the Internet, and as a partner at a large firm he didn't have time to go to lots of social events searching for women" (*New York Times Magazine,* Feb. 13, 2005, 40).

31. "Who's Sari Now?," *Miss Match*, NBC, season 1, episode 11.

32. While her parents are pressuring the subject of the show, Rashmi, Kate's relationship with her father is one that combines business (she works in his firm) with the shattered ideals of romance (he is a divorce attorney who is divorced). Her dilemma, however, is undercut by humor, when she reveals that to date someone, they have to be astrological matches in order to satisfy her and her parents. The story does not discuss Kate's own family and instead deflects the discussion by focusing on Kate's consultation of an astrologer. Though Kate ends up following the pop spiritual advice of an astrologer as her compromise (rather than thinking about her family and their relationship to the people she might date), her willingness to try something different exposes the problems in American mediated visions of romantic love and offers a somewhat alternative view of arranged marriage as a viable and successful approach to marriage.

33. Another alternative is what scholar Martin Manalansan, in his work on the nature of love and sexuality, identifies as "queer love," a practice that involves the community and the individual to challenge the national narrative of the American family as a heterosexual couple with children, a dog, and a house with a white picket fence. Queer love allows for a more expansive definition of marriage relations that include extended families as part of the everyday life of life partners.

WORKS CITED

Abraham, Margaret. *Speaking the Unspeakable: Marital Violence among South Asian Immigrants in the United States.* New Brunswick, NJ: Rutgers University Press, 2000. Print.

Alvarez, Lizette. "Arranged Marriages Get a Little Rearranging." *Nytimes.com.* 22 June 2003. Web. <http://www.nytimes.com/2003/06/22/world/arranged-marriages-get-a-little-rearranging.html?pagewanted=all&src=pm >.

Bonilla-Silva, Eduardo. *Racism without Racists: Color-Blind Racism and the Persistence of Racial Inequality in the United States.* Lanham, MD: Rowman and Littlefield, 2003. Print.

Chocano, Cariana. "TV Review of Miss Match." *Ew.com.* 10 Oct. 2003. Web. <http://www.ew.com/ew/article/049241800.html>.

Coontz, Stephanie. *Marriage, A History: From Obedience to Intimacy, or How Love Conquered Marriage.* New York: Viking, 2005. Print.

Cott, Nancy. *Public Vows: A History of Marriage and the Nation.* Cambridge: Harvard University Press, 2002. Print.

Davé, Shilpa. "Apu's Brown Voice: Cultural Inflection and South Asian Accents." *East Main Street: Asian American Popular Culture.* Ed. Shilpa Davé, LeiLani Nishime, and Tasha Oren. New York: NYU Press, 2005. 313–36. Print.

———. *Indian Accents: Brown Voice and Racial Performance in American Television and Film.* Champaign: University of Illinois Press, 2013. Print.

———. "'No Life without Wife'? Masculinity and Modern Arranged Marriage for Indian Americans." *Catamaran: South Asian American Writing* 5 (2006): 53–66. Print.

"Diwali." *The Office.* NBC. WHGH, Boston. 2 Nov. 2006. Television.

Dow, Bonnie. *Prime Time Feminism: Television, Media Culture, and the Women's Movement since 1970.* Philadelphia: University of Pennsylvania Press, 1996. Print.

Espiritu, Yen. *Asian American Women and Men.* Thousand Oaks, CA: Sage, 1992. Print.

Leonard, Karen. *Making Ethnic Choices.* Philadelphia: Temple University Press, 1994. Print.

Lopez, Ian Haney. *White by Law: The Legal Construction of Race.* New York: NYU Press, 1997. Print.

"Who's Sari Now?" *Miss Match.* NBC. WVIT, Hartford. 15 Dec. 2003. Television.

12

Mainstreaming Latina Identity

Culture-Blind and Colorblind Themes in
Viewer Interpretations of Ugly Betty

PHILIP A. KRETSEDEMAS

Depictions of Latina/os in the U.S. media have veered in many directions. Leo Chavez has observed that from the seventies onward there
has been a steady pattern of news media coverage depicting Latina/
os as a cultural and demographic threat (21–43). But during this same
period, an unprecedented number of Latina/o pop stars and celebrities
have crossed over into mainstream media culture (Beltrán 1–3; Valdivia
1–30, 131–61). This Latina/o celebrity phenomenon has countered some
of the anti-Latino messages advanced by the new nativism, by making
Latina/o culture "fun" for a largely white, non-Latino audience. Arlene
Davila has explained that this process of mainstreaming Latina/o culture has been driven by a corporate interest in Latina/o populations as
a lucrative consumer demographic (*Latino Spin; Latinos, Inc.*). Davila
also observes that this process has given rise to media framing strategies that "whiten" Latina/o culture and bodies (*Latino Spin* 25–45).

These framing strategies, which treat Latina/o identity as an
upwardly mobile ethnicity (that is comparable to the cultural identities
of earlier cohorts of European immigrants), hold out the promise that
suitably assimilated Latinos will be able to escape the stigma of racial
otherness. It bears noting, however, that media constructions of white
(or near-white) Latina/os sit alongside another history of media stereotypes—stretching to the early twentieth century—that depicts Latina/os

as dangerous, hypersexualized, and buffoonish racial minorities (Beltrán 17–39; Benavides 1–24, 111–31; Greco Larson 59–66).

These stereotypes resonate with the Latino threat narrative that has been documented, more recently, by Chavez. It is also important to note that these stereotypes tend to conflate the cultural and racial difference of Latina/os. They do not always target a subset of darker-skinned bodies within the Latina/o population (exempting Latina/os who are suitably "white"). Instead, they evoke the same kind of racialized cultural imaginary that has historically defined anti-Semitic and specifically anti-Islamic racism (Balibar 21–27; Lampert 394–400). Racialized distinctions between white and nonwhite culture can be used to make sense of racialized bodies, but these distinctions also become abstracted from the body. The fulcrum of racialization shifts from the body to cultural diacritica that can be "carried" by bodies (but not always), and it is the possession of these cultural diacritica that ultimately determines the person's whiteness (or nonwhiteness). Under these conditions, it is possible for culture to have a "darkening effect," irrespective of the individual's physical appearance. As a result, all persons who emit signs of Latina/o culture or who identify as Latina/o become racialized as members of a nonwhite cultural and demographic formation.

Unstable Intersections: Constructions of Race, Ethnicity, and Latina/o Culture

This chapter takes a closer look at the unstable intersections of race, ethnicity, and Latina/o culture that were introduced earlier. It does this by way of a group interview study of viewer interpretations of the network television show *Ugly Betty* (2006–10), which made U.S. television history for its portrayal of a working-class, Latina lead character. My analysis focuses on the way that the respondents interpreted the racial and ethnic-cultural identity of the show's lead character, as well as the racial undertones of her relationships with other characters on the show.

My analysis uses the colorblind racial ideologies that have been documented by other race scholars as a starting point for conceptualizing the interpretations of the research participants (Bonilla-Silva *Racism without Racists* 25–52; Carr 107–39; Gallagher 22–37; Guinier and Torres 32–66; Neville et al. 27–43). But the subject matter and design of my study also required me to take the colorblind racism thesis in some new directions. Most of the research and theory on colorblind racial ideologies has focused on the way that white people talk about race, and on racial differences that are associated with non-Latino, black populations. This study, in contrast, examines how a multiracial and multiethnic sample of television viewers talked about Latina/o culture and identity. So it bears noting that my analysis does not just provide additional empirical verification of colorblind racial ideologies. I also use the data to rethink what colorblindness means when it is applied to Latina/o populations. Unlike most of the research on colorblind racial ideologies, this study required me to examine the dynamic interplay between the research participants' perceptions of race and their interpretations of Latina/o ethnicity and cultural identity. Furthermore, it required a theoretical framework that could account for the racialization of Latina/o cultural difference. These demands led me to develop the concept of culture-blindness, which is informed by the colorblind racism thesis (and can be regarded as a companion concept), but which I use to examine patterns of racial interpretation that have not been addressed by the research on colorblind racism.

Colorblind and Culture-Blind: Extending the Colorblind Racism Thesis to Latina/o Racialization

A key theme of the colorblind racism thesis is that the racial inequalities of the present day are perpetuated by ideologies that avoid the subject of race. As a result, the claim that "racism is a thing of the past" is a much more important organizing theme than the claim that racial minorities are "inherently inferior." Lawrence Bobo advances a similar argument with his theory of laissez-faire racism (38–55). Bobo also observes that the desire to proclaim the "end of racism" can still be articulated with a coded discourse on racial inferiority. It is possible, in one breath, to take a stand against racism (by celebrating the end of de jure segregation) and also to imply that there must be something inherently deficient about the minorities who are still struggling with chronic unemployment and social marginality (since these social problems can no longer be explained by the racism of the mainstream society). The possibility that institutional racism could be responsible for disproportionately high incarceration, joblessness, and high school dropout rates of black youth is displaced by a focus on individual culpability and personal responsibility (Ernst 19–64; Wise 132–52).

This emphasis on personal responsibility also crops up in the neoliberal policy discourse that has shaped the restructuring of the U.S. and global economy over the past few decades. The downsizing of the American social service system and the expansion of the prison system were guided by a policy discourse focused on personal responsibility that also included coded references to the deviance of racial minority populations (Hancock 23–64; Peck 83–128; Roberts 202–45). When viewed in this light, it becomes more apparent that colorblind racism and neoliberal or laissez-faire racism are different faces of the same body of discourse. Colorblind racial ideologies shift the discussion of difference and inequality away from macro-level racial disparities and toward a field of deracialized, individual subjectivities. Liberal or laissez-faire racism supplies a language that rationalizes the existence of disparities among these individuals, as well as framing efforts to change these disparities as "illiberal" interventions (Bobo 38–55; Menchaca 285–90).

These connections between racial colorblindness and the individualized subjectivities of neoliberal discourse have also been examined by migration and Latino studies scholars. Jonathan Inda (29–31) has explained how immigration enforcement practices have been informed by a neoliberal discourse on prudentialism that frames deportation as a consequence of excessive risk-taking behavior on the part of the migrant—a rationale that implicitly treats deportation as a punishment, despite the fact that it is not officially regarded as such by the U.S. immigration system (Dow 29–32). But this description of the imprudent deportee has its own coded, racial subtext. Racial profiles (and, specifically, Latino-Mexican profiles) can be used to determine who local police and federal agents will question for suspected violations (Goldsmith et al. 93–123; Kretsedemas 333–40; Shahani and Greene 36–42).

Arlene Davila has explained how neoliberal strategies for urban renewal have produced a different kind of marginality that is affected through a strategic embrace of Latino neighborhood culture (*Barrio Dreams* 97–127). Davila observes that, in the context of these renewal projects, Latino culture is valuable, primarily, as an exotic difference that can be marketed to upscale consumers. As a result, the very same development strategies that affirm the unique Latino heritage of these neighborhoods also convert the neighborhood's culture into a commodity that becomes detached from the places and populations it purportedly represents. As noted earlier, Davila has shown how the U.S. media and marketing companies have used similar strategies to construct the idea of the Latino consumer demographic (*Latino Spin; Latinos, Inc.*).

Isabel Molina-Guzmán provides another insight into this process in her discussion of media depictions of Latinas (119–50). She explains that Latina identity is not entirely erased by these depictions. Instead, it is sublimated—being abstracted from the cultural politics of Latina/o communities and converted into an "ethereal form" that can be more easily disseminated to global audiences (Molina-Guzmán 120–21). Like the corporate marketing of Latino neighborhood culture, Latina identity is converted into a cultural commodity that can be disseminated to an audience of individual consumers.

These observations about the mass marketing of Latina/o culture dovetail with some of the critiques that race theorists have levied at ethnicity theory. According to its critics, ethnicity theory presented an optimistic narrative about immigrant mobility, which explained how the identities of cultural minorities could be used strategically to enhance their integration into the host society (Omi and Winant 14–23; Steinberg 111–48). In this regard, ethnicity becomes the medium through which immigrants adapt to the competitive, individualistic culture of advanced industrialized societies. By comparison, critical race theory has placed more emphasis on how race functions as an imposed hierarchy that overdetermines the pathways for social mobility that are made available to ethnic actors (Bonilla-Silva "Rethinking Racism" 465–80; Jung 375–95). From this vantage point, ethnicity can be explained as an ideological maneuver that obscures and justifies the dynamics of race and class stratification (Williams 401–10).

These analyses have made important contributions to the politics of race and culture among minority populations, but they also tend to pit racial and ethnic identities against one another. An attachment to ethnicity, presumably, signals a denial of race and class inequality, and, conversely, the embrace of a racial identity presumes that one has rejected ethnicity.

A limitation of these analyses is that they focus on the ideological connotations of ethnicity theory as it has been defined by academics and policy makers. They do not account for the meanings that ethnicity can take on in the public sphere and "on the ground," in the social settings where Latina/os encounter nativist and anti-Latina/o racism. In these contexts, Latina/os (and nativists) can advance interpretations of Latina/o culture that, unlike the scholarly literature on ethnicity, are *not* abstracted from race. As noted earlier, anti-Latina/o racism often targets Latina/o culture as a whole, and not simply darker-skinned Latina/o bodies. As a result, nativist references to Mexican culture are always, implicitly racialized (even though they may target the very same cultural traits that are associated with Latina/o ethnicity). Latina/o cultural identities can also be mobilized in ways that respond to this racialization of Latina/o culture.

This is one reason why analyses of Latina/o identity often take an intersectional approach toward the analysis of race and ethnicity (Duany 147–72; Itzigsohn and Dore-Cabral 225–47; Landale and Oropesa 231–54; Rodriguez and Cordero-Guzman 523–42). These analyses start with the premise that culture and ethnicity add an important dimension to Latina/o racialization, instead of distracting attention from the reality of racism (in which ethnicity is treated as the equivalent of a "false consciousness").

This does not mean, however, that the problematic features of ethnic identity, identified by race scholars, should be overlooked. Instead, it becomes important to distinguish between different interpretations of Latina/o identity. This can be understood as distinction between the truncated interpretations of Latina/o identity, which have been criticized by Latina/o studies scholars, and a more complex cultural identity, which is not abstracted from race and is informed by the collective, political interests of Latina/o populations. This is the kind of distinction that Avila (*Barrio Dreams* 1–26) and Molina-Guzmán (3–7, 119–25) make in their critical analysis of the Latina/o identities that have been circulated by the mainstream media. This commodified cultural identity can be likened to the ethnic identities that have been criticized by race scholars. It bears noting, however, that the other type of Latina/o identity that Avila and Molina-Guzmán contrast it against is not the "opposite" of an ethnicity; it is just a more expansive version of this same identity (which has not been "edited down").

These observations carry important consequences for the application of the colorblind racism thesis to interpretations of Latina/o identity. It is important to understand how the desire to avoid seeing race leads people to overlook the racialized dimensions of Latina/o culture (preferring to see Latina/os as bearers of a deracialized ethnicity and not of a racial-cultural identity). I propose that culture-blindness is a more accurate description of this phenomenon than colorblindness because it is informed by an understanding of race that is not simply defined by skin color or other forms of physiognomic difference. It is also important to emphasize that perceptions of Latina/o culture in the United States are always-already racialized. The meaning of culture-blindness must be situated in light of this body of coded, cultural racism.

Colorblind racism insists that, underneath the skin, "we're all the same," while ignoring the social barriers that black and darker-skinned minorities continue to face due to interpretations of their physiognomic difference. Culture-blindness, on the other hand, ignores social barriers caused by racialized perceptions of cultural difference—and suppresses those aspects of minority cultural identity that attempt to speak to these problems. In the same way that African Americans can be viewed as "incidentally black," Latina/os can be viewed as "incidentally Mexican," their cultural difference being a superficial garnish for a set of norms and values that are presumably universal, but which are also understood to be normatively white.

It is not difficult to see how the interpretive logics of colorblindness and culture-blindness parallel one another. But it is important to note that these interpretive frameworks subject Latina/o cultural identity to a different kind of visibility. Because colorblindness is oriented toward discounting the social significance of physiognomic racial differences, it is possible for discourses on colorblindness to embrace ethnicity as a way of suppressing the discussion of race and racism. Discourses on culture-blindness, on the other hand, are oriented toward minimizing the significance of racialized cultural differences. Even though they may appear to embrace the ethnic identities of racial minorities, their overarching tendency is to erase the cultural difference that distinguishes the minority from the white mainstream. Even those traits that are practically indistinguishable from "ethnicity" must be sublimated and incorporated within an interpretive framework that understands the cultural identity of the minority as being derivative of the majority culture.

Depictions of Race, Gender, and Latina/o Culture on *Ugly Betty*

Ugly Betty provides a compelling insight into the divergent perspectives on Latina/o culture that were described earlier. Notably, Molina-Guzmán's argument about the sublimation of Latina identity was derived from her analysis of *Ugly Betty*. She explains that the show's lead character is situated in a Horatio Alger narrative that "assumes the hard-working Betty . . . will eventually achieve . . . success regardless of [her] class or ethnic background" (121). This immigrant success narrative was an important feature of the show's initial appeal (Poniewozik). Shortly after its debut on ABC in fall 2006, *Ugly Betty* became one of the most popular shows on network television.

Betty Suarez, the lead character, is a U.S.-born child of a single-parent, Mexican immigrant father who lives with her family in a working-class neighborhood in Queens, New York. Her aspirations are to become a journalist, but she lands an unlikely position as administrative assistant to the editor in chief of a fashion magazine in Manhattan. The ensuing plotlines explore the tension between Betty's naive integrity (epitomized by her awkward physical appearance) and the urbane sophistication of her Manhattan workplace.

Ugly Betty is an adaptation of a telenovela that originally aired in Colombia (*Yo Soy Betty la Fea*) that has since been adapted to several other national television markets. In the Colombian version of the show, Betty eventually wins the heart of her employer. The story also involves a love triangle between Betty, her employer, and her employer's original fiancée (the beautiful daughter of one of the cofounders of the fashion company). In this context, the questions that the show raises about the meaning of beauty have as much to do with class culture as they do with gender. In her group interview study, Yeidy Rivero observed that the narrative themes of *Yo Soy Betty la Fea* both affirmed and challenged this gendered class culture (66–68).

Ugly Betty borrows some of these same narrative themes by associating Betty's "ugliness" and moral integrity with her working-class roots. But in the U.S. version of the show, these associations become explicitly ethnicized and implicitly racialized. Betty still struggles to prove herself in the workplace, and, as in the Colombian telenovela, she enters into a series of conflicts with a beautiful and powerful female character. In *Ugly Betty*, however, this character is not the employer's love interest but an ambitious career woman who wants to push Betty's employer out of his job. As a result, the romantic conflict between Betty, her employer, and the "other woman" is converted into a desexualized power struggle over status in the workplace. Moreover, each of these characters represents a different racial-ethnic population. Betty is a second-generation Mexican immigrant, her employer (Daniel Meade) is a non-Latino, white man, and his workplace nemesis (Wilhelmina Slater) is a light-skinned African American woman.

Betty's workplace struggles are embedded in narratives that operate on at least two levels. First, there is the Horatio Alger narrative, which focuses on her struggle for recognition in a treacherous workplace. In this context, Betty's Mexican heritage can be interpreted as a cultural resource that she draws on to overcome adversity. But it also so happens that many of the difficult people that Betty has to deal with are women and other racial minorities. As a result, the Horatio Alger narrative also becomes interwoven with a second set of narrative themes, in which the pathway to success requires the successful navigation of the race and gender hierarchies of the professional workplace (avoiding contact with disgruntled minorities and overly ambitious women).

Favorable interpretations of the show's treatment of Latina/o culture have focused on the first set of narrative themes, which depict Betty as a hard worker who will prevail in time (notably, these same themes are echoed by the show's creative team; Beck; Levin). In contrast, critical interpretations have focused on the second set of narrative themes, observing that Betty's success is contingent on conforming to the race and gender hierarchies of her workplace and that she is ultimately limited by these hierarchies (Gonzalez).

These differences among television media critics also surface in scholarly analyses of the show, though it bears noting that most of the academic scholarship has been critical. Some studies have concluded that *Ugly Betty*'s narrative themes are poised ambiguously between a hegemonic discourse on assimilationism (that reinforces dominant race/class/gender hierarchies) and a potentially innovative reading of Latina/o cultural agency (Avila-Saavedra 144–45; Benavides 211–16). Other scholars have argued that the show's discourse on multiculturalism and critique of beauty norms are ultimately derivative of the discursive regimes of global capitalism (Amaya 801–17; Vincent 346–50; Shufeldt Esch 180–81).

Hector Amaya explains, for example, that the discourse on diversity portrayed by *Ugly Betty* "is a perfect example of corporate liberalism, under which diversity becomes morphed from a term rooted in the racial and sexual struggles of the civil rights movement, to an ethnocentric term that is valued because of the benefits it can provide to the majority who identify with our current racial patriarchy" (810). Amaya goes on to explain that "diverse" television shows like *Ugly Betty* become valuable to network television mainly because they are profitable, and that they avoid narrative themes that would draw attention to racism and sexism because of fears that these sorts of narratives might turn off viewers (in addition to the fact that such narratives may run counter to the worldview of the show's producers and media executives). Amaya also observes that "the recasting of diversity as a self-centered economic tactic ... precludes Latinas/os from using the language of justice [and] forces Latina/o narratives to become 'universal' rather than particular" (813).

With this reference to "universal" Latina/o narratives, Amaya advances a critique that is similar to Molina-Guzmán's explanation of sublimation. In both cases, Latina/o identity becomes palatable to a diverse audience of individual consumers because it has been abstracted from any of the political and cultural contexts that would draw attention to the singularity of the Latina/o experience in the United States (and that would highlight what makes Latina/os different from the mainstream). Instead, Latina/o culture is converted into a cultural difference that can be consumed by viewers without requiring them to reflect on their own race, gender, or class positionality. Furthermore, the act of consuming this "difference" actually underscores the "sameness" of Latina/o culture (by affirming culturally dominant norms and values).

For example, ethnicity can be used to add value to the marketing of consumer items. In *Ugly Betty*'s pilot episode, the Betty character salvages an advertising campaign by incorporating images and themes that represent her own Mexican family values (which resonate with her audience because of their "universal" appeal).[1] But in a later episode, when Betty learns that she has become a beneficiary of affirmative action, she dutifully turns down the opportunity until a white, male officemate is granted a similar offer.[2] As Jennifer Esposito has explained, this is just one example of how the narrative themes of *Ugly Betty* delegitimize gender and Latina/o culture as a collective claims-making strategy (521–35). The gender and ethnicity of the Betty character are desirable as an audience draw, but the plotlines of the show remain stubbornly colorblind and culture-blind to the social barriers that Betty might face, precisely because she is a Latina.

In this regard, the narrative themes of *Ugly Betty* tend to send mixed messages about the Betty character's Mexican ethnicity—as a desirable kind of cultural difference, but also as a difference that ultimately should not "make a difference." Furthermore, the plotlines of the show isolate Betty from other nonwhite characters, including (with the exception of her immediate family) other Latina/os. Throughout the four seasons of the show, Betty does not develop a lasting friendship or a romantic relationship with another Latina/o character.[3]

These mixed messages draw attention to the multivalent nature of all media texts. As Stuart Hall has explained, media texts do not just communicate their messages "openly" but do so through connotations that are embedded within their narrative themes (128–32). It follows that the ideological content of the media text cannot be fully realized until the television viewer actively decodes these subtextual messages. This is why it is important to examine the way the media text is interpreted by an audience. This kind of research also allows researchers to examine the social process through which people interpret media texts, shedding light on how their interpretations are shaped in reference to other fields of discourse (that stretch beyond the narrative themes of the television show). So it becomes possible to examine how the narrative themes of the show resonate with discourses on race that are circulating in the public sphere.

The Group Interviews: Sampling Method and Research Design

The interview phase of this study was carried out between July 2008 and February 2009 in the greater Boston area. Discussants were recruited through a self-selected sampling method that has been used by other qualitative studies of media audiences (Ang 41–50). Research subjects were expected to have viewed at least one episode of *Ugly Betty* prior to participating in the study, but the wording of the advertisements encouraged participation from people who were regular viewers of the show.

The sampling method yielded a cross section of discussants that was predominantly white but contained a slightly larger proportion of racial-ethnic minorities than the national audience for *Ugly Betty*. According to May 2009 demographics, the national audience for *Ugly Betty* was 80 percent white non-Latino, 12 percent Latino, 5 percent black, 2 percent Asian, and 1 percent "other" ("Ugly Betty"). In contrast, the sample for this study was 62 percent white non-Latino, 16 percent Latino, 12 percent black, 6 percent Asian, and 4 percent multiracial or "other." The gender composition was more skewed than the national audience for *Ugly Betty*. Although female viewers composed 51 percent of the national audience, they accounted for approximately 65 percent of the sample for this study.

The distribution of foreign-born persons in the sample was similar to the national average, at approximately 12 percent (as of 2010, the U.S. national average was 12.9 percent; "Number of Immigrants"). There are no national statistics on the size of the "second-generation" immigrant population, but this group composed an additional 21 percent of the sample, the remaining 67 percent being native-born children of native-born parents.

The majority of the discussants were young, single adults with no children. Seventy-seven percent of the discussants fell in the nineteen- to thirty-five-year age range, 85 percent of them had never been married, and 58 percent had no children in their household. Household income of the sample was much more diverse. The modal annual household income category was under $20,000 (accounting for 28 percent of the sample, many of whom were college students), but the remaining 54 percent of the sample was spread fairly evenly across the next three income categories (ranging from $20,000 to $80,000 per year). A small number of the discussants (9 percent) listed themselves in a higher income bracket (exceeding $80,000 per year).[4]

A total of nineteen interview sessions were carried out for the study, involving fifty-two discussants. The recruitment process was designed to assemble discussion groups composed of people who normally viewed the show together.[5] Whenever possible, interviews were conducted in the living spaces of the discussants, but this was only arranged at their discretion. For participants who preferred being interviewed elsewhere, arrangements were made to interview them either on the university campus with which the researchers were affiliated (the University of Massachusetts-Boston) or at another location of their preference.

The group interviews were structured around viewings of selected excerpts from episodes of *Ugly Betty*, which were all taken from season 1. All these excerpts were representative of broader patterns in the depiction of Betty's Mexican heritage and the racial dynamics of her workplace that were identified through a content analysis of every episode of season 1.[6]

The excerpts that the discussants viewed (in chronological order) included (1) several scenes from the pilot episode, which featured the Betty character's initial interview for the position at *Mode* magazine, her first encounter with the Daniel and Wilhelmina characters at a staff meeting, and a business meeting at the end of the episode at which Betty averts Wilhelmina's first attempt to sabotage one of Daniel's projects; (2) a sequence of scenes from episode 6 ("Trust, Lust, and Must") that contrast Wilhelmina's strained relationship with her only daughter to Betty's close-knit family ties—during which Betty's father reveals that he is undocumented; (3) a sequence of scenes from episode 17 ("Icing on the Cake") in which Betty, her date (a white male), and the mother of her employer (Claire Meade, a wealthy white female) make an unexpected stop at Betty's home to find her father being accosted by an overly controlling and buffoonish black female immigration officer; (4) the opening scene from episode 22 ("A Tree Grows in Guadalajara"), featuring Betty talking with her sister in a beauty salon (her sister's workplace) about their plans to visit Mexico to rectify the legal status of their father, only to be interrupted by Betty's sister's supervisor, an irascible, dark-skinned Latina.

These excerpts provided a stimulus for discussion, but it bears noting that all of the discussants had viewed the show prior to participating in the study (and 65 percent of the discussants had been following the show for at least one season). So although the excerpts allowed the researchers to focus the conversations on particular themes, they were also propelled by the discussants' general knowledge of the show.

The interview protocol was organized into two sections, beginning with an open-ended series of questions that asked the discussants to describe their general impressions of the show, and closing with a series of directed questions that were focused on the show's racial subtext.

After viewing the first two collections of scenes, the discussants were asked to describe how they felt about the show's main characters. This section of the interview concluded with a series of questions that asked the discussants to reflect on Betty's Mexican heritage and her degree of acculturation to an "American" lifestyle and value system. After viewing the last two collections of scenes, the discussants were asked to reflect on how they would racially categorize Betty and the significance of her racially exclusive friendship networks.

The interviews were conducted by the lead researcher and a research assistant, both of whom were males of color (one non-Latino and the other Latino).[7] Prior research has shown that when the race/ethnicity of the interviewer is different than that of the interviewee, the general tendency is for interviewees to respond in ways that they think will meet with the approval of the interviewer (see Campbell). Given these dynamics, it is reasonable to expect that interview-based research conducted by racial minorities with a diverse sample of interviewees may have a polarizing effect for white and nonwhite discussants. White interviewees may be more inhibited in the way they frame their opinions. Racial minorities, in contrast, may be emboldened to develop more critical framing strategies than they would in discussion groups led by a white moderator.

One limitation of this research design is that it could produce a body of racial discourse that exaggerates the critical framing strategies of racial minorities. Another limitation is that it does not allow for a rigorous comparison of white versus nonwhite or Latino versus non-Latino responses—because it does not attempt to interview these populations under equivalent conditions (i.e., in a homogeneous discussion group led by a moderator of the same race/ethnicity as the discussants).

An advantage of this approach, however, is that it allows researchers to examine the kind of racial discourse that whites and racial minorities are most likely to produce in "mixed company." It also bears noting that colorblind racial discourse has been intended for these sorts of environments (making it possible to make public statements about race that avoid the use of openly racist language). This means that discussants are probably not always being completely candid about what they "really think," and this pressure to self-censor could have been most severe for white discussants. But for precisely this reason, these discussions can provide a valuable insight into the way that Latina/o identity is being interpreted in light of discourses that have currency in the public sphere.

Analysis of the Group Interviews

The following analysis focuses on the culture-blind themes that surfaced in the group interviews, and the way they were articulated with discourses on colorblindness. As I will explain, culture-blind themes surfaced in the majority of the discussion groups, but they were also a complex body of ideas. Despite their pervasiveness, culture-blindness interpretations were sometimes articulated in an uneasy tension with other perspectives that were more open to "seeing" the racial and gendered dimensions of Betty's Latina identity. And even though both white and nonwhite discussants gravitated toward culture-blind themes, they often framed and justified their interpretations in different ways. The connecting thread that ran through all these variations on culture-blindness was a desire to distance the Betty character from her "ethnic particularity."

Mexican Ethnicity and Americanization

Observations about Betty's degree of Americanization were the most common way that culture-blind themes entered into the discussions. All the groups had approving things to say about Betty's Mexican heritage. Even so, in seventeen of the nineteen groups, most of the discussants agreed that Betty was primarily American. One example is provided by the following excerpt. The discussants produced these comments after viewing the first two collections of scenes, that introduced the main characters of the show (from the pilot episode) and Betty's home life and Mexican family values.

GROUP 17

INTERVIEWER: How would you define Betty, as Mexican, as Mexican American, or American?

INTERVIEWEE 1 (WHITE FEMALE): I just see her as American, I guess. I mean—

INTERVIEWEE 2 (WHITE FEMALE): Yeah.

INTERVIEWEE 1 (WHITE FEMALE): We hear her sister like speak more with a Spanish accent. Her dad a little, too, but you don't really ever hear her speak it.

INTERVIEWEE 2 (WHITE FEMALE): Outside of her house, like you really couldn't tell what generation being in America she is, like you'd have no clue. Her family could have been there for like twenty generations or whatever.

INTERVIEWER: How do you define being American?

INTERVIEWEE 2 (WHITE FEMALE): Definitely like the fact that she like speaks without like any kind of accent is a factor. She's aware of things that are going on like culturally in America.

INTERVIEWEE 1 (WHITE FEMALE): I think she's proud of her roots but— well, when she was in—was she in Mexico in that episode, I think that was your stereotypical like, you know, "I'm going back to my roots" moment where she gets this hallucination and she has to follow the bird or something. I forget but it was . . . I think she's proud of [her culture], I just don't think that she waves a flag or anything.

This excerpt provides a good illustration of the sublimation of Latina identity, described by Molina-Guzmán. Betty's ethnicity can be reconciled with an American identity because it has been abstracted from any qualities that might distinguish it from the preferred identities of the discussants. This is why one discussant observed that Betty seemed to be proud of her ethnic roots, but takes care to emphasize that Betty is not excessively attached to these roots.

This qualified acknowledgment of Betty's Mexican heritage is underscored by the statement "I just don't think that she waves a flag or anything." This indirectly references the complaints that many conservative pundits have made about Mexican immigrants who have waved Mexican flags at protest marches and other public events on U.S. soil. A clear line is drawn between Betty's Latina identity and this more "extroverted" or controversial cultural politics.

It is also notable that the discussant described Betty's desire to connect with her Mexican heritage as "stereotypical." In this context, becoming a stereotype has to do with the amount of interest that the Betty character seems to show in her Mexican heritage. These comments draw attention to the latent concerns about Latina/o cultural identity that underlie the discussants' qualified acceptance of Betty's ethnicity.

In the other groups, observations about Betty's Americanization made it possible for the discussants to bracket their knowledge of her Mexican ethnicity. Consistent with the interpretive priorities of culture-blindness, the overriding desire was to focus on those aspects of Betty's character that made her indistinguishable from the American mainstream. So it was possible to acknowledge Betty's Mexican heritage while also insisting that she was not *really* Mexican. A white male discussant from group 13 observed, for example, "I never saw [Betty] as anything but a Brooklyn girl."

This description of Betty as a Brooklyn girl evokes an identity that transcends Betty's ethnic particularity. But later on in this same conversation, the discussants made comments which indicated that the American culture they were describing was normatively white. Furthermore, their interpretations of Betty's Americanness were resistant to inquiries about racial and gender inequality in Betty's workplace. A good example is provided by the following two excerpts. At one point in the discussion, one of the members pondered whether Betty's workplace difficulties might be linked to social barriers that are specific to Latinas. This exchange occurred midway through the interview, after the group had viewed the first two collections of scenes (but interviewee 5 begins within his own recollection of an *Ugly Betty* episode that was not viewed during the interview).

GROUP 13

INTERVIEWEE 5 (WHITE MALE): Like, I was watching last week's episode or the last two weeks. Like, Lindsay Lohan gets promoted, and [Betty's] like [Daniel's] little assistant and nothing happens. I mean they get to know each other better and stuff, but it's all the same as in the other episodes.

INTERVIEWEE 1 (WHITE MALE): Well, it's also that entry-level kind of position—so you want to make your boss look good so maybe you'll be promoted along with him or her.

INTERVIEWEE 5 (WHITE MALE): But look at Kimmie [the Lindsey Lohan character]. She got promoted in like twenty-four hours. She was blonde, you know, and then—and she's been—I mean why hasn't she—she got her business card finally and like it didn't even have a title on it. I mean she's been on the show for three years, so she's been overlooked and it's 'cause she's Latino and 'cause she doesn't dress right and 'cause she doesn't—you know, and she's the smartest one at the whole magazine.

A few minutes later, the conversation shifted decisively away from this analysis. The other members of the group began to insist that Betty's

Mexican heritage was irrelevant to the themes of the show. Notably, the discussant who originally introduced the subject of Betty's unfair treatment (interviewee 5) agreed with the rest of the group as the conversation began to turn in this direction:

INTERVIEWEE 5: [Betty's Mexican American family] makes it more interesting as a show to watch.

INTERVIEWEE 1: But would it be any different if it was a little Amish girl? You know, I mean is—I guess.

INTERVIEWEE 2: Well, I tend to put anybody in that, you know, role and they would—they could write the same character. I don't think it has to be Mexican.

INTERVIEWEE 3: But I think Amish would be a good message.

INTERVIEWEE 2: You know, you'd have the same fashion issues. You'd have the same—

INTERVIEWEE 3: She could speak German.

INTERVIEWEE 5: So, you'd have like this, you know, minority church girl who could also be the all-American girl.

The reference to Betty's Americanness appears at the very end of this excerpt (by way of the "all-American girl" comment). Even so, the themes communicated through the entire excerpt are consistent with the culture-blind interpretation of Americanization that surfaced in most of the interviews. It is also noteworthy that the other cultural identities that the discussants thought Betty could pull off were both white ethnicities. Americanness surfaces as a quality that appears to transcend ethnicity but is normatively white. In this regard, the desire to see Betty's ethnicity as being incidental to who she really is—and as being interchangeable with other ethnicities—underscores the racial subtext of the discourse on Americanization.

Even so, the ambivalences of this exchange are just as significant as its culture-blind themes. The comments of interviewee 5 demonstrate that the plotlines of *Ugly Betty* allowed some openings for critical observations about racial and gender inequalities in the workplace. Even when the conversation turned away from this critical direction, it was not to justify Betty's marginal situation at work. To the contrary, the discussants wanted Betty to succeed, and earlier in the conversation, they expressed their frustration about the fact that the Betty character seemed to be stuck in a subordinate position. But they also interpreted these difficulties as generic features of the professional environment that anyone would encounter. This interpretive tendency surfaced in many of the other groups, in which the discussants expressed an interest in Betty's "empowerment" but only as long as this was expressed in a universalizing language that effaced the singularity of her racial and gendered experience as a Latina.

Interpretations of Race, Culture, and Latina/o Family Values

The discourse on Americanization was not the only interpretive framework that was used to express culture-blind themes. Interpretations of Betty's family values were used in a similar manner. This discourse on the family was not as pervasive as the discourse on Americanization, surfacing in just eight of the nineteen groups. Even so, it provided a compelling insight into how culture-blind themes could be articulated with the identities of white and nonwhite discussants. Consider the following comment from one member of a group composed of black females of Afro-Caribbean, immigrant ancestry. This comment was made midway through the interview after the group had viewed the first two collections of scenes:

> I just want to talk from the point of view of an immigrant family because we are Haitian because you can relate to that like that close-knit type of family except you've seen how other families interact with each other, then you can, that's what happens in the Caribbean world, how close they are. The family is a universal world.

This discussant identified with Betty on the basis of their shared difference from mainstream American culture. For her, Betty was not an exemplary model of an Americanized Latina. But, like the discourse on Americanization, her description of the immigrant family transcended ethnic particularity, which made it possible for Betty's family values to be interchangeable with Haitian/Caribbean family values.

This statement can be read as an expression of pan-ethnic solidarity and not as a worried observation about the "flag-waving" side of

Mexican ethnicity. But it still participates in the sublimation of Mexican ethnicity described by Molina-Guzmán. Betty's family can represent a value system that transcends her Mexican heritage precisely because of the show's thinned-out depiction of Mexican culture (in which Betty's Mexican-ness is always signifying a quality that is other than Mexican).

It is also telling that this pan-ethnic discourse on immigrant family values was resistant to the discussion of race and racism. In the following excerpt, the discussants were asked to think about Betty's racial-ethnic self-concept and to consider why the show's plotlines embed her in white-exclusive friendship networks. These comments were made after the group had viewed the final two collections of scenes.

GROUP 2

INTERVIEWER: How do you think Betty sees herself in racial terms?

INTERVIEWEE 2 (BLACK FEMALE): I don't think, they don't characterize her on that. She just realizes that she's Spanish throughout the show. She doesn't put effort into seeing herself as a lighter Hispanic or darker Mexican.

INTERVIEWER: In the show it doesn't seem that she has any friends or romantic relationships with any racial minorities, including other Latinos. Does this tell us anything about how she might see herself, in racial terms?

INTERVIEWEE 2 (BLACK FEMALE): I don't think the show is saying that.

INTERVIEWEE 1 (BLACK FEMALE): I don't think the show is necessarily saying anything about race. I think she still identifies as a Mexican person but you know she was around, her working environment everything else she's around is white. So she is naturally gonna socialize or socialize herself with people who are white than Mexican. But I think that her identity as a Mexican American is still intact.

This exchange illustrates that the discourse on colorblindness was not far removed from the discourse on culture-blindness. Before questions about Betty's racial identification were raised, the discussion gravitated toward culture-blind themes, emphasizing the universality of Betty's immigrant family values. But when the subject of race was broached by the interviewer, the discussion turned toward a more conventional discourse on colorblindness, which emphasized that Betty and her family (and the show in general) did not pay attention to differences in skin color. The discussants also produced a stronger interpretation of Betty's ethnicity (emphasizing the pride she had in her Mexican heritage). But, notably, this emphasis was not being used to affirm the singularity of her Latina identity but to underscore the insignificance of race.

This exchange demonstrated that the pan-ethnic immigrant identity that was affirmed by the discussants was not grounded in a shared racial experience. Ironically, this was the one moment in the conversation in which the desire for universality did not apply. Instead of being open to seeing how the racialization of Latinas and Afro-Caribbean migrants might be related, the discussants produced a discourse on immigrant ethnicity that was "united" in its rejection of the significance of race.

Other groups produced a culture-blind discourse that drew attention to the similarities of Betty's family values and those of the American mainstream. Notably, these interpretations were typical of all-white or predominantly white discussion groups. The following excerpt provides one such example. These comments were produced near the end of the interview, after the discussants had viewed all the selected scenes from season 1.

GROUP 7

> INTERVIEWER: In racial terms are Betty and her family white, nonwhite brown, or something else?
>
> INTERVIEWEE 1 (WHITE MALE): I don't think I can do the whole family. The whole family seems to represent different aspects of . . .
>
> INTERVIEWEE 2 (WHITE FEMALE): Mexican American experience.
>
> INTERVIEWEE 1 (WHITE MALE): Um, I don't think I have ever thought about defining whiteness before.
>
> INTERVIEWEE 3 (WHITE MALE): Defining whiteness on TV seems redundant.
>
> INTERVIEWEE 1 (WHITE MALE): Yeah.
>
> INTERVIEWEE 3 (WHITE MALE): Because it's the standard in a certain way.
>
> INTERVIEWEE 2 (WHITE FEMALE): Yeah, you could say that.
>
> INTERVIEWEE 1 (WHITE MALE): You could say that, but her home life seems very unified. She still has her home life and influence and her dad is

always there to bring up how it was. With what they had to go through, it's not like she's forgotten. It's not that she's moved on from there.

INTERVIEWEE 2 (WHITE FEMALE): I think everything is much more simplified on TV. So in terms of TV they are trying to represent them as the standard family

INTERVIEWEE 3 (WHITE MALE): . . . and emphasize the universal nature . . .

INTERVIEWEE 1 (WHITE MALE): Yeah.

INTERVIEWEE 3 (WHITE MALE): The universal struggle.

This group produced one of the more ambivalent renditions of the discourse on culture-blindness. It acknowledged Betty's family's Mexican American heritage but also observed that the television show was trying to emphasize the "universal nature" of their struggle. Unlike most of the other groups, these discussants noted that these universalizing themes were encoded in the media text itself. But there was never a point in the conversation when the discussants veered away from this interpretive framework.

Another distinguishing feature of this conversation is that the discussants openly acknowledged that the "standard American" family was normatively white (instead of making comments that merely connoted this white racial subtext). Once again, the discussants did not endorse or criticize the white family norm. Even so, their willingness to acknowledge this racial subtext indicates that they were not as invested in colorblindness as the discussants from group 2. Furthermore, they expressed sympathy for Betty's struggle (and her family's struggle) throughout the interview. But there was no acknowledgment of how these struggles might be specifically connected to a Latina/o experience of social marginality or racialization (despite the fact that all the groups had viewed scenes that drew attention to Betty's father's status as an undocumented migrant).

Points of Departure

A small minority of the discussion groups deviated from the culture-blind themes that have been reviewed here. It bears noting, however, that these conversations differed only by a matter of degree. They were distinguished by the fact that at least one member of the group consistently produced an interpretive framework that violated the premise of culture-blindness (in groups where the discourse on culture-blindness dominated, individuals who produced "deviant interpretations" always recanted and affirmed the majority opinion of the group before the end of the interview—as illustrated by the excerpt from group 13).

These deviations from culture-blindness occurred in four of the nineteen discussion groups. Even though most nonwhites in the sample produced culture-blind interpretations of the Betty character, it also happens that the groups that deviated from culture-blindness contained at least one racial minority (or were composed entirely of racial minorities). This included group 5 (composed of one Latina and one white male), group 8 (composed of one Asian female and one Latina), group 9 (composed of one Asian female and one black male), and group 19 (composed of one Latina and two white females). Furthermore, the individuals in these groups who produced interpretations that deviated the most from culture-blindness were racial minority females (and were often Latinas, though it bears noting that an equal number of Latinas produced culture-blind interpretations of the show).

Consider the following excerpt from group 8, which was composed of a Latina and an Asian female discussant. This exchange occurred in the latter portion of the interview, after the discussants had viewed all four sets of scenes.

GROUP 8

INTERVIEWER: Do you think the show is realistic in its portrayal of Betty's social networks, in racial terms?

INTERVIEWEE 1 (ASIAN FEMALE): For me, when I'm at home with my family I have my Filipino values and all that. But once I go outside, I sort of become an American in terms of my judgment and all that. It seems that I'm trying to fit in by trying to be American, but it's just I know people wouldn't understand if I try to be myself.

INTERVIEWEE 2 (LATINA): I don't think it's realistic because being from an immigrant background, most of my friends are, I have friends that are white, I have friends that are black. The majority are black. I have Spanish friends obviously, but my friends are from all different backgrounds, and when I go home, obviously my culture is, there I have to speak Spanish, that's my ethnicity and I have to at home. And my friends go over, and I speak Spanish to my mom, but I speak English to my friends. It's common sense, and like everybody is OK with it because, you know, they know.

INTERVIEWEE 1 (ASIAN FEMALE): When I was in high school—I'm from western Massachusetts, it's like a country place, and I was the only Asian in my high school. And everybody was rich, like 90 percent of the people. But I never felt awkward. Whenever my friends were at my house, [my family] will be speaking my language, you know, talking in my language in front of them. . . . But what was strange for me was that when I was back home, I never experienced discrimination and all that. Maybe because I managed to Americanize myself, but when I was here in Boston, that's when I experienced something like that—which is weird because here in Boston you see a lot of people with different backgrounds.

In this excerpt, the Filipina discussant uses the same language of Americanization that surfaced in groups that produced culture-blind interpretations of the Betty character. It is also worth noting how the idea of Americanization evokes an individualizing frame of reference that separates the immigrant from his or her cultural group. By implication, the process of becoming American is something that immigrants must work out on their own. Hence, the pressure to "be American" starts once she "goes outside" (leaving the home space that is associated with her family and her inherited culture).

This discussant is not overtly critical of Americanization (or of its racial subtext), but unlike most of the groups that produced a discourse on culture-blindness, she engages Americanization from the vantage point of the immigrant. As a result, she produces an auto-ethnographic reflection that implicitly sympathizes with the situation of the Betty character, but which is not concerned with making statements about "how American" she is. Her closing comment also indicates that she values her cultural difference (i.e., the freedom of "talking in my language" at home in front of her friends, which is contrasted against the discrimination she experienced in the Boston area).

The Latina discussant, on the other hand, directly engages the matter of race. Her comments operate completely outside the majority/minority framework of the discourse on Americanization. She also produces an account of her lived experience that is more collectivist in its orientation—describing her relations with friends and family who are all, presumably, accepting of each other's cultural and racial difference. Furthermore, by describing the racial composition of her friendship networks (observing that most of her friends are black), she also answers the question about the "racial realism" of Betty's friendship networks. But, again, the most significant thing about this exchange is the way that both discussants went about answering the question, by drawing on interpretations of their lived experience.

This use of lived experience was not unique to the groups that deviated from the discourse on culture-blindness (as evidenced by the discourse on "immigrant family values" produced by group 2), but it was most concentrated in these groups. Groups that produced culture-blind (and colorblind) interpretations of *Ugly Betty* were much more likely to confine their analysis to the media text. In contrast, *all* the groups that deviated from culture-blind themes drew on their lived experience to recontextualize the show's narrative themes.

It is important to emphasize, however, that this use of lived experience was an interpretive framework in its own right. It cannot be presumed that these discussants were producing interpretations of *Ugly Betty* that were more grounded in empirical reality than the others. This tendency to draw on lived experience is best understood as an interpretive priority that was tied to a different kind of subjective orientation than those of the other discussants. These interpretations disrupted the private relationship between the individual media consumer and the media text, situating the interpretation of the media text in light of other social relations and experiences that occurred outside of the act of media consumption. The following excerpt provides another example of these interpretive priorities. This exchange was also produced near the end of the interview, after the group had viewed all the scenes (but, like many of the other groups, the discussants drew on their recollections of prior episodes that had not been viewed during the interview session).

GROUP 19

INTERVIEWEE 1 (LATINA): You know, it's very interesting that with Betty, it's like she's only allowed to have white boyfriends on the show.

INTERVIEWEE 2 (WHITE FEMALE): And white friends.

INTERVIEWEE 1 (LATINA): Well, I—first of all, as someone who grew up in New York City, I tend to get offended that the family was made to be Mexican as opposed to being Caribbean which is the predominant Latino population—

INTERVIEWER: Oh, you mean like Puerto Rican.

INTERVIEWEE 1 (LATINA): Like Puerto Rican, Dominican, who knows: make them Haitian. (Laughter) For me it raises a lot of issues about race within the Latino community, just the fact that that was the route that they went and just also the fact that you don't really get the other flavors of other Latino communities in New York.

INTERVIEWEE 2 (WHITE FEMALE): Yeah, and even their friends, right?

INTERVIEWEE 1 (LATINA): Yeah exactly. Not, it's just kind of like it's interesting because it's a Latino show, but, you don't even see like Latinos in the rest of New York City except for the Salma Hayek character.

INTERVIEWEE 3 (WHITE FEMALE): Yeah, and that's the kind of weird part about the whole thing is, I think that to some extent they're allowed to be a Mexican family in these kind of stereotyped ways that are all about like nostalgia and tradition and all this stuff that is—you know, it's about making the immigrant family respectable, but they're not allowed to have a community at all.

INTERVIEWEE 1 (LATINA): Right. Exactly.

This was the only group that directly critiqued the racial subtext of the show and that consistently challenged the culture-blind themes that were expressed by the other discussants. Their discussion also illustrates how interpretations of Latina/o identity that were open to seeing the intersections of race and culture were more collectivist in their orientation. Hence, the "whitening" Latina/o culture is inextricably bound up with the isolation of the Betty character from the New York Latina/o community, along with constructions of this community that distort or oversimplify its cultural diversity (which leads to the erasure of Latino-Caribbean populations).

It is also notable how the Latina discussant includes Haitian migrants within the New York Latina/o community to draw attention to its cultural singularity and racial diversity. Unlike group 2, the Latina discussant is not including Haitians, Mexicans, Dominicans, and Puerto Ricans within a pan-ethnic immigrant identity that transcends race and culture. She insists that Haitian migrants could be authentic cultural representatives of New York Latin-Caribbean culture. This observation violates the principles of colorblindness, by associating Latina/o cultural authenticity with the bodies of black migrants. Just as important, it speaks to the racialization of Latin-Caribbean culture.

By suggesting that Haitian New Yorkers could be culturally interchangeable with Puerto Rican and Dominicans, the discussant is not implying that race "doesn't matter." Instead, she is drawing attention to the fact that Latino-Caribbean populations tend to be racialized in ways that Mexicans are not (Mexicans being perceived as a "whiter" Latina/o population). But, again, this type of racialization is not just focused on the site of the body—it is also oriented around distinctions between white and nonwhite culture. Hence, the black bodies of Haitian migrants can become symbols of the racialization of New York Latin-Caribbean culture—the point being that the reason the show's producers would never have portrayed Betty as the child of a Haitian family is not far removed from the reason they chose not to make her the child of a Puerto Rican or Dominican family. In order for the Betty character to be believable as an "all-American girl," she must be associated with a Latina/o ethnicity that is distanced from these other, more racialized aspects of New York Latina/o culture.

Conclusion

This study examined how depictions of Latina/o cultural identity in *Ugly Betty* were interpreted by a racially diverse sample of television viewers. The analysis was organized around the concept of culture-blindness that was adapted from theories of colorblind racism.

The colorblind racism thesis has focused on the way that antiblack racism has been recoded into a race-neutral language. As the term "colorblind" implies, it prides itself on overlooking the physiognomic differences that have been used to racialize black minorities. It also bears noting that colorblind racism can be used to deny the significance of all kinds of racialized physiognomic attributes (regardless of whether the racial minority is black, Latina/o, or Asian). But there is another dimension to anti-Latina/o racism, which blurs the lines between race and ethnicity—being organized around the racialization of Latina/o culture, more so than the racialization of Latina/o bodies. The concept of culture-blindness was used to examine this particular kind of racial subtext.

As I explained in the analysis, most of the discussion groups used a culture-blind interpretive framework to make sense of the cultural identity of *Ugly Betty*'s lead character. This closing discussion reflects further on these findings, with three summary observations.

The first observation concerns the complex relationship between culture-blind and colorblind themes in the discussants' interpretations. Most of the discussants used culture-blind themes to illustrate what was most universal about the Betty character. Furthermore, in most of the groups that produced culture-blind interpretations, the desire to "look past" Betty's ethnicity paralleled the desire to "look past" race. In this regard, culture-blind interpretations seemed to be informed by a colorblind common sense. Even so, the desire for sameness that was communicated through most of the culture-blind interpretations had its own racial coordinates. Among most of the groups, it was informed by the tacit understanding that the American mainstream was normatively white (the one exception being group 2, which articulated culture-blind themes with a discourse on immigrant family values that transcended race).

Other moments in the discussions drew attention to subtle differences in culture-blind and colorblind framing strategies. Discussion groups that produced culture-blind themes were most approving of Betty's ethnicity when the issue of racism and Betty's racial difference was broached. In these moments, culture-blind themes receded into the background, being displaced by a discourse on ethnic pride that was contrasted against race. This competitive framing of race and ethnicity corroborates some of the observations that race theorists have made about the racial subtext of ethnic identity. But it bears noting that this favoring of ethnicity (which occurred in tandem with a shift toward colorblind themes) was situational. When race and racism were no longer the topic of discussion, culture-blind themes resurfaced—and the same ethnicity that had been embraced moments earlier was treated with more ambivalence. The Betty character was not expected to be too invested in her "Mexican-ness," and her ethnicity was always interpreted in light of qualities that transcended its particularity. The value of culture-blindness, as a conceptual framework, lies in examining these attitudes toward ethnic-cultural identity that are not (as) immediately apparent when ethnicity is being contrasted against race.

A second observation concerns the relationship between culture-blindness and racist ideologies. Research on colorblind racism has shown that colorblindness correlates with the internalization of negative stereotypes about racial minorities and an antipathy toward policies that attempt to correct racial injustices and disparities (Bobo 38–42; Bonilla–Silva *Racism without Racists* 25–52; Neville et al. 39–43). Because this study did not directly examine the self-concept and racial belief system of the discussants, I cannot make these sorts of claims. Hence, I have been careful not to describe these culture-blind interpretations as culture-blind racism. It is possible that there is a relationship between culture-blindness and anti-Latina/o racist ideologies (or attitudes toward immigration policy). Even so, the examination of the precise relationship between these ideas is a subject for future research.

It is likely, however, that culture-blind themes are embedded within a racial subtext that is more diffuse than a Latino threat narrative. The treatment of immigration on *Ugly Betty* was politically progressive in many respects. The plotlines of season 1 provided a sympathetic depiction of an undocumented Mexican immigrant (Betty's father) who was victimized by unscrupulous immigration lawyers and immigration enforcement officers.[8] By depicting Betty's efforts to correct her father's legal status, the show also offered implicit support for legalization programs for unauthorized migrant workers. It is still significant, however, that these immigration plotlines were articulated alongside other plotlines that embedded Betty in mostly white social networks and narrative themes that treated her Mexican heritage as an incidental feature of her social identity. It is also significant that discussants rationalized these depictions in their culture-blind interpretations of the show.

Again, these findings cannot be used to make generalizations about public attitudes concerning Latina/o populations, but they do illustrate how television viewers navigated discourses on Latina/o culture (and the racial subtext of these discourses) that are being disseminated by the mainstream media. On this front, the interview data did provide some compelling insights into how television viewers grappled with the commodified constructions of Latina/o identity that have been examined by Latina/o studies scholars—which leads to the third summary observation.

Most of the groups that produced culture-blind interpretations derived their assessments of the Betty character entirely from their television viewing experiences. There is nothing unusual about this mode of interpretation, which privileges the media consumer's personal (and private) relationship to the media text. Media studies scholars have observed that this is the norm for media consumption in Western societies (Srinivas 155–73). And as Molina-Guzmán has observed, the sublimation of Latina/o identity caters to precisely these types of media consumption habits (119–21). Latina/o identity is abstracted from its collective cultural and political contexts in order to make it more digestible for a global audience composed of individual consumers.

Discussants who deviated from culture-blind interpretations related to the media text in a notably different way. None of the discussion groups were encouraged by the researchers to integrate their lived experience into the interpretation of the show. Even so, the discussants who did not produce culture-blind interpretations of Betty's ethnicity were more likely to interpret the media text in light of their lived, social relationships. As I cautioned in the analysis, it cannot be assumed that these discussants produced interpretations of the show that were more empirically valid than those of other discussants. But it certainly appeared that they had not been as thoroughly socialized into the role of the private media consumer as had discussants who produced culture-blind interpretations of the show. Their social identities and social relationships seemed to play a more pivotal role in mediating their interpretations of the media text.

Critical analyses of the racial subtext of *Ugly Betty* were also brought into the conversations by discussants who related to the media text in this way. In this regard, the discussants' willingness to see race can be understood as an effort to fill in important pieces of the social context that they thought had been left out of the show's plotlines and narrative themes—and they used their own social experiences and relationships to identify these "missing pieces." This interpretive process may have been shaped by a particular kind of racial identity politics (but, again, it must be noted that the research was not designed to evaluate the relationship between the discussants' interpretive decisions and their self-concept). The interview data do show, however, that these critical interpretations emerged from a process in which the content of the media text was evaluated in light of a more complex social reality.

This process may offer a helpful vantage point for conceptualizing the social and political orientations that foster these critical sensibilities. Instead of presuming that these sensibilities are being propelled by a racial identity politics, it could also be that a critical racial consciousness is the outcome of these interpretive practices (or that it emerges in tandem with them). But this still leaves open the question of how these critical, interpretive practices are fostered and sustained. This study does not have a tidy answer for this question, but the findings do indicate that these critical sensibilities emerged from a way of producing knowledge that operated outside of the individualized subjectivities that have been idealized by neoliberal cultural marketing strategies.

Notes

This research was made possible by a Joseph P. Healey Grant that was awarded by the University of Massachusetts–Boston. I am also indebted to the contributions of the graduate research assistants for this project: Diego Gomez-Aristizabal, who helped with the literature review and the recruitment of participants, conducted many of the focus group interviews, and assisted in the data analysis; and Ijeoma Njoku, who helped with the content analysis of Ugly Betty and transcribed many of the group interviews.

1. "Pilot," *Ugly Betty* (season 1), ABC, 28 Sept. 2006, Television.
2. "When Betty Met YETI," *Ugly Betty* (season 3), ABC, 20 Nov. 2008, Television.
3. Besides her boss, Daniel Meade, Betty's only lasting friendship with a character who is not an immediate family member is with a white Scottish immigrant, Christina McKinney. For all four seasons of the show, all of Betty's romantic interests have been white, non-Latinos, though—ironically—one of these characters was played by a light-skinned Latino male who was portraying an Italian American.
4. Eight percent of the participants chose not to disclose their annual household income.
5. Sixty-one percent of the sample had been following the show since the first season (it was in its third season when this research was conducted). Forty-two percent watched the show every week or almost every week, and 57 percent watched the show at least once or twice per month.

6. The content analysis included a description of the race and gender of every character with speaking lines in every scene of each episode, followed by a brief description of the type and quality of interaction between the characters in the scene. The descriptions provided in note 4 are derived from this content analysis.

7. Both of the interviewers were visible minorities, but they did not disclose their race or ethnic heritage to the discussants (and they were never asked to do so by any of the interviewees). The non-Latino interviewer was of Afro-Jamaican and Greek heritage, and the Latino interviewer was of Colombian heritage.

8. The legal status dilemmas of Betty's father was a running theme throughout season 1 of *Ugly Betty*. The most pivotal episodes dealing this issues include episode 6, "Trust Lust and Must," 2 Nov. 2006; episode 17, "Icing on the Cake," 15 Mar. 2007; and episode 22, "A Tree Grows in Guadalajara," 10 May 2007.

WORKS CITED

Amaya, Hector. "Citizenship, Diversity, Law and Ugly Betty." *Media, Culture and Society* 32.5 (2010): 801–17. Print.

Ang, Ien. *Watching Dallas: Soap Opera and the Melodramatic Imagination*. New York: Routledge, 1985. Print.

Avila-Saavedra, Guillermo. "A Fish Out of Water: New Articulations of US-Latino Identity on *Ugly Betty*." *Communication Quarterly* 58.2 (2010): 133–47. Print.

Balibar, Etienne. "Is There a Neo-Racism?" *Race, Nation, Class: Ambiguous Identities*. Ed. E. Balibar and I. Wallerstein. New York: Verso, 1991. 17–28. Print.

Beck, Bernard. "Come into My Parlor: Rendition, *Ugly Betty* and Rude Awakening from the American Dream." *Multicultural Perspectives* 10.3 (2008): 150–54. Print.

Beltrán, Mary. *Latina/o Stars in US Eyes: The Makings and Meanings of Film and TV Stardom*. Champaign: University of Illinois Press, 2009. Print.

Benavides, Hugo. *Drugs, Thugs and Divas: Telenovelas and Narco-Dramas in Latin America*. Austin: University of Texas Press, 2008. Print.

Bobo, Lawrence. "The Color Line, the Dilemma and the Dream: Race Relations in America at the Close of the 20th Century." *Civil Rights and Social Wrongs: Black-White Relations since World War II*. Ed. John Higham. University Park: Pennsylvania State University Press, 1999. 33–55. Print.

Bonilla-Silva, Eduardo. *Racism without Racists: Color-Blind Racism and the Persistence of Racial Inequality in the United States*. 3rd ed. Lanham, MD: Rowman and Littlefield, 2010. Print.

———. "Rethinking Racism: Toward a Structural Interpretation." *American Sociological Review* 62.3 (1997): 465–80. Print.

Campbell, Bruce. "Race-of-Interviewer Effects among Southern Adolescents." *Public Opinion Quarterly* 45.2 (1981): 231–44. Print.

Carr, Leslie. *"Color-Blind" Racism*. New York: Sage, 1997. Print.

Chavez, Leo. *The Latino Threat: Constructing Immigrants, Citizens, and the Nation.* Stanford, CA: Stanford University Press, 2008. Print.

Davila, Arlene. *Barrio Dreams: Puerto Ricans, Latinos and the Neoliberal City.* Berkeley: University of California Press, 2004. Print.

———. *Latinos, Inc.: The Marketing and Making of a People.* Berkeley: University of California Press, 2001. Print.

———. *Latino Spin: Public Image and the Whitewashing of Race.* New York: NYU Press, 2008. Print.

Dow, Mark. "Unchecked Power against Undesirables: Haitians, Mariel Cubans, and Guantánamo." *Keeping Out the Other: A Critical Introduction to Immigration Enforcement Today.* Ed. David Brotherton and Philip Kretsedemas. New York: Columbia University Press, 2008. 29–43. Print.

Duany, Jorge. "Reconstructing Racial Identity." *Latin American Perspectives* 25.3 (1998): 147–72. Print.

Ernst, Rose. *The Price of Progressive Politics: The Welfare Rights Movement in an Era of Colorblind Racism.* New York: NYU Press, 2010. Print.

Esposito, Jennifer. "What Does Race Have to Do with *Ugly Betty*?" *Television and New Media* 10.6 (2009): 521–35. Print.

Gallagher, Charles. "Color-Blind Privilege: The Social and Political Functions of Erasing the Color Line in Post Race America." *Race, Gender and Class* 10.4 (2003): 22–37. Print.

Goldsmith, Pat, Raquel Goldsmith, Manuel Escobedo, and Laura Khoury. "Ethno-Racial Profiling and State Violence in a Southwest Barrio." *Aztlan: A Journal of Chicano Studies* 34.1 (2009): 93–123. Print.

Gonzalez, Ed. "Ugly Betty: Season One." *Slant Magazine* 14 Oct. 2006. Web. 24 January 2012.

Greco Larson, Stephanie. *Media and Minorities: The Politics of Race in News and Entertainment.* Lanham, MD: Rowman and Littlefield, 2005. Print.

Guinier, Lani, and Gerald Torres. *The Miner's Canary: Enlisting Race, Resisting Power, Transforming Democracy.* Cambridge: Harvard University Press, 2003. Print.

Hall, Stuart. "Encoding/Decoding." *Culture, Media, Language: Working Papers in Cultural Studies, 1972–79.* Ed. Centre for Contemporary Cultural Studies. London: Hutchinson, 1980. 128–38. Print.

Hancock, Ange-Marie. *The Politics of Disgust: The Public Identity of the Welfare Queen.* New York: NYU Press, 2004. Print.

Inda, Jonathan Xavier. *Targeting Immigrants: Government, Technology, and Ethics.* Malden, MA: Blackwell, 2005. Print.

Itzigsohn, Jose, and Carlos Dore-Cabral. "Competing Identities? Race, Ethnicity and Panethnicity among Dominicans in the US." *Sociological Forum* 15.2 (2000): 225–47. Print.

Jung, Moon-Kie. "The Racial Unconscious of Assimilation Theory." *Dubois Review* 6.2 (2009): 375–95. Print.

Kretsedemas, Philip. "What Does an Undocumented Immigrant Look Like? Local Enforcement and the New Immigrant Profiling." *Keeping Out the Other: A Critical Introduction to Immigration Enforcement Today*. Ed. David Brotherton and Philip Kretsedemas. New York: Columbia University Press, 2008. 333–64. Print.

Lampert, Lisa. "Race, Periodicity, and the (Neo-) Middle Ages." *MLQ: Modern Language Quarterly* 65.3 (2004): 391–421. Print.

Landale, Nancy, and Salvatore Oropesa. "White, Black or Puerto Rican?" *Social Forces* 81.1 (2004): 231–54. Print.

Levin, Gary. "Plot: Pretty Is as Pretty Does." *USA Today* 15 Aug. 2006. Web. 24 Jan. 2012.

Menchaca, Martha. *Recovering History, Constructing Race: The Indian, Black and White Roots of Mexican Americans*. Austin: University of Texas Press, 2001. Print.

Molina-Guzmán, Isabel. *Dangerous Curves: Latina Bodies in the Media*. New York: NYU Press, 2010. Print.

Neville, Helen, M. Coleman, Jameca Falconer, and Deadre Holmes. "Color-Blind Racial Ideology and False Consciousness among African Americans." *Journal of Black Psychology* 31.1 (2005): 27–45. Print.

"Number of Immigrants and Immigrants as Percentage of US Population, 1850–2010." *MigrationInformation.org*. Migration Policy Institute, n.d. Web. 24 Jan. 2012.

Omi, Michael, and Howard Winant. *Racial Formation in the United States*. New York: Routledge, 1994. Print.

Peck, Jamie. *Workfare States*. New York: Guilford Press, 2001. Print.

Poniewozik, James. "Ugly, the American." *Time* 20 Nov. 2006. Web. 24 Jan. 2012.

"Ugly Betty: US Demographics, May 2009." *Quantcast.com*. Quantcast, n.d. Web. 5 Oct. 2009.

Rivero, Yeidy. "The Performance and Reception of Televisual 'Ugliness' in Yo Soy Betty la Fea." *Feminist Media Studies* 3.1 (2003): 65–81. Print.

Roberts, Dorothy. *Killing the Black Body: Race, Reproduction and the Meaning of Liberty*. New York: Vintage, 1998. Print.

Rodriguez, Clara, and Hector Cordero-Guzman. "Placing Race in Context." *Ethnic and Racial Studies* 15.4 (1992): 523–42. Print.

Shahani, Aarti, and Judith Greene. *Local Democracy on ICE: Why State and Local Governments Have No Business in Federal Immigration Law Enforcement*. New York: Justice Strategies, 2009. Web. 22 Jan. 2012.

Shufeldt Esch, Madeleine. "Rearticulating Beauty, Repurposing Content: Ugly Betty Finds the Beauty in Ugliness." *Journal of Communication Inquiry* 34.2 (2010): 168–82. Print.

Srinivas, Lakshmi. "The Active Audience: Spectatorship, Social Relations and the Experience of Cinema in India." *Media, Culture and Society* 24.1 (2002): 155–73. Print.

Steinberg, Stephen. *Race Relations: A Critique*. Stanford, CA: Stanford University Press, 1997. Print.

Valdivia, Angharad. *Latino/as in the Media*. London: Polity Press, 2009. Print.

Vincent, Brook. "Convergent Ethnicity and the Neo-platoon Show." *Television and New Media* 10.4 (2009): 331–53. Print.

Williams, Brackette. "A Class Act: Anthropology and the Race to Nation across Ethnic Terrain." *Annual Review of Anthropology* 18 (1989): 401–44. Print.

Wise, Tim. *Colorblind: The Rise of Post-Racial Politics and the Retreat from Racial Equity.* San Francisco: City Lights, 2010. Print.

13

Race in Progress, No Passing Zone

Battlestar Galactica, Colorblindness, and the
Maintenance of Racial Order

JINNY HUH

She is your friend and confidante. She is your lover. She fights battles with you. She showers next to you. She beats you at poker. She eats her meals with you. She shares stories of childhood, romantic intrigue, and flight maneuvers. She is like a daughter to you until one day, without any forewarning, she stares squarely into your eyes and shoots you with the intent to kill. She is not who you thought she was. As a matter of fact, she is not even human but a "skin-job" or human replicant. She is a Cylon who has been living in your midst for years, occupying your workplace and socializing in your home, waiting for the signal to seek revenge on the human race.

While the audience witnessed Sharon "Boomer" Valerii's revelation as Cylon at the end of the reenvisioned *Battlestar Galactica* (hereinafter BSG) miniseries pilot, it is not until the end of season 1, when Boomer shoots her father figure, Admiral Adama, that her Cylon identity is revealed to her friends and colleagues. Up until this point, Boomer's character could be read as passing for human. Boomer's shooting of her father is what Eve Bennett calls "the most shocking thing we ever see an individual Cylon do throughout BSG" (30). Boomer's act, Bennett claims, can only be understood in terms of Cylon (i.e., inhuman) programming. In other words, we can only begin to understand Sharon's cold behavior by relegating her to machine status, distancing her from "normal human terms" (30). Sharon's reduction to a calculating robot illustrates our own insecurities about Sharon's passing for human. First, only a nonhuman would coldheartedly kill her father figure. Second, and perhaps more important, how could we not have known Sharon was Cylon?

Through Sharon's outing as Cylon and the emergence of humanoid Cylons (versus the robotic Centurion Cylons of the past), the reenvisioned BSG can now be read as a narrative about detection anxieties. The inability of Boomer's friends, lover, and father figure to discern her nonhuman identity after years of coexistence builds upon our own current cultural anxieties of detection and undetection. The fact that Boomer is played by Korean Canadian actor Grace Park, who is positioned in what Juliana Hu Pegues calls the "post-9/11 Oriental," where she is marked "simultaneously as a (South)East Asian and West Asian, specifically Arab" (196), further evokes a discomforting unease. As a Cylon sleeper agent embodied by an Asian actor, Boomer's passing is now racialized and builds upon the long and vexed history of racial passing in American culture. This chapter situates BSG within a detection-passing dialectic as illustrated in American literary history, particularly between detective fiction and passing narratives, to explore our current state of detective and undetective angst. Further, although BSG illustrates our current state of race detective anxiety, it does so within a cultural moment that promotes a colorblind ideology. Thus, the exploratory question running throughout this chapter is: How do we detect race when race itself is not supposed to be acknowledged?

At the most basic level, detection is about policing. Hence, my interest here is not only in how Cylons are discovered but also in how certain Cylons function as instruments of detection. How is race used to detect, police, and maintain certain cultural hegemonies, customs, and behaviors? While "race" may not be overtly discussed in BSG, how is it visually and narratively utilized to illustrate continuing racial fears as well as preserve certain restrictions of racial behavior and conduct? This chapter explores the role of detection on two levels: (1) how Cylons are detected on a literal level, and (2) how detection functions at a meta-narrative level to uphold certain boundaries of race and gender/sexuality. In BSG, the policing of certain racial behaviors includes interracial sex and reproduction, the "cause," if you will, of the current anxiety of race detection (i.e., racial erasure via mixed-race individuals). While the premise of BSG may be a colorblind one, its narrative reveals the not so blind inevitability of racial difference.

Before examining BSG, a brief history of both detective and passing genres is necessary in order to delineate the interrelatedness of detection and undetection. While many critics date the commencement of the detective tale to Edgar Allan Poe's "Murders in the Rue Morgue" (1841), it was not until the end of the nineteenth century that both the detective and passing genres (particularly African American passing tales) became highly popular. Further, the partnership between detection and passing is not an arbitrary gesture; it is telling that several early authors of detective fiction—Poe, Mark Twain, Arthur Conan Doyle— all include the anxiety of race detection via passing in their detective tales ("Murders in the Rue Morgue," *Pudd'nhead Wilson,* and "The Yellow Face," respectively), undermining the ratiocinative and deductive reasoning skills of superhero detectives like C. Auguste Dupin and Sherlock Holmes and their abilities to detect race. It is important to note here that all three of these early narratives display the intimate connection between anxieties of race detection and fears around black-white sexual mixing. As argued by Lindon Barrett and Elise Lemire, the not so subtle hidden message in Poe's "Murders," in which two white women are viciously murdered by a knife-wielding orangutan, is one that displays the fear of black male bodies and the threat of miscegenation.[1] Further, Lemire argues that the detective genre, while keeping the sexual violence center stage, ensures that the reader and the detective "will never have to confront their own involvement in the violent and erotic spectacle from which they cannot avert their eyes" (199). This absolution, then, is what makes the detective genre a conservative one and one that also plays out in BSG's relation to its audience via current and very controversial storylines such as terrorism and torture, religious freedom, technology, and reproductive rights. Interestingly, while members of the audience are forced to confront and often redefine their own ideological and political positions on these issues, the topic of race is not a central concern due to the show's colorblind casting and storylines. But, as I reveal in the following, racial anxieties hover throughout BSG's narrative arc, and ultimately these anxieties are alleviated by maintaining conservative racial formations.

In addition to Poe, Doyle and Twain also reveal the destabilization of undetectable black bodies and their relation to law, crime, and detection in "The Yellow Face" (1893) and *Pudd'nhead Wilson* (1894) respectively. Published less than one year apart, both "The Yellow Face" and *Pudd'nhead* explicitly illustrate the fears and results of cross-racial breeding and the subsequent destabilization of the detection of racial borders. In Doyle's short story, the superhuman Sherlock Holmes fails in his detection due to little Lucy Hebron, a passing girl who is the product of a white British woman and a free man of color.[2] While Doyle simultaneously critiques and scandalizes American race relations by creating an open assault on white femininity as well as empowering the black male (he is free and a lawyer by trade), Twain's tale illustrates the ultimate unmentionable threat to race passing: race switching. As such, both Doyle's and Twain's tales result in failed detections: Holmes completely miscalculates in his solution, and although the race switching is discovered at the end of *Pudd'nhead* by Pudd'nhead Wilson's fingerprinting technique, white Tom is forever tainted in his blackness.[3]

The mutual connection between the detection and passing tropes is further illustrated in the passing tale, in which the threat of detection is almost always the implied subtext (hence, the hidden nature of passing).[4] As such, the narrative desire (à la Peter Brooks) of BSG is the need to detect the passing figure(s): the biggest mystery (after the search for the mythical Earth) running throughout the storyline is "Who is a Cylon?," which climaxes with the revelation of the Final Five to both humans and Cylons alike in the series' final season. As Brooks argues in *Reading for the Plot*, we are driven to read in order to create meaningful order out of chaos. In the passing narrative, I would add that this narrative desire of closure may or may not be realized by detection due to the difference between the act of passing and the act of undetection.

Here, James Weldon Johnson's *Autobiography of an Ex-Colored Man* (1912) is a telling example. Autobiography may be an example of unrealized narrative closure or one that maintains the threat of passing because the unnamed narrator continues to pass undetected at the conclusion of the story. Hence, for the conservative race reader, the desired closure is not achieved because the unnamed narrator maintains the threat of racial indecipherability and an intrusion into whiteness. However, Johnson's tale of successful passing also assuages some of the threat of detective failure by the narrator's admission that his passing was like "selling his soul for a mess of pottage" (207). This admission as well as his self-identification as an "unfound-out criminal" disclosed in the very first paragraph of his narrative place Johnson's passer into the role of wrong-doer. The narrative, in fact, reads like a criminal's confession, and while he may still wander the streets in his passing identity, this confession of guilt negates some of the subversive gain of the passing act. Hence, I differentiate between the act of passing and undetection in that pass-ing may not always be acknowledged or discovered (i.e., the successful pass), thus the absence of detection.[5] It is at the moment of discovery and self-chastisement (such as the unnamed narrator in Johnson's *Autobiog-raphy*) that detection and undetection come into play. By the conclusion of BSG, it would seem that the narrative desire of revelation/detection is achieved because all passing Cylons have been revealed and contained (by either death or assimilation). Narrative closure is achieved, and, in turn, any racial anxieties that have been imposed upon the Cylon as Other are assuaged. However, BSG's ultimate passing revelation—that humanity is, in actuality, part Cylon—requires a more nuanced and race-sensitive reading, which I address in the following.

BSG's use of the passing motif differs from early African American passing narratives (such as William Dean Howells's *An Imperative Duty* [1891], Charles Chesnutt's *The House behind the Cedars* [1900], Johnson's *Autobiography of an Ex-Colored Man* [1912], Walter White's *Flight* [1926], and Nella Larsen's *Passing* [1929]) because BSG displays detective anxiety in a post-racial, colorblind moment. This difference in historical context and political climate is key because, unlike early passing narratives that occur within a racialized framework of Jim Crow segregation where race is the immediate signifier of difference, the basis of colorblind ideology denies the relevance of race. Colorblind ideology is a type of science fic-tion where, in a strange twist of Ralph Ellison's *Invisible Man* (1952), what is visible is not seen or acknowledged. By not seeing or drawing attention to racial difference, colorblind ideology declares (in a misappropriation of Martin Luther King Jr.'s "I Have a Dream" speech) racism is eradicated and everyone is judged based on his or her merits alone. Not seeing race today is the politically correct answer to racism.

Critics of colorblind ideology such as Leslie G. Carr, Eduardo Bonilla-Silva, and Stephanie Wildman have warned that the prem-ise of colorblindness depends on a post-racial ideology where race is construed as no longer mattering or, for that matter, even existing. Colorblindness, critics argue, ignores the continuation of systematic inequality and oppression sustained by power hierarchies, including such recent examples as racial profiling and the imprisonment of Arab, South Asian, and Muslim immigrants since 9/11; increased anti-immigrant xenophobia, particularly against Latinos and Asians, as evidenced by Arizona's SB 1070 law; the mass incarceration of black men in what legal scholar Michelle Alexander calls the "New Jim Crow"; and the acquittal of George Zimmerman for the 2010 killing of seventeen-year-old Trayvon Martin in Florida. It is this very contradiction, claims Bonilla-Silva, that has transformed colorblind ideology into a new form of colorblind racism that reproduces racial inequality.

I agree that colorblindness promotes the negation of difference while simultaneously and systemically assaulting certain communities. But, ironically, the basis of colorblind theory—that race is not seen—is, in actually, a reality that is in our near future, for we are approaching a demographic tipping point. Recent headlines such as "The Beige and the Black," "Minorities Expected to Be Majority in 2050," "The End of White America," and "Census: Fewer White Babies Being Born" mark this social transformation. Concurrently, headlines also cite the increasing rates of mixed-race couplings: "Interracial Couples at an All-Time High, Study Says," "More Marriages Cross Race, Ethnicity Lines," and "Census Shows Big Jump in Interracial Couples." These headlines display the beiging and browning of America and, if the trend continues, the erasure of racial difference as we know it. For the headlines threaten not a world where we do not see race but one in which race cannot be seen. In some ways, then, BSG utilizes the science fiction genre in order to return the threat of race erasure to a "safer" science fiction universe where race is reinstated into its nonthreatening and prescribed roles. Hence, BSG's narrative regarding race is not a colorblind one but rather one that attempts to continually blind us against the racist ideologies underpinning colorblind rhetoric.

The Racial Speculations of Colorblindness

The beginning of the twenty-first century is an odd and confusing moment for the understanding of race. Declarations of the demise of race (and, presumably, racism itself) were professed with the completion of the Human Genome Project in 2003 and peaked with President

Obama's election in 2008. In response, the question "Is Race Real?" sparked international debate, including headlines by the *New York Times, American Scientist,* and *Psychology Today,* among many, many others. The Social Science Research Council even created a web forum in 2006 debating the topic, including race scholars and experts from fields including biology, anthropology, zoology, and sociology. "RACE: Are We So Different?," a traveling exhibition developed by the American Anthropological Association in collaboration with the Science Museum of Minnesota, is currently on tour throughout the United States. In conjunction with the Human Genome Project's announcement that race does not exist, PBS televised *Race: The Power of an Illusion,* a three-part series documenting the role of race in science, history, and society. In the same year that an early draft of the Human Genome Project was announced (2000), American artist Nancy Burson's "Human Race Machine" made its debut in the London Millennium Dome. The "Human Race Machine" is an interactive machine that utilizes morphing technology[6] to allow viewers to see themselves as six different races (African, Asian, white, Latino, Indian, and Middle Eastern, an added category after 9/11). Described on nancyburson.com as a "diversity tool," the "Human Race Machine" "gives us the opportunity to have a unique personal experience of being other than what we are, allowing us to move beyond our differences. We are all one race, the human race; one nationality called humanity. We are all the different hues of man." The "Human Race Machine" suggests that by seeing ourselves in the embodiment of various races, we will arrive at sameness. But Burson's progressive intentions, Jennifer González writes, are in actuality a "thinly veiled fantasy of *difference*" (49, emphasis in original) offering users a "false promise of universality through the visual mechanics of race" (50). Burson's racial tourism "does not offer users any insight into the privileges or discriminations that attend racial difference" (49). Instead, the "Human Race Machine" proposes that by merely seeing ourselves in other racial embodiments, we will conclude that "we are all human" and live harmoniously, immediately erasing the social, political, and legal realities of everyday lives. This is the dangerous and false promise of colorblind ideology.[7]

The irony of colorblind logic, states black feminist critic and scholar Patricia Hill Collins, is that we have to see color in order to be post-racial. In other words, in a paradoxical twist of the visual, difference must first be seen in order to negate its presence or viability. The absence of difference is, by default, "normative" whiteness. But how do we negotiate the collapse of what is simultaneously seen and silenced in a cultural moment when even mentioning race is to be identified as racist? Whether or not we can acknowledge the emperor's new clothes, then, has created a system of coded language and euphemisms (e.g., "urban community" and "welfare mother") through which we must decipher and detect the real anxieties of race. In this regard, BSG reflects our current colorblind moment where race is both everywhere and nowhere. However silent race may be in this critically acclaimed show, racial anxieties pervade the entire series from the initial Cylon attack to the discovery of Earth in the highly anticipated series finale. But to understand this, we need to understand that "Cylon" is a code word for "otherness." As Christopher Deis explains, "BSG is driven forward by a conception of racial difference where the Cylons are a carefully constructed Other" (157). In fact, the science fiction genre, notes film scholar Ed Guerrero, relies heavily on "abundant racialized metaphors and allegories of dependence on difference or otherness. . . . Taken together, these themes . . . give free associative range and symbolic play to the pent-up energies of society's repressed racial discourse" (56–57). With this reading, the racial anxieties veiled behind a racial silence become much more apparent.

Additionally, the science fiction genre is the perfect arena to discuss the visible invisibility of race because a central premise of the genre is to ponder the "What if?" question. What if we lived in a world where race neither matters nor is even acknowledged? What if skin color is not used to determine one's intelligence, athletic prowess, or strength of character? BSG offers us that world through colorblind casting and storylines that include "obvious" diversity peppered throughout the show, ranging from lead characters such as Admiral Adama (played by Mexican American actor Edward James Olmos) and Sharon/Number Eight (played by Korean Canadian actor Grace Park) to secondary characters including Anastasia "Dee" Dualla (mixed-race South African Kandyse McClure),[8] Felix Gaeta (played by multiracial Chinese Canadian actor Alessandro Juliani),[9] Bulldog (African American Carl Lumbly), and Simon/Number Four (African American Rick Worthy).

Although visually evidenced by a multiracial cast, the word "race" or "racism" is rarely used in the show. In fact, while there are no allusions to racial identity or discrimination because all twelve colonies derived from one single planet (Kobol and/or Earth), the very brief mention and sporadic application of "race" is telling in its own regard. "Diversity" alludes to a type of national, colonial difference (such as Gamenons and Sagittarons). This is suggested in "The Woman King" (season 3, episode 14) when Captain Helo describes Dr. Robert as "racist" for hating and attempting to kill off Sagittarons. It is important to note here that Sagittaron is one of the poorest colonies due to years of exploitation from other colonies. Further, Sagittarons practice a strict religion that abhors traditional medicine and is antimilitary. As a result, many colonies dislike Sagittarons for their seemingly backward nature. In addition to national distinctions, another specific reference to race occurs when Number Six and Helo (a human married to a Cylon) declare that "toaster" is a derogatory racist epithet for Cylons in "Resistance" (season 2, episode 4) and "Flight of the Phoenix" (season 2, episode 9). Here, Cylons are marginalized not only as machines but as racialized others.

With the simultaneous vision of what we understand as racial diversity on-screen and a narrative silence on race, BSG's colorblind stance seems apparent. In the *Battlestar Galactica* series bible, creator Ronald D. Moore describes the characters thus:

> Our characters are living breathing people with all the emotional complexity and contradictions present in quality dramas like *The West Wing* or *The Sopranos*. In this way, we hope to challenge our audience in ways that other genre pieces do not. We want the audience to connect with the characters of Galactica as people. Our characters are not super-heroes. They are not an elite. They are everyday people caught up in a [*sic*] enormous cataclysm and trying to survive it as best they can. They are you and me.[10]

Moore's understanding and characterization of "everyday people" are confined within the limitations and rules of a racialized landscape that even the most well-intentioned author cannot seem to escape. This is evidenced by the fact that certain characters are racially coded and not just a mere happenstance of colorblind casting. The series' bible description of Sharon is telling in this regard:

She applied to flight school, hardly daring to hope that she would be admitted, but the bureaucratic wheels had been greased for this child of the doomed settlement, and she was accepted over several more qualified candidates. Flight school was rough on Sharon. Not a born pilot by any means, she labored long and hard with her technique, but once again, by the time she graduated, she had managed to earn the second chances that she seemed fated to be given.

According to this background information, Sharon is a product of affirmative action. Although race is never mentioned, coded phrases and terminology as well as specific racialized allusions—"she was accepted over several more qualified candidates," "she labored long and hard with her technique"—read Sharon not only as unfairly receiving an affirmative action handout but also as doing so within a specific Asian American context. The narrative dangerously conflates the anti–affirmative action rhetoric of the unqualified who are "fated to be given" benefits due to "bureaucratic wheels" (stereotypically associated with African Americans) and the Asian American stereotype of the model minority whose success is achieved through hard work and overcoming constant struggle. Hence, it is no coincidence that the character of Sharon is embodied with a visually Asian-identified face.[11] Concurrent with the characterization of Sharon as the epitome of yellow peril threat when she is revealed to be a traitorous sleeper agent, she is also symbolic of the invading Asian hordes when we witness dozens of naked Eights confronting her (who at this point is ignorant of her Cylon identity) on a Cylon basestar. The nakedness of the Eights in this scene also reinforces the stereotype of the sexualized Asian female in what Eve Bennett refers to as a "techno-butterfly." Although the final edited series may not allude to Sharon's racialization, more of which will be examined later, Ronald E. Moore's bible reveals its original intent.

Detecting While Blind (or the Other DWB)

In BSG's colorblind stance, what is the relationship between race and detection? Like DWB, or "driving while black" (the popular abbreviation for racial profiling of black drivers that depends on a visibility of blackness), this chapter utilizes another DWB, or "detecting while blind," to comment upon the legal and cultural contradiction of detecting the visible while maintaining an act of unseeing. This section examines how race is detected across different racial fields (specifically Asian and black) and focuses on the visibly raced humanoid Cylons: Sharon (Eight) and Simon (Four). But, before elaborating on the humanoid Cylons, I would like to first offer a theoretical framework of paranoia to illuminate the relationship among race, paranoia, and detection. Anthropologist John L. Jackson Jr.'s study of racial paranoia is a helpful theoretical framework here. In *Racial Paranoia: The Unintended Consequences of Political Correctness* (2008), Jackson explains that colorblindness and paranoia often go hand in hand. Because political correctness produces a subtler form of racism where racist acts may not be as obvious as separate drinking fountains, a resulting effect is racial paranoia. One definition of racial paranoia is a type of intuitive feeling where certain acts, behaviors, and conversations necessitate a particular reading and suspicion.[12] President Laura Roslin calls for this very reliance on intuition in Cylon detection when she declares, "If anyone can be a Cylon and it's hard to tell us apart, then we only have one thing left to trust—our instincts, feelings" (season 1, episode 7).

But what is racialized intuition and instinct, and how does it affect detection? Is the turn to intuition and instinct always objective, without biases and preconditioning? While the act of detection as popularly applied in detective fiction is the art of solving the mystery and often relies on intuition, detection also includes acts of careful discernment that work in very nuanced ways and in very fleeting moments. A reliance on instincts and feelings is key here. Like racial paranoia, the need to detect may occur as a result of a look, a statement, a seemingly innocent act, or even silence and the evasion of a look.

Understanding racial paranoia is central to understanding the link between detectio[...] G is a narrative about paranoid anxieti[...] out discerning Cylons from humans ar[...], about rediscovering and redefining [...] re than this, it is also about the threat[...] result, a fight for survival that conclu[...] Earth. However, BSG also reveals an[...] fear of obsolescence: the extinction o[...] nifest themselves most revealingly when on the brink of danger and possible destruction. Within our current cultural moment, whiteness and racial boundaries are under threat of erasure, eradicating how we have understood "race" for centuries. It is within this racially paranoid framework that a "paranoid" or racially sensitive and attuned reader could discern racial codes and euphemisms amid or perhaps in spite of their absence.

Unlike the other humanoid Cylons who exude whiteness (e.g., the other female humanoid Cylons—Three, Six, and Ellen Tigh—are all very blond),[13] the visibly racialized Cylons on BSG—Sharon, Simon, and Tory—are coded differently along the show's racial spectrum. Juliana Hu Pegues, Eve Bennett, and Leilani Nishime have recently explored Sharon's Orientalist positioning while Nadine Knight and Christopher Deis have examined Simon's status as black sexual threat. This chapter builds upon these critics' readings to explore a cross-racial configuration within a colorblind framework. As such, the remainder of the chapter will explore how the "raced" humanoid Cylons and their multiple variations work as instruments of detection to illustrate how detection functions differently for Asians and blacks and, finally, to reveal how race is not blind but color-coded. Finally, my analysis concludes with a different variation to BSG's potential for colorblind ideology—racial invisibility—that is simultaneously the show's intended message *and* its downfall.

(Un)Detecting Racial Maintenance

Cylon detection is possible. In the miniseries, Commander Adama and Executive Officer Saul Tigh order Dr. Gaius Baltar to create a Cylon detector in which blood and plutonium are mixed (Cylons are susceptible to certain kinds of radiation). Test results are either red (= Cylon) or green (= human). While the test proves successful when Baltar screens Boomer in "Flesh and Bone" (season 1, episode 8), Baltar keeps the results to himself and tells Boomer she is human. After Sharon shoots Adama, the test is believed to be a failure for not previously detecting her Cylon nature and thus is ignored for the remainder of the series.[14] What is the narrative purpose of including and then almost immediately abandoning a storyline about a Cylon detector that actually works? As Baltar coyly admits regarding the blond Cylon Ellen's test results, "I'll never tell" (season 1, episode 9). While Baltar's comment is a playful jest, it is also a telling one. In short, BSG illustrates that what is at stake is not merely about accessing knowledge (Who is Cylon? Who is human?), but also maintaining certain racial formations amid the fear of racial erasure. In other words, detection is too quick and easy a solution and one that precludes the continued security of racial expectations. In detection, there is a difference between telling versus knowing in which the former reveals while the latter does not necessarily expose the secret. Depending on context, there is power in both telling (to announce a revelation) and knowing without telling (with the power to choose revelation or not). In a strange twist, then, BSG temporarily maintains the detective angst produced by (racial) passing in order to safeguard certain racial codes that assuage that very anxiety. In other words, to reveal too quickly is to strip away the audience's narrative desire (Baltar's Cylon detection test proves successful in the middle of season 1, too early to divulge the suspense of revelation) as well as to eliminate the opportunity for a "safe" racial maintenance. By denying full disclosure, detection is achieved concurrent with the observance and continued fulfillment of specific racial roles.

For the Cylons, maintaining certain racial formations must include their assimilation into a human identity. In order to succeed in their infiltration of humanity, Cylons must mirror the humans who created them by enacting "normative" codes of behavior that make them indistinguishable from their creators. In this regard, BSG is often praised for going against expectations, especially regarding gender and sexuality.[15] However, what is the normative racial code of behavior, and how does BSG reflect, maintain, and possibly counter it? Further, how are Cylons narratively programmed to enact these racial codes? A parallel analysis of the Asian and black Cylon models (Eight and Four, respectively) reveals BSG's reflection of our continued cultural anxieties of cross-racial mixing as well as questions of lineage and inheritance for the series commences with the danger of human extinction and, subsequently, a call to breed. Just moments after the Cylons attack Caprica, resulting in fewer than 50,000 human survivors, we witness a discussion between Commander Adama and President Roslin regarding humanity's survival. As President Roslin declares, "If we are going to survive as a species, we need to get the hell out of here and start having babies"

("Miniseries"). Looking at Billy (President Roslin's assistant) and Petty Officer Dualla/Dee, Commander Adama concurs by declaring, "They better start having babies" ("Miniseries"). This desperate need to procreate becomes a gentle reminder with each episode via the fluctuating numbers of the survivor count posted on Colonial Fleet One. The subtle reminders are, however, quickly replaced with unrestrained commands when President Roslin, going against her long-held feminist beliefs, declares a ban on abortion. As Gaius Baltar, the fleet's brilliant scientist and unintended cause of humanity's holocaust, declares, "If continuing on our present course, the human race will be extinct in eighteen years" (season 2.5, episode 7). Breeding has become a duty for the survival of the species, but, as BSG illustrates, the call to breed is not a colorblind decree; rather, partners in procreation are color-coded and adhere to not-so-uncommon racialized couplings reflective of our own cultural and legal histories.

Simon/Four

Much has already been written (both critically and in online forums) about BSG's problematic representation of blackness. In terms of the human characters, one has only to look at Dee, Bulldog, Phelan, Elosha, and Sue-Shaun to notice that the black characters have all dropped off into the inevitable black hole. Dee commits suicide; Bulldog is literally abandoned to the Cylons by Adama, only to return and be abandoned again; Phelan is a criminal (aka "felon") who is killed off by Apollo for being the immoral leader of, yes, the Black Market;[16] the priest Elosha dies after triggering a Cylon land mine on Kobol; and Sue-Shaun begs Kara for death while hooked up to the Cylon fertility machine. Even the series finale sees an absence of blackness, with our common ancestor replaced by a nonblack, half-Cylon child. As one online commenter remarked, "Every single black character was killed, murdered and mutilated in the BSG Universe. Adolf Hitler could not have dreamed up a more inspirational script."[17] The lack of black humans is further emphasized by the treatment of the only black humanoid Cylon, Simon. Here, we have to remember that Cylons were initially created as slave labor. "They were created to make lives easier for humans," reads the miniseries opening lines. As such, perhaps the quintessential humanoid

Cylon to represent slavery is the only black Cylon, Simon. If BSG shows that Asian-white mixing is acceptable (via the revelation of Hera as our common ancestor), it also reveals the nonrelenting fears of black-white miscegenation in existence since American slavery. In this sense, Simon's blackness is signified multiple times (as Cylon slave, as visibly black, and as black sexual threat).

The emphasis on breeding creates an interesting dilemma between humanity's survival and the policing of procreation. While Adama's initial reaction to the blossoming romance of Billy and Dualla (who are white and black, respectively) calls for babies, white-black unions are not the intended or desired solution. This is clearly demonstrated in season 2 with the episode titled "The Farm." When Starbuck, the fleet's blond and blue-eyed gifted Viper pilot, becomes a prisoner at a Cylon hospital, she discovers that the Farm is a breeding ground where human women are used as "baby machines" in the Cylons' plan to create human-Cylon hybrids. As the black humanoid Simon, who stands over a half-dressed, vulnerable Starbuck, declares:

> Gotta keep that reproductive system in great shape. It's the most valuable asset these days. . . . Finding healthy childbearing women your age is a top priority for the Resistance and you'll be happy to know that you're a very precious commodity to us. . . . You do realize that you're one of the handful of women on this planet actually capable of having children. That is your most valuable skill right now. . . . The human race is on the verge of extinction. And to be quite frank with you, potential mothers are a lot more valuable right now than a whole squadron of viper pilots. (season 2, episode 5)

The symbolism of this scene is clear. As Christopher Deis states, "While Starbuck is not penetrated by Simon sexually, she is symbolically raped, penetrated surgically in her abdomen (and, likely, also penetrated medically through vaginal examinations while unconscious)" (165). The haunting of slavery reinforces the fears of black male–white female relations when Starbuck encounters Sue-Shaun, a black female resistance fighter, hooked up to machines that are harvesting her eggs. After Starbuck escapes, Athena tells Starbuck that the Cylons are "conducting research into human-Cylon breeding programs" because Cylons cannot

reproduce biologically and procreation is one of God's command-
ments. While Starbuck kills both Simon and Sue-Shaun, albeit for very
different reasons, the message here is unmistakable: any suggestion of
black-white procreation results in death. This is further emphasized
when another variation of the Simon Cylon is literally shackled like a
slave, perhaps as punishment for his role in cross-racial/species breeding, later in the season (season 3, episode 7). Arguments against black-
white mixing are again underscored when black female officer Dualla's
relationship to two white men (Billy and Apollo) ends with the death
of the one who proposes to her and her own suicide in the middle of
season 4.[18] BSG's limited visions of black-white mixings reveal a fear of
blackness that continues to circulate today. Perhaps this fear (and the
subsequent rewriting of our genealogical past) is what is referred to in
the very beginning of the series when Doral (who later is revealed to be
Cylon Five) explains the Galactica's refusal to be networked: "Galactica
is a reminder of a time when we were so frightened by our enemies that
we literally looked backward for protection" ("Miniseries").

Eight

"Looking backward for protection" occurs with a genetic reimagining of
our ancestral (and racialized) past. If black-white mixing is the utterly
unmentionable, Asian mixing is the "shape of things to come" as mixed-
race Hera is often identified throughout the show. The parallel storylines
of the two main cloned versions of the Eight model (Boomer and Athena)
are significant in their racialization as Asian because they simultaneously
evoke the fear of yellow peril paranoia within a storyline already centered
on terrorism with an Orientalized sexual mixing/reproduction (Hu Pegues, Bennett, and Nishime). That the multiple Eights confront Boomer
while naked is revealing in its own regard. First, this is the only time multiple copies of a Cylon model are revealed to the audience in a significant
way, implying not only the threat of the never-ending horde of Asians but
also one that makes Asians (especially Asian women) inseparable from
their sexuality. This allusion to Asian female sexuality continues with
the Athena parallel story in which she seduces her victim and becomes
pregnant (a miracle in Cylon fertility) because her pregnancy is the literal
and symbolic future of humanity. For as the Boomer/Athena storylines

are coming to a close in the episode that deemed Asians as the yellow peril horde, we see Messenger Six taking Baltar to the Opera House on Kobol. As they approach a baby in a crib enveloped in bright, heaven-like lighting, Six tells Baltar that he is "the guardian and protector of the new generation of God's children. The first member of our family will be with us soon, Gaius. . . . Come . . . see the face of the shape of things to come." Although the baby is unseen by the audience, the strong implication is that it is Athena and Helo's as yet unborn baby, Hera, and the "shape" is mixed-raced on multiple levels (Asian-White, Cylon-human, alien-earthling).

Conclusion: It's Not about Race!

In "Strategic Ignorance," Alison Bailey writes:

> A central feature of white ignorance is the ability to ignore people without white privilege. White ignorance is a form of not knowing (seeing wrongly), resulting from the habit of erasing, dismissing, distorting, and forgetting about the lives, cultures, and histories of peoples whites have colonized. Consider the all-too-common, color-blind responses to racism, such as: "We all bleed the same color," or "We're all human." . . . Color blindness is essentially a form of ignoring that equates seeing, naming, and engaging difference with prejudice and bigotry, and not seeing, naming, noticing, and engaging difference with fairness. Purity is at work here. To be color blind you must learn to split and separate race from humanity. Color blindness relies on the cognitive habit of training the multiple (racial diversity) into a fictitious unity (we are all human). . . . So, color-blind responses to racism are an agreement to misinterpret the world. They are a perfect instance of how whites can act in racist ways while at the same time believing they are behaving rightly! (85–86)

Defining colorblindness as an act of ignorance or not knowing is in direct opposition to the rules of the detective tale commented on earlier. While the detective plot depends on the centrality of knowing, colorblindness is a strategic not knowing or, in Bailey's words, a misinterpretation of the world. Although BSG tackles many current hot-topic issues such as religion, homosexuality, war and terrorism, and the nature of democracy, and is critically acclaimed by *Time*, the *New York Times*, the *New Yorker*, *National Review*, and *Rolling Stone* magazine, among many others, its representation of race is disappointing at the least and dangerous at the extreme. By attempting to blind its viewers to race through its seemingly colorblind storylines while simultaneously playing off our current insecurities around detection, BSG's message is clear and perhaps best illustrated by a line from The Book of Pythia, one of the oracles in the Sacred Scrolls of the Colonial religion: "All this has happened before, and all this will happen again."

But, I conclude with some observations on BSG's unintended final message, one that is readily apparent to the observant and discerning reader. If BSG's ending demonstrates certain restrictions around race and racial mixing, what is actually revealed is the racial nuances—the potential of race mixing—that are unintended by BSG creators. The revelation that we are all part Cylon echoes the seemingly antiracist message reminiscent of current colorblind ideology. As a result of the Human Genome Project's findings that we are 99.9 percent the same, common responses are "See? We're all just human! There is no such thing as race!" But discerning scholars of race will recognize that there is an anxiety of detection and undetection occurring at the final moments of BSG. While Athena's character is most often read as the butterfly stereotype of an Asian woman with a white man, what is usually not noticed is that Athena's coupling is not an Asian-white one but a multiracial mixing, for Tahmoh Penikett (the actor who plays Helo) is of mixed-race background (his mother is First Nation and his father is British). In a recent interview, Penikett reveals his struggle with his mixed-race identity, especially as someone who can pass for white. "The irony is that I hated my white skin as a kid. I grew up in the Yukon. . . . I grew up in a lot of small northern communities, the majority of time with my native cousins. So I was the funny looking one, I was the minority, and oftentimes I just hated it when I was younger, I wish I grew up with darker skin. . . . I got ribbed and teased a lot because I was the 'white boy'" (Kayne). Penikett is the unintentional passer whose racial decodings are often misread. In addition to Penikett's undetectable racial background, Hera's own racial mixings problematize BSG's limited possibilities of mixed-race identity. According to *Battlestar* wiki, Hera is played by three young actresses: Lily Duong-Walton, Alexandra Thomas (older Hera), and Iliana Gomez-Martinez (older Hera). As

I attempt to play detective in Hera's racial decoding, I read the actresses as mixed Asian (Vietnamese, according to "Duong"), white with possible Latina background according to the wiki photo, and Latina (also according to the surname), respectively. Of course, it is very possible that my own decoding of Hera is flawed. My point here is that this is the message BSG seems to have lost or ignored. Leilani Nishime argues that the Athena-Helo-Hera family reflects the familiar trope of the Asian-white interracial family, but this threesome, in actuality, represents the multiracial family of our present and future in which racial markers are not so easily seen or discernible. Thus, it is not that "there is no such thing as race!" but that race is not so easily detectable. Perhaps this is the future BSG is hoping to avoid?

Notes

1. See Lindon Barrett's "Presence of Mind: Detection and Racialization in 'The Murders in the Rue Morgue'" and Elise Lemire's "'The Murders in the Rue Morgue': Amalgamation Discourses and the Race Riots of 1838 in Poe's Philadelphia." Both are published in *Romancing the Shadow: Poe and Race*, ed. J. Gerald Kennedy and Liliane Weissberg.

2. For an extended analysis of Doyle and his relationship to race and detection, see my essay on Doyle (*Modern Fiction Studies*, Fall 2003).

3. I label Twain's narrative as a failure only in that whiteness is not preserved by the detective results. While the scientific method of detection (here, fingerprinting) works to distinguish between Tom and Chambers, it does not succeed in creating a clear racial distinction between whiteness and blackness (Chambers is sold down the river, and Tom will never be able to reaccess his white purity). In this sense, Twain's story concludes with a narrative and racial unease.

4. This is narratively evidenced in Nella Larsen's *Passing*, in which the audacious tragic mulatta, Clare Kendry, suddenly dies when her passing is discovered by her white husband. The significance of Clare's death at the novel's conclusion is that the passing tale becomes a murder mystery with Clare's literal and metaphoric fall. In terms of the anxiety of undetection, whether or not Clare's death is suicide or murder (was she pushed by her part-time passing friend and rival, Irene?) takes a backseat with the realization that her death is a necessary conclusion to the legal/social/cultural criminalizing of race passing. Thus, the detection of Clare's passing is twofold: she is discovered by her duped husband, *and* her passing is punished by her death.

5. A recent example of unacknowledged passing is Madeline Albright's discovery of her Jewish ancestry. Not revealed until late in life, Abright's passing as non-Jewish was not enacted with the fear of detection as a constant threat. Hence,

I label her act as passing rather than undetection. Examples of undiscovered passing may include anyone who is ignorant about their own genetic history. While recent popular shows like PBS's *African American Lives* illustrate how DNA testing can illuminate us about our invisible racial pedigree, there are many more people who have not undergone the test and live unawares of their own racial makeup. Some estimates claim one-third of white Americans have black ancestry. As such, undiscovered passing is a much more practiced and continuing phenomenon than previously thought. The unraveling of BSG's ultimate concluding mystery of humanity's own Cylon admixture plays into this.

6. Nancy Burson is best known for creating photographs using computer morphing technology, such as the Age Machine, which gives a visual prediction of what someone will look like as he or she ages. Utilizing this technology, Burson's work gained publicity beyond the art world when she helped find missing people, prompting both the FBI and the National Center for Missing Children to acquire her software.

7. On a side note, after the recent controversy surrounding the use of yellowface performance in *Cloud Atlas* (directed by the Wachowski siblings of *The Matrix* fame), Google received thousands of protests after launching its "Make Me Asian" app, a visual tool that "racializes" a photographic image similar to the "Human Race Machine." Described as a "fun app" that lets you and your friends "indulge," you can turn yourself into "a Chinese, Japanese, Korean, or any other Asians!" Particularly offensive to this app is the intentional use of broken English alongside the use of slanty eyes, a Fu Manchu mustache, and rice paddy hats. Similarly, the "Design Your Dream Asian Girl" is another app that offers three ethnicities (Chinese, Taiwanese, and Korean) for whom one can choose eyes, nose, and lips. The use of technology to promote and practice racial tourism in these examples demonstrates that race is far from being unseen.

8. Kandyse McClure reveals an interesting experience of racial deciphering when, as a baby, she was taken to the government office in order to get her race "measured" according to skin color and hair texture. Of the nine possible colored categories, McClure was declared "Colored Other" of West Indian and European descent. For more, see kandysemcclure.com.

9. The case of Gaeta is interesting because his racial background is not easily discernible. Played by an actor who is of mixed-race ancestry, Juliani can also pass for Muslim, Latino, or Italian. I read Gaeta's racial ambiguity as directly relevant to his characterization throughout the series. Both Gaeta's and Helo's (played by Tahmoh Penikett) racial ambiguity will be discussed in the conclusion of this essay.

10. http://www.harvardwood.org/resource/resmgr/hwp-pdfs/battlestar_galactica_series.pdf.

11. Asian American success can never seem to escape affirmative action rhetoric of the model minority stereotype. One has only to read the recent headlines regarding emerging NBA basketball star Jeremy Lin to witness the racialization of Asian Americans. Lin is not only smart (he is a graduate of Harvard) but also extremely diligent and hardworking (after eighteen months of training

and practice, the previously ignored Lin scored twenty-five points—as a substitute!—for the New York Knicks, leading them into a winning streak). This moment of "Linsanity" has resulted in what Asian American studies scholar Claire Jean Kim calls the discomforting notion of the "Great Yellow Hope."

12. For instance, Jackson offers the example of Congresswoman Cynthia McKinney, who accused a Capitol Hill police officer of racial profiling when he grabbed her in a congressional office building. Although McKinney never accused the police officer, Paul McKenna, of making inappropriate racist slurs, the officer's nonrecognition of the congresswoman (who had been traversing the same governmental offices for more than a decade) and subsequent grabbing is what Jackson calls de cardio racism or a "racism [that] pivots on the subtle slight as telltale indication of hidden ill will" (101). Did the officer grab her because as a black woman she did not belong there? Or, was the officer's nonrecognition of McKinney an enactment of Ellison's *Invisible Man* syndrome? Or, was this occurrence not racially inflected at all? How to discern racism's "subtle slights" is where the problem of paranoia and detection become inextricably linked.

13. See Richard Dyer's *White*.

14. In an interesting essay on cylon detection, Chris Bilder (associate professor of statistics at the University of Nebraska–Lincoln) argues that Baltar's sixty-one-year projection of testing can be resolved by group testing a number of blood samples together. Group testing, according to Bilder, would have taken about 100 days to complete. See Bilder's "Human or Cylon? Group Testing on *Battlestar Galactica*."

15. For instance, one of the points of praise is the gender switch occurring with the characters as well as the storylines. For instance, both Boomer and Starbuck were men in the original series, played by African American actor Herbert Jefferson Jr. and Dirk Benedict, respectively. Further, the president and leader of humanity is a woman, Laura Roslin (played by Mary McDonnell), speculating on the very real possibility of a female president at a historical moment that witnessed Hillary Rodham Clinton vying for the White House with Barack Obama in 2008. Even language reflects our own cultural implementation of gender bias (in BSG, "Sir" is used to refer to both male and female alike).

16. Phelan's characterization is particularly vexing because his death is justified due to his dealings in child prostitution. And if the connection of blackness to criminality is not clear enough, this black man who is the leader of the Black Market is even darker in an episode that is especially dark and gloomy in lighting in the Black Market scenes. Thus, Phelan is triply marked as "black."

17. To emphasize the complete disregard of blackness even further, the long-anticipated series finale ("Daybreak," parts 1 and 2), reveals the Galactica fleet finally landing on what looks like Africa without any black Africans. Rather than dark-skinned natives, the fleet witnesses a group of pale-skinned, spear-yielding humans wandering the plains. Although our glimpse of the natives is very brief, the only recognizable blackness (dark blue?) is the paint marks covering their bodies. As Dr. Cottle reveals, the natives are genetically compatible with the

humans (i.e., for breeding purposes). The unexplained absence of blackness, again, seems to support Cottle's findings.

18. We see another version of the Simon/Four cylon model in *The Plan* (2009), a film released after the series' finale but set during the time period of BSG's miniseries to season 2. *The Plan* is told from the cylon perspective and as such we observe Simon, now married with an adopted stepdaughter, as a medic onboard Cybele. This version of Simon is interesting because it furthers the anti-black/white mixing of "The Farm" with a slight twist. Simon's wife, Gianna O'Neill, is played by Lymari Nadal (an American actress of Puerto Rican descent and wife of Edward James Olmos, or Commander Adama). In a show without racial distinction, Gianna is obviously "Othered" in that her speech is strongly accented. Simon's black threat is further buried when after a scene of lovemaking, he releases himself out of the airlock while he declares his love for his family. Out of reach from any Resurrection Ship, Simon's death is permanent.

WORKS CITED

Alexander, Michelle. *The New Jim Crow: Mass Incarceration in the Age of Colorblindness*. New York: New Press, 2010.

Bailey, Alison. "Strategic Ignorance." *Race and Epistemologies of Ignorance*. Ed. Shannon Sullivan and Nancy Tuana. Albany: State University of New York Press, 2007. 77–95. Print.

Barrett, Lindon. "Presence of Mind: Detection and Racialization in 'The Murders in the Rue Morgue.'" *Romancing the Shadow: Poe and Race*. Ed. J. Gerald Kennedy and Liliane Weissberg. New York: Oxford University Press, 2001. 157–76. Print.

Bennett, Eve. "Techno-Butterfly: Orientalism Old and New in Battlestar Galactica." *Science Fiction Film and Television* 5.1 (2012): 23–46. Print.

Bilder, Chris. "Human or Cylon? Group Testing on Battlestar Galactica." *Chance* 22.3 (2009): 46–50. Print.

Bonilla-Silva, Eduardo. "The Linguistics of Color Blind Racism: How to Talk Nasty about Blacks without Sounding 'Racist.'" *Critical Sociology* 28.1–2. (2002): 41–64. Print.

Brooks, Peter. *Reading for the Plot*. Cambridge: Harvard University Press, 1992. Print.

Broughton, Ashley. "Minorities Expected to Be Majority in 2050." *CNN.com*. Aug. 13, 2008. Web. Jan. 25, 2013.

Carr, Leslie G. *"Color-Blind" Racism*. Thousand Oaks, CA: Sage, 1997.

Chen, Stephanie. "Interracial Marriages at an All-Time High, Study Says." *CNN.com*. June 4, 2010. Web. Jan. 25, 2013.

Chesnutt, Charles. *House behind the Cedars*. New York: Modern Library, 2003. Originally published in 1900. Print.

Collins, Patricia Hill. "Are We Living in a Post-Racial World?" The Blackboard Jungle 5 Conference. Teaching to Cultural Diversity: A Realm of Possibilities. University of Vermont, Burlington, VT. Mar. 30, 2012. Print.

Deis, Christopher. "Erasing Difference: The Cylons as Racial Other." *Cylons in America.* Ed. Tiffany Potter and C. W. Marshall. New York: Continuum, 2008. 156–68. Print.

Doyle, Arthur Conan. "The Yellow Face." *The Complete Sherlock Holmes: All 4 Novels and 56 Short Stories.* New York: Bantam, 1986. 350–61. Originally published in 1893. Print.

Dyer, Richard. *White.* New York: Routledge, 1997. Print.

Ellison, Ralph. *Invisible Man.* New York: Vintage International, 1995. Originally published in 1952. Print.

González, Jennifer. "The Face and the Public: Race, Secrecy, and Digital Art Practice." *Camera Obscura* 24.1 (2009): 37–65. Print.

Guerrero, Ed. *Framing Blackness: The African American Image in Film.* Philadelphia: Temple University Press, 1993. Print.

Howells, William Dean. *An Imperative Duty.* New York: Harper and Brothers, 1891. Print.

Hsu, Hua. "The End of White America." *Atlantic* January/February 2009. Web. Jan. 25, 2013.

Huh, Jinny. "Whispers of Norbury: Sir Arthur Conan Doyle and the Modernist Crisis of Racial (Un)detection." *Modern Fiction Studies* 49.3 (2003): 550–80. Print.

Hu Pegues, Juliana. "Miss Cylon: Empire and Adoption in *Battlestar Galactica.*" *MELUS* 33.4 (2008): 189–209. Print.

Jackson, John L., Jr. *Racial Paranoia: The Unintended Consequences of Political Correctness.* New York: Basic Civitas, 2008. Print.

Jayson, Sharon. "Census Shows Big Jump in Interracial Couples." *USA Today* Apr. 26, 2012. Web. Jan. 25, 2013.

Johnson, James Weldon. *Autobiography of an Ex-Colored Man.* New York: Vintage, 1989. Originally published in 1912. Print.

Jordan, Miriam. "More Marriages Cross Racial, Ethnicity Lines." *Wall Street Journal* Feb. 17, 2002. Web. Jan. 25, 2013.

"Kandysemcclure.com." Kandysemcclure.com RSS. N.p., n.d. Web.

Kayne, Evan. "What the Frack? Interview with Tahmoh Penikett and Aaron Douglass." *Gaycalgary.com.* May 2010. Web. Jan. 25, 2013.

Knight, Nadine. "Black Markets and Black Mystics: Racial Shorthand in *Battlestar Galactica.*" *Science Fiction Film and Television* 5.1 (2012): 47–66.

Larsen, Nella. *Passing.* New York: Norton, 2007. Originally published in 1929. Print.

Lemire, Elise. "'The Murders in the Rue Morgue': Amalgamation Discourses and the Race Riots of 1838 in Poe's Philadelphia." *Romancing the Shadow: Poe and Race.* Ed. J. Gerald Kennedy and Liliane Weissberg. New York: Oxford University Press, 2001. 177–204. Print.

Lind, Michael. "The Beige and the Black." *New York Times* Aug. 16, 1998. Web. Jan. 22, 2013.

Moore, Ronald. *Battlestar Galactica* Series Bible. http://www.harvardwood.org/resource/resmgr/hwp-pdfs/battlestar_galactica_series.pdf. Web.

"Nancy Burson." Nancy Burson. N.p., n.d. Web.

Nishime, Leilani. "Aliens: Narrating U.S. Global Identity through Transnational Adoption and Interracial Marriage in Battlestar Galactica." *Critical Studies in Media Communication* 28.5 (2011): 450–65. Print.

Poe, Edgar Allan. "The Murders in the Rue Morgue." *The Complete Tales and Poems of Edgar Allan Poe.* New York: Vintage, 1975. 141–68. Originally published in 1841. Print.

Siek, Stephanie, and Joe Sterling. "Census: Fewer White Babies Being Born." *CNN.com.* May 7, 2012. Web. Jan. 25, 2013.

Twain, Mark. *Pudd'nhead Wilson.* New York: Norton, 1980. Originally published in 1894. Print.

White, Walter. *Flight.* Baton Rouge: Louisiana State University Press, 1998. Originally published in 1926. Print.

Wildman, Stephanie M. "The Persistence of White Privilege." *Washington University Journal of Law and Policy* 18 (2005): 245–65. Print.

Evelyn Alsultany is Associate Professor in the Department of American Culture at the University of Michigan. She is the author of *Arabs and Muslims in the Media: Race and Representation after 9/11* (NYU Press, 2012). She is coeditor (with Rabab Abdulhadi and Nadine Naber) of *Arab and Arab American Feminisms: Gender, Violence, and Belonging* (2011), winner of the Arab American Nation Museum's Evelyn Shakir Book Award. She is also coeditor (with Ella Shohat) of *Between the Middle East and the Americas: The Cultural Politics of Diaspora* (2013). She is guest curator of the Arab American National Museum's online exhibit "Reclaiming Identity: Dismantling Arab Stereotypes" (www. arabstereotypes.org).

Austin Ashe is a graduate student in the sociology department at Duke University. His research interests and specialty are race and ethnicity, policing, and delinquency. His work focuses on how aggressive policing impacts youth and the functioning of the criminal justice system.

Eduardo Bonilla-Silva is Chair and Professor of Sociology at Duke University. His first article, "Rethinking Racism: Toward a Structural Interpretation," appeared in the *American Sociological Review* in 1996 and challenged social analysts to abandon the prejudice problematic and anchor race analysis structurally. His books include *White Supremacy and Racism in the Post–Civil Rights Era* (2001), *White Out: The Continuing Significance of Racism* (2003), *Racism without Racists* (2003), *White Logic, White Methods: Racism and Methodology* (2008), and *The State of White Supremacy: Racism, Governance, and the United States* (2011). Recently he has worked on the idea that racial stratification in the United States is becoming Latin America–like, on a critique of Obama and the post-racial logical that orients his politics, and on a book tentatively titled "The Racial Grammar of Everyday Life in America."

Shilpa Davé is Assistant Professor of Media Studies and American Studies at the University of Virginia. Davé is the coeditor of *East Main Street: Asian American Popular Culture* (NYU Press, 2005). Her work has been published in several venues, including *Amerasia*, *Catamaran*, the *Journal of Asian American Studies*, *Literary Interpretation Theory*, and *Contemporary Literature*. Her book *Indian Accents: Brown Voice and Racial Performance in American TV and Film* (2012) explores political and cultural citizenship in contemporary South Asian American literature and popular culture.

Ashley ("Woody") Doane is Associate Dean for Academic Administration, Chair of the Department of Social Sciences, and Professor of Sociology at the University of Hardord. He has taught courses on race and ethnic relations for twenty-five years. He is coeditor (with Eduardo Bonilla-Silva) of *White Out: The Continuing Significance of Racism* (2003) and has written numerous articles and book chapters about whiteness, racism, dominant group ethnicity, and public dialogues on race. Woody is a past president of the Association for Humanist Sociology and a past Chair of the American Sociological Association's Section on Racial and Ethnic Minorities. He was the 2012 recipient of the Founder's Award for Scholarship and Service from the Section on Racial and Ethnic Minorities.

Bruce Lee Hazelwood is currently a doctoral student in Cultural Studies and Social Thought in Education in the Teaching and Learning Department of the College of Education at Washington State University. His research currently focuses on employing critical discourse analysis to commentary during Ultimate Fighting Championship (UFC) events.

Jinny Huh is Assistant Professor of English at the University of Vermont. She received her PhD from the University of Southern California in 2005 and was a Postdoctoral Fellow at UCLA's Institute of American Cultures. She has published articles in *Modern Fiction Studies* and *MELUS*. Her current book project, *The Arresting Eye: Race and the*

Anxiety of Detection, explores narratives of passing and detection in twentieth-century American literature and culture.

Dina Ibrahim is Associate Professor of Broadcast and Electronic Communication Arts at San Francisco State University. Her research includes Middle Eastern Media Coverage and Western media representations of Islam and Muslims. Her publications include *The Framing of Islam on Network News Following the September 11th Attacks* (2010).

C. Richard King is Professor of Critical Culture, Gender, and Race Studies, Washington State University. Dr. King has written extensively on the changing contours of race in post–civil rights America, the colonial legacies and postcolonial predicaments of American culture, and struggles over Indianness in public culture. He is the author/editor of several books, including *Team Spirits: The Native American Mascot Controversy* (a CHOICE 2001 Outstanding Academic Title) and *Postcolonial America*. He has recently completed *Native American Athletes in Sport and Society* and *The Encyclopedia of Native Americans and Sport*.

Philip A. Kretsedemas is Associate Professor of Sociology at the University of Massachusetts–Boston. He is the author of *The Immigration Crucible: Transforming Race, Nation, and the Limits of the Law* (2012), *Migrants and Race in the US: Territorial Racism and the Alien/Outside* (2013), and coeditor of *Migrant Marginality: A Transational Perspective* (2013).

David J. Leonard is Associate Professor and Chair in the Department of Critical Culture, Gender, and Race Studies at Washington State University, Pullman. He is the author of *After Arrest: Race and the Assault on Blackness*, as well as several other works. You can follow him on Twitter @drdavidjleonard.

Roopali Mukherjee is Associate Professor of Media Studies at the City University of New York, Queens College. She is the author of *The Racial Order of Things: Cultural Imaginaries of the "Post-Soul" Era* (2006) and coeditor of *Commodity Activism: Cultural Resistance in Neoliberal Times* (NYU Press, 2012).

Sarah Nilsen is Associate Professor in Film and Television Studies at the University of Vermont. She is the author of *Projecting America: Film and Cultural Diplomacy at the Brussels World's Fair of 1958* (2011). Her research has been published in various journals and books on critical race theory in film and television, Disney studies, and Cold War culture. Her current book project is a history of the Disney princess franchise.

Janice Peck is Associate Professor of Media Studies at the University of Colorado at Boulder. She conducts research and teaches in the areas of critical theory, communication history, television studies, the social meanings and political implications of popular culture, the sociology of news, media representations of class, race and gender, and U.S. political and cultural history. Peck is the author of *The Age of Oprah: Cultural Icon for the Neoliberal Era* (2008) and *The Gods of Televangelism: The Crisis of Meaning and the Appeal of Religious Television* (1993), coeditor of *A Moment of Danger: Critical Studies in the History of U.S. Communication since World War II* (2011), and a coeditor of *Handbook of Communication History* (2012).

Sarah E. Turner is Senior Lecturer of English at the University of Vermont. A Canadian by birth, she has been teaching at the University of Vermont for the past fifteen years. Her areas of research include constructions of race in popular culture, contemporary black women writers, and the rhetoric of twenty-first-century racism. Her work has appeared in *MELUS, Diversity in Disney Films,* and *The Films of Stephen King.*